Psychosocial Aspects of the H

For Mary Bernadette
thank you for everything (yet again)

and for

Genevieve Rebecca

and

Seraphina Oriana

and

Zenoushka Leonora

Psychosocial Aspects of the Health Care Process

Robert J. Edelmann

PRENTICE HALL

An imprint of **PEARSON EDUCATION**

Harlow, England · London · New York · Reading, Massachusetts · San Francisco · Toronto · Don Mills, Ontario · Sydney
Tokyo · Singapore · Hong Kong · Seoul · Taipei · Cape Town · Madrid · Mexico City · Amsterdam · Munich · Paris · Milan

Pearson Education Limited
Edinburgh Gate, Harlow
Essex CM20 2JE
England

and Associated Companies throughout the World.

Visit us on the World Wide Web at:
www.pearsoned-ema.com

First published 2000

© Pearson Education Limited 2000

ISBN 0-582-35724-1

British Library Cataloguing-in-Publication Data
A catalogue record for this book can be obtained from the British Library

Library of Congress Cataloging-in-Publication Data
Edelmann, Robert J.
    Psychosocial aspects of the health care process / Robert J.
Edelmann.
        p.   cm.
    Includes bibliographical references (p.) and index.
    ISBN 0-582-35724-1 (alk. paper)
    1. Medcial care--Social aspects. 2. Medical care--Pyschological
aspects. 3. Public health--Social aspects. 4. Public health-
-Psychological aspects. 5. Social medicine. I. Title.
RA418.E33 1999
362.1--dc21   99-33761
                                                 CIP

10 9 8 7 6 5 4 3 2 1
05 04 03 02 01 00

Set by 30 in 10/12pt Sabon
Produced by Addison Wesley Longman Singapore (Pte) Ltd.,
Printed in Singapore

CONTENTS

PREFACE

This book developed from a lecture course entitled 'Psychological aspects of health care', which I presented as part of the Masters Programme in Health Psychology I directed from 1990 to 1997 at the University of Surrey. The aim in developing this course was to create a new perspective within which otherwise seemingly divergent topics could be assembled. It soon became apparent that there were rather more key references in sociology, anthropology and medical journals than there were in psychology journals. In this context it was evident that the relationship between psychosocial issues and various aspects of the patient's passage through the health care system was a central research issue for a number of disciplines and was of central importance to a number of professional groups as well as the lay public. While there were discipline-specific texts and books targeted towards specific professional groups, or specialist texts which covered certain topics of relevance to psychosocial aspects of health care, there was not one core text which presented an accessible overview of the topic. Hence, the idea for a book developed. In addition to the lecture course, the writing of such a book was facilitated by my involvement with health professionals through my research and teaching.

The first aim of this book is thus to draw together a disparate literature examining psychosocial aspects of the patient's passage through the health care system and their interactions with health care providers. The second aim is to provide an overview of this literature which is accessible not only to undergraduate and postgraduate psychology students and academics and researchers from a number of disciplines, but also to a range of health professionals including medical students, student nurses, mid-wives and health visitors as well as other qualified practitioners. I hope I have succeeded in this aim and that the chapter outlines and summaries as well as highlighted material and suggestions for further reading facilitate this process.

The book itself is organised so that chapters reflect both the patient and health care providers' passage through the health care system. The first chapter outlines the various official and lay definitions for and theoretical perspectives taken to examine health and illness. The second chapter explores preventive health actions ranging from exercise and dietary control to self-examination and screening. In this context the various models of health beliefs and health behaviour are outlined. The third chapter discusses issues relating to the perception and interpretation of symptoms. Chapters from the middle section of the book cover topics dealing with the use of health care services, interactions between health care providers and patients and adherence to treatment advice. Issues discussed include lay care in illness; factors mediating the decision to use health care facilities including delay and overuse of such provision; factors influencing the pattern of communication in doctor–patient interactions; problems in health care consultations and outcomes from health care; the relationship between adherence and treatment outcome; factors influencing adherence to treatment advice and measures for improving adherence. Chapters from the final section cover topics relating to hospitalisation and reducing the stress of medical care, chronic illness and terminal care. Issues discussed include preparation for surgery and coping with unpleasant treatment; the impact of chronic illness and coping and adjustment to chronic illness; informing the terminally ill; adjustment to and care of the dying; bereavement and grief and support for the survivors. The final chapter in the book examines the potential cost of caring upon both lay and professional carers.

The initial stages of writing this book were facilitated by Laura Woodall who undertook literature searches and organised references, and I would like to thank her accordingly. The process of completing this book was unfortunately delayed by several factors beyond my control which conspired to lead me to question my faith in human nature – I have retained it and am a wiser person as a result. I would like to express a particular debt of gratitude to Sarah Caro, who prior to her departure to pastures new, was Senior Commissioning Editor at Addison Wesley Longman. Without her assistance and encouragement it is fair to say that this project may not have seen the light of day. I would also like to thank her successor at Pearson Education, Jane Powell, for so swiftly taking up the mantle and facilitating the rapid completion of the production process. Finally, I would like to thank my wife, Mary Bernadette, who makes everything in life worthwhile, and Zenoushka, Seraphina and Genevieve whose interruptions were always welcomed (well, almost!).

CHAPTER 1

Understanding health and health behaviour

CHAPTER OVERVIEW

This chapter begins with a brief comment on the overall aims of the book. The first substantive section evaluates various definitions of health and illness, firstly, exploring conceptual differences between disease, sickness and health and, secondly, commenting upon both official definitions of health and lay beliefs about health and illness. The second section of this chapter evaluates the broader social context of health; explanations and implications of social and geographical variations in health status are presented. The final section of the chapter reviews the various approaches and models which have been offered as frameworks for understanding health and illness. Each section emphasises the need to incorporate biological, psychological and social factors in any model which claims to provide an understanding of health and illness.

This chapter covers:

Definitions of disease, illness and sickness
Definitions of health
Lay beliefs about health and illness
Health variations
Explanations/models of health and illness

Aims and rationale of the book

This book has two broad aims: firstly, to unravel the complex set of issues involved in making decisions about our health and the way we use health care systems; and, secondly, to explore the interaction between 'patients' and providers of health care and the broader health care environment. In the process of executing this task, topics are covered sequentially to reflect the person's potential passage through the health care system. Thus, while initial chapters deal with the process of symptom recognition and interpretation, subsequent chapters deal with factors influencing the person's decision to use the health care system and their interactions with health care providers, leading finally to chapters dealing with concerns raised by chronic illness and bereavement and the impact of caring upon caregivers.

In order to place such issues in context it is important, firstly, to seek to define health and illness, secondly, to comment upon health within the broader social context and, thirdly, to introduce the various theoretical explanations which have been offered to explain health and illness. Both social and psychological factors, including the beliefs and attitudes people hold about health and illness, contribute to the actions they subsequently take in terms of self-care or health care utilisation, preventive action and adjustment to chronic illness. The extent to which beliefs do or do not correspond with those held by health care providers will also clearly influence behaviour and outcome. Placing this within a broader framework is essential given that beliefs are shaped by the cultural and societal context in which we live.

Definitions and beliefs about health and illness

Defining disease, illness and sickness

A number of authors have discussed distinctions between such labels as disease, illness and sickness (see box 1.1). Barondess (1979) defines disease as:

> a biological event, characterised by anatomic, physiologic or biochemical changes, or by some mixture of these. It is a disruption in the structure and/or function of a body part or system. . . . due to a variety of causes, may persist, advance or regress . . . and may or may not be apparent clinically. (p. 375)

Box 1.1 Definitions of disease, illness and sickness

Disease – a condition diagnosed on the basis of anatomical, physiological or biochemical changes and most usually treated by a medical practitioner (in Western societies at least).

Illness – the individual's own personal and subjective experience of symptoms and suffering.

Sickness – acceptance and labelling by others of the ill or diseased person.

(See Barondess, 1979; Cott, 1986; Eisenberg, 1977; Kleinman, 1988; Kleinman, Eisenberg and Good, 1978; Lupton, 1994; Posner, 1991; Turner, 1984.)

Disease is thus that condition which is diagnosed on the basis of bodily signs and treated, at least in Western society, by the doctor.

Illness, on the other hand, relates to the way in which the individual experiences that disease and is defined by Barondess as consisting of:

> an array of discomforts and psychosocial dislocations resulting from interaction of a person with the environment. The environmental stimulus may be a disease, but frequently it is not. (p. 375)

In a similar vein, Eisenberg (1977) refers to illness as experience and disease as an abnormality in the structure and function of body organs and systems. As Corr (1986) notes, illness is behaviour and hence is a response or effect of which disease is only one possible determinant. Thus, the experience of illness resulting from an underlying disease is affected by a range of psychosocial factors including conditioning and learning experiences, beliefs, culture and social norms (Eisenberg, 1977; Cott, 1986; Kleinman, Eisenberg and Good, 1978).

As Lupton (1994) notes:

> illness refers to the social, lived experience of symptoms and suffering which is innately human. It includes recognising that bodily processes are malfunctioning and taking steps to rectify the situation, such as seeking treatment. Disease, on the other hand, is not limited to humans: we can speak of a diseased apple, for example, but would not describe an apple as ill or sick. (pp. 92–3)

In sum, definitions of disease and illness imply that the former is an objectively identifiable biological event while the latter is a variable subjective experience. However, as Lupton further notes, it is wrong to assume that the diagnosed biomedical disease is a rational scientific reality. Diagnosis is based upon the medical history, examination and pathology tests, all of which are open to interpretation. This is illustrated in an example quoted by Helman (1985). He refers to a male patient with chest pain which was diagnosed as muscular aches by a general practitioner, as a heart attack by a junior doctor, as angina by a senior registrar and as pseudo-angina by a cardiologist; the complaint being caused by external stressors, coronary artery thrombosis, narrowing of the coronary arteries or hyperventilation depending upon the diagnosis offered!

While illness is the individual's experience of disease, sickness, by contrast, tends to refer to the label applied by others to the ill or diseased person. It is the acceptance by others of a social condition whereby the person is expected to take to their bed, take time away from work and so on; that is, be admitted to the 'sick role' (Parsons, 1951). Young (1982) defines sickness as:

> the process through which worrisome behavioural and biological signs, particularly ones originating in disease, are given socially recognizable meanings, i.e. they are made into symptoms and socially significant outcomes. (p. 258)

As Radley (1994) notes, 'ill health' can then operate at three levels, the level of the body, the individual or society, which correspond with identification or labelling of disease, illness and sickness respectively. It is quite possible to have a disease, for example hypertension or a cancerous tumour, without feeling ill. The person does not experience any symptoms and is unaware that high blood pressure or cancer exists. It is also possible to feel ill, or indeed to have profound illness, in the presence of minimal disease or in the absence of diagnosable pathology. An all too common example is the presence of extreme lower back pain or upper limb disorders resulting in job loss, limitations to one's family and social life and consumption of analgesics in the presence of minor soft tissue damage or an absence of clearly identifiable organic pathology. It is also possible to have a disease and/or illness without accepting the sick role or allowing oneself to be defined or identified as sick: for example, soldiering on at work in spite of a head cold and headache or tissue damage and pain. The converse can also apply, where people are sanctioned as being sick while not feeling particularly ill and where disease is no longer present; someone reluctant to relinquish their 'sick role' might comment that: 'I do not feel that bad but I thought I should rest a bit longer just to make sure.'

In Western society it is necessary to have the symptoms viewed as illness confirmed as disease by a health care provider. That is, strictly speaking symptoms are subjective, apparent only to the affected person. Signs are detectable by another person and sometimes, as in the case of hypertension, not by the patient themselves (MacBryde and Blacklow, 1970). The person is also likely to be admitted to and released from the 'sick role' by a health care provider. It is not unusual for a recovering person to comment that: 'I think I am better now, I certainly feel a lot better, but I will wait to see what the doctor says.'

It is important to bear in mind that different cultures provide different structured vocabularies for health and illness which serve to validate a label given to a set of symptoms. This is particularly true with regard to mental health but is also very evident in relation to physical health. A frequently cited example of differing labels for comparable symptoms is provided by Kleinman's (1982) study of Chinese medical practice. He reports that, while no formal diagnosis for depression exists in the Chinese diagnostic lexicon, the majority of patients diagnosed with 'neurasthenia' in that culture have symptoms which would be labelled as depression in Western society (dizziness, headaches, appetite and sleep disturbance and lethargy).

In addition, definitions of both disease and illness vary from culture to culture; what is thought of as disease within Western society may be considered to be a normal phenomenon in other cultures (Kellert, 1976). While clinical features of disease (such as tissue damage or viral infection) will be invariant, the variability rests with the differing experiences of illness and the label, meaning and understanding applied to particular symptoms (Fabrega, 1974; Mechanic, 1978). An example of the differing meanings attached to disease is provided by Mechanic's (1968) reference to a study of a skin disorder (dyschromatic spirochetosis) in a South American tribe. The disease was so prevalent 'that Indians who did not have [it] were regarded as abnormal and were even excluded from marriage' (p. 16).

In sum then, variations in the meaning attached to the terms disease, illness and sickness illustrate the themes inherent in this book. Ill health is more than just an identifiable disease, it is in part the person's perception and interpretation of a particular symptom or cluster of symptoms. Ill health is not merely something which happens to us; as human beings we actively process information in an attempt to make sense of it. The perceptions or representations we construct in relation to health threats determine our responses. When faced with a symptom or diagnostic information, the manner in which we interpret it will determine our subsequent behaviour (Petrie and Weinman, 1997).

Defining health

One might assume that health is simply the opposite of illness; health is often defined as the absence of illness and, in this sense, is in opposition to it. However, as Radley (1994) notes, as individuals, we only tend to be aware of health as a state of being when symptoms of ill health appear, disease is diagnosed and illness experienced. The fact that health seems to be an assumed state is no doubt one reason why it is difficult to persuade people to work at maintaining it. In addition, the historical focus has been upon the biomedical model, and hence the identification of disease processes has been the focus of much research. It is only within the last three decades that the balance has shifted towards identifying factors which promote and maintain good health and hence improve one's quality of life. Both official definitions of health and lay beliefs about health and illness reflect the fact that health refers not just to an absence of illness but to a broad spectrum of social and physical functioning.

Official definitions of health

The World Health Organization (WHO), in its 1948 constitution, proposed that health should be seen as 'a complete state of physical, mental and social well-being, and not merely the absence of disease or infirmity' (WHO, 1948). With the launch in 1978 of the WHO's *Global Strategy for Health for All by the Year 2000*, the aim was 'the attainment by all citizens of the world by the year 2000 of a level of health that will permit them to lead a socially and economically productive life' (WHO, 1981). This was developed in England in the *Health of the Nation* (White Paper, Department of Health, 1992), which sets out a number of such targets to be achieved by the beginning of the twenty-first century.

The underlying assumption is that there is a clear relationship between people's behaviour, lifestyle and health. Patterns of living and personal relationships affect our health status. The aim is that everyone should work together to promote health, prevent disease, alleviate unavoidable disease and disability and ensure that everyone is able to be sufficiently healthy to work and to participate in the social life of the community. The WHO definition paints a positive vision of health as complete well-being, in which a preoccupation with disease is replaced by a recognition of the interaction between the individual and their environment in determining health. This signals the move away from a disease or biomedical model of health to one emphasising the interaction between biological processes and psychological and social factors.

Lay beliefs and health and illness

As with official definitions, research evaluating people's beliefs about health indicate that, to the lay public, health is not merely the converse of illness. Lay beliefs about health and illness are derived from a range of sources including 'folk-models', the mass media, alternative medical practice and 'common sense' understandings derived from both personal experience and consultation with family and friends (Lupton, 1994). A number of studies have investigated what people mean when they talk about health. One of the earliest of such evaluations was conducted by Herzlich (1973) who interviewed a middle-class sample in Paris and Normandy. Health was identified as having three dimensions: absence of illness, a 'reserve' of health, which was determined by temperament and constitution, and 'equilibrium' or a state of well-being. Illness was seen as the product of an interaction between the person's individual characteristics and their 'way of life', especially urban life. Health then is a complex entity which is experienced in relation to one's broader social environment.

Similar constructs to describe health were identified by Williams (1983) from his interviews with a group aged sixty and above in Scotland. The three main conceptions identified were: health as the absence of disease, health as a continuum of strength–weakness and health as being fit for work. Involvement in everyday activities was seen as being not only an index of current health status but also a way of maintaining future health (Williams, 1990). A broader view of health, expanding upon constructs obtained by Herzlich and Williams, was obtained from the Health and Lifestyles Survey (Blaxter, 1990) which questioned 9,000 people. In this survey nine discrete dimensions of health were identified (see box 1.2). Health is clearly more than a unitary concept and more than just absence of illness; health involves behavioural, social and interpersonal elements.

Box 1.2 Lay beliefs about health

The nine discrete dimensions of health derived from the *Health and Lifestyles* survey conducted by Mildred Blaxter in 1990:

   (i) 'not-ill' (or without disease)
  (ii) in spite of disease (for example, 'I am very healthy although I do have diabetes')
 (iii) as a reserve (for example, 'when ill I recover very quickly')
 (iv) as a behaviour or living a healthy life (such as being a vegetarian, or a non-smoker and non-drinker)
  (v) physical fitness
 (vi) vitality ('full of get up and go' or 'full of life')
(vii) social relationships (for example, relating well to other people)
(viii) function (that is, an ability to do things)
 (ix) psychosocial well-being (for example, being mentally and spiritually as one)

In a further study which generated descriptions of health and illness from eleven to eighteen year old adolescents, Millstein and Irwin (1987) found that, although somatic feeling states (feeling good/feeling sick) were the most frequently mentioned category for both health and illness, descriptors of the two states differed in a number of ways. Health was more likely to be described in terms of functional status (easy to run a mile/go out and play), preventive-maintenance behaviours (eating a good diet) and restrictions of the health concept (not having too many illnesses). Illness was more likely to be described in terms of indicators of illness (swollen joints/appendicitis), role functioning (not going to school) and dependence on the evaluation of others (mom says I'm sick). Within the older age groups in the sample, health concepts tended to place less emphasis on 'the absence of illness' and more on the behavioural and interpersonal elements.

More recently, Stainton Rogers (1991) found that descriptions of health derived from seventy participants could be divided into internal and external explanations. Internal explanations included those based on behaviour (e.g. looking after oneself), mind (e.g.

positive attitudes), heredity (healthy constitution), and the body's defences (fighting off disease). External factors involved chance, social policy (e.g. good living standards) and medical advances (e.g. inoculations). Explanations for illness resulted in similar internal factors (unhealthy behaviour, belief and heredity factors) but with more external factors which included chance, other people (e.g. exposure to germs), disease organisms (infections), products of social forces (e.g. pollution) and medical intervention.

A further finding to emerge from qualitative analyses of lay beliefs is that social class differences exist in the way in which health and illness is explained and experienced. D'Houtarud and Field (1984) analysed the responses of a large sample in France and found that middle-class respondents were more likely to think of health in positive and expressive terms, such as 'good physical equilibrium', whereas urban and rural workers were more likely to think in negative and instrumental terms, such as 'avoiding excesses' and 'being able to work'. Studying a smaller sample in the UK, Calnan (1987) found that working-class women tended to use functional definitions, such as 'the ability to get through the day', whereas their professional counterparts were more likely to use multi-dimensional definitions, which included the absence of illness and being fit.

In a further study, Calnan and Johnson (1985) found that middle-class women living in London, when describing health, were likely to talk about engaging in exercise, being fit and active and eating the right food. In contrast working-class women emphasised the importance of getting through the day without feeling ill as being central to feeling healthy. Both groups emphasised that being healthy meant not having to take time away from work or visiting the doctor. Blaxter (1983) notes that illness was viewed by her working-class middle-aged female interviewees as a weakness, as 'giving in'.

Accounts reflect personal experience and it is perhaps inevitable that there are class differences in the descriptions offered. Other findings similarly reflect the influence of personal experience upon accounts offered. For example, a sample of mothers with young children interviewed by Pill and Stott (1982) put forward the belief that, because of their responsibilities as wife and mother, they 'did not have time' to be ill and had to 'carry on' in spite of illness. Given that people differ in their beliefs about health and illness it is perhaps not surprising that there are also individual differences in the way in which health complaints are presented to practitioners and in the treatment expectations people have.

Other studies have evaluated the way in which people conceptualise the causes of illness. In general, such studies suggest that people distinguish between causes which are germ related and those which are lifestyle based. Thus, Pill and Stott (1982) found that the main causes of illness described by a group of young Welsh working-class women included transmission by germs and individual behaviour, including the importance of food, hard work and mental attitudes in maintaining resistance to disease, while a smaller group emphasised hereditary factors. Blaxter (1983), on the basis of interviews with middle-aged working-class Scottish women, similarly notes that infection, heredity and external agents, such as damp housing or stress, are referred to as causal agents of illness.

Both health and illness are seen as being influenced by internal and external factors. In general, health can be defined either negatively (i.e. as the absence of illness), as a general constitutional aspect of the person or in positive functional terms (i.e. physical fitness and the ability to do things). Thus, while health is defined with regard to illness it is also defined with regard to a spectrum of social and physical functioning.

In sum, disease is the diagnosed abnormality of functioning, illness is the experience of that disease, while sickness is the label applied by others to the ill or diseased person. Lay beliefs about health and illness seem to reflect these distinctions. In addition, lay beliefs reflect not only the myriad of factors likely to influence the states of disease (constitution or germs), illness (state of well being) and sickness (vitality or fitness for work), but also the important causative role played by social factors in relation to ill health. Indeed, a full understanding of health and illness can only be achieved by taking into account variations in cultural and societal beliefs and expectations.

Health in a wider social context

A person's beliefs about health and illness are connected to wider social and cultural factors. Definitions of health are affected by age, gender and social background because they reflect aspects of that person's life situation. Actual health is also dependent upon personal behaviour which is in turn influenced by social and economic factors. Within the Western world this century has witnessed a steady improvement in health for much of the population. However, it has become increasingly apparent since the 1970s that these improvements are not equivalent across different social groups or geographical regions. Research has highlighted two major lines of enquiry as explanations for such variations in health status, one focusing upon deprivation (poverty, poor housing, unemployment), the other highlighting personal behaviour or lifestyle factors (smoking, diet, alcohol consumption). Inevitably these are interdependent rather than being mutually exclusive (Whitehead, 1990).

In investigations of health variations, death rates are often used as a measure of health. Although not a particularly sensitive measure of health, death rates have the advantage of being accurate and objective. While not providing any direct index of the prevalence of non-life-threatening conditions, there is some indication that population differences in death rates are closely related to self-report measures of illness, including day-to-day minor ailments (Arber, 1987).

Numerous studies in the United Kingdom including *The Black Report* (1980) (Townsend and Davidson, 1982; Townsend, Davidson and Whitehead, 1992) and *The Health Divide* (Whitehead, 1990) have consistently shown differences in mortality rates according to income and social class. Similar relationships have been found in other European countries and beyond, including New Zealand, Australia and Japan (Davey Smith, Bartley and Bane, 1990). National figures for the UK consistently show two- to threefold differences in death rates between professional occupations (social class I) and unskilled manual occupations (social class V) (Wilkinson, 1996). Sixty five of the seventy eight most important causes of death among men are more common in manual than non-manual occupations and sixty two of the top eighty two among women (Townsend *et al.*, 1988). If manual workers experienced the same death rates as the non-manual classes, there would be 42,000 fewer deaths each year in the sixteen to seventy four age group (Jacobson, Smith and Whitehead, 1991). The life expectancy for children born to parents with unskilled manual occupations is on average seven years less than the life expectancy of children born to parents with professional occupations. This contrast is even more marked in the case of children of single mothers who are not in paid employment (Judge and Benzeval, 1993).

In addition to social class variations there are marked geographical variations in death rates within countries. Within the United Kingdom there are increases in death rate in the north and west of the country which cannot be explained purely on the basis of social class differences (Jacobson, Smith and Whitehead, 1991). While such variations may be explained in part by climatic differences or dietary variations, it seems that socio-economic factors are the primary cause (Whitehead, 1992). That is, in more prosperous regions there seem to be social and economic advantages that benefit people from all occupational groups.

A number of theories have been advanced to explain these socio-economic and geographical variations in mortality. Some authors have argued that social class differences in mortality are more apparent than real, reflecting a bias in the way in which statistics are collected (Bloor, Samphier and Prior, 1987). However, this is not borne out by a number of studies including those within single occupational groups which show clear health differences between higher and lower occupational grades in terms of both longevity and morbidity (Marmot *et al.*, 1991). An alternative explanation, the 'downward drift' hypothesis, proposes that people are not more vulnerable to illness and death because they have a manual occupation but have a manual occupation because they have a greater prevalence of illness. While there is no doubt some element of truth to such claims, such theories cannot explain the extent of the difference between social classes (Marmot *et al.*, 1991).

Other explanations have emphasised social class variations in behavioural or in social factors. At a behavioural level, people on lower incomes have a higher consumption of cigarettes and a poorer diet (Blaxter, 1990); children of parents in social class V are also more likely to suffer from accidents in comparison to children of parents of any other class. However, it is clearly inappropriate to consider any such influence of behaviour upon health in isolation from the wider social context. Social class indices reflect work-related inequalities (Jones, 1994), such as working conditions, pay, prospects of unemployment and risk of accidents at work. For example, there is a clear relationship between unemployment and morbidity and mortality rates (Wilson and Walker, 1993). In addition, social class relates to income and poverty as highlighted by the Black Report. In this context the homeless appear to be particularly susceptible to a range of health problems. Wright and Weber (1987) report that the homeless are particularly susceptible to hypertension, gastrointestinal ailments and disorders of the extremities, as well as acute respiratory conditions.

Although absolute poverty (insufficient nourishment to avoid starvation) is relatively rare in the Western world, subsistence poverty (insufficient resources to meet basic requirements for food, shelter and clothing) is not uncommon. Just over 5 per cent of the population in Britain are judged to be below the 'poverty line' while 20 per cent are judged to be on the margins of poverty (George and Howards, 1991). Those most likely to fall into these categories are older people, the low paid, unemployed people, single parent families and the long-term disabled. As income rises in the lower-income groups so the ratio of those suffering from disease or reporting symptoms of ill health falls sharply (Blaxter, 1990).

Hence, one reason why social class differences are important is the assumption that they arise from social and economic factors and hence are preventable. This emphasises the critical interaction between social and individual factors and biological elements in determining health and illness. In line with lay beliefs, health is not only an absence of disease but is determined in part by behaviour, attitudes and affective state, which is in turn influenced by aspects of the broader social environment, such as employment and living standards. Any model or explanation which does not take into account this multiplicity of factors is likely to provide an inadequate representation of health and illness.

Explanations of health and illness

A number of models and explanations of health and illness have been elucidated which vary in the emphasis they place upon biological, psychological and social factors (see box 1.3). The various theoretical stances are outlined and critiqued in the following sections.

The biomedical model

Disease as a concept, derives from medical concerns with classification based upon characteristic constellations of symptoms and the conditions underlying them, which will enable an effective course of treatment to be applied. Health complaints are thus understood in terms of disordered biology and interventions are guided by biological principles based on 'either/or' and single cause explanations (Engel, 1977). A key assumption of the biomedical model is thus that health and illness are contrasting states of bodily functioning with health representing 'normal' biological functioning and illness representing a deviation from this norm. The cause of illness is typically viewed as being a pathogen, such as a virus or bacteria, or due to some inherent malfunction resulting from genetic factors. Treatment consists of rectifying biological functioning, usually by chemical means, or by eliminating/removing faulty parts by surgery or radiation. Within Western societies such explanations in medical terms predominate and have governed the thinking of most health practitioners for the past three centuries.

The biomedical model incorporates the assumption of mind–body dualism, viewing the mind and body as separate entities. It is reductionist in nature in that it reduces illness to a low-level process such as biochemical imbalances; the role of social or psychological processes is ignored. It is also a unitary model of illness, seeking explanations in terms of just disordered biological functioning rather than recognising the multiplicity of factors involved, of which one might be biological in nature. The emphasis also tends to be on failed or failing health and the identification and treatment of disease processes rather than upon the promotion or maintenance of health.

While medical technology has achieved tremendous success in understanding the pathophysiological basis of disease and in offering appropriate treatment, the biomedical model has been widely criticised and a number of its limitations highlighted (e.g. Eisenberg, 1977; Fabrega, 1975; Kleinman, 1980; Leigh and Reiser, 1985; Mechanic, 1980). Firstly, it is clear that health is partly determined by social factors (e.g. living conditions) and personal habits (e.g. smoking) rather than disordered biology. In addition, treatment efficacy is also influenced by social and psychological factors. Secondly, much medical help seeking results from distress (illness) associated with 'problems of living' and occurs in the absence of identifiable disease processes; medical help seeking is also largely shaped by cultural background and past experience. Thirdly, biomedicine deals poorly with the patient's experience of illness and in some instances, for example when

Box 1.3 Explanations of health and illness

Biomedical model

assumptions
    illness explained as a variation from 'normal' biological functioning

    psychological and social processes largely independent of the disease process

Medical anthropology

Biological anthropologists are concerned with the causes and impact of disease in various cultures
    assumption
        as per the biomedical model

Cultural anthropologists are concerned with cultural variations in the meaning and definition of illness
    assumption
        psychological and social processes shape one's understanding of health and illness

Medical sociology

assumption
    socio-economic, socio-cultural and socio-political factors influence health care use, the distribution of illness and lay explanations of health and illness

Health psychology

assumption
    psychological, including lifestyle and personality, as well as broader social factors influence susceptibility to disease, the experience of illness and the process of recovery

Biopsychosocial model

assumption
    mind and body together determine health – health is a complex interplay of:

        biological factors: for example, genetics, viruses, bacteria and structural defects

        psychological factors: for example, cognitions, emotions and motivations

        social factors: for example, society, community and family

disease processes are not evident, can actually increase the patient's level of distress (illness). As more than 50 per cent of GP visits are for non-disease-based complaints, it is perhaps not surprising that a biomedical perspective will frequently result in unsatisfactory treatment and a continuation of the patient's illness.

As a result, many authors have argued that psychological and social dimensions, in addition to biological dimensions, must be taken into account in order to understand illness and help-seeking behaviour. Indeed, there is a long tradition of theory and research offering explanations for health and illness from other than a biomedical perspective, with interest in such work having increased dramatically in the past three decades. Medical anthropology during the 1960s, medical sociology during the 1970s and behavioural medicine and health psychology during the 1980s have emerged to offer differing but interlinked accounts of health and illness. As Mechanic (1986) noted:

> cultural definitions, social development, and personal needs shape the experience of illness and meanings attributed to physical factors that serve as its basis. (p. 101)

A brief reflection on each tradition will help to illuminate the diversity of factors influencing health and illness.

Medical anthropology

> Medical anthropology is about how people in different cultures and social groups explain the causes of illness, the types of treatment they believe in, and to whom they turn if they become ill. It is also the study of how these beliefs and practices relate to biological and psychological changes in the human organism, in both health and disease. (Helman, 1990, p. 1)

Two distinct and opposing anthropological models have been used to analyse disease; these are biological anthropology and cultural anthropology (Armelagos *et al.*, 1992; Helman, 1990). Biological anthropologists, with a background in a variety of subfields of medical science, such as genetics or epidemiology, are interested in understanding the causes and impact of disease in various population groups. Although the basic approach has changed over the years, this perspective has been criticised even recently as too medical (Singer, 1989) and overly concerned with physical, biological factors (Armelagos *et al.*, 1992).

In contrast, cultural anthropology has drawn attention to cultural meanings associated with symptoms and illness behaviour. Within this framework research has focused on the way in which cultural groups categorise and define illness (Young, 1981) and make decisions to resort to the variety of popular, folk or professional therapies available in most societies (Young and Garro, 1982). Various groups of 'healers' exist in most societies and it is important to understand from the perspective of any given society how people are recognised as being 'ill', how they present their illness to recognised 'healers' and the way in which the 'illness' is managed. As Angel and Thoits (1987) note, we inherit from our culture a shared understanding of health and illness which places a limit on the range of possible explanations we have for our physical and psychological states and the structure of our help-seeking options. Helman (1990) comments that:

> one cannot understand how people react to illness, death or other misfortune without an understanding of the type of culture they have grown up in or acquired. (p. 7)

From an anthropological perspective, biomedical explanations are part of Western culture and hence not only determine health care provision but also shape the manner in which lay people within such cultures understand, describe and seek care for symptoms. This is highlighted by Armelagos and his colleagues (1992) who argue that biomedicine can be conceptualised 'as one of many world-wide ethnomedicines, that of Western cultures and empiricist scientific thought' (p. 40). Just as it may be the norm in some cultures to view ailments as a result of sorcery or witchcraft, it is the norm in Western societies to experience bodily ailments in medical terms (Radley, 1994).

The cultural context

The health beliefs of professionals and lay persons alike are structured and informed by a cultural context from which they cannot be separated and without which they cannot be fully understood (Fabrega, 1974). Thus, in Western societies illness is viewed as a 'person centred, temporally bounded and discontinuous' event (Fabrega, 1974, p. 198) with less reference to family, community or the gods (Landrine and Klonoff, 1992). The basis of Western concepts of health and illness is to assume that disease is caused by naturally occurring agents (e.g. bacteria, viruses, stress) and that the person who 'has' the disease will seek help from a trained expert who possesses the knowledge about how to diagnose and treat that disease. Within Western societies there is thus a:

> prominence and pre-occupation with the technological and biomedical aspects – the technological fix – of health and illness. (Heggenhougen and Shore, 1986, p. 1236)

Rather than adopting such a person-centred view, many other cultures draw upon interpersonal or supernatural explanations for their illness and hence have their own cures for illness and their own healers. This cultural distinction between natural and supernatural explanations has been examined in an extensive survey of 189 cultures (Murdoch, 1980). Theories of supernatural causation involving mystical retribution (punishment by the gods), animistic causation (loss of soul for wrongdoing) and magical causation (witchcraft, sorcery and the 'evil eye') were invoked by most cultures in the world. Few cultures believed in theories of natural causation involving viruses, bacteria, ageing, accidents and stress. Numerous reports of such belief systems are provided in the literature. For example, within the Twsana culture in Botswana three main causes of sickness are recognised: witchcraft, ancestor's anger and pollution through breaking of taboos. The cause is usually divined by healers through the use of bones. Oracle bones may tell the healer that a disease is 'modern' (i.e. one that arrived after contact with humans) or that it 'just happened' (i.e. implying the absence of discernible social or moral causality). In such cases the healer may refer the patient to the hospital or nearby clinic. Lack of cure is usually attributed to 'the will of God' (Ingstad, 1989). More recently Farmer (1990) has found that many rural Haitians understand AIDS not in terms of viral explanations but as a disease caused by (a) malign magic 'sent' to those who violate social and behavioural taboos and (b) most likely to emerge in those with a diathesis of 'bad blood'.

Such variations clearly have major implications for understanding and treating illness across cultures and particularly within culturally diverse societies. Thus, many ethnic minority groups within Western societies have their own indigenous folk healers whose cures are consistent with the beliefs held by many, dependent upon age, acculturation and so on, within that cultural group (e.g. Bullough, 1972; Snow, 1978; Spector, 1991). Ethnic minority groups may thus understand and explain their symptoms in terms which differ from those offered by Western health care professionals. Such differences inevitably have major implications for health education and treatment and yet are often poorly understood or ignored by Western health care professionals. As Snow (1978) noted, if the doctor is not aware of the group's beliefs, they may not ask the questions which would elicit the patient's real fears and, if they are insensitive to alternative ways of viewing symptoms, they may not create a climate in which the patient will feel able to talk about their fears. Many ethnic minority groups may thus be ill served by Western medical provision. It is unlikely that the past two and a half decades since Snow's comments have witnessed anything other than a small change in this regard.

Interpretations of and explanations for bodily symptoms and the form of help considered appropriate can thus only be understood by reference to the cultural context in which the behaviour occurs. In this vein biomedical explanations are part of Western culture, not only determining health care provision but shaping lay understanding of health and illness.

Medical sociology

Medical sociology (as the subdiscipline was first named and which term is still preferred in the United States) or the sociology of health and illness (the term preferred in the UK and Australia) has drawn attention to the implications of broader societal issues for understanding health and illness. This includes study of the influence of socio-economic and socio-political factors upon health care use, the effect of social relationships upon the distribution of illness and the way in which different groups in society explain health and illness. During its history, the sociology of health and illness has drawn upon three dominant theoretical perspectives: functionalism, political economy and social constructionism (Lupton, 1994).

The functionalist approach

The functionalist approach to medical sociology discusses social relations in the health care setting in relation to defined roles and functions by which social order is maintained. The classic functionalist position is to view illness as a potential state of social deviance accompanied by feelings of stigma, shame and vulnerability. Hence the role of the medical profession is to act as an institution of social control using its power to distinguish between normality and 'deviance'. Medicine and the medical profession are thus viewed as instrumental factors in the control or maintenance of social order. Parsons (1951a), one of the first to direct the attention of sociology to such issues, introduced the term 'sick role' to describe the accepted actions (e.g. remaining in bed, taking time away from work) taken by people who are ill. The seriously ill person is thus deviating from the expectations of social roles, their deviation being legitimised by conforming to the norms of the 'sick role'. There are four main components inherent in the 'sick role'. Firstly, the sick person is exempt from performing their normal duties; secondly, they are exempt from a certain degree of responsibility for their own state; thirdly, the 'sick role' is only legitimate for a certain unspecified length of time; and, finally, being sick means being in need of help. Parsons argued that the aim of medicine is not only to help the person to recover their physical health but also to re-establish their normal social role. The original 'sick role' paradigm was based on an acute illness model in which individuals readily self-diagnose their symptoms, seek professional help within a short time after recognising their symptoms, begin a successful treatment programme, co-operate with the doctor and return to full health. Patients are expected to be co-operative, pleasant and quiet and to cede to medical personnel who are responsible for treating them. In this context medicine is viewed as part of the social order with practitioners afforded status and resources to ensure patients follow orders.

The functionalist perspective is, however, not without its critics. Gerson (1976), for example, points out that the picture of the passive, compliant, grateful patient dealing with the powerful, competent doctor is not necessarily a true reflection of reality. The doctor–patient relationship is not only influenced by dynamics which go beyond the sick role, it involves negotiation and a struggle for power.

The political economy perspective

The political economy perspective, which was particularly influential during the 1970s and 1980s, viewed medicine as a device for perpetuating social inequality. The basic tenet of this theory is that the aim of medicine is to ensure that the population remains healthy enough to contribute to the economic system, hence, there will be marginalised groups who have restricted access to health care provision and suffer from poor health as a result. Writers such as Freidson (1970) have argued that, as the remit of medicine has broadened and as social resources have been directed towards illness, so medical power and influence, and hence the control of the medical profession within society, have increased dramatically. Other sociological theorists have developed competing and complimentary versions of social control theory. Zola, for example, argued that medicine had become a 'major institution of social control' (Zola, 1972, p. 487), while Illich (1976) contended that the increasing dependence upon medicine as cure tended to obscure the political conditions which gave rise to ill health and removed consideration of the individual's ability to control their health.

The political economy approach thus gives rise to two alternative views. The first is that medicine is fundamentally good and hence it is important to seek more and better provision for the less privileged. The second is to view biomedicine as seeking to narrow the cause of ill health to a single factor, which can be treated by pharmaceutical or technological means, while ignoring central socio-economic factors contributing to health and which result from capitalist production. These include pollution, occupational hazards, stress and over-processed foods treated with chemicals (McKee, 1988).

Social constructionism

Social constructionists have argued that all knowledge, including our understanding of health and illness, is a social construction. Thus, symptoms only become meaningful as signs of illness because of the way we define them. Hence lay explanations of health and illness are no less legitimate or valid than any other explanation (Dingwall, 1976). Indeed, as noted, lay explanations have formed the focus of numerous research studies which have attempted to ascertain what people mean by the terms health and illness. A rather more formal approach to lay representations has been adopted by psychologists, following an influential paper published by Leventhal and his colleagues (Leventhal, Meyer and Nerenz, 1980). They argued that:

> public representations are important, but as patients experience an illness in themselves, shared public beliefs will be substantially modified to fit the patient's own concrete experiences. (p. 27)

A large body of research investigating and analysing illness representations has developed since that date (Petrie and Weinman, 1997; Skelton and Croyle, 1991).

The societal context

It is thus widely recognised that to understand health and illness requires an acknowledgement of the wider socio-political dimensions. Access to both the opportunity to live a healthy lifestyle and to health care facilities themselves is determined in part by both the macro- and micro-cultural context in which we live. As Baer, Singer and Johnsen (1986) note, health involves:

> access to and control over the basic material and non-material resources that sustain and promote life at a high level of satisfaction. (p. 95)

Hence the struggle for life consists of having access to uncontaminated drinking water and food, adequate housing and sanitation, as well as access to health care provision. These issues apply both between and within societies, as witnessed by social class differences in health and illness.

Beliefs about what is and what is not healthy are shaped by social, moral, economic and interpersonal factors. Just as health and illness cannot be considered without reference to the broader cultural context so they cannot be considered in isolation from the broader socio-cultural or socio-political framework in which we live. Health is shaped by access to material resources while beliefs about what is and what is not healthy are in turn shaped to some extent by social factors. Signs and symptoms are interpreted in the context of the culture within which we live.

Health psychology

Health psychology, as the most recent contributor to the field, has emerged within the past two decades to reflect the growing application of psychological theory and practice to understanding health and illness. It has been defined as:

> the aggregate of the specific educational, scientific, and professional contributions of the discipline of psychology to the promotion and maintenance of health, the prevention and treatment of illness, and the identification of the etiologic and diagnostic correlates of health, illness, and related dysfunction. (Matarazzo, 1980, p. 815)

There are now numerous textbooks devoted to the subject (e.g. Sarafino, 1994; Taylor, 1995) as well as specialist journals. Such texts place great emphasis on the biopsychosocial model (Engel, 1977, 1980; Schwartz, 1982), which highlights the fact that any health or illness outcome is the consequence of the complex interaction between biological, social and psychological factors. Both body and mind, as well as the person's broader social environment, affect their state of health. Susceptibility to disease, the experience of illness and recovery patterns are influenced by both psychological and social factors. Psychological factors include lifestyle and personality; the way in which people perceive and feel about signs and symptoms. For example, those whose emotions are relatively positive are less disease prone and recover more quickly from illness than those whose emotions are relatively negative. Our behaviour and hence our lifestyle is also influenced by family, friends and the broader society in which we live. If groups value and promote health activities, such as exercises, then such activities are more likely to increase; the same applies to unhealthy activities such as smoking or drinking.

In applying the biopsychosocial model many health professionals refer to the need to 'understand the whole person' or to adopt a 'holistic' approach (Lipowski, 1986). Engel

(1980) has outlined the interplay of biological, psychological and social systems which interrelate within the biopsychosocial model. Each large, complex system consists of smaller simpler systems. The biological system, including the immune and nervous system, consists of organs, tissues and cells. The psychological system, including experience and behaviour, consists of cognitions, emotions and motivation. The social system includes society, community and family as subsystems. As systems they are constantly changing and have components which interrelate. Health then operates as a complex interplay of factors within factors. A person may have a genetic predisposition to develop heart disease, for example an inherited tendency to high cholesterol, but may increase his or her risk through lifestyle factors, such as sedentary living, smoking, consumption of high fat foods and a 'stressful' work environment. If his or her broader social environment, such as work colleagues, encourages and values such activities, rather than alternative health-promoting activities, then the person's risk of developing ill health is likely to be increased still further.

Given that the biopsychosocial model is the prevailing model within the health psychology literature, it is perhaps surprising that broader cultural and societal factors often receive little attention. As recent specialist texts note (Radley, 1994; Stainton Rogers, 1991), many psychological theories of health and behaviour are framed without any consideration for the way in which culture and society mould our understanding. Indeed, a Western cultural tradition has largely informed health psychology's research on illness behaviour and beliefs. As Marteau (1989) comments in a review of psychological theories, 'there is a danger that health psychology will become a health psychology of the detached individual, without regard to the social, economic and environmental context'. This is perhaps illustrated by the fact that in 326 articles published in forty five issues over the first nine years of the journal *Health Psychology* only one article dealt with culture and health (Landrine and Klonoff, 1992). Only rarely are attempts made to integrate psychological with broader social factors (Carroll, Bennett and Davey Smith, 1993).

Other concerns with the biopsychosocial model have also been raised (Reynolds, 1996). For example, the emphasis on personality and lifestyle may lead to an overemphasis on the possibility of individual control. Similarly, the emphasis on 'healthy' behaviours may lead to decreased tolerance for those whose behaviour is health jeopardizing. Indeed, there may be occasions when access to biomedical care is restricted for such people. For example, heart surgery may be denied to someone who smokes excessively or who is overweight, unless they change their lifestyle.

Although there are shortcomings which need to be acknowledged, a wealth of research within health psychology has been directed towards understanding and predicting the relationship between health beliefs and health behaviours or other health-related actions. Many models of health beliefs assume that human beings are rational information processors and that health-related behaviour is a consequence of a series of rational stages, each of which can be measured. Health behaviours are those actions taken by someone who believes themselves to be healthy to prevent disease or detect it in its asymptomatic stage. Such actions can involve the adoption of behaviours beneficial to health (such as exercise), the giving up of actions likely to compromise one's health (such as smoking) or actions taken to identify and treat an illness at an early stage with the aim of stopping or reversing the problem (such as breast or testicular self-examination or screening). Other health-related actions include the recognition and interpretation of symptoms, decisions to seek medical care and whether to adhere to treatment provided.

If human beings were indeed rational information processors and carefully weighed up the pros and cons of performing a particular behaviour, reflecting upon the seriousness of, or their susceptibility to, a particular illness, then the relationship between health beliefs and behavioural outcomes would be relatively straightforward to predict and assess. For example, if I am informed by a reliable source of the dangers of taking a particular substance or eating a particular diet and am aware of the advantages of altering my habit or diet, then, if I were a rational decision maker, one would predict a corresponding change in my behaviour. However, not only may we be unduly influenced by specific aspects of our environment, we also tend to hold beliefs which are not entirely rational in nature. Indeed, one of the reasons people continue to practise unhealthy behaviours is their inaccurate perception of risk and susceptibility; as human beings we are unrealistically optimistic about our health (Weinstein, 1983, 1984, 1987).

In comparison to others who are the same age and gender as ourselves, we tend to think we are less likely than they are to develop health problems. Firstly, human beings seem to have an exaggerated sense of their ability to control their health and hence may ignore potential health risks. For example, they tend to ignore behaviour that increases their health risk (I don't take much exercise but that does not matter) and focus instead upon behaviour that reduces their risk (but at least I do not smoke). Secondly, we may have little direct experience with health threats and so may under-estimate our own vulnerability. We also tend to assume that if a problem has not yet appeared, it is not likely to do so in the future.

Hence, while many theories in health psychology assume that human beings are rational decision makers, this is clearly not the case. While beliefs and expectations shape health care decisions, these also need to be framed within the broader context of the person's cultural and social life.

Summary

Thus, in attempting to understand health and health behaviour two issues are noteworthy. Firstly, there are a number of differing yet complementary theoretical explanations for understanding health and health behaviour. A number of authors have pointed out that in order to understand the process through which individuals identify and evaluate illness it is necessary to take into account the theories and research of psychology, sociology and anthropology (Angel and Thoits, 1987; Landrine and Klonoff, 1992; Stainton Rogers, 1991). While psychology may provide information about the way in which we think about health and illness, such knowledge must, of necessity, be informed by both the culture and society within which such beliefs are formed. Unfortunately, because theories have been developed within specific disciplinary frameworks, there is a tendency for researchers to draw on one set of explanations while failing to acknowledge others.

A second issue is the assumption, partly rooted within Western cultural tradition, that the 'patient' is a passive recipient of 'care'; hence the notion of compliance with medical care. Within the Western medical context the 'good' patient is generally regarded as one who is passive, co-operative and uncomplaining, accepting the views of the 'expert'.

Even within a Western cultural context the person actively interacts with the health care system, making assumptions about the diagnosis and treatment. People actively seek to make sense of signs and symptoms and build their own understanding of their illness and the disease process. Such understanding is shaped by a range of psychological processes and influenced by beliefs and expectations, which in turn are shaped by cultural and societal factors. The extent to which assumptions and understandings are shared by the patient and health care provider will clearly determine the extent to which they accept and/or adhere to treatment offered and cope with the illness experienced.

Health and illness can only be understood by examining the interaction between social and individual factors with biological elements. Health is determined in part by behaviour, attitudes and affective state, which is in turn influenced by aspects of the broader social environment, such as employment and living standards. Any model or explanation which does not take into account this multiplicity of factors is likely to provide an inadequate representation of health and illness.

FURTHER READING

M. Bury (1997). *Health and Illness in a Changing Society*. London: Routledge.

D. Lupton (1994). *Medicine as Culture: Illness, disease and the body in western societies*. London: Sage.

A. Radley (1994). *Making Sense of Illness: The social psychology of health and disease*. London: Sage.

R. G. Wilkinson (1996). *Unhealthy Societies: The afflictions of inequality*. London: Routledge.

CHAPTER 2

Preventive health behaviour

CHAPTER OVERVIEW

This chapter examines both health-promoting behaviours, such as exercise and diet, and preventive action including participation in screening programmes and self-examination. The first part of the chapter evaluates research examining the role that exercise and diet play in determining health. Difficulties motivating people to change their lifestyle are also discussed. The second part of the chapter presents a brief overview of social cognition models in relation to health behaviour change. The final section of the chapter overviews issues relating to preventive health behaviours, including an evaluation of the utility of social cognition models in predicting participation in screening programmes and self-examination. While screening allows for the early detection of disease, recent research has raised questions regarding the psychological costs of screening.

This chapter covers:

Exercise and health
Diet and health
Social cognition models and health behaviour change
Participation in screening programmes
Self-examination
Psychological costs of screening

Introduction

Preventive health behaviours include both behaviours which are health promoting and actions which facilitate the detection of disease or disease risk factors and hence increase the likelihood that preventive or therapeutic action can be taken. Health-promoting behaviours include self-directed actions to alter diet, and alcohol and cigarette consumption, or the amount of exercise taken. Preventive actions include participation in screening programmes, breast and testicular self-examination, adherence to dietary advice, compliance with medical regimens and the use of health care services for vaccinations. Health behaviour can thus be defined as:

> Any action undertaken by a person believing himself to be healthy for the purpose of preventing disease or detecting it at an asymptomatic stage. (Kasl and Cobb, 1966, p. 246)

The idea that certain behaviours enhance health or prevent disease has been investigated in a variety of studies. For example, research has evaluated the association of lifestyle factors such as exercise and diet with lower morbidity and higher subsequent longer-term survival. This issue is examined in the first part of the chapter. It is widely recognised in industrial societies not only that behaviour patterns make a significant contribution to life expectancy, but that such behaviour patterns can be modified (Stroebe and Stroebe, 1995). A great deal of research effort has been directed towards evaluating factors predictive of health behaviour. Such knowledge is essential not only to facilitate the design of interventions to change health behaviours but also to target such interventions effectively. A range of factors influence the likelihood that individuals will or will not engage in certain health behaviours, including demographic, social, personality and cognitive factors, that is, beliefs, attitudes and knowledge. The latter in particular have formed a major focus of research as they are assumed to mediate the effects of demographic, social and personality-related factors. Thus the focus of a number of models in health psychology is upon cognitive variables as predictors of health behaviour; such models have been labelled social cognition models (Conner and Norman, 1996). Relevant models are outlined in the second section of the chapter as an introduction to understanding and predicting health behaviour. The final part of the present chapter then overviews studies which have drawn upon these models to evaluate factors predictive of both health-promoting and preventive behaviour.

Exercise, diet and health

There is increasing agreement that exercise and diet play an important role in determining health. As Dubbert (1992) comments:

> the evidence that a sedentary life-style lowers life expectancy for both men and women and contributes independently to the development of many prevalent chronic diseases is substantial and still increasing. (p. 616)

Many studies attest to the utility of exercise in disease prevention and treatment (Bouchard *et al.*, 1990), suggesting, for example, that those who engage in regular exercise are less likely to develop and die from coronary heart disease (e.g. Blumenthal *et al.*, 1980) and have lower blood pressure (e.g. Nelson *et al.*, 1986). In addition, evidence suggests that exercise may provide protection against some forms of cancer (Calabrese, 1990). In a recent commentary Vuori (1998) argues that substantial health benefits can be gained from only moderate daily physical activity, such as cycling or walking to work rather than travelling by car or other motorised transport (Oja, Vuori and Olavi, 1998).

Many have also argued that both the amount and content of Western diets is linked to the development of chronic disease. With regard to the former, during the 1960s and 1970s over consumption of food was thought to be the main contributor to the excessive accumulation of body fat or obesity. While it is now recognised that obesity is due to a multitude of factors, including genetics, metabolic rate and fat cells, as well as physical activity levels and eating behaviour (Brownell and Wadden, 1992), the fact that obesity is associated with an increased risk of coronary heart disease, diabetes, gall bladder disease, stroke, gout and orthopaedic problems, as well as being a major cause of high blood pressure has been well documented (Bray, 1986; Kannel and Gordon, 1979; Wardle, 1989).

With regard to the content of Western diets, high levels of fats and dietary cholesterol have been tied to atherosclerosis and ultimately to coronary heart disease (Stamler, Wentworth and Neaton, 1986), high levels of salt have been linked to hypertension (Falkner and Light, 1986), while diets high in fat and low in fibre have been associated with the development of cancer, particularly cancer of the colon (Levy, 1985).

The following sections examine briefly the extent to which a sedentary lifestyle and the amount and content of one's diet serve as risk factors for chronic disease. While lifestyle change is an important factor in the prevention of chronic illness, motivating people to change their lifestyle remains a problem. Reasons for this are also briefly discussed.

Exercise

Exercise, involving some form of programmed physical activity, results in a similar set of responses to those experienced during stress. In each case blood pressure, heart rate and peripheral blood flow, together with the secretion of such hormones as epinephrine, norepinephrine and cortisol are all increased. Reviewing the differences, Blumenthal and McCubbin (1987) suggest that physical exercise is additionally associated with major increases in oxygen demand, extraction and consumption, which may not be required during stress. On the other hand, stress leads to a neuroendocrine response adequate to maintain moderate levels of exertion, although the levels are not warranted by oxygen demand. This imbalance may explain why stress is not considered to be beneficial whilst exercise is.

The evidence for the beneficial effects of exercise has been evaluated using a range of methods with a variety physical health problems, such as hypertension, coronary heart disease and cancer, and in relation to mental health problems.

Exercise and blood pressure

Evidence for the possible beneficial effects of exercise in reducing the likely incidence of hypertension has been provided by a number of longitudinal studies investigating the effect of exercise during early adulthood with the incidence of hypertension in later life. In one study Paffenbarger, Thorne and Wing (1968) sent a questionnaire to over 8,000 college alumni some twenty two to thirty two years after graduation. Nine per cent of respondents had been diagnosed as hypertensive since graduating. The prevalence of hypertension was significantly lower for those who had been college athletes or reported five or more hours of exercise a week while at college. Whether physical activity per se some twenty or more years earlier is an accurate predictor of later hypertension is inevitably open to question. Those who engage in college athletic activity may, for example, be more likely to engage in physical activity throughout their lives or adopt a more generally healthy lifestyle.

In a further report, Paffenbarger *et al.* (1983) followed, over a six to ten year period, a sample of almost 15,000 Harvard alumni who had entered Harvard between sixteen and fifty years prior to the study. At the start of the study questionnaires were used to exclude hypertensive subjects and to assess leisure time physical activity. At follow up, hypertension was again assessed by questionnaire. The lack of strenuous, current exercise, together with body fat and parental hypertension, were all found to independently predict risk of hypertension. Interestingly, unlike their earlier report, college athleticism was not a predictor of hypertension in later life. In another study, Blair *et al.* (1984) assessed more than 6,000 normotensive men and women who were self-referrals to a preventive medicine clinic and followed them for between one and twelve years (median four years) to assess the development of hypertension. After adjusting for age, sex and follow-up interval, less-fit individuals had a relative risk of 1.52 of developing hypertension when compared with highly fit people.

Exercise and coronary heart disease

A number of epidemiological studies examining physical activity versus sedentary lifestyles have found that physical activity has a protective effect on total mortality in relation to coronary heart disease. Seminal work in this area was conducted by Paffenberger and his colleagues (see box 2.1).

Box 2.1 Exercise and coronary heart disease – longitudinal studies

Key research by Paffenbarger and his colleagues illustrates the importance of physical activity in protecting against heart disease. They investigated a sample of 16,936 male alumni who entered Harvard between 1916 and 1950. For each participant they collected archival material from the original college records detailing student health and participation in athletics, including entrance physical examination records. For alumni alive between 1962 and 1966 they collected questionnaire information concerning post-college physical exercise activities, health status and lifestyle. In a 1972 follow up, surviving alumni also detailed any incidence of diagnosed coronary heart disease and other diseases. For alumni who had died between 1962 and 1978 official death certificates were examined and times and causes of death recorded. Five hundred and seventy two alumni had suffered first attacks of coronary heart disease between 1962 and 1978, 215 fatal and 357 non-fatal. During the same sixteen year period a total of 1,413 alumni had died. The major finding was that habitual post-college exercise, not student sports activity, predicted low coronary heart disease risk. Sedentary alumni, even ex-varsity athletes, had a high risk level and exercise benefit was independent of coronary lifestyle elements, such as smoking, obesity, weight gain and adverse parental life-style history. Men who participated in physical activities using more than 2,000 calories a week had death rates one-quarter to one-third lower than those who were less active.

(Paffenbergar *et al.*, 1984; Paffenbergar *et al.*, 1986.)

Similar positive effects of physical activity have been reported in further studies. For example, in a study conducted by Leon *et al.* (1987), approximately 13,000 men aged thirty five to fifty seven years with no clinical evidence of coronary heart disease were assessed for amount of leisure time physical activity and risk factors. All participants were followed up after about seven years. Moderate leisure time physical activity was associated with fewer fatal coronary heart disease events and sudden deaths compared with low leisure time physical activity. There was no apparent further decrement associated with additional leisure time physical activity.

In a review of twenty five epidemiological studies, Froelicher and Oberman (1977) report that sixteen of the studies revealed a positive effect of exercise and physical activity on the prevention of cardiovascular disease (the remaining nine studies reported no such association). In a further review, the majority of the forty two methodologically adequate studies evaluated, demonstrated a statistically significant relationship between differing levels of physical activity and the onset of coronary heart disease (Powell *et al.*, 1987).

Other studies which have assessed fitness, as measured by treadmill performance, suggest that levels of fitness associated with moderate levels of exercise are associated with a major reduction in mortality (Blair *et al.*, 1989). Studies in Finland (Salonen, Puska and Tuomilehto, 1982), Holland (Magnus, Matroos and Strackee, 1979) and the UK (Morris *et al.*, 1980) all show lower levels of coronary heart disease for men at high risk who self-select moderate amounts of predominantly light and moderate non-work physical activity. As Leon *et al.* (1987) suggest, this may be because the lower exertional heart rate associated with improved physical fitness decreases myocardial oxygen demands. This may reduce the possibility or severity of a myocardial infarction or of a fatal cardiac arrhythmia in the presence of significant coronary artery disease. Certainly it seems that long-term aerobic conditioning appears to produce positive adaptations on the cardiovascular system that may be protective against coronary heart disease.

Cancer

The relatively recent suggestion that exercise reduces mortality from cancer is difficult to verify as cancer represents an admixture of site-specific diseases, with varying clinical features and courses. Nevertheless, some research studies suggest that physical exercise is associated with a reduced incidence of mortality from all cancers (Paffenbarger, Hyde and Wing, 1987) while reviews suggest that increased physical activity may protect against cancer of the colon in men (I-Min, Paffenbarger and Hseih, 1991; Powell *et al.*, 1989) and that it is associated with a lower risk for certain reproductive cancers in women (Kohl, LaPorte and Blair, 1988; Calabrese, 1990).

While such results are promising, it is not possible to deduce whether exercise per se is the important ingredient. Thus, those who are physically active may also have significantly different diets or other attributes and habits which make them different from those who are non-physically active. Differing diets in particular could play an important role in relation to cancers of the digestive system. At best then, given the present state of knowledge, any conclusions about the relationship between physical activity and cancer will of necessity be tentative.

Adherence to exercise regimens

While the balance of evidence suggests that exercise and participation in physical activity have discernible health benefits, not only are there relatively low rates of exercise participation within the general population, but also adherence to exercise regimes, even amongst those who stand to benefit most, is poor. In this context, attendance at exercise sessions is the most common index of adherence. Although this does not take into account whether the exercise is performed at levels of duration and intensity sufficient to achieve the programme's health objectives (Perkins and Epstein, 1988), it does seem reasonable to assume that this would indeed be the case for those who continue to attend.

Within the general population in the US, epidemiological estimates suggest that more than 40 per cent of eighteen to sixty five year old adults are completely sedentary (Stephens, Jacob and White, 1985). Amongst eighteen to thirty year olds in Europe as many as 30 per cent do not engage in regular physical exercise (Steptoe et al., 1997). On average, only half those who initiate a voluntary exercise programme are still maintaining their level of exercise some six months later (Martin and Dubbert, 1982). In fact, the first three to six months appear to be critical; those who adhere beyond this stage are likely to continue to maintain their exercise schedule (Dishman, 1982). For many it is unlikely that exercise in and of itself is sufficiently attractive to motivate adherence. It entails a time commitment, effort and possible need to tolerate pain and discomfort, at least in the initial stages of adaptation.

A range of physiological, environmental and psychological factors have been identified as influencing short-term exercise adherence (Dishman, 1982, 1991). The overweight are less likely to maintain their participation in a fitness programme (Epstein, Koeske and Wing, 1984), while, in contrast, those high in self-motivation, enabling effective goal-setting, self-monitoring and self-reinforcement are more likely to do so (Dishman and Ickes, 1981). Encouragement by friends, family or health care professional can have a positive influence on exercise participation (Dishman, Sallis and Orenstein, 1985) as can convenience, such as exercising at home or as part of one's social activities (Wilhelmson et al., 1975). Those who believe they should take responsibility for their health are more likely to engage in exercise than people without such beliefs (Dishman, 1982).

The correlates of long-term maintenance of exercise behaviour appear to be less clear. A number of recent studies suggest that cognitive factors are likely to play an important role. For example, research suggests that the individual's beliefs or their self-efficacy concerning their perceived capabilities (Bandura, 1977) seems to be an important cognitive mediator in both the adoption and maintenance of exercise behaviour (Duncan and McAuley, 1993; McAuley, 1992, 1993; McAuley and Courneya, 1992; McAuley and Jacobson, 1991). Such factors form the focus of social cognitive models of health behaviour discussed later in the chapter.

Increasing exercise adherence

A number of studies have evaluated a range of strategies for increasing and maintaining exercise adherence. These include health promotion and education campaigns, as well as behavioural methods, such as written agreements or behavioural contracts, and cognitive-behavioural approaches involving self-monitoring, goal setting and feedback (see box 2.2). In reviewing fifty six studies evaluating behavioural and cognitive-behavioural interventions, Dishman (1991) suggests that these are usually associated with a 10 per cent to 25 per cent increase in frequency of physical activity when compared with no treatment control groups. As he notes, however, many interventions have lasted less than twelve weeks without any demonstrable fitness or health changes, while studies employing attention, placebo or minimally effective comparison conditions are associated with changes in physical activity comparable with the intervention condition. Indeed, he concludes by suggesting that the case for the effectiveness of behavioural interventions for promoting exercise and physical activity remains unclear. In this regard, Dubbert (1992) refers to the 'continuing problem of exercise adherence', adding that there have been 'no major breakthroughs in exercise adherence research'. Thus, in general, there have been more advances in understanding the health benefits of exercise than in encouraging people to participate in exercise programmes. Although the number of people who participate in regular exercise has increased over the past decade, progress in modifying people's exercise habits has been disappointing.

Diet

Excessive accumulation of body fat or obesity is linked to a number of chronic health problems while, conversely, weight loss appears to improve health. For example, weight loss has been found to improve glycemic control and reduce the need for medication in diabetics (Wing *et al.*, 1987), while weight loss is recommended as a treatment for hypertension (Blanchard, Martin and Dubbert, 1988). Others have argued that it is not body fat per se but its distribution in the body, in addition to oscillations in weight, which pose the most serious health risks. Indeed, while certain chronic diseases are undoubtedly more common in the obese, there is some evidence that obesity is associated with a lower incidence of other diseases: for example, respiratory diseases, infectious diseases and osteoporosis (Garner and Wooley, 1991).

With regard to dietary composition, the most frequently cited links with disease are those associating salt intake (assumed to be associated with hypertension and cardiovascular disease) and fat and dietary cholesterol (assumed to be associated with atherosclerosis and ultimately heart disease). Both the links between dietary composition and health and the appropriateness of dietary treatments for obesity have been the subject of considerable debate.

Diet and weight

A range of factors affect weight regulation including genetic factors, early eating and exercise experience, biological set point (i.e. each person has an ideal biological weight that cannot be greatly modified) and, ironically, dieting (Garner and Wooley, 1991). It seems that successive cycles of dieting and weight gain serve to enhance the efficiency of food use and metabolic control and in some cases may pose a greater danger to health than simply being overweight (Hamm, Shekelle and Stamler, 1989). In spite of this, dieting has been the most common approach to treating obesity, although long-term maintenance of weight loss is not impressive. Thus, over the past two decades, more comprehensive behavioural weight reduction programmes have been used, involving exercise, nutritional education, management of the environment (for example, eating only in one room), involving family or spouse and improving self-confidence, in conjunction with dietary restriction (Wardle, 1989). However, reviews of behavioural treatments suggest that at four to five years follow up most individuals will have regained any weight they have lost (Garner and Wooley, 1991). This factor, together with the possibility that the health risks of obesity may not be as clear as generally assumed, has led some to suggest that non-dieting interventions designed to increase exercise, normalise eating, reduce weight fluctuations and bring about qualitative changes in dietary composition are more appropriate than weight reduction programmes per se (Garner and Wooley, 1991). The question of whether it is weight reduction or qualitative changes in diet which serve to reduce health risks is illustrated by research relating to hypertension (Blanchard, Martin and Dubbert, 1988; Jacob, Wing and Shapiro, 1987).

Weight reduction and hypertension

It is generally assumed that weight reduction is associated with a reduction in blood pressure although there have been few long-term investigations. In addition, it has been argued that weight loss is associated with reduced sodium intake and that it is the latter which is responsible for reductions in blood pressure. In this context, many studies have failed to monitor change in sodium intake as a result of weight change or have included both weight change and diet as part of a lifestyle change programme. Thus, in a five year trial, Stamler *et al.* (1989) randomly assigned 201 mildly hypertensive men and women either to a control group or to an intervention group receiving advice aimed at weight reduction, change in diet composition – including salt composition – reduction in alcohol intake and increased exercise. The intervention led to reductions in sodium intake, significant reductions in weight and significant improvements in blood pressure. However, it is impossible to say whether the results were achieved through weight loss, reduced sodium intake or some combination of factors.

Indeed, there are few studies which have assessed the efficacy of weight loss on blood pressure independent of sodium restriction. However, one such study (Wing *et al.*, 1984) provides interesting findings. Mild hypertensives were randomly assigned either to a weight reduction diet or to a diet to alter sodium/potassium excretion. At the end of eight weeks the weight reduction group showed significant weight change but no significant change in sodium and potassium excretion, while the sodium/potassium patients showed significant reduction in sodium and increase in potassium excretion but no overall change in weight. Both groups showed significant decreases in blood pressure. The evidence from this study thus suggested that weight reduction and/or sodium reduction are associated with a reduction in blood pressure.

Dietary composition

With regard to sodium intake independent of weight change, both very low and very high levels have been shown to be related to high blood pressure. The association of high blood pressure with sodium rich diets is particularly evident in results from cross-cultural comparisons, although populations may also differ on variables other than salt intake (Page, 1983). For example, less-industrialised populations with low sodium intake also tend to be more physically active with less weight gain with age. However, a number of empirical studies bear out the contention that sodium-restricted diets have beneficial effects in terms of blood pressure reduction. In one such study MacGregor *et al.* (1982) restricted the sodium intake of nineteen hypertensives over a two week period. Subsequently they received, in random order, either a sodium supplement to return their total intake to baseline levels or a placebo. Blood pressure was lower during the low sodium phase of the study. In a subsequent study MacGregor and his colleagues found a progressive decline in blood pressure with salt restriction alone that was well maintained for sixteen of twenty participants (MacGregor *et al.*, 1989).

In the study by Wing *et al.* (1984) referred to earlier, the group assigned to the sodium-restricted potassium supplemented diet showed significant decreases in blood pressure. As these authors note, however, even if sodium level is related to blood pressure, it is not known whether the effect is related to absolute levels, the ratio of sodium intake to diet or the percentage change in sodium intake.

Taken overall research does tend to suggest that dietary amount and/or content plays an important role in the control of blood pressure. In this regard Blanchard, Martin and Dubbert (1988) contend that:

> Weight loss is a very effective method of reducing blood pressure [which should be] recommended for all obese hypertensives. (pp. 167 and 168)

Others, however, are rather more circumspect. This is partly due to the fact that weight loss is rarely maintained over time and partly due to the fact that dietary restriction can itself be associated with health risks via weight fluctuations. As Garner and Wooley (1991) suggest:

> qualitative changes in diet, rather than weight loss, may have a positive effect on health risk factors. (p. 764)

The extent to which qualitative aspects of diet play an important role is, however, difficult to evaluate given the relatively few well-controlled studies. In addition, it is very difficult to induce people to modify their diet and, should they initially comply, even more difficult to encourage them to adhere to dietary recommendations over time (Carmody, Matarazzo and Istvan, 1987). Adherence is not helped by the controversy surrounding some dietary advice. For example, although the relationship between sodium intake and hypertension is generally accepted, other proposed links, such as that between cholesterol levels in the blood and atherosclerosis, are more controversial. This debate is in the public as well as the academic domain. Thus, even though a number of studies have found that reducing cholesterol through dietary interventions reduces the incidence of coronary heart disease morbidity and mortality (e.g. Caggiula *et al.*, 1981), public controversies may undermine advice based upon such evidence.

Adherence to dietary restrictions

As is the case for exercise, adherence to dietary restrictions is low. Some dietary recommendations are for monotonous or restrictive intakes and may necessitate changes in meal planning or cooking methods. In addition, recommendations to change usually imply the need for life-long change to prevent an illness or occurrence of symptoms which may take years or decades to develop. Dietary change is a goal of treatment for a broad spectrum of chronic disease including hypertension, diabetes and renal disease. It is well documented that adherence generally tends to be poor when the regime to be followed is complex, needs to be followed for a long period of time and necessitates changes in the person's lifestyle. This is discussed in more detail in chapter 6. Hence, although people may initially comply with dietary recommendations, adherence is likely to decrease over time. Indeed, adherence to dietary recommendations is poor even for those, such as diabetics, who are likely to benefit most (Wing *et al.*, 1986). A particular problem associated with investigating adherence to dietary regimens is that dietary adherence is not generally amenable to any direct method of assessment.

As a result, a number of studies have evaluated strategies for promoting adherence to healthy diets (Cormody, Matarazzo and Istvan, 1987). Cognitive-behavioural interventions involving self-monitoring, stimulus control and contingency contracting have been used to help people modify their diet to some effect (Carmody *et al.*, 1982) (see box 2.2).

Box 2.2 Cognitive-behavioural interventions for promoting adherence

Self-monitoring – a client completed record of thoughts, feelings and target behaviours. Behavioural records may include such factors as the amount and timing of exercise, or type, timing and quantity of food intake.

Goal setting – agreed and manageable targets to achieve within a specified time frame: for example, a specified increase in an agreed exercise regimen.

Stimulus control – many health-related behaviours appear to be controlled, at least in part, by their antecedents. Particular stimuli elicit particular behaviours: that is, they serve as prompts or reminders to act in a particular way. Stimulus control techniques are designed to modify the antecedent of the target behaviour. With regard to diet, stimulus control techniques can include reserving only one room for eating, eating at the same time each day and only storing specified 'healthy' food in the house.

Contingency management – the goals of contingency management programmes are to increase desired behaviours, such as exercise or a healthy diet, and to decrease undesired behaviours. A number of contingency management procedures have been used:

social-reinforcement – having someone from the person's immediate environment provide a reward contingent upon achieving a specified goal.

self-reinforcement – the self-administering of rewards set by oneself for achieving specified goals.

behavioural contracting – this may take the form of a specified contract between oneself and another party: for example, a written contract may be agreed between parties to initiate and maintain an exercise programme.

Family-based interventions also appear to improve adherence. In a large-scale evaluation Carmody *et al.* (1986) provided participants with information about dietary change which was then discussed within the family group. A dietary counsellor also met with the families while certain family groups met with each other to discuss suggestions and problems. Families were also encouraged to share recipes; in addition they received regular printed information. Although such family interventions are clearly promising, they emphasise the degree of involvement required to influence lifestyle change.

In sum then, the balance of research evidence suggests that exercise and diet play an important role in maintaining health and well-being. There is also ample evidence to indicate that motivating people to change their activity levels or the amount and composition of their diet is not without its difficulties. This is true even amongst those who stand to benefit most. A range of social and psychological factors have been suggested as likely to influence decisions to adhere to exercise or dietary recommendations. However, research over the past two decades indicates that cognitive factors – that is, beliefs, attitudes and knowledge – are the most important determinants of health-related actions. Such factors are central to models of health behaviour, which have accordingly been termed social cognition models.

Social cognition models

'Social cognition is concerned with how individuals make sense of social situations' (Conner and Norman, 1996, p. 5). Social cognition models seek to describe important cognitions or thought processes and the role they play in the regulation of behaviour. Conner and Norman suggest there are two broad types of social cognition model. The first, which they label attribution models, are concerned with individuals' causal explanations of health-related events. As they note, the focus of much research within this tradition is upon how people respond to serious illness rather than preventive health behaviour in otherwise healthy individuals (see chapter 10). In contrast, the second type of social cognition model specifically seeks to predict future health behaviour on the basis of appraisal and processing of available information. The most widely cited social cognition models are social learning theory and the health locus of control construct which derives from it; self-efficacy theory, the theory of planned behaviour and the theory of reasoned action from which it derives; the health belief model; protection motivation theory; subjective expected utility theory; and the transtheoretical model of behaviour change (see box 2.3). Each model will be described briefly, prior to discussing research applying the models to specific examples of preventive health behaviour, such as self-examination and screening.

Social learning theory

Social learning theory (Rotter, 1954) proposes that the likelihood that a behaviour will occur in a given situation is a function of two factors: firstly, an expectation that that behaviour will lead to a particular reinforcement; and, secondly, the extent to which that reinforcement is valued. One particular expectancy, that of locus of control, has been the focus of much research. The assumption is that either one's own behaviour or external factors control reinforcements. Various locus of control scales have been developed to assess generalised expectancy either as one dimension (internal–external) (Rotter, 1966) or as three orthogonal dimensions (internality, powerful others and chance) (Levenson, 1973) in relation to various health-related situations (e.g. Wallston, Wallston and DeVellis, 1978).

However, studies examining the relationship between health locus of control beliefs and preventive health behaviours have, in general, produced disappointing results (Wallston and Wallston, 1982). This is no doubt due, in part, to the fact that few studies

Box 2.3 Social cognition models – a summary

Social learning theory – focus: the importance of health beliefs and health values

Self-efficacy theory – focus: efficacy beliefs
  A belief in one's ability to perform a particular behaviour in a particular situation.

Theory of reasoned action/planned behaviour – focus: behavioural intentions
  These are determined by our attitude towards a particular action and
  assumptions about others' expectations.

  An additional dimension – perceived control over the behaviour – was
  subsequently added to the original theory.

Health belief model – focus: multiple determinants of health behaviour
  The likelihood that someone will engage in a particular health behaviour is
  a function of:
      demographic variables
      sociocultural variables
      perception of susceptibility to a particular illness
      perceived severity of the illness
      benefits and barriers of taking a particular health action
      cues to action

Protective motivation theory – focus: perceptions of threat and coping resources
  Threat is determined by perceived severity and susceptibility.
  Coping is determined by a belief in the efficacy of a particular response
  and one's ability to cope.

Subjective expected utility theory – focus: the individual as an active decision
  maker, evaluating the desirability of alternative actions.

Transtheoretical model – focus: the process of change people go through in
  thinking about and changing behaviour
      precontemplation – not intending to adopt a particular action
      contemplation – thinking about adopting a particular action
      action – undertaking the particular behaviour
      maintenance – sustaining change over time

(See Conners and Norman, 1996.)

have included an assessment of the value placed on health by the individual. Beliefs should only predict those behaviours where health is highly valued. Thus, 'internals' who also value health highly tend to have stronger intentions to perform a range of health-related actions such as breast self-examination (Seeman and Seeman, 1983).

In addition, Kristiansen (1987) has argued that much of the work drawing upon the health locus of control construct has done so at the expense of other aspects of social learning theory. She argues that, in addition to health beliefs and health value, it is important to assess the individual's belief about the efficacy of certain behaviours in promoting health. Thus, Norman (1991) found that belief in the efficacy of screening, together with health locus of control and health value, predicted attendance at general health screening. However, as the overall amount of explained variance was small, he concludes by calling into question the utility of social learning theory in the prediction of preventive health behaviour.

Self-efficacy theory

The core feature of self-efficacy theory is that the initiation and maintenance of behaviours is determined primarily by judgements and expectations concerning behavioural skills and capabilities and the likelihood of being able to cope successfully with environmental demands and challenges (Bandura, 1977, 1986). Two basic cognitive mediating processes, efficacy expectations and outcome expectations, are important in determining which behaviours people initiate and the extent to which they persist with their actions when barriers or obstacles are encountered. Efficacy expectations or self-efficacy involve beliefs concerning one's ability to perform a particular behaviour in particular situations that leads to the outcome in question. Outcome expectations are beliefs concerning the probability that this specified course of action will lead to certain outcomes or consequences. A number of studies suggest that self-efficacy expectations are good predictors of behaviour. Self-efficacy influences the adoption of healthy behaviours, including exercise (e.g. McAuley, 1992, 1993; McAuley and Courneya, 1992) in a variety of population groups, for example the elderly (Grembowski et al., 1993), as well as influencing the cessation of unhealthy behaviours and the maintenance of these behavioural changes in the face of challenge and difficulty (Strecher et al., 1986). Thus, McAuley (1992) found, for a group of previously sedentary middle-aged adults engaged in a structured exercise programme designed to last for three months, that efficacy cognitions were predictive of exercise frequency and intensity over the first three months of the programme but that at five months previous exercise behaviour was a stronger predictor of exercise participation. However, four months after the termination of the exercise programme, efficacy cognitions were predictive of continuing exercise behaviour (McAuley, 1993).

However, someone who does not believe they will be able to maintain a behaviour, such as exercise, will probably not initiate that behaviour even though they might recognise that health problems are associated with a sedentary lifestyle or that exercise is beneficial to health.

Self-efficacy theory has many features in common with the theory of reasoned action. Both have a strong expectancy-value foundation: that is, they focus upon what individuals think about their actions and what they believe others think about their involvement in those actions.

The theories of reasoned action and planned behaviour

The theory of reasoned action (Fishbein and Ajzen, 1975) assumes that a health behaviour results directly from an intention to perform that behaviour. Behavioural intentions are determined by two factors: our attitude towards the action and subjective norms about its appropriateness. Our attitudes about a particular action are a function of our beliefs about the likely outcome and evaluations of that outcome. Subjective norms derive in part from our assumptions about what other people expect us to do and our motivation to comply with these expectations. To take a simple example, someone who believes that lack of exercise can have serious health consequences, such as increased risk of hypertension and heart disease, who believes that other people think he or she should exercise more and who is motivated to comply with these expectations of others, is more likely to engage in an exercise programme than someone who does not hold such attitudes and beliefs. By the use of rating scales it is possible to quantify both attitudes and subjective norms in order to arrive at a mathematical representation of behavioural intentions and hence to predict actual behaviour.

Although there are those who argue that the use of mathematical formulae dresses up a rather trite formulation (Klein, 1988; Stainton Rogers, 1991), the model does have a number of important elements. Firstly, behavioural intention can be measured at a specific rather than a general level. For example, a question assessing intention to use specific birth control methods may produce a different response from a question assessing intention to use birth control in general. Secondly, the separation of attitudes and subjective norms is also important and can provide useful information for counselling or for the targeting of health campaigns. For example, Manstead, Proffitt and Smart (1983) found that subjective norms were less important than attitudes for women's choice between breast- versus bottle-feeding, while Smetana and Adler (1980) found that a woman's decision to have an abortion was more strongly affected by perceived social pressure than by personal attitudes. Indeed, the model has been successful in predicting a range of behaviours including blood donation, dental hygiene, cigarette smoking and drug use (see review by Eagly and Chaiken, 1993).

Nevertheless, the model has been criticised on a number of grounds. Firstly, the model omits a number of factors which might potentially affect intention and actions. Perhaps the most important of these is past behaviour. Indeed, a number of studies have found that past behaviour in comparison with intention is a better predictor of future behaviour (Bentler and Speckart, 1981; Schaalma, Kok and Peters, 1993). These studies have tended to evaluate behaviours that could be regarded as influenced, at least in part, by habit (e.g. exercise and condom use). Indeed many health-related behaviours (e.g. smoking) are only partly under voluntary control. Others have pointed out that much of the research supporting the theory has involved relatively simple behaviours which do not require much in the way of resources and skills (Eagly and Chaiken, 1993).

These concerns led Ajzen and his colleagues to revise their theory which has been renamed the theory of planned behaviour (e.g. Ajzen, 1991). As well as the elements from the theory of reasoned action, perceived control over the action is added as a further element. This is similar to Barndura's (e.g. 1977) concept of self-efficacy – people's judgements that they are able to perform a certain behaviour and that this will have the intended effect. Perceived control can be influenced by both internal factors (e.g. skills, abilities, urges) and external factors (e.g. opportunities and dependence on others) (Ajzen, 1988). A range of studies published in the past decade (see Ajzen, 1991 for a review of some of these) suggest that incorporation of perceived control as an element in the equation improves the prediction of both intentions and behaviour. Health behaviours studied include use of oral contraceptives (Doll and Orth, 1993) and mammography use (Montano and Taplin, 1991). In spite of the added predictive value of perceived control there are occasions when intentions to act do not relate directly to actual behaviour. Thus, Godin, Valois and Lepage (1993) found that, although attitudes and perceived behavioural control predicted intentions to exercise, these variables did not relate to actual exercise behaviour. Although exercise may be more likely to be influenced by situational factors (e.g. time and facilities) than other health behaviours, such findings nonetheless serve to raise a note of caution about the predictive utility of the model. Indeed, Sutton (1998) concludes, from a review of research evaluating the theories of reasoned action and planned behaviour, that these models only explain between 19 and 38 per cent of the variance in behaviour.

Health belief model

The health belief model (Rosenstock, 1974; Janz and Becker, 1984) assumes that the likelihood that someone will engage in a given health behaviour is a function of demographic and socio-cultural variables as well as the following four factors:

(i)   peceived susceptibility – the extent to which the person believes that they will contract a particular illness;

(ii) perceived severity – how serious the consequences will be of getting a particular illness;

(iii) perceived benefits/barriers – the extent to which the person perceives the potential benefits of taking a particular health-related action (e.g. screening, health checks) as outweighing the potential costs (e.g. inconvenience, pain);

(iv) cues to action – either internal cues, such as bodily symptoms, or external cues, such as media campaigns or reminder letters from the GP which might serve to prompt health-related actions.

Janz and Becker (1984) reviewed forty six studies based on the health belief model. The studies reviewed covered preventive health behaviours, compliance and health service utilisation. They concluded that there was substantive support for the predictive utility of each of the dimensions of the model with perceived barriers being the most powerful dimension influencing whether or not people actually practise a particular health behaviour. Health belief model dimensions were significantly associated with perceived barriers in 89 per cent of papers, perceived susceptibility in 81 per cent, perceived benefits in 78 per cent and perceived severity in 65 per cent. A range of subsequent studies also suggest that the health belief model is a useful predictor of health behaviour. For example, the model helps predict the practice of preventive dental care (Ronis, 1992) and breast self-examination (Champion, 1990).

However, not all components of the model have proven useful in predicting variance in preventive health behaviours; thus, Janz and Becker (1984) report that of twenty four studies which focused on preventive health behaviour only 50 per cent reported significant levels for perceived severity. Also a number of research studies either do not support the health belief model (e.g. Weisenberg, Kegeles and Lund, 1980) or only lend it partial support. For example, Cody and Lee (1990) found that while health beliefs, particularly perceived barriers, were significant predictors of knowledge, intention and behaviour in relation to skin cancer prevention, other variables, such as skin type and previous experience with skin cancer, were more important. Indeed, even amongst those studies which find significant positive relationships between health belief model dimensions and health behaviours, the amount of variance accounted for by any one dimension tends to be relatively small. In a selective review of sixteen published studies which had included all four health belief model elements, Harrison, Mullen and Green (1992) report that 'at best less than 10 per cent of the variance could be accounted for by any one dimension' (p. 113).

A number of additional criticisms have been levelled at the health belief model. Firstly, the fact that different questions have been used across studies to elicit information about the same beliefs makes it difficult to compare results. It has also been argued that the health belief model is 'more a collection of variables than a formal theory or model' (Oliver and Berger, 1979). Also, as Stainton Rogers (1991) notes, 'models based on lists of potential influences … in having to pre-determine what is to be included and what excluded … they are inevitably culturally and historically highly specific and constrained' (p. 55).

Protective motivation theory

Protective motivation theory (Rogers, 1983) incorporates the health belief model but also makes use of Bandura's concept of self-efficacy. Decisions to engage (or not engage) in health-related behaviours are influenced by two primary cognitive processes: threat appraisal and coping appraisal. According to Rogers' model, protective motivation and, subsequently, adaptive or coping responses are evoked when (i) the threat is perceived as severe (severity); (ii) the individual feels vulnerable (susceptibility); (iii) the adaptive response is believed to be an effective means for averting the threat (response-efficacy); and (iv) the person is confident in his or her ability to complete the adaptive response successfully (self-efficacy).

A number of studies suggest that susceptibility, response-efficacy and self-efficacy are predictive of health-related intentions and behaviour (Wurtele and Maddux, 1987) while, as with the health belief model, severity is a less robust variable.

Subjective expected utility theory

Subjective expected utility theory (Edwards, 1954) postulates a simple mathematical model of decision making in which people evaluate the expected utility (desirability) of alternative actions and select the action with the highest subjective expected utility. According to the theory, people evaluate the costs, benefits and probabilities of courses of action in a situation and choose the behavioural alternative most likely to maximise their subjective expected utility: that is, the sum of the perceived probability of each outcome multiplied by the desirability of that outcome. The theory complements the health belief model (Ronis, 1992; Ronis and Harel, 1989) and has generated a vast body of research which supports its general usefulness. However, a number of limitations of the model have also been identified (Fischoff, Goitein and Shapira, 1982). For example, people frequently use simpler decision rules than implied by the theory.

Transtheoretical model

Recent research has recognised that models which do not take account of the processes people go through in thinking about and changing their behaviour may only partially explain health behaviours. It is important to recognise the series of stages people go through in formulating their actions. Such a model has been developed by Prochaska and DiClemente (1984). Originally formulated as a general model of intentional behaviour change, the transtheoretical model has been most extensively applied to smoking cessation (DiClemente et al., 1991). However, the model has more recently been extended to other health-related behaviour including exercise (Marcus and Owen, 1992; Marcus et al., 1992) and mammography (Rakowski et al., 1992).

The model has two basic elements: stages of change and process of change. People move through a sequence of change: from pre-contemplation (not intending to adopt the target health practice), to contemplation (considering adoption of the practice), to action (initiating the new behaviour), to maintenance (sustaining the change over time). Clearly, progression through the stages may not be strictly linear and behaviour change may have cyclical properties of success and reversal along the path to final adoption.

Complementing the stage-of-adoption element are elements of decision making regarding the adoption of the target behaviour. One of these is a pair of perceptual or judgemental factors, the pros and cons, together with a decisional balance measure derived from them. The pros and cons as used in the model are comparable to perception and belief dimensions included in other approaches referred to earlier; decisional balance and intention also parallel concepts included in other models. As an example of one study, Marcus and Owen (1992) found that, in contrast to those who exercised regularly, those who had not yet begun to exercise had little confidence in their ability to exercise and saw exercise as having nearly as many costs as it had benefits.

In sum, the model has the advantages of treating health behaviour as a dynamic entity which may change from time to time and of 'providing a framework in which concepts from apparently competing theories can be integrated' (Rakowski et al., 1992, p. 112).

The utility of models of health beliefs and behaviour

The various models outlined, while differing with regard to certain key features, show considerable overlap in factors identified as predictors of health behaviour. As Norman and Connor (1996) note, this could be taken as evidence that the key cognitions have been identified. As they further note, the models also provide a clear theoretical background to guide research, and a wealth of such research has indeed been conducted. However, in addition to issues raised in relation to the various models, the models as a whole are not without their critics (e.g. Schwarzer, 1992; Stainton Rogers, 1991). The emphasis of the models is upon the individual and the role of broader social and environmental factors is largely ignored. Even when social factors are considered, as in the theory of planned behaviour, this tends to be in the context of the individual's cognitions in relation to their personal social world. In non-Western societies health-promoting activities will be of a very different nature to those in the Western world. Hence, the applicability of such models to other than Western societies is questionable.

The models also tend to assume that human beings are rational processors of information. As noted, most people are unrealistically optimistic about the likelihood they will develop major health problems. They feel less vulnerable towards health threats than they should, and believe that others of comparable age, gender and so on face greater risks to their health than they do themselves (Weinstein, 1982, 1983, 1987).

Many health threats also seem remote in terms of time in relation to a given health behaviour. The rewards of exercise or of a healthy diet may not manifest themselves, if they become evident at all, for twenty or thirty years. In addition, people either fail to acknowledge or do not see the relationship between their actions and their risks of poor health (Weinstein, 1984).

These factors, together with variations in the variables assessed across models and methods of assessment used, no doubt explain in part why studies obtain mixed results and why the models only explain a relatively small percentage of the variance in actual behaviour (Harrison, Mullen and Green, 1992; Sutton, 1998).

These issues not withstanding, the various models outlined have provided an important framework in guiding attempts to predict and understand who will perform health behaviours. A selective overview of this research is presented in relation to the self-examination and screening literature.

Self-examination and screening

The aim of self-examination or screening is for early detection of disease or disease risk factors in order that preventive or therapeutic action can be undertaken prior to, or at the earliest possible stage of, disease onset. When a disease is less advanced, treatment is more likely to be effective The precise benefits of screening can, however, be difficult to estimate. Long-term follow-up studies are required to evaluate differential mortality rates in the screened and unscreened. Given the relative rarity of premature deaths from conditions such as breast or cervical cancer, very large sample sizes would be required to investigate differential mortality rates. In addition, participants in screening programmes tend to be self-selected and hence may differ in disease risk from non-participants. For example, with regard to breast cancer, the literature suggests that, while there is evidence of reduced mortality in women over fifty, the evidence for younger women is more controversial. In reviewing this literature, Wardle and Pope (1992) point out that, although some studies suggest reductions in mortality from cervical or breast cancer following the introduction of screening programmes, a number of studies suggest no evidence for reductions in mortality or only small non-significant reductions. However, as they further comment the majority view is that mammography screening can make a significant contribution to reducing mortality from breast cancer. Similarly, as Vernon, Laville and Jackson (1990) note:

> data are sufficiently convincing that both European and American groups have issued guidelines concerning the recommended frequency of mammography for women in various age groups. (p. 1107)

Self-examination

Self-examination is most frequently advocated and studied in relation to early detection of breast cancer, although more recently research has been directed towards testicular self-examination (Brubaker and Wickersham, 1990; Steffen, 1990; Finney, Weist and Friman, 1995) and skin self-examination (SSE) in a population at increased risk for skin cancer (Friedman *et al.*, 1993). Among women, breast cancer is the most common cause of cancer deaths (OPCS, 1984), and, among men, testicular cancer is the most frequently occurring form of cancer and the second leading cause of death amongst those aged between fifteen and thirty five (Schottenfeld *et al.*, 1980). The incidence of skin cancer has increased steadily over the past two decades particularly in the twenty to forty age group.

Despite medical advances, up to 90 per cent of all breast cancers are detected through breast self-examination (BSE); men tend to be less familiar with testicular self-examination (TSE) and most do not perform it (Cummings *et al.*, 1983; Steffen, 1990; Wardle *et al.*, 1994); SSE is still infrequently performed even in countries where rates of skin cancer are higher.

The practice of self-examination involves self-checking for either tissue irregularities, alteration or swelling and lumps which might be early warning signs for the presence of cancer. Early detection greatly influences the likelihood of survival; self-examination involves a simple procedure, yet relatively few people practise it.

A number of studies have investigated factors predictive of BSE; a few recent studies have also examined such factors in relation to TSE and skin self-examination. A consistent finding in the BSE literature is that many people do not practise self-examination at all, that adherence rates are low and that the practice decreases with age, even though the incidence of breast cancer increases with age. Thus Bennett *et al.* (1983) noted that less than 20 per cent of women performed BSE regularly while Ronis and Harel (1989) report that women who were under thirty five years of age, who were less-educated, unmarried, unemployed and with low incomes were less likely than other women to have performed BSE in the past three months. There is also evidence that TSE is rarely performed with figures from a recent European survey indicating that regular TSE (monthly) was reported by only 3 per cent of the sample with another 10 per cent reporting occasional TSE (Wardle *et al.*, 1994). A number of studies have evaluated factors predictive of self-evaluation, focusing, in particular, upon health beliefs and attitudinal variables.

Predicting self-examination

The health belief model

The health belief model (HBM) has been widely used for predicting BSE with most studies finding that at least one variable is a significant predictor. Perceived benefits and the perception of few barriers have shown the most consistent and highest correlation with BSE (Champion, 1985, 1990; Champion and Miller, 1992; Friedman *et al.*, 1994; Hill, Gardner and Rassaby, 1985; Ronis and Harel, 1989; Shepperd *et al.*, 1990). Indeed, almost all studies which have assessed barriers in relation to BSE have found a significant relationship (Champion, 1992). Perceived benefits and barriers have also been shown to be related to SSE (Cody and Lee, 1990) and TSE (Moore, Barling and Hood, 1998). Common barriers are forgetting, lack of confidence in ability to perform the self-examination, fear of finding a lump and embarrassment. The concepts of perceived susceptibility and seriousness have been related to SSE (Cody and Lee, 1990) and to BSE in some studies (e.g. Calnan and Rutter, 1986; Champion, 1990; Hill, Gardner and Rassaby, 1985; Ronis and Harel, 1989; Strauss *et al.*, 1987) but not in others (e.g. Champion, 1985) and for BSE in younger but not older women (Champion, 1992). Ronis and Harel (1989) note in their study that, although perceived severity had no direct effect upon BSE, severity of outcome given a delayed treatment increased perceived benefit of and intention to perform BSE.

Champion (1985) incorporated a health motivation scale into her HBM measure. This involved asking questions about behaviours, such as seeking new health information, doing things to improve health and exercising. Her health motivation measure distinguished between low, medium and high BSE groups. In a subsequent study (Champion and Miller, 1992), health motivation was related to BSE, the latter being assessed one year after the motivation measure was administered.

Although studies have found relationships between HBM variables and self-examination, the relationships between variables is generally weak. For example, Friedman *et al.* (1994) found that a range of variables assessed, including some derived from the health belief model, accounted for only 37 per cent of the variance in BSE frequency, while Calnan and Rutter (1986) report a figure of less than 25 per cent. The range of variables studied by Friedman *et al.* (1993) in relation to SSE accounted for about 25 per cent of the variance in SSE frequency. Also, the majority of studies assess intention to perform the examination, rather than actual behaviour, and intention tends to be only moderately correlated at best with actual behaviour. For example, Brubaker and Wickersham (1990) report a correlation of 0.30 between intention to perform TSE and actual behaviour. In many studies, past behaviour rather than health belief variables is the best predictor of future behaviour (Calnan and Rutter, 1986; Champion and Miller, 1992).

The inconsistent findings and weak relationships are no doubt due in part to differing conceptualisations of the components of the health belief model and measures used to assess them.

The theory of reasoned action

The theory of reasoned action has also been applied to both BSE and TSE. Calnan and Rutter (1986) found that social normative factors were important predictors of BSE performance, while van Ryn, Lytle and Kirscht (1996) report that intention was related to normative beliefs. Lierman *et al.* (1990) found that perceived social norms and favourable attitudes towards BSE predicted BSE practice. Brubaker and Wickersham (1990), Steffen (1990) and Moore, Barling and Hood (1998) all report findings indicating that intention to perform TSE is related to attitude and subjective norm. Moore *et al.* (1998) report that intentions were predictive of both BSE and TSE behaviours. However, this was assessed cross-sectionally by a self-report questionnaire. In a follow-up study of actual BSE behaviour assessed at one year follow up, Champion and Miller (1992) found no support for an influence of attitudes and intent on behaviour.

Other theories

Other studies suggest that self-efficacy (Lauver, 1987; Friedman *et al.*, 1994), locus of control (Bundek, Marks and Richardson, 1993) and knowledge of the usefulness of BSE (Champion, 1990) relate to BSE practice, although the latter relationship was not obtained by Friedman *et al.* (1994). However, differing methods of assessing knowledge were used in the latter two studies. Self-efficacy and knowledge of usefulness have, however, been found to relate to frequency of SSE (Friedman *et al.*, 1993). Brubaker and Wickersham (1990) report that consideration of self-efficacy and TSE knowledge improved the prediction of intention to perform TSE.

Other studies suggest that internal control and optimism are related to self-examination. For example, Bundek, Marks and Richardson (1993) found that believing that health outcomes are controlled by oneself (internal control) was positively related to BSE frequency, although this variable only accounted for 12.7 per cent of the variance. In a further study, Friedman *et al.* (1993) found that optimists – that is, those who anticipate good outcomes – tended to engage in skin self-examination more than pessimists; although this relationship was not found in the case of BSE (Friedman *et al.*, 1994).

There is also evidence that breast cancer worries result in a curvilinear relationship with BSE frequency, with women with moderate levels of worry more likely to practise monthly BSE than those with either high or low worry (Lerman *et al.*, 1991). However, such a curvilinear relationship was not found in a more recent study; McCaul, Schroeder and Reid (1996) report that the highest level of breast cancer concern was related to a higher likelihood that women performed breast self-examination.

As noted, variations in the variables assessed across models and methods of assessment used, the fact that human beings are not rational decision makers and the lack of attention to broader social and environmental factors no doubt explain in part why studies obtain mixed results and why the models only explain a relatively small percentage of the variance in actual behaviour.

Proficiency in self-examination

While performance of self-examination is clearly of importance, few studies have assessed adequacy of self-examination. Indeed, findings from such studies are that techniques of self-examination are generally poor (Holtzman and Celentano, 1983; Mayer and Solomon, 1992; Shepperd *et al.*, 1990; Strauss *et al.*, 1987). This has led some to point out that unless self-examination is practised correctly and regularly its contribution to survival is seriously limited (Miller, Chamberlain and Tsechkovski, 1985). In one study Shepperd *et al.* (1990) found that while only 37 per cent of their sample performed BSE, only 19 per cent of these were assessed as performing it adequately. In this context, it is of interest to note that knowledge of BSE was the single best predictor of reported BSE quality.

A number of recent studies have evaluated strategies for improving BSE efficiency with positive results. These include training in differing methods of undertaking BSE with vertical strip search proving to be more effective than the more conventional concentric circle or radial search methods (see box 2.4) (Atkins *et al.*, 1991) and the enhancement of self-examination through the use of 'refresher' instructional audiotapes (Jones *et al.*, 1993).

Promoting self-examination

Although most women hold a positive attitude towards and intentions about BSE they often fail to act on their intention (Champion, 1985); intention does not imply either a perceived or an actual ability to perform the behaviour in question. As noted, few men perform TSE while SSE is also infrequently performed. Hence, a number of studies have examined methods for increasing self-examination. Given that intention does not imply ability to perform a behaviour, factors which promote behavioural competence, such as experience with a self-examination, are also likely to increase its frequency. Thus Steffen *et al.* (1994) found that men's experience of performing TSE on a life-like model led to more consistent translation into self-reported behavioural action. Reminders have also

Box 2.4 Methods of breast self-examination

To perform breast self-examination the breasts should ideally be palpated once a month, about ten days into the menstrual cycle. It has been recommended that self-examination should be performed while lying down, while standing and by visual/mirror inspection. All breast tissue should be checked including the nipple and the area under the armpits. Self-examination should be conducted using the pads of the three middle fingers of the contralateral hand, using small circular motions and light, medium and deep pressure.

Three search patterns for coverage of the breasts during examination have been recommended:

Concentric circle patterns – starts with palpation along the outer edge of the breast and continues in smaller concentric circles until reaching the nipple.

Radial spoke pattern (wedge or spoke-of-the-wheel) – involves examining wedges of the breast from the outside of the breast tissue until converging at the nipple.

Vertical strip search pattern – involves examining the breast in vertical strips from the top to below the bottom of the breast area.

(American Cancer Society, 1987; Saunders, Pilgrim and Pennypacker, 1986.)

been found to help people translate their intentions into actions (Brubaker and Wickersham, 1990). In addition, a negatively framed message has also been shown to be more effective than a positively framed message in promoting BSE (e.g. 'By not doing BSE now, you will not learn what your normal healthy breasts feel like so that you will not be prepared to notice any small abnormal changes that might occur as you get older'). However, negative frame was not superior to positive frame in promoting TSE among young men (Steffen *et al.*, 1994).

Screening

Screening for prevention is concerned with actively seeking to identify a disease or pre-disease condition in people who are presumed to be healthy and indeed presume themselves to be healthy (Holland and Stewart, 1990). Screening is available for many different conditions across the life span. These range from screening to detect fetal abnormalities (e.g. maternal-serum alphafetoprotein screening for spina bifida and Down's syndrome), genetic screening (e.g. cystic fibrosis, Tay-Sachs disease), cancer-related screening (the two most common being breast and cervical cancer) and cardiac screening. Research strategies to investigate screening behaviour and intentions have included community surveys, comparisons of attenders with non-attenders and investigations into the characteristics of non-attenders. Although screening is generally viewed in a positive light and is assumed to be associated with a significant reduction in mortality, the psychological costs of screening have recently been documented (Wardle and Pope, 1992). Although this latter paper was restricted to cancer screening, it raises a number of general issues relating to the consequences of undergoing a screening test.

Uptake of screening

The uptake of screening is highly variable depending upon the condition being screened for, the type of screening test, the way in which the test is offered and fears of and beliefs about the test. In relation to type of test, Marteau *et al.* (1992) report that 88 per cent of their sample of over 1,000 women underwent a prenatal screening test. Sutton *et al.* (1994) report that the attendance rate for breast cancer screening from a sample of over 3,000 women was 42 per cent. Hayward *et al.* (1988) report from a 1986 US survey that 79 per cent of women surveyed had had a Papanicolaou smear test (Pap test), 55 per cent had had a physical breast examination performed by a doctor and 20 per cent had had mammograms.

With regard to variations in uptake depending upon method of invitation, Norman and Conner (1993) report that 37 per cent of those offered an open invitation to attend for a general health check took up the offer, this figure increasing to 70 per cent if an appointment was offered with the initial invitation letter. Similar variations in uptake, depending upon method of invitation, have been reported in other studies. For example, Myers *et al.* (1991) report that 27 per cent of their sample who received an invitation letter, screening kit and follow-up reminder letter returned a fecal occult blood test in a colerectal cancer screening programme. This increased to 48 per cent in a similar sample who also received a self-help screening booklet, an instruction call and a reminder call.

As well as such variations in uptake rate, there is evidence that, even amongst those who initially attend for screening, as many as a half may not attend for subsequent annual or other repeat screening programmes (Lerman *et al.*, 1990).

There are inevitably a number of reasons why people fail to attend for both initial or repeat screening. There is some evidence that knowledge of the availability of a screening procedure will determine whether or not someone undergoes it. In addition, with regard to attending for a general health check, those not attending tend to be those with a lifestyle which is associated with an increased risk to their health (i.e. those who smoke, drink, have a poor diet or are overweight) (Thorogood *et al.*, 1993). In general, however, the explanations for failure of uptake are inevitably more complex than this. A number of studies have evaluated the predictive validity of background characteristics or practitioner influence or have drawn more directly upon psychological theories in predicting screening uptake.

Predicting uptake of screening

Demographic characteristics

A number of studies have compared those who attend for screening with those who do not. In relation to mammography, the demographic profile of attenders and non-attenders suggests that women who obtain mammograms tend to be of a higher socio-demographic status and are more likely to be younger and married (e.g. Bostick *et al.*, 1994; Rimer, 1992; Rutledge *et al.*, 1988; Sutton *et al.*, 1994). Attendance for a Pap test for cervical cancer screening is associated with marital status (Calle *et al.*, 1993). Three of five studies reviewed by Rimer (1992) suggested that married women were more likely to complete screening. In reviewing the literature, Vernon, Laville and Jackson (1990) note that eight out of ten studies report an inverse association between age and participation in mammography screening with several studies finding especially low rates for women over seventy years of age. Similar conclusions are presented by Rimer (1992) who points out that older women are less likely to have received a doctor recommendation or referral which, as noted below, is one of the major predictors of attendance for screening. Younger women are also more likely to complete additional examinations. Studies also suggest that there is a decrease in attendance for Pap test with age, in spite of the fact that the highest incidence of invasive cancers occurs in older women (Orbell and Sheeran, 1993). Those tending to undertake repeat screening also tend to be younger (forty to forty nine years of age), and have higher education, income and occupation (Rimer, 1992).

The majority of studies reviewed by Vernon, Laville and Jackson (1990) reported a positive association between social class and screening completion. Some studies also suggest that women are more likely to attend for mammography if they have a higher education level and a positive family history of breast cancer (Bostick *et al.*, 1994). However, in their review Vernon, Laville and Jackson (1990) report a number of studies which found no association between either a relative with a history of breast cancer or a personal history of breast cancer and mammography completion. However, in relation to other cancer screening programmes (colorectal, prostate and cervical), a positive family history of illness and regular medical attendance with consistent care were predictive of participation in the programme (Bostick *et al.*, 1994; Hennig and Knowles, 1990; Hill, Gardner and Rassaby, 1985).

Doctor recommendation

A more consistent finding in the literature is that women who have visited their doctor within the past year and whose doctor has recommended uptake of screening are more likely to be screened. Thus, recommendation by a doctor appears to be an important factor in cervical screening (Peters *et al.*, 1989). Doctor encouragement to get a mammogram has been found to be related both to mammogram intentions (Aiken *et al.*, 1994; Fox, Murata and Stein, 1991; Lerman *et al.*, 1991) and behaviour, both in the short term (Bastani *et al.*, 1994) and in the longer term with regard to having regular mammograms (Rimer *et al.*, 1991; Vernon, Laville and Jackson, 1990). For example, Fox, Murata and Stein (1991) found that rates of mammography were four to twelve times higher for women whose doctors had discussed mammography with them in comparison to women whose doctors had not done so. Aiken *et al.* (1994) report comparable figures of 63 per cent versus 8 per cent, while Rimer *et al.* (1991) report that women are twelve times more likely to have regular mammograms if recommended to do so by their doctor. However, even when doctors refer women for screening, not all women follow these recommendations. Bastani, Marcus and Hollatz-Brown (1991) point out that women who have had a previous mammogram are more likely than women who have never had a mammogram to act in accordance with their doctor's recommendation to agree to get a mammogram. In a further study, Fox, Murata and Stein (1991) report that 48 per cent of women aged fifty to sixty four and 56 per cent of women aged sixty five and older, whose doctor had encouraged mammography, were not obtaining yearly mammograms as recommended by the American Cancer Society.

Health belief model variables

A number of studies have investigated health belief model variables in relation to uptake of screening particularly, but not exclusively, in relation to Pap test and mammography (e.g. Aiken et al., 1994a, 1994b; Bastani et al., 1994; Baumann et al., 1993; Fox, Murata and Stein, 1991; Hennig and Knowles, 1990; Hill, Gardner and Rassaby, 1985; Lerman et al., 1990; Orbell, Crombie and Johnston, 1996; Rutledge et al., 1988; Siegler, Feaganes and Rimer, 1995; Stein, Fox and Murata, 1991; Stein et al., 1992).

In relation to Pap test, perceived susceptibility, health motivation and low perceived barriers have been found to be significant predictors of intention to have the test. The general finding from studies investigating uptake of mammography screening suggest that there is a positive relationship between uptake and perceived susceptibility and perceived benefits and a negative relationship between mammography screening and perceived barriers (Rimer, 1992). However, there may be a point at which fear of a health threat is so great (i.e. a perception of extreme susceptibility) that this has a negative effect upon attendance for screening. Thus, Seydel, Taal and Wiegman (1990) found that intention to attend a mass cancer screening programme was negatively associated with perceived susceptibility.

Perceived barriers include the doctor failing to recommend a mammogram, the perception that a mammogram is unnecessary and that there is no evidence of breast disease. Other barriers mentioned less frequently include fear of the result and concerns about radiation, pain and embarrassment (Lerman et al., 1990; Rimer 1992; Rimer et al., 1991). Thus, breast cancer worries have been found to be related to mammography intentions (Lerman et al., 1991) and a belief that the test will be embarrassing, painful or frightening related to non-participation in cervical screening (Peters et al., 1989). Bastani et al. (1994) found that women who were greatly concerned about radiation exposure were two and half times less likely to obtain a mammogram during the following year than women not so concerned. Other barriers referred to, relate to problems of access, including lack of time, distance and, in some countries, cost, which may be a particular barrier for some social and ethnic groups (Rimer, 1992). Similar barriers were referred to by those who did not participate in a fecal blood test in a colorectal screening programme (Myers et al., 1991). The test was perceived as inconvenient, uncomfortable, unnecessary in the absence of symptoms and too anxiety provoking.

Perceived vulnerability to breast cancer and family history of breast cancer have been found to be associated with repeat mammography participation (Lerman et al., 1990). That perceptions of personal vulnerability relate to increased screening behaviour for breast cancer is also noted in a meta-analytic review of the literature (McCaul et al., 1996). However, there is also evidence that anxiety reduces the likelihood of repeat screening (Lerman et al., 1990). Indeed, a number of studies have found that the feeling that screening induces unnecessary worry is associated with a reduced likelihood of repeat screening (Rimer, 1992).

Drawing on the health belief model, Aiken et al. (1994b) devised an educational programme designed to enhance adherence to mammography screening. Women who received the health belief model-based intervention (an educational programme designed to increase awareness of perceived susceptibility to breast cancer and perceived severity of late detected breast cancer, increase perceived benefits of mammography screening and decrease perceived barriers) were two to three times more likely to obtain a mammogram than women in a control condition who had not received the intervention.

However, while there is predictive utility of health belief model variables in relation to screening uptake, as with self-examination, the amount of variance explained by the variables examined tends to be small. Thus, Aiken et al. (1994a) found that, taken together, the health belief model variables accounted for 16 per cent of the variance in mammography compliance. In a further study, Marteau et al. (1992) found that nine variables selected accounted for only 21 per cent of the variance in uptake behaviour in relation to prenatal screening.

Theory of reasoned action

A number of studies have drawn on the theory of reasoned action to examine predictors of screening uptake. Marteau et al. (1992) report that a positive attitude towards doctors and medicine were predictive of uptake of prenatal screening. Norman and Conner (1993) report that intention to attend and perceived control were predictive of attendance at a general health check following a general invitation. DeVellis, Blalock and Sandler (1990) report that perceived behavioural control enhanced prediction of intention to complete a colorectal cancer screening test over and above the contributions of attitude and subjective norm, although variables evaluated accounted for less than 25 per cent of the variance. Montano and Taplin (1991) report that attitude, subjective norm and affect were all significant predictors of both intention to take up and participation in a breast cancer screening programme. However, these factors explained only 39 per cent of the variance concerning intention and 20 per cent for behaviour. Baumann et al. (1993) found that social influence was a significant predictor of mammography intention. In two further studies, variables derived from the theory of reasoned action were predictive of intentions to have a smear test, although again the amount of variance explained by these variables was small (12 per cent and 26 per cent respectively) (Hennig and Knowles, 1990; Hill, Gardner and Rassaby, 1985).

Other factors

Other variables investigated in relation to screening uptake include the general tendency to practise preventive health behaviours, knowledge about the screening test, anxiety, personality and locus of control. Thus, in relation to mammography screening, the variable most predictive of uptake is the tendency to practise other preventive health behaviours, such as regular dental check-ups and having previously had other medical tests and procedures (Vernon, Laville and Jackson, 1990). Other studies emphasise the role played by knowledge of the test in predicting uptake (Marteau et al., 1992). In reviewing the literature in relation to cervical screening, Orbell and Sheeran (1993) conclude that knowledge of the preventive purpose of the test is reliably related to uptake.

Past behaviour is also a good predictor of future action. Thus, Baumann et al. (1993) found that habit (previous mammography behaviour) was a significant predictor of intention. However, contrary to this Montano and Taplin (1991) found no relationship between habit and behaviour or between habit and behavioural intention.

Finally, a number of studies have investigated various aspects of personality and psychological state in relation to participation in screening programmes. Kreitler, Chaitchik and Kreitler (1990) compared, on a number of psychological measures, women who had attended for screening with a sample of women matched on demographic variables who had heard of the breast screening but who had not participated. They interpret their findings as suggesting that women with a cancer-prone personality (e.g. higher on negative emotions and repression and lower on positive emotions, daydreaming and neuroticism) were more likely to attend for breast cancer screening. However, data presented in the paper make it difficult to gauge the accuracy of this interpretation. For example, they are based on the results of a series of tests, administered to subsamples of a study group; each subsample was administered a random selection of five out of a total of ten tests. In a further study, Siegler, Feaganes and Rimer (1995) report that measures of conscientiousness, extraversion and lower depression predicted adoption of regular mammograms reported two years later, while Bundek, Marks and Richardson (1993) report that beliefs in control by powerful others was related to recency of having had a Pap smear and a breast examination conducted by a doctor.

There are then a range of factors influencing attendance at a screening programme. The factors discussed above have been broadly characterised by Marteau (1993) as organisational (method of invitation and whether screening is voluntary or mandatory), patient related and doctor related. As she notes, these factors will influence and be influenced by each other and will affect uptake accordingly. It is perhaps not surprising then that, in relation to uptake of screening, the amount of variance explained by any cluster of variables investigated in any one study tends to be small.

The psychological costs of screening

Until recently there has been a general and unequivocal enthusiasm for screening. For example, in the United Kingdom, The Forrest Report (1986) recommended a breast screening programme undertaken at three yearly intervals. In many countries within the Western world mandatory screening programmes exist, while in the United Kingdom new contracts for general practitioners have increased screening in certain contexts where payment is dependent upon meeting set targets. However, as Ogden (1996) notes, over the past decade the possible negative aspects of screening have emerged as a new dimension in the screening literature. Such negative aspects can be broadly characterised into four areas involving (i) merely participating in screening, and obtaining (ii) negative results, (iii) false positives or inconclusive results and (iv) positive results (see box 2.5)

Participating in screening

While one might anticipate anxiety for those receiving positive results, even if these later transpire to be negative, the fact that negative results are also associated with anxiety would seem to be less expected. However, the actual invitation to take part in a screening programme can itself provoke worry and anxiety possibly generated by a fear that receipt of the invitation must imply to the person that they have the illness concerned (Marteau, 1993). Other anxieties may relate to concern about the possible stressfulness

Box 2.5 The psychological costs of screening

(i) *Negative effects of merely participating in screening*
worry about the stressfulness of the procedure
anxiety about the possibilities of distressing results being obtained
fear that the invitation to attend for screening implies the person has the illness concerned

(ii) *Negative effects of obtaining negative results*
alerts people to their lifestyle and possibly their mortality
confers inappropriately high levels of reassurance

(iii) *Negative effects of obtaining false positive results or inconclusive results*
anxiety about the possibility of having a disease
anger at the emotional distress occasioned by screening

(iv) *Negative effects of positive results*
anxiety, fear and depression

(See Marteau, 1993; Wardle and Pope, 1992.)

of the procedure or the risk that upsetting results will be obtained. Thus, in a retrospective study of women's responses to receiving a request to attend a breast screening session, although 93 per cent reported being pleased, 55 per cent reported feeling worried (Fallowfield, Rodway and Baum, 1990). While some concern and anxiety may be inevitable, a survey of 1,500 fifty to sixty four year old women, assessed before attending for breast screening at the screening clinic and nine months later, suggests that changes in anxiety level are only very small (Sutton *et al.*, 1995). However, given that many people may be tested for a relatively small reduction in mortality, it could be argued that some people are unnecessarily burdened by anxiety and worry even if, on average, levels of anxiety are relatively low.

Negative results

As Marteau (1993) notes, the meaning of a negative result varies according to the screening test under consideration. For a genetic test where all mutations are known, a negative result means the individual is free from risk of ever developing or passing on the disease. In genetic tests where all mutations are not known, a negative test result implies a residual risk that the person is a carrier. Negative results in relation to diseases which an individual is vulnerable to across a period of time (e.g. breast, cervical or bowel cancer) implies absence of disease or risk of disease at the time of the test. It is in this latter context where there is some evidence that even receiving negative test results is associated with anxiety. For example, Stoate (1989) found that 215 healthy adults attending a coronary heart disease screening clinic by invitation had significantly lower subjective psychological distress than an unscreened group of matched controls. However, three months after screening the screened group had significantly higher levels of distress compared with the controls who showed a non-significant decrease in distress. Stoate argues that participation in screening made people aware of their lifestyle and perhaps their own mortality. The fact that people tend to under-estimate their vulnerability to health threats (Weinstein, 1984) may mean that participation in screening (irrespective of a negative result) serves to alert at least some people to the fact that they may be vulnerable to a particular condition.

There is also some evidence that a negative result confers inappropriately high levels of reassurance (Tymstra and Bieleman, 1987). However, such results would seem to be the exception rather than the rule and, in reviewing the evidence in relation to cancer screening, Wardle and Pope (1992) comment that:

> overall there is no strong evidence that participation in screening followed by a negative result, poses any psychological threat. (p. 619)

As they further note, however, such a conclusion needs to be interpreted in the context that populations attending cancer screening programmes are self-selected and hence may have different beliefs about health and preventive behaviour than non-attenders.

False positives or inconclusive results

The possibility inevitably exists that some results will be inconclusive or suggestive of abnormality which subsequent further testing or examination reveals to be negative. With regard to breast cancer screening, Wardle and Pope (1992) estimate that about twelve women are faced with the threat of cancer for every true case. The Forrest Report (1986) suggests that 10 per cent of attendances for breast screening are for women who are recalled for further mammograms after initial mammograms were unsatisfactory or inconclusive. In a study of PKU screening for congenital hypothyroidism in Sweden, 137 out of 144 positive tests were later proved to be false positive (Bodegard, Fyro and Larsson, 1982). Suspicions of abnormality or inconclusive results can inevitably have adverse psychological consequences. As Wardle and Pope (1992) note:

> the high false positive rate confers a high psychological cost on screening. (p. 611)

Thus, Lerman et al. (1991) found that women with suspicious abnormal mammograms, in comparison with those receiving a negative result, exhibited significantly elevated levels of mammography-related anxiety and breast cancer worries which interfered with their mood and functioning. These concerns persisted even after these women had received additional tests ruling out cancer. The authors suggest that women with abnormal mammograms perceive themselves to be at greater risk of developing breast cancer in the future even though this perception is inaccurate. In a further study, false positive results on routine screening for fetal abnormalities were associated with raised maternal anxiety and concern for the baby even after subsequent testing indicated that no abnormalities were present (Marteau et al., 1988). Indeed, some women were still anxious and concerned even after the baby had been born (Marteau et al., 1991). Parents whose children had been screened for metabolic or endocrinological disorders exhibited persistent anxiety following a false positive result (Sorensen et al., 1984). In a further study false positive screen results for congenital hypothyroidism resulted in acute short-term distress for the majority of parents concerned, parental anxiety persisting five years later

(Fyro and Bodegard, 1987). Although the initial response to false positive results may be relief at not having a serious disease, anger at the emotional distress occasioned by the screening may be a common reaction (Wardle and Pope, 1992).

Psychological effects of positive results

> Receipt of a positive result on certain screening tests, later confirmed by diagnostic investigations, is frequently associated with a mixture of shock, anger, and anxiety. (Marteau, 1993, p . 161)

Wardle, Pernet and Stephens (1995) found that women with positive smear test results had higher scores on measures of psychopathology, general anxiety and screening-related anxieties than women with mild abnormalities or negative results. Paskett and Rimer (1995) report that abnormal Pap tests and mammograms could result in anxiety, fear, depression and failure to comply with treatment and future routine screening tests. Even mildly abnormal results, which involve a recommendation for early repeat screening, caused raised concern about cancer for the recipients. In addition, length of wait for the smear test result was associated with greater distress for those receiving a positive or mildly abnormal result. A positive smear is thus associated with a marked level of what could be viewed as unnecessary anxiety. As Wardle, Pernet and Stephens (1995) note:

> a positive smear result is *not* a diagnosis of cancer, the treatment required (if any) is minor, and the long-term risks after treatment are minimal. (p. 193)

In summary, research has only recently been directed towards the question of the psychological costs of screening. It is clearly important to establish exactly what the costs are and to establish who is most vulnerable. This has implications not necessarily for the ethos of screening but for the manner in which screening information is conveyed and for dealing with the concerns of screening participants.

Summary

The key issues explored in this chapter relate to two aspects of preventive health behaviour: firstly, actions which are health promoting, diet and exercise being discussed as key examples, and, secondly, actions which facilitate the detection of disease or risk factors, with discussion focusing upon self-examination and participation in screening programmes. With regard to the former, many studies attest to the utility of exercise in disease prevention and treatment. Exercise reduces the likely incidence of hypertension and has a protective effect on total mortality in relation to coronary heart disease. Recently it has been argued that exercise reduces mortality from cancer although this may be due to the fact that those who are physically active differ from those who are less active on a number of other attributes relating to cancer. In spite of the increasing evidence for the discernible health benefits of physical activity, adherence to exercise regimens, even amongst those who stand to benefit most, is poor. A number of studies have evaluated both the factors predictive of adherence to exercise regimens and the strategies for increasing and maintaining exercise adherence.

Rather more controversial than the role of exercise are the suggested links between dietary composition and health and the appropriateness of dietary treatments for obesity. Whether quantitative or qualitative aspects of diet are more important in relation to health is difficult to evaluate given the relatively few well-controlled studies which have been conducted. It is also difficult both to induce people to modify their diet and to encourage them to adhere to dietary recommendations over time.

Rather than being aimed at disease prevention, the purpose of self-examination and screening is for early detection of disease or disease risk factors. Numerous research studies drawing on a range of theories and models have evaluated factors predictive of both self-examination and the uptake of screening. Of particular relevance in this regard are social cognition models, which focus upon beliefs, attitudes and knowledge which might prompt particular health-related actions. The health belief model in particular has been widely used for predicting both self-examination and uptake of screening with most studies finding that at least one variable is a significant predictor, although the amount of variance explained by the variables examined tends to be small.

Self-examination is being increasingly promoted and, until relatively recently, there was general and unequivocal enthusiasm for screening. Both clearly play an important role; there is evidence that, despite medical advances, up to 90 per cent of all breast cancers are detected through breast self-examination. Screening clearly allows for the early detection of disease which can be readily treated in its early stages. However, recent research has raised the question of the psychological costs of screening, not only with regard to positive and false positive results but also in relation to anxieties raised by the mere participation in screening programmes. It is clearly important to establish exactly what the costs are and who is most vulnerable in order that the concerns of screening participants can be dealt with effectively.

FURTHER READING

C. Bouchard, R.J. Shepherd, T. Stephens, J.R. Sutton and B.D. McPherson (eds) (1990). *Exercise, Fitness and Health: A consensus of current knowledge*. Champaign, IL: Human Kinetics.

M. Conner and P. Norman (eds) (1996). *Predicting Health Behaviour*. Buckingham: Open University Press.

P. M. Dubbert (1992). Exercise in behavioral medicine. *Journal of Consulting and Clinical Psychology*, 60, 613–618.

T. M. Marteau (1993). Health-related screening: Psychological predictors of uptake and impact. In S. Maes, H. Leventhal and M. Johnston (eds), *International Review of Health Psychology*, Vol. II. Chichester: Wiley.

W. Stroebe and M. S. Stroebe (1995). *Social Psychology and Health*. Buckingham: Open University Press.

CHAPTER 3

Perception and interpretation of symptoms

CHAPTER OVERVIEW

This chapter examines the various psychosocial factors which influence how we perceive and interpret bodily symptoms. The first part of the chapter examines cognitive representations of illness and the way in which such common-sense models provide explanations for variations in health- and illness-related behaviour. Subsequent sections examine the influence of individual differences in self-awareness and negative trait affectivity and gender and cultural factors, in addition to the role of attentional, social and emotional factors, upon symptom perception. Mass psychogenic illness and the efficacy of placebo treatments are discussed as illustrative examples of the combined influence of such variables. The final section of the chapter examines factors influencing the interpretation of symptoms.

This chapter covers:

Illness representations
Labelling symptoms
Individual differences in symptom perception
Attention and symptom perception
The effects of stress and mood upon symptom perception
Mass psychogenic illness
Placebo effects
Interpreting symptoms

Introduction

An essential first step in an individual's decision making relating to their use of health care is their perception and interpretation of the symptom(s) being experienced. While certain signs of disease may be observable (bumps, breaks, temperature changes), symptoms of illness usually involve a subjectively sensed component of bodily responses (Cacioppo and Petty, 1982) – that is, feeling sick, tired or in pain – which are not available for public scrutiny or verification. In this context it is perhaps not surprising that, while people experience symptoms on a regular basis (Bishop, 1984; Pennebaker, 1982; Verbrugge and Ascione, 1987), there is marked individual variability in the extent to which such symptoms are attended to, reported and acted upon. For example, Bishop (1984) found that while healthy subjects reported experiencing symptoms, ranging from headaches to rectal bleeding, on an average of one in every five days, they sought help for less than 7 per cent of the symptoms reported. In a further study, Verbrugge and Ascione (1987) found that, for a sample of almost 600 people, only 5 per cent of women and 11 per cent of men reported no symptoms over a six week period, yet only 5 per cent of symptomatic days involved any kind of medical contact. Of importance then is the process by which a sensory event is transformed into an indicator or representation of an underlying threat of disease or injury.

Most recent explanations for variations both in symptom perception and symptom reporting have emphasised the fact that the information-processing system that translates sensory experience into symptoms is influenced by a complex interaction of sensory, cognitive and emotional factors. As Cioffi (1991) notes:

> symptom interpretation is a multiprocess elaboration upon a real or perceived physiological state. (p. 29)

The process is initiated by an awareness of a physical sensation, awareness that can be experienced in the absence of detectable physiological change (e.g. phantom limb pain; Skelton and Pennebaker, 1982). In this context Cacioppo and his colleagues (e.g. Cacioppo et al. 1986; Cacioppo et al., 1989) have argued that motivation to detect signs and symptoms is a function of their salience, personal relevance and perceived consequence; the extent to which cognitive resources are allocated to the appraisal process is posited to be proportional to the strength of this motive (see box 3.1).

Cacioppo's explanation overlaps with the self-regulation/information-processing model of responses to health threats proposed by Leventhal and his colleagues (Leventhal, 1983; Leventhal, Meyer and Nerenz, 1980; Leventhal, Nerenz and Steele, 1984; Leventhal et al., 1997).

> This model views health related behaviour as the result of an iterative process by which the person integrates both internal and external stimulus information with existing cognitive structures to give meaning to the person's experience. (Bishop, 1991, p. 33)

Awareness of and subsequent interpretation of symptoms is thus influenced by a range of factors including individual differences and social, emotional and cognitive parameters. Of prime importance in this regard is how the individual thinks about health and illness: that is, their health and illness representations.

Box 3.1 Perceiving and interpreting symptoms

Imagine you have a slight cramp in your stomach – what factors influence your perception and interpretation of it?

While specific attributes of the cramp, such as its intensity and duration, will make you more or less aware of it, other personal or environmental factors also exert an influence. Thus, you are more likely to notice the stomach cramp if there is not a great deal of activity going on around you. You are also more likely to be aware of it if you are feeling under pressure or if you are in a negative mood.

Once aware of the sensation, you will apply a basic somatic label to it and initiate an attributional search in order to self-diagnose possible causes and consequences of the sensation. These may result in the application of a symptom label or a decision that the sensations are understandable responses to situational or personal circumstances. Hence your stomach cramp may be used as evidence that something is wrong with you and you may self-diagnose your illness or you may believe that it is a normal response to some specific event such as missing lunch or eating too much. This attribution in turn is likely to be influenced by social, emotional and cognitive parameters. Hence you may respond very differently to your stomach cramp if a close friend or relative has recently been diagnosed with stomach cancer.

Illness representations

There is a long tradition within medical anthropology of investigating cross-cultural variations in the meaning assigned to a disease (Chrisman and Kleinman, 1983). However, it was not until the 1980s (Leventhal, Meyer and Nerenz, 1980) that psychology began to explore the notion that individual representations of health and illness vary within a culture and that such variations may help to account for variations in health- and illness-related behaviour (Skelton and Croyle, 1991; Petrie and Weinman, 1997). For an individual to assume they have an illness and/or a disease the initial step involves the perception of a bodily state which is recognised as differing from their normal state: that is, they perceive a symptom. They may or they may not subsequently interpret this symptom as being a possible sign of disease. Hence, we are not:

> passive victims of illness, we actively process, evaluate, and act upon illness-related information. (Croyle and Barger, 1993, p. 29)

The term illness cognition has been used to refer to:

> mental activity (e.g. appraisal, interpretation, recall) undertaken by an individual who believes himself or herself to be ill, regarding the state of his or her health and its possible remedies. (Croyle and Ditto, 1990, p. 32)

By acquiring information through the media, personal experience and from family and friends we construct personal models of health and illness which will inevitably vary in their complexity and technicality. Such cognitive representations of illness or common-sense models that people hold, influence how they react to symptoms and illness (Bishop, 1991; Lau and Hartman, 1983; Lau, Bernard and Hartman, 1989; Meyer, Leventhal and Gutmann, 1985).

The structure of illness representations

In their groundbreaking article, Leventhal, Meyer and Nerenz (1980) argued that there were four components to people's illness representations. Subsequent research using a variety of methodologies suggests that such representations have at least five attributes (box 3.2). Illness cognitions appear to develop quite early in life and can be identified even in young children, although the content is less mature and less informed (Goldman *et al.*, 1991).

Box 3.2 Cognitive dimensions of illness attributions

Five cognitive dimensions of beliefs or representations about illness have been identified:

(i) *Illness identity* – this refers to the label one gives to a disease (the medical diagnosis) and the symptoms which indicate it: for example, I have influenza (the diagnosis) characterised by a high fever (the symptom).

(ii) *Causes and underlying pathology* – ideas about how one gets the disease such as from an injury, infection or genetic weakness. In addition, we hold beliefs about the relevance of biological or psychosocial causes: for example, I may feel my influenza was caused by a virus but also feel that I was more susceptible to contracting it because I was run down at the time.

(iii) *Time line* – views about how long a disease takes to appear or lasts: that is, whether it is acute, cyclic or chronic; for example, my influenza should only last for a few days.

(iv) *Consequences* – the expected effects and consequences of an illness, which may be physical (pain, discomfort), social (dislocation from friends) or economic (loss of income): for example, I have a headache and my body aches because I have influenza and it will prevent me from working and socialising.

(v) *Cure and controllability* – assumptions about how one recovers from the disease and the extent to which symptoms can be controlled either by ourselves or by external sources: for example, if I take my analgesic medication and rest I will soon recover from my influenza.

(Bishop, 1987; Croyle and Jemmott, 1991; Lau and Hartman, 1983; Lau, Bernard and Hartman, 1989; Leventhal, Meyer and Nerenz, 1980; Meyer, Leventhal and Gutmann, 1985.)

A range of studies have produced supportive evidence for the five components of illness representations and the extent to which they guide an individual's response to a somatic sensation, and influence health care seeking and the subsequent monitoring of change as a symptom progresses, is managed or cured (Petrie and Weinman, 1997). In a recent review, Scharloo and Kaptein (1997) identified over one hundred published studies which evaluated at least one of the dimensions into which illness representations are organised in relation to a range of chronic illnesses. A few selected studies indicating how specific dimensions relate to specified outcomes will serve as illustrative examples.

With regard to diabetes, Hampson, Glasgow and Toobert (1990) found that perceived importance of treatment and perceived seriousness of the condition enhanced the prediction of diet level and exercise. With regard to osteoarthritis, Hampson, Glasgow and Zeiss (1994) report that patients with higher perceived seriousness reported higher levels of self-management and more utilisation of medical services and experienced poorer quality of life. In a further set of studies with hypertensives, it was found that those who believed their disease was acute rather than chronic (time line) were more likely to drop out of treatment (Baumann and Leventhal, 1985; Meyer, Leventhal and Guttmann, 1985). Fear of the possible consequences of diagnosis has been related to failure to seek medical attention for self-identified breast lumps (Taylor, Lichtman and Wood, 1984). People with strong identity (a clear label) and cure (belief that a cure is possible) components are more likely to visit a doctor when feeling ill than people who have weak identity and cure components (Lau, Bernard and Hartman, 1989).

In addition to the component approach researchers have also sought to identify the underlying dimensions people use to think about disease. In their factor analytic study, Lau and Hartman (1983) argue that attributions for getting sick and getting better can be conceptualised along three dimensions: stability, locus and controllability. Stability refers to the temporal consistency of symptoms; locus relates to attributions which are internal or external to the person; while controllability is the person's perception of the extent to which they believe they can control their symptoms or the cause of their symptoms. While the component approach looks at the differing content of disease representations, the dimensional approach examines different ways in which people evaluate that content (Bishop, 1991). Both provide information about the way in which people perceive and respond to symptoms. For example, persistent but stable symptoms are more likely to be noticed while changing symptoms are more likely to prompt health care seeking.

Labelling symptoms

Our interpretation of symptoms is inevitably influenced by a range of factors including expectations and illness assumptions and the context in which the symptoms occur. A number of research groups using differing approaches have evaluated such issues. The influence of expectations has been evaluated by Croyle, Ditto and their colleagues, illness assumptions have been evaluated by Bishop and his colleagues, while Pennebaker and others have investigated the influence of various contextual factors on symptom perception and reporting.

Belief that one has a disease

The belief that we have an illness or that we might be susceptible to it is likely to lead to a search for and focusing upon symptoms which might be consistent with such a diagnosis. In the light of new information, everyday symptoms may be interpreted in a manner which is consistent with a given diagnosis. This is illustrated by the results of an experimental study using undergraduate volunteers who were told they were taking part in a health attitude study (Baumann et al., 1989). Half the subjects were informed that they had normal blood pressure and half that they had high blood pressure. At the conclusion of the study subjects completed a questionnaire which included a symptom checklist. Subjects told that they had high blood pressure reported more symptoms than those told they had normal blood pressure. In addition, symptoms reported by the former group were those reported by hypertensives: that is, headache, heart beating and tension. Labelling someone as hypertensive led to higher levels of reporting of assumed symptoms.

In a further series of experimental studies Croyle, Ditto and their colleagues (Croyle and Jemmott, 1991) investigated symptom perception and reporting in individuals informed they had a risk factor for a disease. In each study subjects were tested for a recently discovered enzyme deficiency and told that the absence of the critical enzyme placed them at risk of developing a complex of mild but irritating pancreatic disorders (Croyle and Ditto, 1990). In one such study, after subjects had received their test results, they were asked, firstly, to list any symptoms or ailments they had experienced within the past month and, secondly, to complete a symptom check list, the symptoms supposedly being associated with the enzyme deficiency (Croyle and Sande, 1988). Subjects who were told they had the enzyme deficiency tended to report more symptoms during the previous month that were associated with the disorder, while diagnosis did not affect the free recall of general symptoms. Similar effects of labelling on symptom reporting have been noted in other studies (Baumann *et al.*, 1989; Pennebaker 1982).

Disease prototypes

Bishop and his colleagues have argued that people process information about physical symptoms according to certain preconceived notions they have about how symptoms fit together. These elements or illness schema provide the basis for disease prototypes which help people organise and evaluate information which they might otherwise have difficulty interpreting (Bishop *et al.*, 1987). This is illustrated in a study by Bishop and Converse (1986) in which subjects presented with a symptom set recalled a greater number of symptoms when the set was closely related to a disease prototype than when the set contained irrelevant symptoms. Hence, when people experience physical symptoms they interpret these symptoms by retrieving from memory prototypes of various diseases. People are then more likely to interpret a set of symptoms as indicating a particular disease when all the symptoms in the set relate closely to the commonly held prototype for that disease. In reporting symptoms to medical personnel, patients may well be biased in reporting symptoms consistent with their pre-existing disease prototypes, possibly ignoring those perceived as not relevant to the prototype. This may result in a distorted report of symptoms experienced (Bishop and Converse, 1986).

As well as influencing the perception and reporting of symptoms (Bauman *et al.*, 1989; Matthews *et al.*, 1983) prototypes provide clues about how to deal with the illness and what to expect in terms of length of illness, outcome and so on. On the basis of such interpretation people may seek treatment, change treatment, vary their behaviour or construct views about their future health (Bishop and Converse, 1986).

Contextual factors

In addition to illness beliefs and illness schema, the context in which symptoms occur can also be an important source of information which influences the perception and interpretation of symptoms. In this regard Pennebaker and Skelton (1981) have argued that the perception of symptoms is partly guided by a hypothesis the person has about what symptoms they feel they should be experiencing. In two experimental studies they found that subjects who were led to believe that an experimental manipulation would result in a particular symptom were more likely to report having experienced it. This also relates to the notion of prototypes described earlier; once the person has made a decision about the identity of an illness, on the basis of initial symptoms, they will check for further symptoms which are consistent with that prototype. Ambiguous bodily reactions are then more likely to be interpreted as prototype consistent symptoms. For instance in one study, half a group of subjects running on the spot were told it was the time of year when there was an increased incidence of flu. After exercising, those given the flu information were more likely to report flu-like symptoms in relation to exercise symptoms than those not given the flu information (Pennebaker, 1982).

Other researchers have similarly emphasised the influence upon symptom interpretation of the social and personal context in which they occur. Thus in a study by Croyle and Jemmott (1991), subjects were run in groups and were told either they were the only ones to test positive or that they were one of several receiving a positive test. Subjects who were uniquely affected judged the disorder to be quite serious, whereas those who shared the disorder with others judged it to be relatively minor. Perceiving the threat as shared reduces its judged severity. In a further study, Lalljee, Lamb and Carnibella (1993) found that when subjects were asked to make a diagnosis from an imaginary description they were more likely to relate the symptoms to the type of person, and make a diagnosis on that basis (e.g. mumps for children, typhoid for those who had visited Third World countries and stroke for older adults).

In summary then, the way in which we become aware of, organise and understand symptoms is influenced by our cognitive representations of illness or the common-sense models we hold. A belief that we have an illness is likely to result in a (possibly selective) search for symptoms to enable us to confirm our suspicions. Our beliefs about which symptoms should be associated with each other, given a particular illness label, can similarly lead to a further (possibly selective) search for symptoms. Finally, symptom perception and interpretation are influenced by the particular social and personal context in which they occur. Such models are not invariant, however, and symptom perception is influenced by a number of additional factors including personality, gender, culture and mood.

Individual differences in symptom perception

Research assessing the role of personality differences in the perception and reporting of physical symptoms suggests that two personality variables in particular seem to play an important role. These are individual differences in self-awareness and neuroticism or trait negative affectivity (see box 3.3).

Self-awareness

A high degree of self-awareness is associated with a tendency to focus on one's feelings and reactions, including somatic information (Duval and Wicklund, 1972). Indeed, research suggests that individuals with a dispositional tendency to focus attention

Box 3.3 Factors influencing symptom perception

Personality
Self-awareness – a dispositional tendency to focus on one's feelings and reactions is related to a particular awareness of one's bodily sensations.

Neuroticism and trait negative affectivity – such people tend to be introspective, apprehensive, negativistic and vigilant and hence are more likely to attend to and notice bodily sensations and minor discomforts.

Gender
Women in comparison with men tend to report more symptoms and illnesses.

Culture
Attention to and interpretation of bodily states is influenced by culture specific child-rearing practices.

Attention
Lack of environmental stimulation results in a greater awareness of bodily symptoms.

Salient environmental stimuli can induce selective attention to bodily sensations.

Social and emotional factors
Stress – relates to perceived vulnerability to illness and hence attention to bodily changes.

Mood – depressed mood relates to more illness-related memories and enhanced perception of bodily symptoms.

inwards towards themselves rather than outwards towards external events are particularly aware of their bodily sensations (Pennebaker, 1983). Inward focus can result in an overestimation of bodily functioning: for example, an overestimation of heart rate in relation to actual heart rate. In this context, Hansell and Mechanic (1984) found that introspectiveness, defined as a relatively large degree of attention focused diffusely and inward, was related to symptom reporting by adolescents. It has also been argued that a tendency to internal focus combined with a tendency to catastrophise about physical sensations is related to hypochondriacal problems (Barskey and Klerman, 1983).

Related to self-awareness is the tendency for some people to monitor specific bodily sensations. Monitoring or vigilant scanning for threat-relevant cues induces a greater sensitivity to new and changing physical symptoms. Thus, monitors tend to seek medical care with less-severe symptoms and perceive their recovery as being slower (Miller, Brody and Summerton, 1988).

In sum, those with a dispositional tendency to internal focusing of attention will have more somatic information available to them. As a result such information is likely to be more salient and hence potentially more distressing.

Neuroticism and negative affectivity

A number of studies have demonstrated a relationship between neuroticism and either concurrent or retrospective self-reports of illness symptoms (Smith *et al.*, 1989; Parker, Bagby and Taylor, 1989). Other studies and reviews conclude that neuroticism is related to health complaints, even though those health complaints may not reflect actual diagnosable physical illness (Costa and McCrae, 1987; Larsen and Kasimatis, 1991; Watson and Pennebaker, 1989).

A further characteristic, trait negative affectivity, has also been extensively investigated in relation to health complaints (Watson and Pennebaker, 1989). Trait negative affectivity closely resembles neuroticism. According to Costa and McCrae (1987), neuroticism is centrally defined by individual differences in the tendency to experience negative emotional states. Across a range of studies stable individual differences in negative affect correlate with measures of symptom reporting. Several researchers argue that this is a function of the relationship between neuroticism and symptom perception.

Thus Costa and McCrae (1985) state that:

> we conclude ... that ... neuroticism influences perceptions of health, but not health itself. (p. 24)

Similar conclusions were reached by Holroyd and Coyne (1987) who stated that neuroticism reflects: a biased style of perceiving ... physiological experiences' (p. 372). In reviewing the evidence, Watson and Pennebaker (1989, 1991) conclude that this relationship is due to the perceptual style of high negative affectivity populations. That is, such populations are introspective, apprehensive, negativistic and vigilant. Hence, rather than differences in actual diagnosable health problems between high and low negative affectivity populations, high negativity subjects are more likely to notice and attend to normal bodily sensations and minor discomforts which they then erroneously interpret as possible signs of illness.

Unfortunately, most of the studies investigating personality and health rely on retrospective measures of physical symptoms. This provides data on perception but not recall of symptoms which can only be accurately assessed by longitudinal studies. Such a research design was used by Larsen (1992) who obtained both concurrent daily symptom reports over a two month period in addition to retrospective reports of symptoms' severity. Not only was neuroticism associated with a tendency to be more perceptive of concurrent physical sensations; it was also associated with a tendency to recall physical symptoms as worse than they really were.

In addition to neuroticism and trait negative affectivity a number of other dispositional characteristics have been investigated in relation to symptom perception. For example, Larsen and Kasimatis (1991) note that people who do not respond with aggressive responses to anger-provoking or frustrating situations report having symptoms of shorter duration than those who do respond with anger. They also found that high Type A individuals (those showing a behaviour pattern marked by impatience, excessive drive, competitiveness and exaggerated achievement motives) reported less unpleasant affect during symptom episodes than low Type A individuals. The authors suggest this is due to the fact that Type A's are task oriented and hence less inclined to allow symptoms to interfere with activities.

Gender differences

A number of reports suggest that women report more symptoms and illnesses than men. For example, Celantano, Linet and Stewart (1990) found significant gender differences in perceived pain associated with headaches. One explanation for this, which is frequently advanced, is that women may be more sensitive than men to bodily discomforts and more willing than men to report symptoms of distress and illness. Such gender differences are assumed to result from childhood socialisation as well as adult expectations (Nathanson, 1975). However, in the absence of objective measures of discomfort it is difficult to judge whether such differences are due to biological or social factors or due to the possibility that women have lower thresholds for perceiving and reporting symptoms. Even comparing patient self-reports with doctor ratings of patient discomfort tells us more about the influence of patient's gender upon doctor's expectations than about any real differences in symptoms which might exist.

Others have argued that gender differences in attribution of somatic sensations and personality variables explain gender differences in physical symptoms (van Wijk and Kolk, 1997). Further studies provide some evidence that men and women differ in their perception of symptoms depending upon the illness or symptom under consideration (Mechanic, 1976). Thus, Marshall and Funch (1986) in a study of illness behaviour in people with cancer of the colon or rectum found that women were no more likely than men to recognise and respond to cancer symptoms. In a report of chronic joint symptoms, men with osteoarthritis were more likely to report pain irrespective of the severity of the disease (Davis, 1981). Finally MacIntyre (1993) in a study of common cold symptoms found that men were significantly more likely to over-rate their symptoms in comparison with a clinical observer than were women.

Cultural differences

Cultural differences in symptoms experienced and reported have been documented over a number of years, particularly in relation to pain (Lipton and Marbach, 1984; Zola, 1966; Zborowski, 1952). Zola (1966) found that Italian Americans were much more likely to report a number of symptoms while Irish Americans mentioned only a few. Zborowski (1952) found significant ethnic differences in the interpretation of and response to pain. Italian American males tended to complain about the pain itself, whereas Jewish American males tended to express worries about the implications of the pain for their future health. Subsequent interviews revealed that the Italian Americans felt free to complain in hospital, a liberty denied them at home, while the Jewish Americans, who were allowed to complain at home, were more concerned with eliciting the doctor's concern for their condition. Zborowski speculated that culturally specific child-rearing practices influence an individual's attention to and interpretation of bodily states. In a further study Lipton and Marbach (1984) found statistically significant differences between Black, Irish, Italian, Jewish and Puerto Rican American facial pain patients in the pain they reported experiencing. Degree of assimilation into American society and of acculturation to medical norms were strongly related to patients' symptom reporting and their behaviours and attitudes about these symptoms.

Thus, there is some evidence that symptom perception varies as a function of personality, gender and culture. The latter two factors are no doubt instrumental in shaping expectations and assumptions about health and hence, in turn, symptom perception. The extent to which we are aware of physiological responses is no doubt influenced by enduring biases in style of perceiving.

Attention

Attentional focus not only varies as a result of individual differences; environmental factors can also serve to direct attention towards or away from sensations (Pennebaker, 1983). People are more likely to be aware of and/or to report symptoms when they are understimulated by their environment; a stimulating environment provides a great deal of sensory information which serves to decrease the degree of attention which can be allocated to internal sensations. Observations of sports men and women who continue their sporting activity after suffering apparent injury during a game and whose injury is confirmed subsequent to that game seem to testify to this fact. There is also evidence from experimental research that symptom reporting can be varied by manipulating attentional focus. Thus, Pennebaker and Lightner (1980) relayed either noise or their own breathing to subjects who were taking part in an exercise task. Relative to control subjects (who heard no sound) paying attention to distracting sounds (i.e. noise) tended to decrease perception of fatigue and accompanying symptoms while subjects forced to attend to their own breathing were more likely to report symptoms. The fact that there were no actual physiological differences between the groups emphasises the fact that cognitive/attentional factors were influencing symptom perception. In a further study, subjects were instructed either to focus externally by listening to words repeated over headphones or to focus internally by attending to their breathing and heart rate during a mile run. Participants reported significantly less exercise-related symptoms when focusing attention externally (Fillingim and Fine, 1986).

There is also evidence that salient environmental factors can induce selective attention to and pathological interpretation of what might otherwise be merely background somatic information. That is, certain factors seem to activate health-related thoughts which in turn result in a greater reported frequency of symptoms. Such a process has been demonstrated experimentally by Skelton and Strohmetz (1990). In two studies, subjects reported more symptoms on a standardised symptom frequency inventory if they completed it prior to rather than after taking part in a health-decision task (which of two words is health related).

In sum then environmental factors affect attentional focus which in turn influences the perception of symptoms. In addition, a number of studies suggest that social and emotional factors also play a prominent role in symptom perception and interpretation.

Social and emotional factors

It has long been noted that stress and mood influence health, both in terms of signs of illness and also in relation to symptom reporting.

Stress

Mechanic (1974) has proposed that stressful experiences lead to an increase in health care seeking by altering sensitivity to and/or appraisal of physical symptoms. Thus, people who are stressed may believe they are more vulnerable to illness and so attend more closely to bodily changes. They may also experience stress-related physiological changes, such as increased heart rate, and interpret these as symptoms of illness (Gortmaker, Eckenrode and Gore, 1982).

Mood

A number of studies suggest that people in a positive mood rate themselves as healthier and report fewer illness-related memories and fewer symptoms in comparison to those in a negative mood. People in a negative mood also believe they are less capable of doing anything about their symptoms and are pessimistic about the likelihood of actions they take being effective in relieving them (Persson and Sjoberg, 1987; Salovey and Birnbaum, 1989; Salovey et al., 1991). The relationship between depressed mood and symptom appraisal holds both for individuals who merely feel relatively unhappy as well as for those with diagnosable clinical depression. Persson and Sjoberg conclude that:

> to feel bad is characterized by lower ratings on all mood aspects and higher ratings on all aspects of somatic symptoms as well. (p. 509)

Even quite transient mood states can affect symptom reporting. Thus, Salovey and Birnbaum (1989) randomly assigned undergraduates suffering form flu or flu like symptoms to happy, sad or neutral mood-induction conditions, obtaining physical symptom reports both before and after the five-minute mood-induction procedure. Although there were no differences in mood or symptom reports prior to the mood induction, after the mood-induction subjects in the sad mood condition not only reported twice as many aches and pains as those assigned to the happy condition; they also reported more physical symptoms from the previous week and attributed greater discomfort to these symptoms. In a clinical context, Funch (1988) reports that depressed mood at the time of interview was a significant predictor of symptom reporting in colorectal cancer patients.

A number of mechanisms have been suggested by which mood might influence symptom reporting. These relate to (i) the influence of mood upon memory; (ii) the influence of mood upon focus of attention; and (iii) the possibility that mood directly alters physiological processes, such as immune system functioning, hence affecting health (Salovey et al., 1991).

Mood and memory

A relatively robust finding within the literature is that mood can serve as a retrieval cue for mood-congruent material (Blaney, 1986). With regard to physical symptoms there is some evidence that negative mood increases recall of illness-related memories. Thus, Croyle and Uretsky (1987) found that subjects in a negative mood-induction condition judged their health to be poorer in comparison to those in a positive mood-induction condition. Symptom recall was significantly correlated with judgements of health status, suggesting that the effect of mood on judgement was mediated by the increased availability of mood-congruent memories.

Mood and attention of focus

As noted, there is evidence that self-focus of attention increases perception of symptoms and sensations, while external focus serves to decrease symptom perception. Increased self-focus is also associated with depressed mood (Ingram, 1990). This has led Salovey *et al.* (1991) to suggest that when sad mood produces body-oriented self-focused attention, symptoms will be more likely to be noticed and experienced more intensely.

Mood and immune system functioning

Finally, there is evidence that depressed mood is directly related to immunity so that, with greater intensity of depressed affect, there is more compromise of cellular immunity (Herbert and Cohen, 1993). Hence, the relationship between mood and symptom reporting may be due to an increase in illness rather than being mediated by mood-congruent recall or self-attention.

The powerful influence of socio-emotional factors in influencing symptom perception is attested to by two specific 'illnesses' documented in the literature: medical student's disease and mass psychogenic illness. As medical students learn about the symptoms of various diseases, more than two thirds believe they have had the illness at some time or another (Mechanic, 1972). The literature is also replete with many documented outbreaks of symptom reporting and physical complaints for which no organic pathology is evident. In both cases, factors such as attentional focus, mood, modelling or stress are likely to play a prominent role in enhancing symptom perception and increasing the importance people attach to them.

Mass psychogenic illness

Mass psychogenic illness involves a widespread perception of symptoms amongst a large group of people even though tests indicate that there is no medical basis for their symptoms (e.g. Alexander and Federuk, 1986; Brandt-Rauf, Andrews and Schwarz-Miller, 1991; Colligan, Pennebaker and Murphy, 1982; Elkins, Gamino and Rynearson, 1988; Gamino, Elkins and Hackney, 1989; Small and Borus, 1983; Small *et al.*, 1994). Symptoms most frequently reported include headache, hyperventilation, fainting or feeling faint and abdominal distress, symptoms which tend to be vague and subjective (Boxer, 1985).

Typical settings for such occurrences are those where individuals are in close proximity to each other, such as schools, hospitals or factories (Sirois, 1982). It has been argued that mass psychogenic illness is part of a spectrum of workplace disorders encompassing sick building syndrome, building-related illness and neurotoxic disorders, as well as mass psychogenic illness (Ryan and Morrow, 1992), and that psychological factors play a prominent role in both triggering and maintaining the unique pattern of somatic and neuropsychiatric symptoms which occur.

Mass psychogenic illness is thought to be relatively rare although its incidence and prevalence is unknown. Boxer (1985) reports that between 1972 and 1979 the National Institute of Occupational Safety and Health in the USA estimated that 1.7 per cent of their health hazard evaluation requests were thought to be mass psychogenic illness.

It is inevitably difficult to differentiate outbreaks of mass psychogenic illness from epidemics due to physical causes. This is illustrated by cases in environments where there are known hazards, such as in chemical or other industrial complexes, but where investigations have shown noxious agents to be present but within acceptable levels even though many people report the presence of noxious agents and symptoms of illness. The picture is further clouded by the fact that many such illness episodes occur after an initial 'real' event. Subsequent investigations of who reports the presence of noxious agents and who falls ill suggests a number of common elements (Hall and Johnson, 1989). Small and Borus (1983) suggest eight central factors. Four of these appear to be symptom related: (i) an absence of laboratory results or physical findings that would confirm a specific organic cause; (ii) apparent transmission of the illness by sight or sound; (iii) hyperventilation and faintness as typical symptoms; (iv) rapid spread followed by rapid remission of symptoms. Indeed, mass psychogenic illness tends to be transmitted within specific social networks. There is usually an index case who firsts develops one or more dramatic symptoms to whatever substance is believed to be the environmental trigger. Symptoms then spread rapidly to other individuals, with friends of the index case most often affected first. Rest, reassurance and suggestion of improvement tend to be adequate to alleviate symptoms. The remaining four factors appear to relate rather more to elements of suggestion and include: a predominance of females and adolescents or pre-adolescents; a predominance of physical or psychological stress; and relapse of illness in the setting of the original outbreak (see box 3.4).

Box 3.4 Examples of mass psychogenic illness

That the effects of mass psychogenic illness are dramatic is illustrated by examples of such outbreaks which have been documented in the literature:

Small and Borus (1983) document a case in which seventy school children complained of nausea, abdominal pain and shortness of breath during the rehearsal for and performance of a musical programme. Several suspected toxins were investigated and judged not to be responsible, with symptom development subsequently attributed to mass psychogenic illness.

Elkins, Gamino and Rynearson (1988) document a case in which thirty students amongst a number attending an evening football game were seen in hospital with supposed 'food poisoning' after one of their number became ill and collapsed. Symptoms of genuine food poisoning were absent in all but the first, index person, who collapsed and who was known to be ill prior to watching the game.

Gamino, Elkins and Hackney (1989) describe a case in which over one hundred people were seen in two hospitals following the escape of toxic smoke. Only twenty showed symptoms of poisoning characteristic of those resulting from the toxin in question (e.g. constricted pupils and breathing difficulties) which required medical treatment (e.g. eyewashes, medication). Prominent symptoms for the remainder were hyperventilation, agitation, abdominal distress and headache with treatment largely consisting of reassurance and positive suggestion.

Small et al. (1994) document a case in which a number of school children reported symptoms of illness after an odour was reported that was thought to emanate from a nearby oil refinery. The origin of the suspected fumes could not be located. The authors report many of the characteristic symptoms and other features of mass psychogenic illness.

Various explanations have been put forward to account for the development and spread of mass psychogenic illness. Pennebaker (1982) has speculated that those who are most likely to become symptomatic are those who are tense, anxious and stressed, and hence have heightened levels of autonomic arousal. In their effort to explain their non-specific physical symptoms such people inappropriately attribute them to some likely environmental event. A number of authors have argued that suggestion or imitation may play a role in mass psychogenic illness (Freedman, 1982). It seems that symptoms are more likely to spread if the first victim is held in high esteem, if their actions are reinforced through receipt of attention, sympathy or medical care, and if the initial situation is accompanied by stress or conflict. Indeed, visual or auditory contact between affected individuals and others seems to reinforce and intensify symptoms.

Many of the issues discussed in this chapter serve to shed some light on the question of mass psychogenic illness. The central feature is the way in which psychological factors serve to produce an apparent illness (Spurgeon, Gompertz and Harrington, 1997). Given that we experience symptoms on a regular basis it seems reasonable to assume that we will also engage in a search for meaning. If those symptoms occur in a context where other people have suffered similar symptoms to which a diagnosis has been applied (the disease prototype) we may then selectively search for other symptoms consistent with this diagnosis. This is more likely to occur given a particular set of environmental parameters (individuals in close proximity in a stressful or highly charged atmosphere) and personal characteristics (negative affectivity and low mood).

Placebo effects

The extent to which psychological factors influence symptom perception and interpretation is also attested to by responses to placebo treatments. A placebo or non-specific treatment procedure has been defined as:

> any therapy or component of a therapy that is deliberately used for its non-specific, psychological, or psychophysiological effect, or that is used for its presumed specific effect, but is without specific activity for the condition being treated. (Shapiro and Morris, 1978)

It has been referred to as the most consistently effective and widely used procedure in the history of medicine (Shapiro, 1960). The literature lists a wide variety of conditions for which placebos have been reported to produce symptom relief. These include allergies, asthma, diabetes, migraine, skin diseases, ulcers and warts (Richardson, 1989). Interestingly placebos can also produce side effects, with headaches and dizziness the most frequently reported adverse symptoms. The placebo response would appear to be a complex chain of events involving both psychological and physiological parameters which, as with symptom perception and interpretation in general, is affected by a range of individual, social and situational factors.

A number of studies have investigated patient variables in relation to placebo responding. Although there is some evidence that a high need for approval and external orientation is related to stronger placebo affects (Shapiro, 1964), it seems likely that such characteristics will interact with other factors in determing overall responses. Thus, there is good evidence that practitioner characteristics can have a profound effect upon placebo effectiveness. Placebo efficacy is enhanced if they are administered by high status, confident practitioners, who take an interest in the patient (Shapiro, 1964) and who emphasise the placebo's effectiveness (Roberts *et al.*, 1993). Placebos which resemble medications, which include precise instructions and which are administered in a medical context are also more effective (Shapiro, 1964).

A range of explanations have been offered for the placebo effect (White, Tursky and Schwartz, 1985) including expectancy, motivation/dissonance and anxiety-reduction theories. The most common explanation for placebos is that placebos alter people's expectations. Hence, given an expectation that a medication will operate in a particular way, drug and placebo effects should be similar. In summarising double-blind drug outcome studies Ross and Olson (1981) concluded that (i) the direction of the placebo effect paralleled that of the drug under study; (ii) the strength of the placebo effect was proportional to that of the drug under study; (iii) reported side effects of drug and placebo were similar; (iv) the time taken for the placebo to become maximally effective and to decrease in effectiveness was similar to that of the comparison drug; (v) placebos and drugs have similar dosage effects.

The expectancy hypothesis is also supported by findings that placebo instructions can alter the perception of symptoms. For example, Gelfand, Ullman and Krasner (1963) found that subjects given placebos reputed to be analgesics reported less pain than no-treatment control subjects. Although numerous studies support the expectancy hypothesis, others suggest limited or no expectancy effects (e.g. Jensen and Karoly, 1991). However, such differing findings are no doubt due to a range of factors, including subject characteristics, comparison of experimental versus naturalistic studies, the type of experimental manipulation used and so on. For example, expectations of treatment outcome will no doubt differ between undergraduate volunteers and patients with chronic illness, whose expectations will no doubt also differ from those of patients with acute illness. That expectancy effects are undoubtedly important is illustrated in an intriguing review. Roberts *et al.* (1993) examined five medical and surgical treatments once thought to be effective but no longer considered effective following results of later trials. For the five treatments, outcomes of 40 per cent excellent, 30 per cent good and 30 per cent poor were reported by their proponents. Roberts *et al.* conclude that when both practitioner and patient believe in the efficacy of a treatment, placebo effects:

> exert considerably more influence than commonly believed and reported in many controlled studies. (p. 387)

There have been relatively few studies of the motivational/dissonance hypothesis of placebos and symptom perception. In one experimental study Totman (1975) informed one group of subjects injected with an 'analgesis' (which was actually just a slight pin prick) they would be paid for their participation in the study while another group were not being paid. He argued that the non-paid group would have greater motivation to respond to the placebo, since a response would justify the discomforting injection they had undergone. Motivation would thus create a greater analgesic effect in these subjects. Although the non-paid group did indeed display the greater analgesic effect, motivation was unfortunately not assessed and hence it is not possible to say if this was indeed the crucial variable. In a more recent study, Jensen and Karoly (1991) manipulated motivation by telling subjects that responses to a particular sedative were linked to a particular personality which was described as possessing a range of positive characteristics. For the low motivation subjects, the link between personality and response to the sedative was described as weak. Subjects encouraged to have a stronger desire to respond to the placebo reported a greater sedative effect than those not so motivated to respond. In relation to cognitive dissonance, the belief that no beneficial effect of treatment has occurred could be regarded as inconsistent with the fact that treatment has been received, the doctor was confident that improvement would occur and so on. In order to reduce dissonance, one option for the patient is to alter his or her perception of occurrence of change (Totman, 1987).

Finally, others have argued that placebo effects operate via anxiety reduction. The effect of reducing anxiety may be direct, for example, by allowing bodily resources to replenish themselves, or indirect, by reducing attention to and hence salience of a particular symptom.

In all cases, however, the important factor is that a non-specific treatment procedure can influence symptom perception and interpretation. This attests to the central role played by psychological factors in not only influencing awareness of signs of potential illness but also influencing the likelihood that they will be translated into symptoms of disease.

Interpreting symptoms

As Pennebaker (1982) notes, symptoms and illness signs are notoriously ambiguous; hence, a critical factor determining symptom-related behaviour is the person's subjective interpretation given to the symptoms involved. A range of factors have been suggested as underlying the interpretation of symptoms. For example, Jones *et al.* (1981) suggest that symptom interpretation and the likelihood of seeking medical care is influenced by: (i) the extent to which a symptom is perceived as threatening, serious, disruptive to activities and painful; (ii) familiarity with and perceived responsibility for the symptom's occurrence; and (iii) embarrassment. Other research suggests that symptom interpretation is influenced by perceived cause, site of symptom and the extent to which it disrupts activities. This is illustrated in a study by Bishop (1987) who asked subjects to sort sixty symptoms according to perceived co-occurrence. Four dimensions were obtained: caused by a virus; upper versus lower in the body; physical versus psychological causation; and disruptive to activities. Disruptiveness was related to both reduction in activities and adoption of self-care; viral causation was also related to self-care; physical causation and symptoms in the lower part of the body were related to use of professional care. Other research, predominantly with elderly people, suggests that symptom interpretation is influenced by familiarity with the symptom, state of health when the symptom was experienced (Haug, Wykle and Namazi, 1989) and situational factors (Alonzo, 1984).

Much of the available research can be interpreted in relation to Leventhal's (1986) bio-psychological model of symptom processing. He argues that illness representations are coded through sensory motor channels, perceptual memory (in the form of schemas) and abstract semantic or conceptual codes. Schematic processing is immediate and involves the interpretation of current symptoms in relation to representations of specific illness episodes in memory (prior illness experience). In contrast semantic or conceptual processing relates to reflections about memories of labels, such as heart disease, cancer and colds (Leventhal and Leventhal, 1993). Thus both abstract semantic and concrete perceptual memories are involved in the processing or transformation of a sensation into a symptom and the subsequent interpretation of this symptom. Factors influencing such processing include expectations, learning experiences, prior experience, general state of health and social factors (see box 3.5).

Box 3.5 Factors influencing symptoms interpretation

Expectations – assumptions about bodily symptoms will influence how we interpret them. However, our assumptions may not be accurate and can themselves be influenced by a range of factors including our age, the timing of the symptom and our knowledge base.

Learning experiences – parental reactions to signs and symptoms may subsequently be acquired by their children.

Prior experience – our prior experience with a symptom will influence how we interpret it should it re-occur.

State of health at symptom onset – those whose general health is poor are more inclined to interpret a new symptom as threatening, perhaps as an indicator that their health is deteriorating further.

Situational factors – factors leading to a greater tendency to interpret bodily symptoms in a negative light are:
    loneliness
    bereavement
    unemployment
    poverty
    a strong belief in the power of medicine

Expectations

A widely researched topic of relevance relates to menstrual symptoms. A substantial number of women report experiencing physical, psychological and behavioural change during the pre-menstrual phase of the menstrual cycle. Symptoms occurring during this phase have been referred to as the pre-menstrual syndrome, which consists of a specific cluster of severe symptoms, or simply as pre-menstrual symptoms, which refer to a mild to moderate experience of symptoms (Brooks-Gunn, 1986). Only a minority of women suffer from the pre-menstrual syndrome whereas many women report pre-menstrual symptoms (Haskett and Abplanalp, 1983). One explanation for why many women report symptoms as menstruation approaches is based on cultural expectations. There is considerable evidence that in Western cultures people believe menstruation to be associated with a variety of unpleasant physical and psychological symptoms. For example, women are believed to experience more headaches, abdominal pain, irritability, mood swings and tension during the menstrual phase of their cycle (Brook-Gunn and

Ruble, 1986). Women holding such negative expectations for bodily change during the pre-menstrual phase may attend more closely to normal bodily sensations and consequently will be more likely to interpret them as pre-menstrual symptoms when they think they are approaching menstruation.

Indeed, there is evidence that the more a woman believes in the phenomenon of menstrual distress, the more exaggerated, in recall, will be the negativity of perceived symptoms during the preceding period (McFarland, Ross and DeCourville, 1989). There may then be a tendency to misattribute at least some aspect of negative feeling to a salient physical cause: that is, menstruation. The influence of demand characteristics on symptom reports is illustrated in a study by AuBuchon and Calhoun (1985). They found that women reported more menstrual symptoms if they knew the study concerned menstruation-related symptoms than if they did not know it concerned such symptoms. In addition, perception of cycle phase is related to symptom reports. Thus, women led to believe they are in the pre-menstrual phase report more symptoms than those led to believe they are in the intermenstrual phase regardless of whether they were actually premenstrual or intermenstrual (Ruble, 1977; Klebanov and Jemmott, 1992).

Learning experience

A further explanation for differing symptom reports relates to differing learning experiences. Thus, Whitehead *et al.* (1986) asked student nurses how their mothers reacted to menstrual symptoms and cold symptoms during their adolescence and how their mothers themselves behaved when they themselves had menstrual symptoms. Mothers of respondents were independently asked the same questions. Nurses who had been encouraged to adopt the sick role during menstruation or whose mothers modelled menstrual distress reported significantly more menstrual symptoms, clinic visits and disability during menstruation as adults.

Prior experience

Prior experience with a symptom will inevitably influence how re-occurrences of a symptom are intrepreted, perhaps either leading the person to pay little attention to it or alerting them to possible danger. One of the best predictors of mothers' making correct decisions to seek medical care for their children was prior experience – whether or not their child or a relative had had a similar problem in the past (Turk *et al.*, 1985). In some instances prior experience and expectations can lead people to interpret their symptoms incorrectly. Elderly people tend to have more symptoms than younger people, but, even when they consult their doctor, they tend to report fewer symptoms (Hickey, 1988). It has been suggested that older people may attribute new symptoms to previously diagnosed chronic conditions or with the ageing process, assuming, for example, that tiredness and weakness are symptoms of old age rather than signs of illness (Leventhal and Prohaska, 1986; Prohaska *et al.*, 1987; Stoller, 1993).

State of health at the time of symptom onset

State of health at the time of symptom onset also influences symptom interpretation. Thus, people who believe they are in good health have more confidence in their own resilience and are less likely to interpret any particular symptom as threatening (Haug, Wykle and Namazi 1989); they are also likely to normalise and hence minimise the importance of new and unfamiliar symptoms. In contrast people in poor health are more likely to assess any new symptom as a bad sign, as it may indicate further deterioration in health (Stoller, 1993).

Situational factors

People who have experienced stressful life events, are widowed or divorced, live alone, are unemployed, have low incomes, who rely on their GP for advice with non-medical problems and who express strong beliefs in the capacity of medical science to protect their health tend to report more symptoms, which they are more likely to view as severe (Dean, 1986). In contrast, those with satisfactory social support, effective strategies for coping with stress, and confidence in their own ability to influence their health tend to report fewer serious symptoms (Vergruuge, 1987). Social support may buffer the effect of new symptoms either by providing emotional or practical assistance or because people in one's social network suggest treatments to alleviate symptoms.

Summary

The key issues explored in this chapter involve the wide individual variations in the extent to which people attend to bodily signs of potential illness and the manner in which they subsequently interpret them. Most recent explanations for such variations have emphasised the fact that the information-processing system which translates sensory experience into symptoms is influenced by a complex interaction of sensory, cognitive and emotional factors. This is illustrated by the various paradigms that have been advanced in the context of cognitive representations of illness. Thus, we tend to hold beliefs about which symptoms should be associated with each other and given a particular illness label, while a belief that we have an illness is likely to result in a search for symptoms compatible with that illness. Hence, beliefs about illness shape our search for, awareness and subsequent interpretation of symptoms. In addition, there is evidence that symptom perception is influenced by personality, attention and mood. Less clear results are obtained for the influence of gender and culture upon symptom perception, although culture certainly influences the interpretation and labelling of symptoms.

The varied factors influencing our perception and interpretation of symptoms are attested to by both the phenomenon of mass psychogenic illness and the efficacy of placebo treatments. The former involves the widespread perception of symptoms amongst a large group of people even though tests indicate that there is no medical basis for their symptoms. Placebo or non-specific treatment procedures have been referred to as the most consistently effective and widely used treatment procedures in the history of medicine. Once we acknowledge the existence of a bodily sign which differs from our usual experience of our bodies, the manner in which this sign will subsequently be interpreted will largely depend upon our prior experience of the symptom, expectations, learning experience, our general state of health and social factors.

The essential first step in an individual's decision making relating to their use of health care is thus a complex one; it is not surprising that although symptoms occur on a regular basis there is marked variability in the extent to which we attend to, report and act upon them. A clear understanding of health and illness is not possible unless we also seek to understand why signs become salient for a given individual and which factors subsequently serve to shape the meaning given to particular symptoms.

FURTHER READING

M. J. Colligan, J. W. Pennebaker and L. R. Murphy (eds) (1982). *Mass Psychogenic Illness: A social psychological analysis*. Hillsdale, NJ: Erlbaum.

K. J. Petrie and J. A. Weinman (eds) (1997). *Perception of Health and Illness*. Amsterdam: Harwood Academic Publishers.

P. Salovey, A. O'Leary, M. S. Stretton, S. A. Fishkin and C. A. Drake (1991). Influence of mood on judgments about health and illness. In J. P. Forgas (ed.), *Emotion and Social Judgments*. Oxford: Pergamon Press.

J. A. Skelton and R. T. Croyle (eds) (1991). *Mental Representation in Health and Illness*. New York: Springer-Verlag.

D. Watson and J. W. Pennebaker (1989). Health complaints, stress, and distress: Exploring the central role of negative affectivity. *Psychological Review*, **96**, 234–254.

CHAPTER 4

Seeking health care

CHAPTER OVERVIEW

This chapter examines the various psychosocial factors which influence our use of health care facilities. The first part of the chapter examines the extensive use of self-care and lay referral networks within the community as an initial response to possible signs of illness; the use of 'complementary therapies' is also considered in this regard. The following section discusses conceptual frameworks seeking to explain individuals' decision-making processes relating to their use of health care; pathway and determinants models are discussed. Factors mediating the decision to use health care facilities are evaluated; age, gender, culture, social and emotional factors are discussed. The second half of the chapter examines delay in seeking professional medical care, discussing the prevalence, consequences and determinants of such delay. The final section of the chapter examines overuse of health care facilities by those with excessive health care concerns or who exhibit abnormal illness behaviour.

This chapter covers:

> Lay care in illness
> Seeking health care; conceptual frameworks
> Variables affecting decisions to use health care
> Delay in seeking medical help
> Excessive health concerns and the overuse of health care

Introduction

A bodily symptom which is interpreted as a possible sign of disease may provoke a range of subsequent responses: the sign may be ignored; the person may opt for self-treatment either in the form of medication or lifestyle change; friends, family or a variety of 'alternative' practitioners (for example, homeopaths, aromatherapists and acupuncturists) may be consulted; or the person may seek Western biomedically based health care. Within our own cultural framework it is only the latter practitioner who legitimises the 'sick role': that is, makes acceptable certain actions, such as taking time away from work, by people who are ill (Parsons, 1959).

Seeking and securing treatment is thus a complex process. A frequently taken first step is to ask one's family or peer group for advice. This may involve the person seeking to establish whether the physical changes or discomfort should be regarded as potentially serious, discussion about the need for professional advice and identifying an appropriate provider, who may or may not be a recognised medical practitioner. Complementary or alternative medicine is widely and increasingly used within the Western world. Friends and family may also be involved in making arrangements for seeing and communicating symptoms to the health professional or other provider as well as facilitating adherence with recommendations which might be made.

Responses to signs and symptoms are largely determined by the circumstances and social setting in which they occur. Cultural background and familial influence may determine whether professional or other practitioners are consulted. Demographic, interpersonal and emotional factors also play a role. In addition, utilisation is inevitably influenced by access to health care, determined by availability and financing issues. A range of factors thus influence an individual's decision to use or not use professional or lay care in illness. As Kleinman, Eisenberg and Good (1978) note:

> the medical encounter is but one step in a more inclusive sequence. The illness process begins with personal awareness of a change in bodily feeling and continues with the labelling of the sufferer by family or by self as 'ill'. Personal and family action is undertaken to bring about recovery, advice is sought from members of the extended family or the community, and professional and 'marginal' practitioners are consulted. This sequence may or may not include registration within the legitimized health system. (p. 251)

Lay care in illness

Self-care has been defined as involving a lay person acting on his or her own behalf to promote their health, or detect, limit, prevent or treat their symptoms of ill health (Dean, 1986; Levin and Idler, 1983; Levin, Katz and Holst, 1976). Self-care can thus range from actions taken to care for oneself more effectively, for example by exercise or dietary control, to immediate and continuing responses to illness, as well as an individual's coping ability when confronted by ill health (see box 4.1).

Dean (1986) suggests that lay care consists of at least four components: individual self-care; family care; care from one's extended social network; and mutual aid responses to health problems such as self-help groups.

Box 4.1 Self-care practices

We engage in a range of self-care practices in order to promote our own health and well being; we also seek to self-diagnose and self-treat; typical self-care actions we take include:

seeking the advice of family or friends or speaking to someone else with the same problem

changing our behaviour:

taking exercise

altering our diet

avoiding stressful situations

giving up smoking

self-medication – most usually in the form of over-the-counter preparations

non-medication interventions; home-made preparations such as herbal infusions

change in activity level: for example, taking bed rest or having a holiday

consulting 'folk healers' or using non-traditional remedies

(See Dean, 1986; Levin and Idler, 1983.)

Self-care in response to symptoms of illness is widespread. In one report it was estimated that 96 per cent of patients obtained lay advice or care prior to consulting a medical practitioner (Elliott-Binns, 1973). This led the report's author to question the appropriateness of characterising the family doctor as the primary source of health care. In a further study, Freer (1980) reported that women practised some form of self-care on 80 per cent of days on which bothersome symptoms were experienced. Indeed, research in both the USA and UK indicates that between 70 and 90 per cent of illness episodes are never seen by a doctor (DeFriese and Woomert, 1983; Demers *et al.*, 1980; Zola, 1973). Thus, DeFriese and Woomert (1983) found that only 10 to 25 per cent of illness episodes actually resulted in contacts with professional health care providers and that a large proportion of those who had sought medical care had treated themselves before seeking such professional advice. In a diary study, Demers *et al.* (1980) found that nearly 95 per cent of health problems recorded did not involve contact with professional medical care. Many such episodes are likely to be treated within the family, while others may be treated by folk healers or by a variety of non-traditional remedies.

Although some studies suggest that self-care rates do not differ as a function of age (Haug, Wykle and Namazi, 1989), a number of other studies suggest that for older people in particular self-care assumes special significance (Hickey, 1988; Rakowski *et al.*, 1988). Although older people are more likely than their younger counterparts to present for physical checks and minor complaints, they will not necessarily present with serious symptoms despite the higher prevalence of chronic conditions experienced by older people. Using a diary method, in which respondents recorded daily illness symptoms and responses, Rakowski *et al.* (1988) found that self-treatment and no action decisions were the overwhelming responses to symptoms of illness among their elderly respondents. In reviewing the literature relating to self-care in the elderly, Hickey (1988) concludes that self-care is a prominent illness response in the elderly, but when symptoms are considered serious, as determined by how long they last and how much pain and dysfunction they cause, older people are as likely as younger respondents to seek help or shift from self-treatment or no treatment to professional care.

Dean (1986) argues that the fundamental aspect of self-care behaviour in illness is the recognition and evaluation of symptoms. Once symptoms are recognised and judged sufficiently serious for direct action, one or more of four types of illness behaviour are undertaken: decisions to do nothing about the symptoms, self-medication, non-medication self-treatment or decisions to consult professional providers. Self-medication involves the use of both over-the-counter preparations and medications prescribed during previous medical consultations. Non-medication intervention strategies include the use of appliances (e.g. thermometers, enemas), home-made preparations (e.g. herbal teas, hot baths), activity (bed rest, change in exercise level), avoidance behaviour (e.g. not lifting, not smoking, avoiding stressful situations) or changes in diet. Little is known about an individual's decision to do nothing about symptoms although this is clearly bound up with issues relating to recognising and interpreting symptoms discussed previously. The question of ignoring symptoms and the problem of unnecessary delay in seeking medical care are discussed later in this chapter.

The use of self-medication as treatment for symptoms is extensive (Levin and Idler, 1983). For example, Prohaska, Funch and Blesch (1990) found that over 80 per cent of their sample of older adults used at least one over-the-counter medication in response to symptoms later diagnosed as colorectal cancer. Indeed, a number of studies have found that self-medication with non-prescribed medicines exceeds the use of prescription drugs, while behavioural responses to symptoms, such as alteration to diet, more or less exercise, having a rest or taking a holiday, are frequently practised (McEwan, 1979).

A number of studies have evaluated factors predictive of self-care versus professional health care in relation to health belief model variables. Thus, Haug, Wykle and Namazi (1989), in a survey of over 700 older adults, found that self-care was more likely when the individual perceived the symptom as mild rather than severe. Good health was related to self-care for ailments viewed as minor, but low faith in doctors was a contributing factor for the decision to self-treat for symptoms viewed as more serious. Similarly, Stoller, Forster and Portugal (1993), in a survey of over 600 elderly people, found that symptoms which had little disruptive impact on desired activities or were dismissed as not serious were more likely to be ignored. As these authors note, however, we do not know whether these lay assessments are accurate and, hence, we do not know whether taking no action is an appropriate response or whether people are putting themselves at risk by ignoring potentially dangerous symptoms. However, others have argued that self-care decisions are generally appropriate and self-treatment helpful.

Lay referral network

One of the most frequent actions taken in response to symptoms is to talk about concerns with family or friends who may help interpret the symptom, give advice about seeking medical care, recommend a remedy, or recommend seeing another lay person. After consulting with family and friends the next step is often to consult with someone known to have a similar problem (Hayes-Bautista, 1976). While lay referral frequently incorporates medical rumour and gossip about effective remedies, it can also provide reassurance, or be a prompt to seek professional health care (cf. Zola's 1973 social sanctioning trigger). Research suggests that the elderly in particular seem to prefer care from informal rather than formal sources, with kinship being the preferred source of support. Indeed, the lay referral network (Freidson, 1960) can be highly systematic and is widely used.

Thus Scambler, Scambler and Craig (1981) found that for a sample of working-class women, 71 per cent of symptom episodes which resulted in a medical consultation were first discussed with a lay person. Sanders (1982) found that, in a student sample, during the course of the preceding year, an average of three non-experts (family and friends) had been consulted about symptoms the respondents had experienced. In 68 per cent of cases this advice was felt to have been influential. In addition, 87 per cent of the respondents had themselves acted as lay advisers to others in the preceding year. In a further study, Prohaska, Funch and Blesch (1990) found that of 254 patients diagnosed with cancer of the colon 80 per cent had spoken with at least one other person before initiating professional care.

The important role played by network advice is attested to by the fact that network advice to see a doctor is a significant predictor of health care use (Berkanovic, Telesky and Reeder, 1981). There is also evidence that people are more likely to seek medical advice for symptoms when both their own beliefs and network advice favour help seeking than when their own and network views are incongruent. However, when one's own views are incongruent with network advice, it seems that one's own views predominate. Thus, Berkanovic, Telesky and Reeder (1981) report that if the person's own beliefs favoured help seeking but network advice did not, then about two-thirds sought medical help; far less did so if their network advised seeking medical care but their own beliefs did not support this behaviour.

Lay care in the community thus constitutes a dominant proportion of 'health care'. Use of home remedies and various types of non-prescription treatments has a long tradition and is common throughout the world. Such care is frequently adequate as a treatment for symptoms and rarely harmful (Williamson and Danaher, 1978). Yet as Dean (1986) notes:

> Professionals providing care in formal medical systems tend to view self-care … as inferior to their own. This tendency persists even when these forms of care prove to be more appropriate and effective than those provided by professionals. Lay care continues to be viewed as residual and supplemental to professional care in spite of the well documented fact that professional care is the supplemental form of health care. (p. 275)

Complementary therapies

Almost half the adult population in Europe has made use of complementary medicine at some time in their lives. If one were to include self-medication with various homeopathic or herbal remedies within this definition then as many as one-third of the population have made use of complementary medical treatment within the past year (Lewith and Aldridge, 1991; Sharma, 1992). Within the USA, Eisenberg, Kessler and Foster (1993) argue that people consult more frequently with providers of unconventional medicine, including complementary therapies, than with physicians in primary care. However, Eisenberg and his colleagues included exercise and relaxation techniques within their realm of unconventional medicines, which no doubt led them to overestimate the use of alternative therapies. There can though be little doubt that use of complementary therapies is widespread. The term covers a range of techniques including homeopathy, acupuncture, chiropractice, acupuncture, osteopathy and a range of herbal medicinal preparations which might be considered as conventional or standard treatment in many non-Western societies or sub-cultures within the Western world.

In addition to the fact that people make widespread use of such therapies there is also evidence, within Western societies, that traditional general practitioners are becoming increasingly likely either to practise complementary medicine themselves or to refer patients to complementary practitioners or to endorse such practices (Anderson and Anderson, 1987; White, Resch and Ernst, 1997).

As with all decision making relating to health care, the decision to use complementary therapy is influenced by a range of factors. A general finding is that patients who use complementary therapies tend to be of higher educational status and with a higher income than non-users (Astin, 1998; Sharma, 1992). This may indicate a greater ability to 'shop around' for health care but also suggests the possibility that use of alternative health care is the end-point of a reflective decision-making process. Complementary therapy also tends to be used for chronic conditions, particularly back problems or chronic pain, rather than life-threatening conditions (Astin, 1998) and is used in conjunction with, rather than instead of, conventional medicine (Thomas *et al.*, 1991). There is also some indication that those holding specific beliefs, such as a holistic orientation towards health or a particular commitment towards environmental or spiritual issues, are more likely to use complementary therapies (Astin, 1998). On the other hand, use of complementary treatments does not seem to be part of a 'flight from science' (Smith, 1983). Dissatisfaction with conventional medicine in general does not necessarily predict use of alternative medicine (Astin, 1998) and complementary medicine and general practice patients do not seem to differ with regard to health beliefs or views about the perceived efficacy of conventional or alternative treatments (Furnham and Smith, 1988; Vincent and Furnham, 1994). However, there is some indication that a belief in the efficacy of a specific complementary treatment and a belief that orthodox medicine has been ineffective in treating their problem does relate to use of that specific alternative therapy (Furnham and Bhagrath, 1993; Furnham and Forey, 1994; Furnham and Smith, 1988; Vincent and Furnham, 1996).

In sum, people make widespread use of both self-care or lay care and complementary or alternative medicine. Indeed, such practices constitute the dominant proportion of 'health care'. Lay care is the usual first step people take in relation to their health care. This may or may not be associated with the use of complementary therapy, which in turn may or may not be associated with the use of conventional medicine. In spite of the predominance of biomedicine within the Western world, use of conventional medicine may only occur after a lengthy process of evaluation and use of over-the-counter remedies or alternative therapies. A central issue then becomes when do people decide to use conventional medical care and what factors influence their readiness to consult medical practitioners.

The decision to seek medical treatment

Two broad conceptual frameworks have been advanced to address the question of how people enter the sick role and make choices regarding their use or non-use of different kinds of health services. They can be broadly termed pathway models, which describe the stages through which people go in the decision-making process, and determinants models, which focus on the explanatory variables or determinants of the choices people make (Kroeger, 1983).

Pathway models

Pathway models describe the series of sequential decision-making steps people take in the process of translating distress into action. A number of pathway models have been proposed (see box 4.2).

Box 4.2 Pathway models to seeking medical treatment

Examples of pathway models are provided by Suchman (1965) and Fabrega and Van Egeren (1976).
  Suchman identified five stages:

Stage I involves the use of folk-medicine, self-medication, denial of symptoms or delay in seeking medical care.
Stage II involves the adoption of the sick role, in which normal behaviours are suspended while lay interventions are continued.
Stage III involves medical care contact and the seeking of professional advice.
Stage IV is termed dependent-patient role when professional treatment is accepted.
Stage V refers to recovery and rehabilitation when normal behaviours are resumed.

Fabrega and Van Egeren describe eight stages:

(i)   illness recognition and labelling
(ii) illness disvalues – change to lifestyle
(iii) treatment plans
(iv) assessment of treatment benefits
(v)   treatment costs
(vi) net benefits or utility – of treatment
(vii) selection of treatment
(viii) set-up for recycling – recovery

While such models provide a useful descriptive framework the description is inevitably stylised; a given individual may not necessarily pass through all the stages and may not follow the stages in an invariant sequence. For example, while someone may opt for self-treatment as an initial step prior to consulting a medical practitioner, they may subsequently return to self-treatment following their medical consultation; the process may not involve the adoption of the sick role. It is unlikely in practice that translating distress into action will be a straightforward process, as specific factors will have differential relevance for any given individual. At best, describing stages provides an account of what might happen, it does not provide an explanatory framework.

Thus, the decision to seek medical treatment often has little to do with an individual's objective physical condition. As noted previously, people experience symptoms but do not necessarily seek medical care. In this context, DeFriese and Woomert (1983) note that only about one-quarter to one-half of all episodes of illness actually result in contact with professional sources of health care. Such variations in medical utilisation require an explanatory framework. One such model which has been proposed to explain medical utilisation is Anderson's Behavioural Model (Andersen and Newman, 1973).

Determinants models

Anderson's Behavioural Model seeks to explain the use of health services as a function of three variables: predisposing, enabling and need factors (see box 4.3)

Box 4.3 Anderson's Behavioural Model and health care utilisation

Anderson's Behavioural Model proposes that the likelihood that any one individual will make use of health care facilities is a function of:

Predisposing factors
    Demographic characteristics
        age, sex, marital status and family size
    Social structures (the individual's lifestyle)
        employment, education and ethnicity
    Health beliefs
        attitudes about medical care, physicians and disease
        worries about one's health

Enabling factors
    Familial resources – individual's ability to provide for him or herself
    Community resources – availability and accessibility of health care facilities

Need
    The individual's perception of their illness
    Professionally evaluated need

(Andersen and Newman, 1973.)

A number of studies have used Anderson's Behavioural Model to guide research examining health care utilisation in the general population (e.g. Wolinsky, 1978) and in sub-sections of the population, such as the elderly (e.g. Jewett, Hibbard and Weeks, 1991/92). Although methods used within such studies have varied, a general finding is that the model explains a relatively small amount of the variance in utilisation, with most of the explanatory power provided by the need variable, while predisposing and enabling factors account for little variation (e.g. Coulton and Frost, 1982; Jewett, Hibbard and Weeks, 1991/92; Hulka and Wheat, 1985; Wolinsky and Coe, 1984; Wolinsky and Johnson, 1991).

For example, in Coulton and Forst's (1982) study, while all the variables together only accounted for 12 per cent of the variance in older people's medical service use, 11 per cent was accounted for by need measures. In Wolinsky and Coe's (1984) study, 18 per cent of the variance in doctor visits was explained by the full range of variables, with 13 per cent contributed by need variables. In a further study incorporating a broad range of social, structural, organisational, social network and social psychological variables as predictors of a decision to seek medical care, Berkanovic, Telesky and Reeder (1981) report that the entire set of independent variables explained 57 per cent of the variance in the decision to seek medical care for symptoms. Forty two per cent of the variance was explained by symptom-specific network advice (i.e. network advice to see a doctor, a factor not included in Anderson's model) and beliefs (i.e. perceived efficacy of care), with a further 12 per cent explained by need variables (e.g. number of chronic health problems and reported disability from symptoms). In a further study, health status (need) factors alone accounted for approximately two thirds of the explained variability (Wolinsky, 1978).

In other words, once physical health status is accounted for, there are few other significant predictors of health care use. The greater the number of symptoms that are perceived and the greater the health concerns, the more likely it is that medical care will be sought irrespective of social structure, community or familial resources or demographic characteristics. However, as Hulka and Wheat (1985) note, need in terms of health is an imprecise concept that has been measured in a variety of ways including using diagnostic methods, based on symptoms or the individual's own perception of themselves. As Hulka and Wheat further note, measures of health care use have also been highly variable, ranging from percentage of the population visiting the doctor, to length of hospital stay, or type of visits to doctor or hospital. The relationship between use and need will inevitably vary according to the combination of need and utilisation variables chosen.

In this context, it is clearly necessary to take account of factors influencing the recognition of and importance attached to the symptom and beliefs about available health care. Such issues are incorporated into the health belief model, which clearly overlaps with the need variable from Anderson's Behavioural Model. Two predictive factors are inherent in the model: firstly, the person's beliefs about their vulnerability to a particular disorder and their beliefs about its seriousness and its consequences and, secondly, the person's beliefs about the efficacy of a particular treatment (Kirscht, 1983). As discussed, the health belief model has been used to predict a range of health-related behaviours. However, as with Anderson's Behavioural Model, although the various components of the model have some predictive utility, the amount of variance explained tends to be relatively small.

Of the health belief model variables investigated in relation to people's decisions to use health care facilities, belief in the efficacy of health care and perceived seriousness of symptoms seem to have the most predictive utility (Crandall and Duncan, 1981; Matthews et al., 1983). With specific regard to myocardial infarction, Matthews and her colleagues proposed five dimensions of symptom experience relevant to the patients' health care seeking decision: firstly, the salience or prominence of the initial symptoms; secondly, the situational context in which the symptom initially appeared; thirdly, the affective reaction to the symptom; fourthly, the attempt to understand what the symptom means; and, fifthly, assessment of the symptom's seriousness. When the appraisal process results in the judgement that a symptom is serious, disruptive of on-going activities and difficult to control, then the person is more likely to seek medical care (Cameron, Leventhal and Leventhal, 1993; Mechanic, 1978).

Individuals appraise their condition and decide whether the symptom warrants treatment based on the processing of information guided by existing cognitive representations of illness. For example, there is evidence that the perceived prevalence of a symptom affects a person's response to it, so that medically significant conditions that are perceived as relatively common often do not prompt treatment seeking or symptom reporting (Zola, 1966). In an experimental study, Ditto and Jemmott (1989) found that among college students who were led to believe they had a fictitious disorder, those who were told it was highly prevalent were less likely to seek information about the disorder than those who were told it was low in prevalence.

In general then the person's need, as reflected by their perception of the symptoms, is a major determinant of health care use. However, important as such factors are, they nevertheless only account for a modest amount of the variance. A variety of other factors, as suggested by both Anderson's model and the health belief model, are likely to be mediators of the decision to use health care facilities.

Factors mediating the decision to use health care facilities

Kroeger (1983) has organised variables mediating the decision to use health care facilities into three groupings: characteristics of the person (cf. Anderson's predisposing factor); characteristics of the disorder and people's perception of it (cf. Anderson's need factor); and characteristics of the health care delivery system (cf. Anderson's enabling factor). Characteristics of the person include sociodemographic variables, such as age, gender, ethnic background, social class and educational background. Characteristics relating to the disorder involve a person's perception of its chronicity, cause, contagiousness, prognosis and impact on the patient's activity level. Finally, characteristics of the health care delivery system include factors which promote or discourage the use of such resources within the community, including accessibility and affordability. The main variables investigated within this framework include age, gender and cultural background.

In addition, a number of social and emotional factors also play a role in determining whether or not medical care will be sought for a particular symptom (Cockerham, Kunz and Lueschen, 1988; Gortmaker, Eckenrode and Gore, 1982; Tessler, Mechanic and Dimond, 1976; Timko, 1987; Zola, 1973).

Age

A number of studies suggest that use of health care is greatest within both the youngest and the oldest age groups. In the former case, greater use is accounted for not only by the range of infectious diseases of childhood and the risk of childhood injuries, but also by routine health checks and inoculations. In the case of older adults while, on average, they make greater use of health care, there is great variability in use within such populations. Thus, there is evidence that a great deal of use by a minority of the older population accounts for much of the excess use by the elderly. Hulka and Wheat (1985) suggest that less than 10 per cent of the older adult population account for more than three quarters of all hospital admissions. The heavy use by a relatively small proportion of older adults serves to skew the data, creating the impression that the elderly as a group make excess demands upon health care. Indeed, most older adults do not consult their doctor, over three quarters not requiring any hospital admissions (Hulka and Wheat, 1985), and many do not consult even when it might be appropriate for them to do so.

Older adults, in comparison to their younger counterparts, do tend to suffer from more chronic illnesses. Yet, investigations of screening programmes for the elderly suggest that elderly people may fail to report as many as 50 per cent of their medical problems to their doctor. Disabilities not reported include correctable functional impairments like hearing and vision deficiencies, urinary incontinence and locomotor dysfunction. Such under reporting of symptoms is frequently explained in the context of attributing symptoms to age rather than disease (Levkoff et al., 1988), a factor also associated with delay in seeking care for potentially serious illness. In contrast to under reporting of chronic illness there is some evidence that older adults are more likely to present for physical checks and with minor ailments (Haug, 1981).

Gender

The fact that women's life expectancy exceeds that of men has been extensively documented. However, numerous studies since the 1950s have found repeatedly that women report more daily symptoms, such as headaches and tiredness, and are more likely than men to seek medical care for symptoms (Mechanic, 1976; Nathanson, 1975, 1977; Verbrugge, 1979, 1980, 1982, 1989; Verbrugge and Ascione, 1987). Nathanson (1977) suggests that women in the reproductive age group use medical services one to one and a half times the rate for men in this age group, excluding use associated with pregnancy. A variety of hypotheses have been suggested to explain such differences (see box 4.4).

The first explanation is based upon the notion that women are at a greater biological risk of suffering ill health. That is, women report more illness because they actually do experience greater disease pathology. After the age of seventeen, morbidity rates for women are higher than those for men, with women presenting more acute conditions, except for injuries, and more chronic diseases, except for fatal chronic conditions. The greater morbidity for women remains even if reproductive-related events are excluded (Waldron, 1983). Thus women are more likely to have arthritis, chronic sinusitis and digestive problems, while men are more likely to have heart disease, atherosclerosis and emphysema (Nathanson, 1977; Verbrugge, 1985, 1989). Hence, it is argued that gender differences in reported health are biologically determined and due to the fact that men are more likely to suffer from fatal conditions while women experience more acute illness, or chronic illness which can persist into old age.

The second hypothesis relates to acquired risks (Verbrugge, 1979), which are largely determined by the differing roles and role expectations and hence the differing behaviours of men and women. Thus, men experience more serious illness because they lead unhealthier lifestyles. They smoke and drink more than women and are often involved in riskier occupational and leisure roles and, as a result, experience more fatal illness. Women's roles by contrast place them at risk of experiencing a range of minor ailments.

Different authors have emphasised differing aspects of women's roles. Verbrugge argued that, in comparison to men, female role options are more limited and have fewer, but more uncertain, time restraints, all of which may constitute psychological stressors. Others have made the contrary point that women's roles, in comparison to those of

Box 4.4 Hypotheses to explain possible gender differences in use of health care

Hypothesis 1 – Women are at greater biological risk of suffering ill health – that is, they report more illness because they actually do experience greater disease pathology.

Findings – Women do suffer more acute and chronic illness which persists into old age, while men are more likely to suffer fatal conditions.

Hypothesis 2 – Health care utilisation is a function of gender differences in role and role expectations.

Findings – contradictory – for example, some suggest that women in child care roles are more likely to come into contact with minor ailments and hence present more frequently with such ailments themselves; however, women without children are as likely as those with children to visit the doctor.

Hypothesis 3 – Sick role behaviour is more compatible with traditional female roles and hence women feel less constrained than men about reporting mild symptoms.

Finding – Women in comparison with men do tend to be more able to talk about emotional problems and health-related difficulties.

Hypothesis 4 – Women are more likely than men to interpret symptoms as sufficiently serious to warrant attention.

Finding – Women do tend to assume responsibility for family health and hence may be both more knowledgeable about and aware of health-related matters.

(See Nathanson, 1975, 1977; Verbrugge, 1979, 1980, 1982, 1989.)

men, are actually more varied, often involving both family and employment responsibilities (Nathanson, 1977) and that such role flexibility itself is more demanding and inherently stressful and hence more likely to be associated with ill health. Gove (1984) argued that, given that women in our society traditionally fulfil a nurturant role, demands from others may impair their ability to rest, meaning they are apt to become physically run down (Gove, 1984). Others have emphasised the acquired risks inherent in women's traditional role expectations (Nathanson, 1975). For example, women in child care roles are more likely to come into contact with minor contagious illnesses. However, Corney (1990) reports that women with children were no more likely to visit a doctor that those without. Indeed, in her study, older women, who were more likely to be familiar with the surgery, were less likely to be high attenders.

The fact that sex differences in health care utilisation seem to be greatest during young and middle adulthood has led some to speculate about the possibility that, at these ages, traditional family roles for men and women are likely to be most divergent (Nathanson, 1977). Thus women at this stage of life may have more time and greater flexibility in scheduling and suffer less cost associated with medical care use than is the case for men who may lose financially if work is missed. However, a number of authors have pointed out that women, particularly if they work part-time, fulfil multiple roles and are often under greater time constraints than their partners. This is supported by the literature which suggests little by way of gender difference in relation to actual access to medical care (Gove, 1984).

The third hypothesis relates to differential illness behaviour. This hypothesis presumes that sick role behaviour is more compatible with traditional female roles and thus women may feel less constrained than men about reporting mild symptoms as illness (Verbrugge, 1989). There is also evidence that women find it easier to confide in others, including medical personnel, about their social and psychological problems, while men tend to limit their reporting to physical ailments (Corney, 1990). Women may be more likely to discuss health concerns, not only with people they know, but also with health care providers and survey interviewers. Indeed, even in circumstances of extreme health risks (e.g. homelessness), women report more symptoms than men (Ritchey, La Gory and Mullis, 1991). Thus, while traditional role expectations restrain men from giving in to illness or making use of health services, traditional female role expectations allow for women to be more responsive to perceived illness.

A fourth hypothesis suggests that women are more likely than men to interpret perceived symptoms as sufficiently serious to warrant medical intervention. Thus Verbrugge (1985) suggests that women have more knowledge about signs and symptoms, are more willing to confront the implications of symptoms, and are more concerned about their health. Women's greater responsibility for family health may increase the salience of health matters and influence symptom perception and response to illness. Indeed, there is some evidence that women are more likely than men to perceive symptoms and that the more symptoms perceived, the more likely it is that the person will seek medical care (Hibbard and Pope, 1983).

The latter suggestions have led some to argue that gender differences are merely a reflection of differences in symptom perception and help-seeking behaviour rather than reflecting 'real' underlying differences (Verbrugge, 1985). In a subsequent paper Verbrugge (1989) argued that when women's multiple roles and associated stress were taken into account men actually appear to use health care facilities more than women. Other studies have also cast doubt both upon the findings of sex differences and explanations for them. For example, Meininger (1986) found that women, particularly from higher social classes and particularly if they were worried about their symptoms, were more likely to make use of lay referral systems rather than professional health care. In a further report, Anson, Carmel and Levin (1991) found that, with the exception of patients aged seventeen to twenty four, significantly more men than women used an emergency department as a primary care service. The authors also report that similar percentages of both sexes were hospitalised during the study period. They argue that the similar emergency department visit rate contradicts the notion that women tend to perceive their symptoms as more severe than men and the similar hospitalisation rates suggest that women are not inclined to magnify the seriousness of their symptoms. A number of other researchers and theorists have argued either that there is no support for the notion that women are more likely than men to seek help for a particular problem (Cleary, Mechanic and Greenley, 1982), or that, while gender differences do occur, they are only evident for less dramatic health problems (Kessler, 1986). Indeed, a number of factors, such as belief that a doctor could do something to relieve the symptoms, number of days of disability and number of component symptoms, affect health care use equally for both men and women (Meininger, 1986).

No doubt some of the differing findings are due to various methods of data collection. For example, some studies focus specifically upon differential morbidity rates based upon clinical observations, while others rely upon reported symptoms and hence depend upon the ability and willingness of the respondent accurately to report their own health. It seems reasonable to conclude that men and women differ in their health reporting behaviour (Mechanic, 1976; Verbrugge, 1985) and that this factor alone may account for differential use of health care facilities. However, in the context of specific ailments rather than diffuse symptoms, men may be as likely, if not more likely, than women to seek medical care.

Cultural background

Cultural factors influence health care use at two levels: firstly, at the level of symptom interpretation, explanation and presentation and, secondly, at the level of perception of the health care delivery system. As noted previously, cultural differences in symptom perception and interpretation have been documented over a number of years, particularly in relation to pain (Lipton and Marbach, 1984; Zola, 1966; Zborowski, 1952). In addition, although symptoms may be regarded as significant or problematic, willingness to report them publicly may vary across cultures according to the social acceptability of either the symptoms or disclosure or expressions of feelings. As Angel and Thoits (1987) note, people may delay seeking treatment for culturally undesirable disorders, such as venereal disease.

Cultural factors may also influence how symptoms are presented to health care providers. For example, Stoeckle, Zola and Davidson (1963) report that Irish patients typically presented with specific, physical complaints in a stoic accepting manner, while Italian patients tended to describe more diffuse complaints with greater emotionality. In a further report Zola (1966) refers to ethnic differences in the likelihood that a patient would deem symptoms worthy of medical attention. Irish Americans were more likely than Italian Americans to present symptoms of eye, ear, nose or throat as their chief complaint. In a more recent study Burnam, Timbers and Hough (1984) found that, in comparison to Mexicans, Anglos reported a greater number of infrequent symptoms but that Mexicans reported symptoms that occurred more frequently.

Because cultural factors influence the person's explanatory model for their 'illness' they will also have an influence upon the relative 'appeal' of traditional versus biomedical healers to members of the community (Kroeger, 1983). Illnesses that are commonly recognised within cultural groups, whose explanatory model differs from that of the biomedical paradigm, have been referred to as 'folk illnesses' (Pachter, 1994). This is one of four key 'cultural' factors relating to choice of health care discussed by Young (1981). He argues that choice is based upon evaluations of the gravity of the illness, knowledge of a home remedy for the illness, 'faith' in the potential effectiveness of folk versus medical treatment and accessibility of health services. With 'folk illnesses', ethnic populations in Western societies may seek biomedical care for symptom relief while simultaneously seeking care from a folk healer to eliminate the cause of the illness (for example, removing the 'hex') (Pachter, 1994). Even within indigenous Western populations it is not unusual for patients simultaneously to seek both medical care as well as treatment from 'alternative' therapies. Pachter (1994) has argued the case for a culturally sensitive health care system: that is, one that not only is accessible, but also respects the beliefs, attitudes and cultural lifestyles of its patients.

Social and emotional factors

In an influential paper Zola (1973) argued that there are five potential 'triggers' for the decision to seek medical attention, three of which were social or interpersonal in nature (see box 4.5).

Box 4.5 Zola's five potential 'triggers' for the decision to seek medical care

The first trigger – the occurrence of an interpersonal crisis
This may prompt treatment either because a symptom threatens a relationship or because treatment can be used as a means of escaping the crisis.

The second trigger – perceived interference with social or personal relations
Prompt treatment may be sought when a valued activity is threatened by the symptoms.

The third trigger – social sanctioning by others who legitimise the condition
People who believe that significant others expect or want them to have treatment are more likely to do so. For example, Bass and Cohen (1982) found that in relation to factors leading parents to bring children in for medical treatment, one contributing factor was the fear of another family member who is pressing for 'answers' about the child's symptoms.

The fourth trigger – perceived interference with work-related or physical activity
It seems that people are most likely to seek medical care when symptoms are perceived as interfering with their lives.

The fifth trigger – the occurrence of similar symptoms to those previously experienced:
for example, recurrent headaches.
Recurrent symptoms provoke increasing distress as a continuing search is undertaken for a satisfactory explanation.

While social triggers are undoubtedly important factors in the decision to seek health care, emotional factors, in particular the degree of concern or worry engendered by particular symptoms, may also be influential. In this context, Bass and Cohen (1982), in a study of factors leading parents to bring children in for urgent treatment, found that important factors were fears relating to family history of serious or life-threatening illnesses, fear of the child's death and fear of loss of a vital function related to the part of the body affected. In a further study, Turk *et al.* (1985) also found that family history of the complaint emerged as an important factor influencing parents to seek medical help for their child. Other important factors found in this study were worry about the symptoms and the child's complaints.

Stress

A number of studies have documented the fact that stress is related to health care utilisation even after controlling for demographic, attitudinal and health status variables, although with a few exceptions the association tends to be modest (e.g. Cockerham, Kunz and Lueschen, 1988; Gortmaker, Eckenrode and Gore, 1982; Tessler, Mechanic and Dimond, 1976). Thus, in a prospective diary study, with a random sample of ninety six female users of a neighbourhood health centre, the presence of stress on a given day was associated with the approximate doubling of the probability of health care contact on that day (Gotmaker, Eckenrode and Gore, 1982). In a further report presenting analysis of data from over 2,000 Americans and West Germans, Cockerham, Kunz and Lueschen (1988) found that psychological distress was related to both greater reporting of physical symptoms and more visits to the doctor.

The evidence seems to point to the fact that people who are distressed or who have difficulty coping with life problems are more likely to deal with such problems by seeking medical care. Mechanic (1972, 1974) argued that distressed individuals often misattribute physical sensations of stress to illness, an attribution which increases the complexity and apparent severity of their somatic complaints, prompting them to seek medical care. A similar argument has been advanced by Cohen and Williamson (1991). Laboratory studies indicate that the same symptoms can be judged as signs of stress or as signs of illness depending upon the presence of a potentially stressful event or information about a particular illness (Baumann et al., 1989). Stress is also related to heightened symptom sensitivity and hence may have an indirect effect upon health care utilisation. In addition, the fact that stress is implicated as a cause of illness, either directly or via stress-induced behaviours (smoking, drinking), has been extensively documented.

It is worth bearing mind, however, that several studies have failed to detect an association between stress and health care use (Berkanovic, Hurwicz and Landsverk, 1988; Cameron, Leventhal and Leventhal, 1995; Sarason et al., 1985). These discrepant findings can partly be explained by Cameron, Leventhal and Leventhal's (1995) research results. These suggest that the effect of stress upon care seeking changes as a function of the characteristics of the symptoms experienced and the duration of the stressful event which occurs. For symptoms that were easily recognised as indicators of illness, stress did not affect care-seeking decisions. Lower rates of care seeking were associated with ambiguous symptoms which were perceived as associated with stress of recent onset, while greater rates of care seeking were evident when ambiguous symptoms occurred along with stressors that were prolonged in duration. The association of a recent stressor with symptoms may provoke a 'wait and see' strategy, whereas chronic stress may lead to care seeking as a way of coping with stress (Leventhal and Leventhal, 1993).

In sum, seeking medical care is the end point of a complex decision process influenced by a number of factors including demographic characteristics, features of the illness and characteristics of the health care delivery system. Although there is variation between various population groups identified on the basis of age, gender or culture, health care utilisation within such groups will depend on an interaction between additional factors, such as characteristics of the illness, attitude towards health care and social support (Linden *et al.*, 1997). The end point of this decision process involves identifying an appropriate provider (who may or may not be a recognised medical practitioner), but may also result in self-care or use of a lay-referral network either prior to, or as an alternative to, seeking professional help. Indeed, lay care provided in the community constitutes the dominant proportion of care for illness (Dean, 1981; 1986) while consulting family or friends is often the preferred action in response to symptoms (Freidson, 1960). Use of complementary therapies is also widespread (Sharma, 1992). Indeed, there is wide individual variation in the tendency to seek formal health care, some people being more inclined to adopt a 'wait and see' strategy, while others seek health care on a regular basis without there being any evident organic pathology to explain their symptoms.

Delay and overuse of health care

Two seemingly contradictory findings are entrenched in the literature: (a) people often 'wait to see what will happen' at the onset of symptoms and may not seek care for potentially serious symptoms until an illness is more advanced and treatment more difficult (Mayou, 1973; Safer *et al.*, 1979); and (b) a large proportion of physician visits (40–65%) are for complaints for which no disease can be detected (Barsky, Wychak and Klerman, 1986; Shapiro and Morris, 1978). Both types of care-seeking decisions are inefficient and taxing to both the individual patient and the health care system. (Cameron, Leventhal and Leventhal, 1995, p. 37)

Given the widespread practice of self-care in illness it seems inevitable that a high percentage of people are likely to 'wait and see what will happen' following the detection of possible signs of illness. Traditionally, when considering the tendency either to ignore symptoms or to delay seeking medical care, such actions have been ascribed to some negative psychological trait of the individual (Dean, 1986). More recent research has been directed towards a broad array of phychosocial factors thought to influence care-seeking decisions. These include demographic factors, type of symptoms, availability of medical or other forms of care, health beliefs and attitudes and emotional factors including denial of symptoms or fear and concern about medical treatment. As a result of such concerns some may fail to obtain urgent medical procedures that could save their lives. A variety of factors influence the person's decision to delay or immediately seek medical care.

Although there is a growing literature on delay in care seeking, little is known about the extent of actual avoidance of medical care and, although this seems less frequent, a number of single case reports document such fear-induced health avoidance. Lloyd and Deakin (1975) describe a fifty one year old woman with a long-standing history of fear of hospitals and medical procedures who avoided hospital in spite of a four-year history of illness eventually diagnosed as uterine carcinoma. Many cases of avoidance of medical treatment have been documented in relation to blood–injury fears. Thus, Thyer *et al.* (1985) in their review of fifteen cases of blood–injury phobia comment that avoidance of medical care was common. Kleinknecht and Lenz (1989) suggest that one-third of their sample of undergraduates, whom they identified as likely to faint in response to blood–injury stimuli, avoided both medical and dental treatment. In relation to blood–injury fears and medical avoidance, Marks (1988) comments that:

> Some patients with blood–injury phobia avoid urgent medical procedures that could save their lives: those who become diabetic may eschew insulin injections, and those who develop cancer may shun surgery ... blood–injury phobia leads some women to avoid becoming pregnant because pregnancy and childbirth are associated with blood and medical procedures. (p. 1208)

Although blood–injury phobia has been extensively studied, little is known about the relationship between this phobia and avoidance of medical treatment or the true extent of such fear-induced medical avoidance.

In contrast to the question of delay and avoidance of medical care is the question of frequent and repeated seeking of medical care in the absence of diagnosable pathology. The existence of a subset of patients who make frequent use of health care facilities and, in the view of their doctor, inappropriately, has long been noted (Pilowsky, 1997). While such medical visits may well be symptom related they are not necessarily disease related. Indeed, it is estimated that at least half of patient visits are prompted by symptoms for which a physical basis cannot be established. For example, between 30,000 and 120,000 patients undergoing coronary angiography for chest pain in the USA each year have either normal or minimally diseased arteries (Marchandise et al., 1978). While there is increasing recognition that many such visits are prompted by psychological or social difficulties and that minor symptoms and sensations can be misinterpreted, hence prompting a single medical visit (the worried well), some patients use health care excessively due to what has been referred to as abnormal illness behaviour, syndromes of which include hypochondriacal concerns and malingering (Pilowsky, 1997). The former includes concerns about specific illnesses in the absence of diagnosable pathology, such as fear of sexually transmitted diseases (venerophobia) including the more recently reported 'pseudo-AIDS' relating to acquired immune deficiency syndrome (AIDS), as well as preoccupation with more diffuse and non-specific symptoms. Two features characterise patients with such concerns: a lack of organic pathology for their symptoms and an unreasonable amount of concern about symptoms which persist despite medical reassurance.

Malingering, on the other hand, is frequently associated with claims for disability or compensation although the numbers involved are likely to be small. When health care seeking for symptoms is narrowed down to those who are considered to be hypochondriacal, prevalence figures are lower, ranging from 3 per cent to 13 per cent (Kellner, 1985). Antonovsky and Hartman (1974) have proposed a continuum between denial of symptoms and hypochondriasis although in reality the picture is inevitably more complicated than such a linear relationship would imply.

Delay in seeking medical help

Types of delay

Delay in achieving appropriate consultation with a health care professional can take many forms. Adam, Horner and Vessey (1980) identified several sources of delay in relation to obtaining treatment for breast cancer. These included missed opportunities, by both the women and their doctors, to detect the symptoms of asymptomatic breast cancer; women not reporting their symptoms immediately; delay in diagnosis by both general practitioners and surgeons; and time spent waiting for both hospital out-patient appointment and hospital admission.

Safer *et al.* (1979) discuss three forms of delay: relating to phases of symptom detection and care-seeking appraisal, illness and utilisation (see box 4.6).

Box 4.6 Forms of delay in seeking health care (Safer *et al.*, 1979)

Appraisal delay – the time the patient takes to appraise a symptom as a sign of illness.

Illness delay – the time taken from deciding one is ill until deciding to seek professional medical care.

Utilisation delay – the time from the decision to seek care until the patient goes to the clinic and uses its service.

The duration of the first two phases is primarily under the control of the patient, whereas provision factors such as availability of an appointment, ease of access to health care and so on, additionally influence the third phase. In an empirical evaluation of variables predictive of length of delay for each of these three stages, Safer and colleagues found that patients experiencing very painful symptoms and those who did not read about their symptoms had short appraisal delay. Patients with old symptoms and those who imagined possible, severe consequences of their illness had long illness delays. Those with painful symptoms, who were certain their symptom could be cured and who were not concerned about the cost of treatment had the shortest utilisation delays. At the appraisal phase the 'wait and see' option is most likely for vague and mild sensations that are not clearly definable as a symptom or disease indicator (Cameron, Leventhal and Leventhal, 1993).

In relation to illness delay, Byles *et al.* (1992), in a community survey of rectal bleeding, found that those who thought the bleeding was not serious and would clear up by itself were most likely to fail to consult or delay. When a mild and vague somatic sensation occurs at the same time as a new environmental stressor, it is likely to be seen as a sign of stress rather than illness (Baumann *et al.*, 1989) and is unlikely to lead to the seeking of medical care. However, if it appears in association with a chronic stressor, it can motivate help seeking because the problem can be seen as serious (Cameron, Leventhal and Leventhal, 1993). In a further study, Caccioppo *et al.* (1986) found that the average total delay for female cancer patients in their study was eighty days and that the period of appraisal accounted for 70 per cent of the total delay. In reviewing the evidence in relation to delay in seeking treatment for heart attack symptoms, Dracup *et al.* (1995) note that the interval from symptom onset to emergency response (i.e. the recognition and action phase) accounted for between 50 per cent and 75 per cent of the total delay from symptom onset to receipt of hospital care.

Defining and assessing delay

Operational definitions of delay remain relatively arbitrary with differing definitions of delay reflecting the condition under investigation. In the field of cancer research, definitions of delay have varied from two weeks to three or more months from the time of symptom discovery to an end point, which may be consulting a doctor, biopsy, diagnosis or first treatment (Facione, 1993). Obviously in the latter instance, there is a compound of patient initiated delay with time waiting for diagnosis or treatment. In a very different field of study with suspected sexually transmitted disease (STD), delay was defined as a wait and see period of four weeks (Leenaars, Rombouts and Kok (1993). While a delay of weeks or months between symptom detection and care seeking may be acceptable in the case of STDs and cancer, a delay of hours can be crucial in the case of cardiac symptoms (Matthews *et al.*, 1983).

With regard to assessing patient-initiated delay, the typical procedure is to ask patients to recall when they first experienced a symptom in relation to their subsequently diagnosed illness. In the case of cardiac patients, interviewing them about symptoms which may have occurred only a few hours prior to hospitalisation may provide reasonably accurate recall data, albeit influenced by emotional state. However, it is obviously questionable to rely on data dependent upon recall of symptoms experienced some two years earlier, which might be the case in assessing the incidence of cancer-related delay. This lack of reliability is illustrated in a study by Owens and Heron (1989). They initially collected information by questionnaire on women's delay in seeking breast cancer diagnosis and treatment for symptoms; patients were subsequently asked questions about symptoms in a guided recall interview. Differing estimates of delay were obtained by the two methods. Among the twenty eight women who originally said they had delayed for less than a week, only three changed their mind. Among the eleven women who originally said they had delayed for more than a month, eight changed their estimates.

Prevalence of delay

Due in part to the difficulties inherent both in defining delay and in its assessment, the proportion of individuals who delay seeking medical attention, or who fail to do so when seeking medical care could prevent discomfort or illness, is unknown. However, a number of studies have documented delay in relation to specific populations. For example, Hinton (1977) reported that 57 per cent of American women and 64 per cent of Canadian women delayed seeing their doctor for more than three months after discovering a suspicious breast lump. Hackett, Cassem and Raker (1973) found that, in a sample of 563 cancer patients, over 25 per cent had waited for more than six months after recognising they had a problem before consulting a doctor. In a community survey of over 1,000 people, of seventy seven who had noticed a first occurrence of rectal bleeding more than three months but less than five years prior to the survey, twenty three (30 per cent) either had not sought medical advice or had only done so after a period of delay over three months (Byles *et al.*, 1992). In a further study, Samet *et al.* (1988) found that of 800 patients over sixty five years of age with newly diagnosed cancer, while 48 per cent had presented within two months of symptom onset, 19.2 per cent had delayed for at least twelve weeks before seeking care, while 7.4 per cent delayed for at least one year. Prohaska, Funch and Blesch (1990), in a study of 254 older adults diagnosed with cancer of the colon or rectum, report that the delay between the first symptom associated with the cancer and the first medical contact averaged seven months. Half the patients had contacted their doctor within five months of symptom onset, but by the end of the first year 21 per cent had still not made medical contact. Facione (1993), summarising twelve studies or breast cancer in which delay was defined as three or more months from symptom detection to treatment initiation, indicates that 34.3 per cent of a total sample of over 8,000 show such delay.

In a further study, Leenaars, Rombouts and Kok (1993) report that 27 per cent of a sample of over 800 attending with suspected sexually transmitted disease (STD) delayed for more that four weeks after experiencing symptoms before consulting their doctor. In a study of one hundred patients with suspected or proven myocardial infarction, over one-third had delayed for more than twelve hours after the onset of chest pain before entering hospital (Hackett and Cassem, 1969). In reviewing delay in seeking treatment for heart attack symptoms, Dracup *et al.* (1995) report delay times from symptom onset to hospital arrival ranging from 2 to 6.5 hours.

In all contexts then delay in seeking formal medical care tends to be the norm. Given that any individual's perception and evaluation of symptoms is influenced by a range of factors and that most people adopt a 'wait and see approach', frequently asking family and friends for advice in the first instance, delay is to be expected. Indeed, in many instances, it is no doubt the best option; many ailments are self-limiting and medical care is unnecessary. However, many people seem to delay for a very long period of time, when such delay, involving hours, weeks or months, depending upon the condition, may be inappropriate and, at worst, life threatening.

Consequences of delay

Delay in seeking treatment can have serious medical consequences. For example, untreated Pelvic Inflammatory Disease can result in later ectopic pregnancies or infertility. In the case of cutaneous malignant melanoma, thin relatively non-invasive tumours can be effectively treated with conservative surgery, while there is no effective treatment for advanced tumours or metastatic disease. As a malignant breast tumour advances in stage the person's chances of survival decrease. Thus, Neale, Tilley and Vernon (1986) found that eight years after their initial contact, 50 per cent of women in their study who had delayed less than three months in seeking treatment for breast cancer were still alive compared with only 31 per cent who had delayed six months or longer.

Determinants of delay

A variety of factors have been identified as contributing to delay (Dracup *et al.*, 1995; Jones, 1990). These include patient characteristics, e.g. age, gender, social class and cultural background; illness-related variables, e.g. the site of the symptom; and the type of symptoms, e.g. pain and physical disability or degree of stigma associated with it (see box 4.7). For certain conditions, such as STDs or incontinence, embarrassment about discussing it can be a factor prompting delay behaviour (e.g. Antonovsky and Hartman, 1974; Leenaars, Rombouts and Kok, 1993).

Other factors investigated include the patient's knowledge of and attitude towards the suspected illness, including fear of the illness and social support (see box 4.7). In an early study, Hackett and Cassem (1969) found that accurate interpretation of symptoms as heart disease and the prompting of an influential person was associated with reduced delay in health care seeking in relation to chest pain. Those having regular medical check-ups tend to delay less in seeking medical care (e.g. Samet *et al.*, 1988).

A range of personality variables, such as repression, have also been investigated in relation to delay. While some studies suggest there may be a relationship between personality and delay, others do not (Keinan, Carml and Rieck, 1991–2). In one study of interest, Matthews *et al.* (1983) found that MI patients who delayed in the early stages of seeking treatment (i.e. between noting initial symptoms and deciding they were ill) were more likely to exhibit Type A behaviours and experienced little pain at a time when their work was quite demanding. Those who delayed in later phases (i.e. between deciding they were ill and deciding to seek treatment) were more likely to be Type B and were more likely to talk to others about their symptoms. Type As may ignore fatigue and physical symptoms when engaged in challenging tasks, but once they decide on the interfering effect of symptoms, they quickly decide they are ill and quickly decide to seek medical care.

Care-related variables are also likely to be influential in determining care seeking. The problem of access to health care in terms of cost and distance clearly differs both within and across cultures. Thus many rural areas even within the Western world may be some distance away from health care facilities. The problem is more extreme in many other parts of the world. For example, in a study of the effects of distance and geographic location on the use of 'Western-type health facilities' in rural Nigeria, Stock (1983) reports that per capita utilisation declined exponentially with increasing distance from the biomedical health centre.

The general tendency for research, however, has been to ignore such factors and focus on socio-demographic and symptom-related beliefs and expectations as determinants of delay in seeking Western biomedical care (see box 4.7).

Box 4.7 Determinants of delay in seeking medical care

Age – contradictory findings – some studies suggest that patient delay increases with age while other studies do not.

Gender – contradictory findings – some studies report no relationship between gender and delay while others report that women delay longer than men.

Culture – due to cultural beliefs some symptoms may be seen as socially undesirable and hence the person may be less willing to report them.

Illness-related factors – symptoms of rapid onset or which are severe are likely to prompt more immediate seeking of medical care.

Health beliefs and intentions – a belief that the symptom will go away has been shown to be positively related to delay while knowledge about symptoms results in less delay.

Anxiety – contradictory findings – some studies have found that anxiety about symptoms results in longer delay, other studies have found that anxiety results in shorter delay while other studies have found no relationship between anxiety and delay.

Age and delay

Although a number of studies suggest that patient delay increases with age (e.g. Battistella, 1971; Prohaska *et al.*, 1987) a number of other studies do not (e.g. Denney, Kole and Matorazzo, 1965; Hackett, Cassem and Raker, 1973; Matthews *et al.*, 1983; Prohaska, Funch and Blesch, 1990). In a review of studies investigating delay in the detection of cancer, Antonovsky and Hartman (1974) report that all the studies indicated that older people delayed seeking help significantly longer for all cancer sites. However, a review of subsequent studies relating to breast cancer found no such age differences (Facione, 1993). Facione suggests that changes in treatment and prognosis in the years between the publication of the two reviews could explain the different findings. In relation to such contradictory findings Levkoff *et al.* (1988) note that:

> clinicians working with older patients ... have noted that some older individuals tend to ignore illness ... others suggest that some elderly inappropriately adopt the sick role, making excessive demands on the health care system, and even receive unnecessary and possibly harmful procedures. (p. 622)

However, there is reason to believe that older adults differ from younger adults in their perception of illness and illness-related behaviour. Disease in old age is often superimposed on normal age-related changes in physiological functioning. Thus, although elderly people experience numerous symptoms on a daily basis, some of which are potentially serious, many are perceived as representing the normal ageing process (Brody and Kleban, 1983; Brody, Kleban and Moles, 1983). As a result, many elderly fail to recognise and seek help for conditions because of the similarity between symptoms of disease and age-related physiological changes (Rowe and Besdine, 1982). Coping strategies for such symptoms include minimisation of the seriousness of the symptoms and adopting a 'wait and see' attitude (Brody and Kleban, 1983; Brody, Kleban and Moles, 1983). For example, symptoms of hypothyroidism such as apathy, lethargy, intolerance of cold and dry skin may be seen as signs of normal ageing and hence professional help may not be sought.

A number of studies provide empirical support for this notion. For example, in an initial interview with two groups of elderly, Brody, Kleban and Moles (1983) found that more than half (56 per cent) of the symptoms they had experienced during the preceding month had not been reported to health care professionals. When asked why they had not reported them, one of the main reasons given related to the respondents' belief that nothing could be done for the symptoms because they were part of normal ageing and hence only to be expected. Prohaska *et al.* (1987) also found that when symptoms are initially attributed to ageing, patients delay longer in seeking care for those symptoms than when no such attributions are made.

In addition, the interaction between normal changes that occur with age and disease contributes to an altered presentation of illness. As a result, many presenting symptoms typically associated with disease may be absent in the aged. Certain older patients, for example, do not experience the pain associated with angina pectoris and may thus not seek care for an underlying heart condition (Day *et al.*, 1987). Others do not feel early pain associated with acute appendicitis and as a result frequently delay obtaining professional attention, hence increasing the probability of their appendix perforating. Another problem noted for older people is that, because of the absence of elevated temperatures, infections such as pneumonia and urinary tract infections can go undetected until they are quite severe (Berman, Hogan and Fox, 1987).

The balance of evidence then suggests that older age contributes to increased delay, although a number of contradictory findings exist. This is due in part to the possibility that older adults differ from younger adults in their perception of illness and, in some instances, symptoms of illness may not be present. Also, as previously noted, older patients may be more inclined to consult initially with family and other lay individuals (Hickey, 1988; Prohaska, Funch and Blesch, 1990; Rakowski *et al.*, 1988).

Gender and delay

As with age, contradictory findings have been reported with regard to gender and delay in seeking medical care. Some have reported no relationship between gender and time of delay (e.g. Marshall, Gregorio and Walsh, 1982; Matthews *et al.*, 1983), while others have concluded that women delay longer than men (Alonzo, 1986; Marshall and Funch, 1986). In one study investigating delay in treatment seeking for symptoms in patients with a variety of cancer types, including cancer of the colon, rectum, stomach, lung, leukaemia and lymphoma, no differences between men and women were found (Marshall, Gregorio and Walsh, 1982). In a further study, no gender differences in delay behaviour were found in patients with cancer of the colon, but for patients with cancer of the rectum, women were more likely than men to delay in seeking care (Marshall and Funch, 1987).

However, in some investigations, in which no statistically significant differences are reported, there are nevertheless large differences in delay times which are potentially of clinical significance. For example, Hackett and Cassem (1969) report a lack of significant gender difference in delay in seeking medical care following the onset of chest pain, although women delayed a median of one hour longer than men. Dracup *et al.* (1995) conclude that all researchers who have documented a difference in delay times between men and women have noted that women delayed longer.

Given that women appear to be more likely than men to make use of health care facilities one might anticipate less appraisal delay for women than men. However, given that there is some evidence that women's problems are treated differently, some suggesting that they may be taken less seriously than men's (Nathanson, 1977), one might expect greater diagnostic delay for women. However, few studies have investigated this issue.

In one such study, Marshall and Funch (1986) note that part of the delay for women seeking care for cancer of the rectum seemed to be a function of female patients needing more appointments before a diagnosis was made. However, in relation to symptoms of acute myocardial infarction, Alonzo (1986) reported increased delay times for women due primarily to a longer self-evaluation phase.

Culture and delay

As noted previously, cultural beliefs influence health care utilisation. This may be due to cultural differences in willingness to report symptoms publicly according to their social acceptability. For example, people may delay seeking treatment for culturally undesirable disorders, such as venereal disease (Angel and Thoits, 1987). Delay in seeking professional health care may also be due to cultural beliefs about the appropriateness of Western biomedical care in comparison with traditional folk remedies.

If such beliefs become an impediment to seeking biomedical care and alternative folk treatments are harmful or inappropriate then such delay in receiving biomedical attention may have dire consequences. For example, the Mexican folk illness *caida de mollera* (fallen fontanelle) has been shown to be a cultural interpretation of significant dehydration in infants (Kay, 1993). With delay in medical attention significant morbidity may occur. However, such cases are the exception rather than the rule and the fact that Western biomedical care is not without its inherent problems and limitations has also been noted. In many instances, seeking alternative remedies – that is, the 'folk remedies' of a given culture (the alternative medicine sought within Western societies should be considered in the same light) – may be both appropriate and beneficial.

Illness-related factors

The main symptom characteristics known to influence patient delay are the speed of symptom onset and the chronicity and severity of the symptoms (Mechanic, 1972; Prohaska *et al.*, 1987). For example, Prohaska and colleagues (1987) reported that individuals experiencing mild symptoms were less likely to seek medical care than those experiencing identical, but more severe symptoms.

Other symptom-related variables have been less extensively documented and little conclusive evidence exists. In one study, Lauver and Chang (1991) found that women with a family history of breast cancer had lower intentions to seek care than women without such a history. Those with a family history had more anxiety about a breast lump and perceived care seeking as less useful. This led the authors to conclude that this may have been due to the fact that such women had seen both the negative side effects as well as the benefits of breast cancer treatment.

Health beliefs and intentions

A number of studies have investigated intention to seek care in relation to social cognition models of health behaviour. Thus, in two studies examining intention to perform a behaviour, well women were asked to imagine a discovered breast symptom and to indicate their likelihood of seeking immediate care. Lauver and Chang (1991) used an eight items 'expectations' scale to assess factors predictive of delay in care seeking. Statements, rated as 'not at all likely' to 'definitely likely', included 'I would lose my breast', 'I would find out what my treatment options are', and 'I would know one way or the other if I had breast cancer'. In addition, respondents were asked to rate the importance of each of the specific outcome expectations (to assess 'value'). A utility score was computed by summing the product of each of the corresponding expectations and values scores and then dividing by the number of questions (eight). The resultant utility score was significantly associated with delay.

In a further study, assessing variables specified by the theory of reasoned action, Timko (1987) found that intention to delay (i.e. monitoring a breast symptom for a time rather than immediately calling the doctor) was positively associated with a favourable attitude toward delay (i.e. a belief that the symptom would go away). She also found that social normative beliefs were significant predictors of intention to seek help. A similar relationship between normative beliefs (a norm score created by adding scores for ratings of personal norm, social norm and interpersonal norm) and intention to seek care was reported by Lauver and Ho (1993). However, Lauver and Chang (1991) found that social norms (a rating of the degree to which eight types of significant others believed she should seek immediate care) were unrelated to delay. It is difficult to explain such differences as both Timko and Lauver and Chang assessed intention while Lauver and Ho assessed actual behaviour. However, other variables such as symptom status and outcome measures did vary between the Timko and Lauver and Chang studies.

Knowledge about symptoms and ability to explain them have also been investigated in relation to delay. In a study of patients seeking medical attention for cutaneous malignant melanoma, Temoshok et al. (1984) found that patients with less knowledge of melanoma or its appropriate treatment had significantly longer delays. In a further study of patients consulting their GP with a suspected abnormality of the breast, half of those who delayed did so because they assumed their symptoms were nothing to worry about and would disappear, while a further substantive proportion of those who delayed did so because they had a rational explanation for their symptoms (Adam, Horner and Vessey, 1980).

Anxiety and delay

A number of studies have investigated the relationship between anxiety and delay in seeking health care, some finding a positive relationship (Lauver and Chang, 1991; MacFarlane and Sony, 1992), others finding no such relationship or a negative relationship (Lauver and Ho, 1993; Timko, 1987). Thus, Lauver and Chang (1991) report that anxiety was a significant predictor of intention to seek care in women asked to imagine a discovered breast symptom. In a further study MacFarlane and Sony (1992) assessed anxiety associated with breast biopsy in forty two women with benign lesions, twenty four of whom had self-discovered symptoms. Anxiety was significantly higher in women who had delayed longer in consulting their doctor, although it is unclear from the study whether anxiety resulted in delay or vice versa. Indeed, the authors note that there were multiple reasons for delay in contacting a doctor.

In contrast, both Timko (1987) and Lauver and Ho (1993) found that anxiety had no direct effect on either intention or actual delay. In the latter study, having a practitioner moderated the relationship between anxiety about care seeking and delay. Among women who lacked a regular practitioner, greater anxiety was associated with less delay, while among women who had a regular practitioner, there was no association between anxiety and delay. Lauver and Ho note that women without a regular practitioner tend to be younger and are less likely to engage in breast self-examination and are, therefore, less likely to be aware of normal and abnormal findings in the breast; hence, a little anxiety may prompt care seeking. In a further study, Temoshok et al. (1984) found that for patients with cutaneous malignant melanoma, those who minimised the seriousness of their condition were more likely to seek treatment sooner. The authors suggest that this may have been due to the fact that such minimisation reduced fear and anxiety about the disease and its treatment.

The question of delay in seeking health care is thus a complex issue. The preceding discussion has briefly examined some of the factors research has investigated. Care seeking seems to be affected by socio-demographic factors, illness-related variables and health beliefs. Given the degree of variability between individuals in symptom perception and interpretation it is perhaps not surprising that such factors will impinge upon the rapidity with which medical care is sought. Such factors no doubt account in part for some of the frequently contradictory findings presented. However, the process of unravelling such findings is not facilitated by methodological differences across studies and study limitations. One problem is that, in retrospective studies, investigators are forced to rely on the patient's memory of symptoms which may have occurred months or even years previously. The accuracy of such recall is clearly questionable. Other studies, which have used hypothetical situations and assessed intentions to seek care, do not necessarily reflect the actual behaviour which might occur in reality. Delay in seeking care remains a major problem, one that may result in unnecessary human suffering, premature mortality and increased medical costs (Jones, 1990). However, the contrary position of seeking to use health care facilities when such action may be inappropriate, and continuing to do so in spite of medical reassurance that there is no identifiable physical pathology to treat, can also be a drain on health care resources.

Health anxiety, abnormal illness behaviour and the overuse of health services

Excessive worry about one's health results in greater use of health care facilities. Both the 'worried well' and the 'worried ill' place greater demands on the system (Wolinsky and Johnson, 1991). The central aspect distinguishing these two groups is the presence or absence of identifiable physical pathology. Unfortunately this is not always a particularly useful distinction to draw as it places greater emphasis upon the accuracy and precision of diagnostic techniques than upon the person's perception and interpretation of the symptom. It is worth bearing in mind that accuracy of diagnosis is likely to be highly variable and this is no doubt one reason for the great variability in estimates of patients presenting for whom obvious pathology cannot be detected. Thus, Garfield *et al.* (1976) refer to estimates ranging from 20 per cent to 84 per cent for the number of patients who seek medical help for which no organic cause can be found. While ruling out organic pathology will, in many instances, involve relatively straightforward diagnostic procedures, there will inevitably be certain cases where a diagnosis of 'no detectable organic pathology' is based upon current knowledge and investigative procedures; as medical knowledge advances and new investigative procedures are developed, organic pathology may be detected in cases previously designated as 'no known cause'.

As noted, whether or not organic pathology is present, there is evidence that a range of factors influence both symptom perception and symptom interpretation as well as the tendency to use health care services. Attendance at a GP surgery depends upon the patient's subjective interpretation of symptoms. However, as noted, patients' assessments of illness may not correspond with the disease-oriented perspective of biomedicine. Thus, while a significant proportion of GP consultations may be regarded as 'trivial' or 'inappropriate' because there is no evident pathology, without a knowledge of patients' beliefs and/or social circumstances, their concerns are unlikely to be addressed.

Abnormal illness behaviour, hypochondriasis, illness phobia and health anxiety

It is widely acknowledged that a small but significant number of patients persist in attending their doctors in the absence of obvious pathology and even though the practitioner has taken all reasonable steps to reassure the patient. Pilowsky (1997) has referred to such patients as exhibiting abnormal illness behaviour which he defines as:

> an inappropriate or maladaptive mode of experiencing, evaluating or acting in relation to one's own state of health, which persists, despite the fact that a doctor (or other recognised social agent) has offered accurate and reasonably lucid information concerning the person's health status and the appropriate course of management (if any), with provision of adequate opportunity for discussion, clarification and negotiation, based on thorough examination of all parameters of functioning (physical, psychological and social) taking into account the individual's age, educational and socio-cultural background. (p. 25)

A number of syndromes are encapsulated within such a definition according to whether the illness is affirmed or denied and whether the focus is somatic or psychological. Within the biomedical framework, many such abnormal patterns of functioning are themselves given 'disease' labels. Thus, a preoccupation with the fear of having a disease in the absence of identifiable organic pathology, with the fear persisting in spite of medical reassurance, is referred to as hypochondriasis. A vast research literature evaluating this 'condition' exists. For example, Barsky and Klerman (1983) suggest that the physical complaints associated with hypochondriasis are usually vague and variable, with pain the most common symptom and bowel and cardiorespiratory symptoms frequent presenting complaints. Kellner (1985) argues that research findings identify two components of hypochondriasis: an unrealistic fear of disease and conviction of having a disease. He further suggests prevalence figures for hypochondriasis of between 3 per cent and 13 per cent.

In hypochondriasis, fears are generally diffuse and not of any particular illness; this has led some to argue for the existence of a focal form of hypochondriasis referred to as illness or disease phobia (Pilowsky, 1967; Marks, 1987). Beunderman and Duyvis (1990) suggest that between 2 per cent and 5 per cent of the general population are excessively preoccupied with the fear of having heart disease in the absence of identifiable pathology, referred to as cardiac phobia, and suggest that 10 per cent of general practitioner lists and 40 per cent of cardiologists' practices are made up of such patients. As noted earlier, as many as 120,000 patients undergoing coronary angiography for chest pain in the USA each year have normal or minimally diseased arteries (Marchandise *et al.*, 1978). In a further report, MacAlpine (1957) describes twenty four 'syphilophobics', all of whom had been investigated repeatedly for syphilis, one having received twenty two negative tests within a year. More recently, Miller *et al.* (1985) have described two 'pseudo-AIDS' patients for whom the degree of concern had reached such levels that they exhibited marked signs of anxiety and depression. Both patients had had extensive negative investigations and received reassurance from a senior venerologist, but persistently misinterpreted minor symptoms as confirmation that they had AIDS since some of the symptoms appeared superficially similar. A series of nineteen similar worried-well patients with AIDS-related fears are presented by Miller, Acton and Hedge (1988). They comment that:

> Almost all subjects showed an unshakeable and anxiety laden conviction that they had HIV infection or disease, as indicated to them by the presence of anxiety-based physical features which they had misinterpreted as signs of HIV disease. (p. 159)

Even more recently, McEvedy and Basquille (1997) have documented two cases of BSE (bovine spongiform encephalopathy) phobia following the recent surge in media attention on BSE. The first patient exhibited overwhelming hypochondriacal worries that she had CJD (Creutzfeldt Jacob Disease) as a result of eating beef while the second presented with a two year history of intrusive hypochondriacal concerns.

There may then be specific identifiable instances when physical pathology is clearly not present and consultation with a medical practitioner is prompted largely by a misinterpretation of signs as illness, fuelled by anxiety about the illness in question and a belief in biomedically based care. However, as Costa and McCrae (1985) point out, hypochondriasis is frequently used in a more general sense to refer to the tendency to make unfounded medical complaints. As they further state:

> categorisation of a patient as a hypochondriac is generally informal, based not on validated tests and procedures, but on the physician's conviction that complaints are exaggerated or unfounded. (p. 20)

This has led some to argue that, rather than seeking to diagnose a patient as hypochondriacal, the central issues relate to the patient's health anxiety and a belief that biomedical care can alleviate symptoms of distress. Salkovskis and Warwick (1986) argue that health concerns follow a continuum from those with mild concerns about some unusual bodily sensation to those who are preoccupied with and fearful of bodily sensations to the extent that all thoughts and activities centre upon their illness. They describe this continuum as reflecting dimensions of 'health preoccupation', with 'morbid health preoccupation' representing the extreme end of the continuum and such behaviours typical of those patients referred to as hypochondriacal. A similar dimensional perspective is advanced by Costa and McCrae (1985), supported by Barsky and Klerman's (1983) contention that some people are prone to transient hypochondriacal concerns and by Garfield et al.'s (1976) reference to the 'worried well'. This quantitative difference in health-related worries receives some support from a study by Kellner et al. (1987) who compared twenty one patients meeting psychiatric classification criteria for hypochondriasis with matched family practice patients, non-patient employees and non-hypochondriacal psychiatric patients. Although all groups reported some level of fear about disease and death, hypochondriacal patients reported more fear of, and false beliefs about, disease, attended more to bodily sensations, had more fears about death and distrusted doctors' judgements more, yet sought more medical care than other subjects.

Determinants of excessive health concerns

As noted previously, most people regularly experience bodily sensations which they may or may not interpret as a potential sign of illness. The biased or inaccurate perception of a symptom will mean that it is less likely to be interpreted as innocuous or irrelevant. A range of studies suggest a relationship between anxiety and symptom concerns. Thus, general somatic symptoms are more prevalent in patients who are anxious (Tyrer, 1976), high symptom reporters are generally more anxious (Pennebaker, 1982), hypochondriacal beliefs and attitudes are associated with anxiety (Kellner et al., 1986) and somatic concerns are related to neuroticism (Costa and McCrae, 1980). The latter authors note that chronic worriers, as indexed by high neuroticism scores, report two to three times as many physical symptoms as those at the lower end of the neuroticism range. It has been frequently noted that symptoms reported by those designated as hypochondriacs are those that commonly occur in association with stress; people who characteristically respond to stressful situations with somatic arousal have higher levels of physical symptoms and seek medical help more often. It is possible that somatic responses to stress are representative of a general sensitivity to bodily sensations (Frost *et al.*, 1986).

Factors influencing the likelihood that bodily symptoms will be interpreted as more dangerous than they actually are, as well as determining which symptom(s) will form the focal concern in vulnerable individuals, include previous experience with illness in oneself or one's family, previous experience with unsatisfactory medical management and media-induced concerns, as in AIDS-related fears. The role of family history of illness is illustrated in a report by Ryle (1948) who describes thirty one cases of cancer phobia of whom twelve had lost a near relative or friend from cancer. In a further report, Bianchi (1971) describes thirty disease-phobic patients, fourteen of whom feared cancer and ten of whom feared heart disease, sixteen of the patients reporting such illnesses in a relative.

A number of authors have pointed to the fact that 'topical' disorders, such as AIDS and BSE which are highly publicised, tend to form the focus of unnecessary concerns (McEvedy and Basquille,1997; Miller, Acton and Hedge, 1988; Warwick, 1989; Warwick and Salkovskis, 1990). The avoidance of disease reminders, such as articles in the media, as well as frequent checking for signs of illness and requests for examination and reassurance from doctors, are typical of such cases.

The association of hypochondriacal concerns with the need constantly to seek reassurance from doctors, family and friends, as well as being preoccupied with bodily health, has been noted by a number of authors (Baker and Mersky, 1983; Barsky and Klerman, 1983). Salkovskis and Warwick (1986) illustrate with two case examples the way in which reassurance provides an immediate but transient reduction in anxiety, leading to further reassurance seeking so that provision of reassurance unwittingly reinforces the patients' condition.

Summary

This chapter has examined factors influencing health care seeking behaviour. Seeking medical care is the end point of a decision-making process which frequently results in self-care or consultation with family or friends either prior to, or as an alternative to, seeking professional help. As many as 90 per cent of illness episodes may never be seen by a general practitioner; many patients may consult complementary practitioners either instead of or as well as conventional medical practitioners. The influence of lay advice is illustrated by the fact that, together with beliefs about the efficacy of medical care, network advice is often the most influential factor in determining whether or not medical care is sought. In fact, lay care in the community and use of complementary medicine constitute a dominant proportion of 'health care'.

Two broad conceptual frameworks for addressing the question of how people make choices regarding the use or non-use of different kinds of health services were examined. Pathway models describe the decision-making steps people take in the process of translating distress into action, while determinants models, such as Anderson's Behavioural Model and the health belief model, seek to provide explanatory frameworks. However, a general finding is that variables incorporated into explanatory models explain a relatively small amount of the variance in utilisation. Health needs, perceived seriousness and belief in the efficacy of health care provide the most predictive utility.

A range of demographic, illness related and social and demographic variables have been proposed as mediators of the decision to use health care facilities. Use of health care is greatest within the youngest age groups and, on average, within the oldest age groups, although there is evidence that a great deal of use by a minority of the older population accounts for much of the excess use by the elderly. Numerous studies have documented that women are more likely than men to seek medical care for symptoms and a number of explanations have been advanced for this finding. However, in the context of specific ailments rather than diffuse symptoms, men may be as likely as, if not more likely than, women to seek medical care. Because cultural factors influence the relative 'appeal' of traditional versus biomedical healers to members of the community, cultural background will inevitably play a role in determining health care use. Finally, social and emotional triggers to health care use have been discussed. A number of studies have documented modest associations between stress and health care utilisation.

Such factors may also influence the person's decision to delay or immediately seek medical care, patient related delay in seeking health care taking many forms. Safer *et al.* (1979) refer to appraisal delay, involving the failure to detect a symptom as a sign of illness; illness delay, for example not reporting symptoms to a practitioner immediately; and utilisation delay, for example the time spent waiting for an appointment. Defining and assessing delay is, however, fraught with difficulties. Definitions are arbitrary and reflect the condition under investigation. In relation to cancer, definitions of delay have varied from two weeks to three or more months from the time of symptom discovery to an end point, while in relation to heart attack symptoms delay is referred to in terms of hours. Delay in symptom reporting tends to be assessed via recall; whether recalling symptoms experienced some two years earlier provides reliable data is obviously open to question. Due in part to such difficulties the proportion of individuals who delay seeking medical attention is unknown, although numerous studies suggest that delay is widespread and can have serious medical consequences.

Conflicting findings have been reported for the role of both age and gender in influencing delay, although the balance of evidence suggests that older adults and females tend to delay longer. Cultural beliefs will inevitably influence decisions about whether to seek Western biomedical health care. With regard to symptom-related variables, symptoms with rapid onset which are chronic and severe are related to less delay in use of health care. Finally, contradictory findings have been obtained for the relationship between the role of both beliefs and anxiety in influencing delay in seeking health care.

In contrast to delay, excessive worry about one's health results in greater use of health care facilities. A number of studies suggest that a large proportion of both general and specialist practitioners' lists consists of repeat attenders who exhibit abnormal illness behaviour, fearing illness in the absence of identifiable pathology and for whom reassurance only serves to prompt further medical care seeking. A range of studies suggest a relationship between anxiety and symptom concerns. Other factors influencing the likelihood that bodily symptoms will be interpreted as more dangerous than they actually are include previous experience with illness in oneself or one's family, previous experience with unsatisfactory medical management and media-induced concerns.

FURTHER READING

L. Cameron, E. A. Leventhal and H. Leventhal (1995). Seeking medical care in response to symptoms and life stress. *Psychosomatic Medicine*, **57**, 37–47.

K. Dean (1986). Lay care in illness. *Social Science and Medicine*, **22**, 275–284.

I. K. Dracup, D. K. Moser, M. Eisenberg, H. Meischke, A. Alonzo and A. Braslow (1995). Causes of delay in seeking treatment for heart attack symptoms. *Social Science and Medicine*, **40**, 379–392.

N. C. Facione (1993). Delay versus help seeking for breast cancer symptoms: A critical review of the literature on patient and provider delay. *Social Science and Medicine*, **12**, 1521–1534.

B. S. Hulka and J. R. Wheat (1985). Patterns of utilization: The patient perspective. *Medical Care*, **23**, 438–460.

L. M. Verbrugge (1989). The twain meet: Empirical explanations of sex differences in health and mortality. *Journal of Health and Social Behavior*, **30**, 282–304.

CHAPTER 5

Health care provider–patient interaction

CHAPTER OVERVIEW

This chapter evaluates research examining interactions between health care providers and patients; most such studies focus upon doctor–patient interactions in primary care settings. After reviewing explanatory frameworks proposed to explain the nature of doctor–patient encounters, the various factors influencing the pattern of communication in such interactions are discussed. These include characteristics of the health care provider or the patient concerned and situational and interactional factors. In this context, factors which contribute to poor communication between health care provider and patient are also examined. Outcome-based research relating to doctor–patient communication is then reviewed with specific emphasis upon understanding and recall and patient satisfaction. The final sections of the chapter examine strategies for improving health care provider–patient interaction and medical decision making.

This chapter covers:

Tasks of medical encounters
Factors influencing the pattern of doctor–patient communication
Problems in health care consultations
Patient understanding and recall
Patient satisfaction
Improving medical communication
Medical decision making

Introduction

Within the biomedical health care context, patients come into contact with a range of health care providers including medical, nursing and paramedical staff. The anticipated aim of such encounters is for the exchange of information between patient and provider in a manner which allows it to be understood by both parties and used in both parties' decisions about treatment or prevention (Weisman and Teitelbaum, 1989). As will become apparent, however, the exchange of information in medical encounters is often unsatisfactory, information provided to patients is frequently misunderstood by them and patients are often not involved in decisions about their own health care.

Although empirical reports and reviews have dealt with a variety of health care provider–patient interactions in a number of contexts, studies have, for the most part, tended to focus upon doctor–patient interactions in primary care settings. This fact will be reflected in the general content of the chapter. Such research tends to focus upon either the process or outcome of doctor–patient communication (Pendelton, 1983; Winefield, 1992). Process studies are concerned with patterns of communication between the health care provider and the patient, describing either the verbal or non-verbal interaction which takes place. Outcome studies, on the other hand, concentrate on factors influenced by such communication processes. Outcome variables assessed include health-related variables, such as cure, survival rates and quality of life, as well as patient satisfaction and adherence. In addition, studies have evaluated the teaching of communication skills to health care professionals in order to modify both the process and the outcome from consultations.

It is worth bearing in mind that most clinical encounters can be analysed as an inter-action between two often quite distinct 'cultures': the 'culture' of medicine and the 'culture' of the patient. These two groups may think quite differently about health and illness, having differing explanatory models and hence differing perceptions, attitudes, knowledge, communication styles and approaches towards health-related issues (Pachter, 1994). Although both 'sets' of explanations should be viewed with equal legiti-macy, a number of authors have pointed to the fact that medical encounters are traditionally structured to reflect medical dominance and the power differential and 'competence gap' between doctors and their patients (Lupton, 1994). In relation to the sick role concept, Parsons (1951) points out that a power differential is an essential part of biomedical care; it is essential in establishing the authority of the doctor and encour-aging compliance on the part of the patient. Thus, the medical consultation is not only a transaction between lay and professional explanatory models; it is also a transaction between two parties with a differential power base in both social and symbolic terms (Kleinman, 1980).

In this context, patients and health care providers often have quite distinct agendas. The patient's will reflect their own unique experience of illness and their ideas and expectations about the consultation and treatment; the health care provider's will reflect their, usually Western, medical training. This is illustrated by empirical findings. Thus, research indicates that the intentions of primary care patients in the USA in seeking care are for the treatment of psychosocial problems, seeking medical explanations, support-ive communication, test results and ventilation and legitimation (seeking to talk about and understand a symptom or symptoms) (Good, Good and Nassi, 1983). A study in the UK, using a modified version of Good *et al.*'s questionnaire, identified four similar categories which the authors summarise as: wanting explanations, emotional support, medical advice or more general information (Salmon and Quine, 1989).

In contrast, doctors often disregard emotional or psychosocial issues because they view the presenting symptoms as signs of an underlying physical pathology. While non-Western and popular health care are primarily concerned with treating the experience of illness and with providing an explanation for it, biomedicine, on the other hand, is primarily concerned with recognising and treating/curing the disease and with explanations based upon physical criteria. The dominant theme on the doctor's agenda is likely to be the 'correct' diagnosis of the patient's complaints. This dichotomy between doctor's assumptions and patient's expectations is illustrated in a study of doctor–patient communication in the context of cancer (Chaitchik *et al.*, 1992). The authors of this study note that doctors were more concerned with defining medical information objectively: that is, with regard to the type of disease, its stage and the type of treatment which might be appropriate. Patients, on the other hand, were more interested in defining it in terms of its personal relevance: that is, whether they would fully recover from it and how much pain they should expect to experience.

This potential conflict between the lay person's mental representations of illness and those of medical personnel goes some way towards explaining prevailing patient dissatisfaction with Western biomedical health care. Lack of attention to personal or social issues is in part responsible for patient non-compliance with Western biomedicine and with patients' and their families' dissatisfaction with primary health care provision (Davis, 1968; Hall, Roter and Katz, 1988).

Doctor–patient encounters

Since the late 1960s a number of observational and descriptive studies of doctor–patient encounters have been published. In two reviews, Hall, Roter and Katz (1988) and Roter and Hall (1989) document the results of approximately fifty observational studies providing descriptions or evaluations of the communication process which occurred during medical visits. Much of this literature is descriptive in nature with little or no theoretical framework guiding the research undertaken (Pendleton, 1983; Inui and Carter, 1985; Ong *et al.*, 1995; Roter and Hall, 1989). As Roter, Hall and Katz (1988) note in their review of this literature:

> [it] is a difficult literature to review; the field appears to be disorganized, with little sense of theoretical cohesiveness or rational progression. (p. 100)

In addition, there is marked variation in the methods used in different studies. For example, there tends to be very little overlap in systems used to code the behaviour observed, questions asked or the range of variables assessed (Roter and Hall, 1989). In one commentary Ong *et al.* (1995) identify twelve coding systems and note that, in conducting research, the coding scheme selected is usually chosen not because of its theoretical relevance but 'because of its availability and/or proven high reliability' (p. 906). As these authors further note, given the nature of the research conducted much of the review literature is organised around the tasks involved in medical consultations and the manner in which these are accomplished rather than their theoretical relevance.

Goals of the medical encounter

Overlapping classifications relating to the purpose of communication between doctor and patient have been suggested by Ong *et al.* (1995) and Hall, Roter and Katz (1988) and Roter and Hall (1989) from their review of the literature (see box 5.1). The latter suggest distinguishing between two basic goals of the medical encounter – instrumental and socio-emotional. A number of process studies have focused upon these different types of interaction, abstracting the percentage of the total interaction time spent on each during doctor–patient encounters (Roter and Hall, 1992).

Box 5.1 Goals of the medical encounter

Ong *et al.* (1995) suggest three different purposes of communication between doctor and patient:

(i)   creating a good interpersonal relationship
(ii) the exchange of information and
(iii) medical decision making

An overlapping classification has been suggested by Hall, Roter and Katz (1988) and Roter and Hall (1989). They suggest two basic goals of the medical encounter:

(i)   instrumental tasks
        information giving
        question asking
        technical competence
(ii) socio-emotional tasks
        partnership building
        social conversation
        positive and negative talk
        interpersonal competence

Roter and Hall (1989) further argue that the two types of task are related to different outcomes from doctor–patient exchanges. Adherence and recall are indicators or outcome measures of task-related features, whereas satisfaction is an outcome of the socio-emotional domain. A feature of any interpersonal encounter is the extent to which it is reciprocal rather than imbalanced. Rotter and Hall argue that the concept of reciprocity provides an explanatory mechanism for doctor–patient interaction. That is, doctor task behaviours generate patient task behaviours and doctor socio-emotional behaviours generate patient socio-emotional behaviours. While the provider's competence at both task and socio-emotional behaviours will predict the extent to which the patient's socio-emotional state is positive or negative, the provider's competence at socio-emotional behaviours will not necessarily be related to a perception of them as task proficient.

A health care provider is expected to be both socially and medically skilled and to use these skills to engage the patient at both an interpersonal and task-oriented level. Given the lack of time usually available for medical consultations, the task of identifying and treating symptoms may become the only goal for the practitioner, who then denies the patient the opportunity to explain their 'illness'. This only serves to reinforce the often discrepant goals of the two parties involved, the resultant imbalanced relationship being a source of dissatisfaction to each.

Theoretical perspectives

Until the late 1980s little of the published literature relating to doctor–patient interaction was guided by any theoretical framework. However, a number of alternative explanatory frameworks have been proposed, ranging from illness or doctor-centred to patient-centred approaches (see box 5.2). Doctor-centred explanations emphasise an asymmetrical relationship between doctor and patient, with the doctor leading by asking for medical 'facts' and giving advice, while the patient provides information about their complaint. Patient-centred approaches place more emphasis upon each patient as a person with unique needs and a unique life history. In the patient-centred approach the doctor aims to determine the patient's agenda and to reconcile this with their own.

Box 5.2 Doctor-centred and patient-centred communication styles	
Doctor-centred	**Patient-centred**
Doctor's position characterised by status and control	Doctor aims to establish the patient's agenda and reconcile it with their own
Doctor acts solely to gather information	Doctor listens and reflects
Doctor asks: direct questions closed questions self-answering questions about medical 'facts'	*Doctor acts by:* offering observation encouraging clarifying seeking patient's ideas indicating understanding
Doctor acts by: making decisions instructing patient	*Doctor acts by:* involving the patient in decision making
Patient expected to: be passive ask few questions not influence the course of the consultation	*Patient expected to:* be active ask questions influence the course of the consultation

(Byrne and Long, 1976; Pendleton, 1983; Stewart, 1984; Waitzkin, 1985)

Two dominant doctor-centred approaches have been proposed, the consensus (Parsons, 1951b) and discrepancy models (Friedson, 1961). The consensus model holds that the relationship between doctor and patient is a harmonious one with the doctor leading and the patient following. The doctor's role is characterised by high status and a position of control with regard to the patient. The doctor is seen as acting in the patient's interests and the patient as co-operating with the advice and treatment given. In contrast, the discrepancy model (Friedson, 1961) argues that there is an inherent mismatch between what the patient expects and what the doctor can deliver. Although the doctor is in a position of control in relation to the patient and uses this to advance the patient's interests, the doctor also uses control to maintain his or her institutional authority.

The notion that the doctor is in a position of control, and indeed the patient's assumptions about their relative hierarchical positions, is reflected by the general finding that patients tend to be passive during medical consultations, asking few questions and making little attempt to influence the course of the interaction (Haug and Lavin, 1981). In an illuminating study which focused on the first ninety seconds of the medical consultation, Beckman and Frankel (1984) found that in only 23 per cent of the visits studied was the patient allowed to complete their response to the doctor's opening question. In 69 per cent of the visits the doctor interrupted the patient's opening statement after an average of only fifteen seconds and in only one of these visits was the patient allowed to return to, and complete, their opening statement. Interestingly, doctors tend to overestimate the length of time they spend with patients and underestimate patients' desire for information (Waitzkin, 1985). However, patients are themselves often reluctant to ask questions. Thus, Roter (1989) notes that only 6 per cent of doctor–patient interaction time involved the patient asking questions. There is some indication though that frequency of patient question asking is in turn related to the prevalence of doctors' information-giving behaviours (Waitzkin, 1984).

The issue of power and control in medical encounters is further emphasised by Blaxter and Paterson's (1982) study of economically disadvantaged women. Older women in their sample had a characteristic attitude towards their doctor of deference, gratitude and trust. Although younger women were less deferential, most women, while feeling that their interaction with their doctor was unsatisfactory, did not have the sense of power to take steps to change their doctor. Similar issues of power and control are raised by Porter (1990) in relation to women patients involved in consultations relating to reproductive health. While the women complained of various factors, such as waiting time and having to undress and be practised upon by medical students, they were most unwilling to comment negatively about what the doctor had said or done. Given the doctor's inherent position of control, it seems reasonable to expect them to take responsibility for initiating engagement with the patient in the interaction.

In contrast to doctor-centred approaches, the patient-centred approach (Stewart, 1984) emphasises the interactive aspect of the doctor–patient relationship and the fact that the doctor is actively interested in the patient's point of view. In a widely cited study, Byrne and Long (1976) investigated doctor-centred and patient-centred styles in their analysis of 1,850 general practice consultations. They found a cluster of patient–doctor styles which could be arranged on a continuum with high use of patient knowledge and experience/low use of doctor knowledge and experience at one end (extreme patient-centred) and the converse balance of knowledge and experience (extreme doctor-centred) at the other. Their main findings were that doctor-centred styles were preferred by GPs and that doctors developed a relatively static style, using the same style with all patients and showing little variation in the style adopted according to patient needs.

In evaluating patterns of control and communication within doctor–patient relationships, Roter and Hall (1992) suggest there are four archetypal forms: paternalism, consumerism, mutuality and default. Default relationships are characterised by total lack of control by either the doctor or the patient and an inability to negotiate a mutually acceptable middle ground. These represent the poorest form of doctor–patient relationship. Paternalism, characterised by a passive patient and a dominant doctor, is most clearly articulated by Parsons (1951a). The doctor has access to medical information which the patient has less knowledge of, while the roles prescribed for doctor and patient are institutionalised. Beyond this inbuilt imbalance, a number of studies have identified 'control' behaviours used by doctors during medical visits. These include behaviours used to dominate conversations, verbally exaggerating to emphasise a point, dramatising, being very argumentative, questioning and interrupting frequently (Buller and Buller, 1987; Kaplan, Greenfield and Ware, 1989). While attempts to exert control introduce a negative element into the medical encounter, the paternalistic model of itself is not necessarily negative. While it may imply a social control function, there are occasions when the doctor taking control, directing care and making decisions about treatment can prove to be supportive, particularly for patients who are very sick or elderly (Ende *et al.*, 1989). Interestingly, while patients desire information about diagnosis, prognosis and treatment, they often do not wish to be involved in treatment decisions (Benbassat, Pilpel and Tidhar, 1998). This seems to be particularly true for those with life-threatening or severe conditions. Blanchard *et al.* (1988) report that while most of the cancer patients they interviewed expressed a desire for information, only two-thirds wished to participate in treatment-related decisions. Rather than being involved in decisions, what patients probably want is more adequate information about why the doctor prefers or recommends one treatment rather than another (Fallowfield *et al.*, 1990). This is borne out by a recent review of research studies both for and against patient participation in medical care (Guadagnoli and Ward, 1998). From an array of studies evaluated the authors conclude that the evidence indicates that patients want to be informed of treatment alternatives and they want to be involved in treatment decisions when more than one effective alternative exists. Clearly patients differ in their readiness to participate in medical decisions, but this should not mean that doctors should adopt a paternalistic stance with such patients. As Guadagnoli and Ward suggest, 'physicians should endeavour to engage all patients in decision making albeit at varying degrees' (p. 337). In this context, Benbassat, Pilpel and Tidhar (1998) argue that the ability to gauge the patient's desire to participate in medical decisions should be regarded as a basic clinical skill.

In contrast to paternalism, consumerism, by focusing upon the patient's rights and the doctor's obligations, is characterised by high patient, low doctor control. Mutuality, on the other hand, is characterised by a sharing of decision-making responsibility by doctor and patient and is the ideal advocated by Guadagnoli and Ward. Brody (1980) discusses four ways in which a doctor can encourage mutuality. These involve establishing an atmosphere conducive to participation by the patient, ascertaining the patient's goals and expectations, educating the patient about the nature of his or her problem and eliciting from the patient his or her informed suggestions and preferences and negotiating any disagreements between doctor and patient.

Although asymmetrical relationships predominate in medical encounters there appear to be marked differences in the nature of the interaction dependent upon a number of factors. For example, female doctors seem to be more patient-centred in their approach than is the case with male doctors (Meeuwesen, Schaap and Van der Staak, 1991; Roter *et al.*, 1991). In addition, several studies suggest that a doctor's interactions with his or her patients is influenced by a range of factors including the patient's ethnicity, social class and presenting problem (Eisenberg, 1977).

Factors influencing the pattern of communication in doctor–patient interactions

Numerous studies have investigated a variety of factors assumed to influence the pattern of doctor–patient communication. Investigations have tended to focus upon either specific characteristics of the health care provider or the patient concerned or upon situational or interactional factors (see box 5.3).

Box 5.3 Factors influencing the pattern of doctor–patient communication

Characteristics of the health care provider

Gender – the communication style of women doctors conveys the impression that they are more empathic and caring than their male counterparts

Characteristics of the patient

Gender – women patients tend to be given more information than their male counterparts and receive a more empathic reaction from their doctor

Social class – patients from higher social classes receive more information from their doctors and have longer consultations with them

Education – more educated patients receive more diagnostic information

Age – while some studies suggest that older patients in comparison to younger patients have more favourable encounters with health care providers, other studies suggest the reverse to be true

Differences between health care provider and patient

with regard to:

>   social class and education
>   attitudes, beliefs and expectations

Situational factors

General patient load and level of acquaintance between doctor and patient

(See Hall, Roter and Katz, 1988; Roter and Hall, 1992; Roter, Lipkin and Korsgaard, 1991.)

Several early studies focused specifically upon doctor-related characteristics, such as their age, social class and attitude. In line with the consensus model previously discussed, a desire to maintain the power imbalance within medical encounters may inhibit some doctors from conveying information to certain patients, thus maintaining the patient's uncertainty (Waitzkin, 1985). A variety of patient characteristics including age, gender, marital status, social class and educational background, attitude, desire for information and degree of uncertainty about diagnosis and prognosis have also been investigated. Hence, differences in doctor's information giving may be due to variations between patient groups in their communicative style (for example, older, more educated patients may ask more questions), or due to differences in the doctor's attitude towards various subgroups of patients (Street, 1991). In an experimental investigation using simulated patients, Gerbert (1984) reported that, even when symptoms were presented similarly across all groups of patients, doctors gave more information to patients they liked as opposed to disliked and to patients perceived to lack understanding in comparison to more knowledgeable patients. Finally, medical encounters are also likely to be influenced by a range of situational factors, including the catchment area, general patient load and level of acquaintance between doctor and patient (Waitzkin, 1985). The context of the interaction and the nature of the presenting problem are also important factors. Much of the research to be described has sought to evaluate factors influencing the pattern of communication. Such studies have rarely been theory driven nor have they led to a coherent framework of research. Nevertheless it is instructive to examine each factor in turn.

Characteristics of the health care provider

It is almost inevitable that the type of training received will influence assumptions and expectations about style of health care delivery. However, there is also evidence to suggest that inherent characteristics of the health care provider concerned, such as their gender, also influence the manner in which consultations are conducted.

Professional role

It has been argued that doctors consider their primary responsibility to be the diagnosis and treatment of disease processes, while nursing traditions and teaching place the patient's life situation and experience as the primary focus of practice (Campbell *et al.*, 1990). Indeed, for many professions allied to medicine their goals are to evaluate and direct intervention towards either the patient's life situation or their personal experiences. At a global level, one would therefore assume that differing styles would be adopted by members of different professional groups. However, relatively few studies have documented differences in behaviour during health care provider–patient interaction dependent upon the professional concerned. In their review of the literature, Hall, Roter and Katz (1988) note that there is some evidence that, in comparison to doctors, nurses give patients more information and communicate more overall, use more open-ended questions and positive talk and give higher quality care. In a study published since the review by Hall and her colleagues, Campbell *et al.* (1990) found few differences between the styles adopted by doctors and nurse practitioners, although nurse practitioners exhibited more psychosocial concern. The perception of patients was also that nurse practitioners exhibited more psychosocial concern. However, these results should be treated with some caution as nurse practitioners were more likely to see patients with psychosocial problems. Although the majority of nurse practitioners in this study were female and the majority of doctors male, gender did not seem to have a significant influence on observed provider action. Given the marked variations in the goals of different professional groups, whether investigating differences in communicative style is a fruitful avenue for future research is clearly open to question.

Gender

In their 1991 review Roter, Lipkin and Korsgaard comment that

> there have been a handful of observational studies investigating the influence of patient sex on communication in the medical visit, and even fewer studies investigating provider sex. (p. 1083)

However, the general literature on communication patterns has identified some consistent gender differences which recent research suggests also typifies medical encounters. While technical aspects of medical care show few, if any, gender differences there appear to be marked differences in communication style (Martin, Arnold and Parker, 1988). Both health professionals and patients perceive female doctors as better able to listen to and empathise with patients; patients seen by female doctors are also more satisfied with care received than those seen by male doctors. In her micro-analyses of encounters between patients and twenty one doctors, four of whom were female, West (1984) found that male doctors interrupted patients more frequently and used interruptions as a means of exerting control over their patients. Female doctors, on the other hand, interrupted their patients no more often than they themselves were interrupted. Obviously the small number of women doctors included in this study raises a note of caution about these findings. However, other more recent studies with larger samples of female doctors have also found gender differences in various aspects of communication during medical encounters.

Thus, Hall *et al.* (1994) and Roter, Lipkin and Korsgaard (1991) found that female doctors tended to spend more time with their patients. Roter and her colleagues analysed audiotapes from 537 adult, chronic disease patients and their 127 doctors (101 men and twenty six women). They found that not only did women doctors engage in more talk during a medical visit but so did their patients. Differences between female and male doctors were evident in several different categories including more positive talk, partnership building, question asking and information giving. Differences were most marked during the initial history-taking section of the interview, a time when several key tasks are undertaken (Frankel and Beckman, 1989). These include developing rapport and defining and understanding the patient's concerns in the context of their overall life situation.

Other studies also suggest that female doctors tend to show more affiliative behaviour while male doctors show more controlling behaviour, female doctors tend to be more empathic than their male counterparts, conduct longer, more talkative medical visits, reflect more partnership orientation and are more positive (Meeuwesen, Schaap and Van der Staak, 1991). There is also evidence that female doctors differ in their attitudes towards health and patient care. For example, in comparison to male doctors, they profess to like their patients more (Hall *et al.*, 1993); female doctors are more sensitive to the doctor–patient relationship, more accepting of the patient's feelings and more open to psychosocial factors in patient care, educating patients about their problems and counselling patients about health matters (Maheux *et al.*, 1990).

The longest consultation time and most productive medical encounters would seem to be between female doctors and their female patients. Roter, Lipkin and Korsgaard

(1991) found that a consultation between a female doctor and female patients was four minutes longer than consultations between a male doctor and female patients. In addition, Hall *et al.* (1994) note that the relative percentage contribution made to medical consultation by doctors and patients is equal for female doctors with female patients, while for male doctors with male patients the doctor's speech predominates. It seems that female patients are more successful in recounting their difficulties to a female doctor, this relationship also exhibiting the most doctor positive verbal and non-verbal statements such as nodding and smiling.

Clearly such findings have important implications both for health care practice and for training. The communication style used by female doctors conveys the impression that they are more empathic and caring but not less technically skilled than their male counterparts. This seems to go beyond the stereotypical notion that women are more caring than men. As a result of such communication differences patients tend to be more satisfied with the care they receive from female doctors. The greater time women doctors spend with their patients to achieve this goal may inevitably impinge upon both their time in clinic and their own well-being. The health care provider's style of communication, patient satisfaction with care received, their subsequent pattern of attendance and the impact of care upon the health care provider concerned are important issues for future research.

Characteristics of the patient

In reviewing the influence of patient characteristics upon communication between doctor and patient, Roter and Hall (1992) hypothesise three mechanisms by which such influences can operate. First, the marked difference which often exists between patients and doctors in social class, education and ethnicity may result in communication difficulties. Second, the doctor may be appropriately tailoring their responses to reflect diverse attitudes, beliefs and expectations of the group to which their patient belongs. Thirdly, doctors may be responding to stereotypes. Inevitably, the amount of information doctors give to patients will be influenced by patients' personal characteristics and communication styles. For example, Street (1991) found that patients who asked more questions, and expressed more concerns, worries and emotions, received more information than patients asking fewer questions, expressing fewer concerns and showing less anxiety. However, rather than examining communication styles, most studies have focused upon the influence of inherent patient characteristics on the nature of the medical consultation which occurs; gender, social class and age being the variables most frequently investigated.

Gender

The available literature suggests a number of differences between the patterns of communication which occur between male and female patients respectively and their doctors. Thus, there is evidence that women patients are likely to be given more information than men (Hall *et al.*, 1988; Hooper, Comstock, Goodwin and Goodwin, 1982) and that this is in response to their more frequent questions (Pendleton and Bochner, 1980; Waitzkin, 1985). Female patients also tend to receive more positive communications and more partnership building than their male counterparts, with doctors being more likely to express 'tension release' (laughter) with female patients, as well as being more likely to ask them about their opinions and feelings (Stewart, 1983). In contrast to widely held beliefs, there is also some evidence that female patients have a more positive experience with their doctor, not only receiving more information than their male counterparts, but also receiving a more empathic reaction from their doctor (Hooper *et al.*, 1982) who interrupts them less and who provides them with more comprehensible information. That is, with women patients, technical matters are explained or reported in simpler language (Pendleton and Bochner, 1980; Waitzkin, 1985). It has been suggested that such differences may reflect women's superior communication skills and hence their ability to express their information needs (Weisman and Teitelbaum, 1989).

However, such findings contrast with those from several studies which have documented systematic biases in the way health care providers perceive hypothetical male and female patients and their complaints (Weisman and Teitelbaum, 1989). For example, health care providers tend to perceive female patients as inherently unhealthy in comparison with a male norm and tend to attribute female complaints to psychosomatic origins. Thus, Bernstein and Kane (1981) suggest that doctors have preconceptions that female patients are 'more emotionally labile than men and have a higher prevalence of psychosomatic illness'. However, there are some instances when such stereotypes may act to the advantage of the female patient who consequently experiences more positive and informative encounters (Hooper *et al.*, 1982).

Social class

In reviewing the literature, Hall, Roter and Katz (1988) conclude that patients of higher social class have longer consultations with, and receive more information from, their doctors. Thus, Pendleton and Bochner (1980) found that, during consultations, doctors spontaneously offered more explanations to patients of higher-class backgrounds in comparison to those from lower social classes. There is also evidence that with patients of higher socio-economic status doctors provide clearer explanations, for example following a technical explanation with one in language more comprehensible to the lay person (Waitzkin, 1985); doctors also tend to provide patients from higher social classes with a clearer justification for the treatment offered.

In summarising the literature, Roter and Hall (1992) conclude that:

> education may play a key role in the differential communication to patients of varying socio-economic groups. (p. 48)

Thus, a number of authors have found that more educated patients receive more diagnostic information (Street, 1991; Pendleton and Bochner, 1980; Waitzkin, 1985). In this context, Street (1991) found that less-educated patients were less likely to express concerns. As a result, doctors may be less informative with less-educated patients in part because they erroneously assume that such patients are not particularly interested in learning about their health (Waitzkin, 1985).

Age

Research studies investigating the effect of patients' age upon doctor–patient communication have produced contradictory results. Some studies suggest that older people appear to have some advantage over younger people in communicating with doctors, while other studies suggest the reverse pattern of results. For example, Greene *et al.* (1986), in a comparison of the interactions of patients aged over sixty five and their doctors with a group of patients aged under forty five and their doctors, found less favourable results for the older adults. With the older patients, doctors discussed more medical topics and fewer psychosocial issues. In addition, when the older patients raised psychosocial issues, doctors tended to be less responsive than when the younger patients raised similar issues. They also tended to be less egalitarian, less patient, less engaged and less respectful when with older patients. In contrast, Hooper *et al.* (1982) found that doctors tended to be more courteous with elderly (over seventy four year olds) compared to younger patients and spent more time with and gave more information to patients over forty. In a further study Street and Bulker (1988) report that doctors tended to be less communicatively dominant, more non-verbally responsive as listeners and more egalitarian in their interactions with middle-aged and older patients relative to their encounters with younger clients. In reviewing the literature Hall, Roter and Katz (1988) reflect these contradictory results by concluding that older patients receive more information, more total communication and less 'tension release' (laughter) than younger patients.

However, is it likely that a range of other factors in addition to age will influence communication patterns during a consultation, perhaps the most important of which will be the doctor's perception of the patient. Although some doctors may develop stereotypical notions of specific groups of patients, dependent upon characteristics such as age, gender and class, and then respond accordingly, many will react to each patient as a unique individual with their own personal characteristics and communication styles. It is thus perhaps not surprising that when the effect of inherent characteristics upon communication patterns is examined contradictory results are often obtained.

Problems in health care consultations

A number of factors contribute to poor communication between health care provider and patient. Unfortunately, research has tended to search for characteristics of either the health care provider or, more usually, the patient which can explain why difficulties occur in medical encounters. This tends to create a climate of 'blame' while ignoring both the broader psychosocial and interpersonal context. It can nevertheless be instructive selectively to explore broad parameters which create negative interactions.

Health care providers

Medicine, as with all professions, has its own specialist language and hence doctors and patients are likely to differ in the way they express themselves. Doctors can switch from medical to everyday language, while patients may be unfamiliar with medical language, or have only a basic understanding of it. Indeed, it is quite usual for doctors to use medical terms which patients do not understand and which leave them confused. In their survey of doctors, nurses and patients, Hadlow and Pitts (1991) found that, for the common health terms presented, 70 per cent were understood by doctors while only 36 per cent were understood by patients. In addition, patients also seem reluctant to ask for clarification (Roter and Hall, 1992). It is of interest to note that Bourhis, Roth and MacQueen (1989) found that, while doctors reported switching to everyday language when communicating with patients, neither patients nor nursing staff perceived such switching. In contrast, while nurses also reported using everyday language, they were also perceived as converging towards the everyday language used by patients. While patients attempted to use the medical language of the health professional, doctors reported being unaware of a change in the patient's language.

Roter and Hall (1992) also note from their own data that jargon is more likely to be used by junior than by senior doctors although the former are more likely to tell patients what they mean. There is also evidence that, although doctors know which terms patients are likely to have difficulty understanding, they nevertheless tend to use these terms in spite of reservations they have about them (McKinlay, 1975). Explanations for the failure of doctors to provide clearly comprehensible information to patients are based upon an assumed desire to maintain the professional–patient power imbalance. By using specialised professional knowledge the doctor maintains the patient's role as a passive participant in what has been termed a 'parent–child' relationship (Szasz *et al.*, 1858). An informed patient who would be able to interact on more equal 'adult–adult' terms with the practitioner is seen as a threat to the doctor's professional status (Roter and Hall, 1992). However, explaining technical matters in readily understandable lay language is not necessarily an easy matter. While all professional training tends to introduce its own specialist language, less emphasis is all too often placed on the skills necessary to communicate to a wider lay audience.

Patients' characteristics

It is not unusual for doctors to experience frustration in relation to patient visits. This may be due to a lack of agreement between doctor and patient, lack of patient adherence to instructions or medication recommended by the doctor or because the patient is seen as demanding or controlling. In one study, more than half the patient visits characterised as frustrating by the practitioner concerned were seen as resulting from the characteristics of the patient (Levinson *et al.*, 1993). Unfortunately, much of the literature devoted to this issue focuses upon anecdotal accounts of the characteristics of patients who are described as 'difficult'. Various terms have been coined to describe such patients. Groves (1978) used the term 'hateful patient' and described four stereotypical categories: dependent clingers, entitled demanders, manipulative help seekers and self-destructive deniers. A similar pejorative term, 'heartsink' patients, who exasperate, defeat and overwhelm their doctor by their behaviour, has been coined by O'Dowd (1988). In such instances it is assumed that the patient is the root of the problem and the doctor must do something with respect to the patient who is difficult. Such an approach ignores the broader interpersonal, psychosocial context and differences between doctors and their patients in their explanations of health and illness. Given the different agenda for doctors and their patients, the former focusing upon disease categories while the latter may be more concerned with emotional support or information needs, it is perhaps not surprising that when a doctor can identify no discernible disease but a patient repeatedly returns in a quest for a medical explanation of their difficulties, the doctor experiences some degree of frustration.

In one of the few empirical studies investigating difficult doctor–patient interactions, Schwenk *et al.* (1989) argue that doctors perceive two domains of difficult patient characteristics which act as sources of frustration: those patients who present with uncertain medical problems and those who are perceived as having an abrasive interpersonal style. The authors suggest that these characteristics are in apparent conflict with the main motivations for practising medicine: medical problem solving and a desire to help people. Thus, a failure on the part of the practitioner concerned to meet their own expectations results in low levels of doctor satisfaction; this is translated into a perception of the patient as being difficult. Schwenk *et al.* (1989) conclude that:

> it is important to reiterate that ... patients themselves are not difficult. Rather, physician–patient relationships can be and frequently are difficult. (p. 63)

The interaction between health care provider and patient

A variety of studies indicate that, although some patients prefer not to be given information or prefer incomplete information, for the most part patients express a desire for information, particularly relating to the prognosis, diagnosis and aetiology of their condition. For example, Blanchard *et al.* (1988) found that 92 per cent of the cancer patients they interviewed expressed a desire to know everything about their condition irrespective of whether the news was likely to be good or bad. In contrast, doctors frequently underestimate the amount of diagnostic and prognostic information their patients desire (Kindelan and Kent, 1987), while overestimating the importance patients attribute to treatment issues. There are also instances, particularly with life-threatening illness, when doctors may withhold information from patients or provide only non-alarming information due to a desire to protect the patient or where they feel that total disclosure will cause strong negative emotional reactions (Chaitchik *et al.*, 1992; Seale, 1991b). Inevitably, the transmission of information from doctor to patient will be dependent, at least in part, upon the doctor's perception of the patient's desire for information. There is evidence that information provision can have negative as well as positive effects, in part depending upon the patient's coping style (Miller and Mangan, 1983). Evaluating information preference from a clinical interview is no easy matter and hence it is not surprising that there are discrepancies between doctor and patient in information disclosed and desired.

While doctors may not disclose as much information as patients require, there is also evidence that patients frequently fail to mention concerns or ask questions during the medical encounter. Anxiety about what the doctor might think is the most frequently given reason for failing to ask questions (Tuckett *et al.*, 1986). This is partly due to the fact that patients regard question asking as disruptive of the basic rules of the 'doctor–patient game' (Chaitchik *et al.*, 1992).

Outcomes from health care

In their review of outcome-based research relating to doctor–patient communication, Beckman, Kaplan and Frankel (1989) refer to four categories of outcome identified by their point of delivery in the process of health care provision. These are process, short-term, intermediate and long-term outcomes (see box 5.4).

Box 5.4 Outcomes from health care

Process outcomes – during the medical encounter

Mutuality
Empathy
Frequency of interruptions
Use of open ended questions
Eliciting patient's concerns
Agreement about treatment options

Short-term outcomes – immediately following the medical encounter

Patient understanding
Patient recall
Patient satisfaction
Doctor satisfaction
Intention to comply with treatment

Intermediate outcomes – patient's response to evaluation or treatment

Adherence to recommendations/treatment
Anxiety reduction
Health or disease knowledge
Increased self-esteem and self-confidence

Long-term outcomes – end point of treatment

Symptom resolution
General well-being/quality of life
Survival

(See Beckman, Kaplan and Frankel, 1989; Pendeleton, 1983.)

An example of process outcomes is provided by Beckman and Frankel's (1984) study of doctors' interruptions of the patient's opening statement. Evaluation of such factors can enable identification of those issues which relate positively or negatively to later stage outcomes and can facilitate the evaluation of interventions designed to increase the efficacy of doctor–patient communication.

Short-term outcomes are those assessed immediately after the completion of the medical encounter and include patient understanding and recall, patient satisfaction and intention to comply with treatment. A number of studies suggest that satisfaction is related to adherence. In addition, satisfaction relates to factors such as 'doctor-shopping' or seeking alternative care. Doctor satisfaction has been less frequently investigated as an outcome measure although this is receiving more attention in recent research.

Intermediate outcomes indirectly measure a response to evaluation or therapy. The achievement of intermediate goals, such as adherence, may not necessarily result in desirable long-term (health) outcomes, such as symptom resolution. Until recently few studies had investigated longer-term health outcomes in relation to the medical consultation.

Understanding and recall

Reviews of the literature suggest that patients often do not recall or understand what they have been told by their doctor. Thus, Ley (1989) notes that between 7 and 53 per cent of patients claim not to have understood what they had been told about various aspects of their condition. In a further publication, Ley (1988) concludes that between 5 and 69 per cent of patients are judged by experts not to have adequate understanding of their treatment regime. While such variability is due in part to the varying complexity of information provided to the patient according to their condition, it also, no doubt, reflects the fact that patient understanding has been assessed in a number of different ways. Thus, some studies have assumed that patients' knowledge of illness is a reflection of, and hence an adequate assessment of, understanding, while other studies have obtained patient self-reports of their actual degree of understanding (Ley, 1989).

In addition to understanding, a number of studies have assessed patient recall of information in a variety of settings as an outcome measure of medical consultations (Ley, 1988, 1989). The general method of assessing such recall involves asking patients, immediately following the consultation, what the doctor has said to them about their problem; the proportion of information given by the doctor which the patient recalls is then calculated. Various methods of recall have been used, such as free recall versus cued recall, while other studies have used recognition tasks. Such data have been collected from a variety of patient groups, such as first attenders or mixed groups of patients.

Inevitably, people have expectations about what they are likely to be told and hence, if such information is indeed imparted during the consultation, are much more likely to recall it. In contrast, when information is particularly upsetting, for example hearing the diagnosis 'cancer', many patients do not subsequently register any further information given to them (Hogbin and Fallowfield, 1989). As Ley (1989) notes, such issues should be kept in mind when reviewing the data. He concludes that the amount of information recalled ranges from 47 per cent for analogue subjects to 65 per cent for general hospital patients.

However, general assessment of recall does not capture the relative importance or quality of different aspects of communication. In a large-scale study of 328 patients seen by sixteen general practitioners (Tuckett, Boulton and Olsen, 1985) only 10 per cent of patients failed to recall all of the key points made to them during the consultation. Thus, it appears, from this study at least, that individual patients appear to forget very little information of central importance to themselves.

Patient satisfaction

Patient satisfaction is assumed to reflect quality of care and is often regarded as one of the major outcome criteria of doctor–patient interactions (Bowman et al., 1992); over 1,000 papers published in 1994 incorporated the term patient satisfaction (Sitzia and Wood, 1997). However, the assessment of patient satisfaction is not without its difficulties and hence some degree of caution is required in interpreting results of empirical research in this area. While there are several measures of patient satisfaction, there are few which are both valid and reliable. In one recent study, Bowman et al. (1992) argue that the Patient–Doctor Interaction Scale (PDIS; Falvo and Smith, 1983) is one of the few instruments which appears to fulfil the requirements for a valid, reliable and useful instrument to assess patient satisfaction in general practice. However, many of the items refer to indices of quality of care (e.g. the doctor explained the reason why the treatment was recommended for me) rather than necessarily referring to satisfaction. The fact that the authors report a significant correlation between this instrument and a single item measure of global satisfaction does not necessarily tell us anything other than that potential determinants of satisfaction relate to global measures of the construct.

In their review, Hall and Dornan (1988a) note that of 221 studies examined, almost 75 per cent had devised 'home-made' instruments: that is, an instrument specifically for their own study. Indeed, the majority of studies used one global satisfaction question. Single-item instruments cannot assess variability in patient satisfaction and tend to concentrate the respondent's mind on the question of favourable versus unfavourable. In such contexts subjectivity of judgement is inevitably a major difficulty. In addition, some studies ask directly about satisfaction while others use indirect approaches, asking about care or quality of care. As Hall and Dornan (1988a) note, the indirect approach blurs the distinction between satisfaction and its potential determinants by assuming that the same items serve both purposes. Indeed, the same item (e.g. my doctor always explains matters thoroughly to me) could be cited as a predictor variable in some studies but as an item of satisfaction in others. Other studies ask about satisfaction in relation to differing dimensions or aspects of health care, ranging from satisfaction with accessibility or physical facilities to satisfaction with provider competence or amount of information supplied by providers (Hall and Dornan, 1988b). The fact that different studies include different aspects of satisfaction clearly raises questions about the comparability of satisfaction as a measure from one study to another. As Hall and Dornan (1988a) note:

> what we learn when we ask about patients' satisfaction is not, however, completely clear. (p. 637)

In addition, as with research relating to doctor–patient communication in general, much of the satisfaction research has a weak theoretical basis. Nevertheless, numerous studies have assessed satisfaction with health care consultations in a variety of contexts, with a variety of different patient groups and in relation to a variety of variables, such as expectations of doctor and patient, patient background, behaviour of the health care provider and characteristics of the setting. In their reviews, Hall and Dornan (1988a, 1988b, 1990) refer to 221 such studies published in a twenty year period between 1966 and 1986. In spite of numerous variations across studies, the proportion of patients who report being dissatisfied has remained remarkably constant at about 40 per cent (Ley, 1988).

Interestingly, patients who are less healthy tend to be less satisfied with their medical care than healthier patients, although this is partly mediated by the doctor's use of social conversation (Hall et al., 1998). Other variables which have been investigated as predictive of patient satisfaction, as with research relating to doctor–patient communication in general, are characteristics of both patient and provider and the interaction between them.

Patient characteristics

With regard to patient characteristics three main parameters have been investigated: background variables, personality and coping style. Results of studies investigating the relationship between patient background characteristics and satisfaction tend to be inconsistent, showing either a weak or inconsistent relationship between the two sets of variables or a complete lack of any relationship at all. Most reviewers agree that older people and women generally report more satisfaction but that for other variables, such as socio-economic status, marital status and race, findings are less consistent. However, in their meta-analytic review, Hall and Dornan (1990) suggest that there is in fact no evidence for gender differences, arguing that previous qualitative literature reviews were based upon selective results. In a similar vein Gabbard-Alley (1995) argues on the basis of her review of the literature that any conclusion about the role of gender in health care interaction is suspect because there are few well-conducted research studies.

Hall and Dornan (1990) also report findings from their meta-analysis indicating that greater satisfaction is significantly associated with greater age and lower educational status and marginally associated with being married and having higher social status. As noted earlier, there is some evidence that doctors are more communicative and informative with older patients, while higher-class patients receive better care. Hence, in these instances the relationship between socio-demographic variables and satisfaction may be mediated by actual differences in health care. However, as Hall and Dornan point out, an alternative explanation for the relationship between socio-demographic variables and health care is that the latter may merely reflect certain socio-demographically influenced response tendencies. For example, older people may be more reluctant to be critical of health care received, while those of higher educational levels may have greater expectations in their evaluation of care. Hall and Dornan's overall conclusion concerning the relationship between patient characteristics and satisfaction is that:

> In general, relations were extremely small even when statistically significant. Sociodemographic characteristics are a minor predictor of satisfaction, at best. (p. 816)

There also tends to be little relationship between satisfaction and personality. Satisfaction does, however, seem to be related to coping style. Thus, Steptoe and O'Sullivan (1986), in a study of women hospitalised for gynaecological surgery, found that blunters (information avoiders) reported that they had a good understanding of their condition and were thus satisfied with the information provided. In fact, their factual medical knowledge (as assessed by an objective test) was not high but their coping style led them to avoid further direct information. In a further study with patients hospitalised because of metastatic cancer, Steptoe *et al.* (1991) found that those reporting greatest satisfaction were more avoidant in their coping style, while factual knowledge was actually greater among patients who were less satisfied with communication. This finding was unrelated to patients' age, education or socio-economic status. In general then it seems that an avoidant coping style is related to less desire for information which in turn influences satisfaction with information.

Provider characteristics

A number of studies suggest that younger and less-experienced doctors receive greater satisfaction ratings than more experienced doctors (Hall and Dornan, 1988a, 1988b). It seems that this is due in part to the fact that they conduct longer visits and show greater technical and interpersonal competence, variables shown in other studies to be related to patient satisfaction. There is also evidence that a facilitating in contrast to a domineering conversational style on the part of the practitioner is related to greater patient satisfaction and adherence to medical instructions (Stewart, 1984).

Doctor–patient interaction

Hall, Roter and Katz (1988) note, in their review of the literature to 1986, that patient satisfaction is related to a number of parameters of the consultation. These include the length of time for the consultation and the amount of information patients receive during a medical encounter, greater patient perceived interpersonal and technical competence of the practitioner, greater partnership building (that is, increased likelihood of patient participation), more positive and immediate non-verbal behaviour and more positive talk and less negative talk from the practitioner.

Dissatisfaction has been related to discrepancies between patients' and doctors' models of the problem and the former's expectations regarding treatment (Tuckett *et al.*, 1986). Inevitably a lack of recognition of patients' concerns and a failure to explore lay models of illness is likely to contribute to overall patient dissatisfaction. Roter *et al.* (1997) found that patient satisfaction was lowest with doctors who adopted a narrow biomedical focus and highest with those who adopted a psychosocially based communication pattern. Other studies have evaluated two components of information exchange between doctor and patient which relate to satisfaction. These are 'patient exposition' – that is, patients talking about their concerns using their own words rather than 'yes' or 'no' answers, and 'doctor explanation' – that is, giving patients objective medical information in addition to instructions and advice (Putnam *et al.*, 1985). Increases in each relate to greater patient satisfaction.

Taken overall, a number of patient, provider or interactional factors relate to patient satisfaction. However, satisfaction has been neither defined nor measured consistently across studies, making it difficult to interpret results. Nevertheless, the consistent finding that as many as 40 per cent of patients are dissatisfied with biomedical health care no doubt reflects in part the differing assumptions of patient and provider about health and illness and the differing agendas they bring to medical encounters.

Health outcomes

Measuring the adequacy of health care interventions in terms of health outcomes is notoriously difficult. The use of mortality and morbidity statistics, symptoms or measures of well-being all have their difficulties. Mortality within a given practice is easy to measure but inevitably can only provide an unreliable index of long-term outcome in relation to quality of care. In the absence of other knowledge, for example about the catchment area and population under study, or in the absence of a carefully matched comparison group, mortality rates would be meaningless. However, obtaining suitable comparison groups is no easy matter. Morbidity, symptoms and well-being can be assessed with decreasing degrees of accuracy; in the latter instances varying degrees of subjective self-reporting add to the difficulty of comparing figures thus obtained.

It is thus perhaps not surprising that there are relatively few studies evaluating the quality of doctor–patient communication in relation to patients' health outcome. Those studies which have been conducted tend to favour *post hoc* reports of patients' conversations with their doctor and subsequent self-reports of symptoms, rather than involving direct observation of consultations and objective measures of health. Nevertheless, in their review of eight studies, published between 1975 and 1987, relating doctor–patient communication to health outcome, Kaplan, Greenfield and Ware (1989) suggest that six indicated a positive relationship between doctor–patient conversations and health outcome. Thus, improvement in or resolution of the patient's health problem was found to occur more often when there was agreement between doctors and patients about the nature and severity of the patients' health problems than when they held discrepant views (e.g. Bass *et al.*, 1986).

Although a difficult area to research, given the importance attached to primary care, it seems important to establish the extent to which health outcome is likely to be influenced by the manner in which such care is provided. There is a general assumption that improved medical communication would enhance not only satisfaction and medical adherence but also, in relation to such factors, health outcome. As a result, a number of programmes have been developed for training practitioners in communication skills; while widely used, there are relatively few carefully conducted studies evaluating the efficacy of such programmes and little evidence that interventions impact upon the outcome of care.

Improving medical communication

A number of intervention studies aimed at enhancing the communication effectiveness of health care providers, particularly doctors, have been conducted. For example, Maguire, Fairburn and Fletcher (1986) randomly allocated medical students to either a video-feedback training group or a conventionally trained group. The skills acquired were evident in practice some five years after training. In addition, the quality of diagnostic information obtained from patients by the former group were superior to information usually gained by practising doctors. However, other studies suggest that while training can be successful in modifying behaviour patterns, it does not necessarily impact upon the outcome of care. Thus, Putnam *et al.* (1988) found that, while training doctors in interviewing skills (patient exposition and doctor explanation) was successful in increasing the amount of time doctors spent listening to and giving explanations to patients as well as increasing the amount of information the patient gave to the doctor, these changes were not related to outcome measures, such as patient satisfaction and compliance.

In spite of the numerous research studies indicating that patients wish to receive health information and the long history of advocacy of patient involvement in health care, few studies have attempted to change patient behaviour during the medical encounter. In one of the few such studies Greenfield, Kaplan and Ware (1985) employed a health educator in the waiting room to assist patients in reading their medical records and coached them to ask questions and negotiate medical decisions. Coached patients were more verbally active during the consultation and made other attempts to control the conversation and elicit information from the doctor. They achieved the latter by strategies other than asking direct questions; these included joking about their uncertainties and concerns and introducing topics attributed to others. The authors suggest that asking direct questions may be threatening for patients, who thus employ more subtle procedures.

Communication skills training has become an integral part of most medical training and is often offered as part of continuing professional training. Medical care has changed a great deal in the past two decades so that paternalistic approaches have largely been replaced by the ideal of 'shared decision making'. Given the complexities of the task at hand this is no easy matter to achieve.

Medical decision making

As Ong *et al.* (1995) note, one purpose of medical communication is to allow doctors and patients to make decisions about treatment. However, any such decisions will be influenced by a range of parameters. These will clearly include medically related variables, for example knowledge about available options, although personal preference may often be a more influential factor. As Verkes and Thung (1990) note:

> doctors choose from an ever-growing array of diagnostic and therapeutic procedures on the basis of habit or convenience rather than after weighing carefully all possible options and outcomes. (p. 81)

Medical decision making is also likely to be influenced by a range of non-medical factors, such as the patient's age, gender, socio-economic status and lifestyle factors. For example, an experimental analysis using videotaped presentation indicated that younger patients presenting with either chest pain or dyspnea were more likely to receive a psychogenic diagnosis while older patients were more likely to receive a cardiac diagnosis (McKinlay, Potter and Feldman, 1996).

In addition, broader social and economic parameters will inevitably enter the equation. The needs of other patients or society as a whole will often have to be taken into account and whether or not a particular intervention strategy is cost effective.

The past two decades have seen the growth of Medical Decision Analysis (Pliskin and Pliskin, 1980; Weinstein and Fineberg, 1990), offering techniques for systematising and rationalising processes of choice and decision under conditions of uncertainty inherent in most medical actions. The concept of quality adjusted life years or QALYs has been incorporated into medical decision analysis as a measure of duration and quality of survival. A QALY is defined as the period of time in perfect health that a patient says is equivalent to a year in a state of ill health. For example, a patient may be expected to live ten years in a poor state of health but with costly surgery could expect one year of full health. In an increasingly cost conscious health system, issues of rationing health care also enter into the equation. Medical decision analysis attempts to impose quantitative parameters on decisions which in reality are influenced by personal values and ethical and moral considerations and as such has not been met with universal enthusiasm.

The literature relating to medical decision making has increased dramatically in the last ten years and encompasses a wide area of health care, ranging from decisions to offer screening tests to diagnostic and treatment issues. The present comment is of necessity very brief and selective and a few studies are cited by way of illustration. The fact that medical decision making is influenced by such a broad range of parameters partly explains the wide variations in surgical rates, speed of both diagnosis and referral to specialists, as well as wide variations in diagnostic tests undertaken and drug prescribing behaviour for various conditions attested to by numerous publications. Such variations are not accounted for by variations in population characteristics and disease prevalence, but are explained by the broad variety of parameters influencing medical decisions. As illustrative examples three specific issues will be briefly examined, practitioner delay in making a diagnosis, geographical variations in care and gender differences in care received.

Practitioner diagnostic decisions

In an early report, Hackett and Cassem (1969) observed that doctors' delay in making a diagnosis caused or contributed to delay in hospital referral of patients with chest pain in twelve of the 100 cases of suspected or proven heart disease they studied. The medical personnel concerned rationalised their delay by blaming other organs or by minimising the pain. The authors conclude that there appeared to be no adequate reason for the doctor to delay. Funch (1985) notes that, for a sample of 294 colorectal cancer patients, 46 per cent experienced doctor-related diagnostic delay due to factors such as misdiagnosis or observing symptoms without direct action. Such factors resulted in an average delay of eighteen weeks before diagnosis.

In reviewing the evidence relating to breast cancer, Facione (1993) comments that the consensus from a range of studies suggests that provider delay is significant and has been underestimated. She further notes evidence to suggest that delay in diagnosis of breast cancer is more common when symptoms are presented by younger women. Adam, Horner and Vessey (1980) found that ten out of forty one women experienced doctor-related diagnostic delay for breast symptoms because of a diagnosis by the doctor of benign breast disease or no breast disease.

Medicine is an inexact science and when there is more than one possible diagnosis on the basis of symptoms presented an initial 'wait and see' decision may be appropriate. With rare conditions or when the symptoms are unusual in a particular age group a decision to delay referral for further investigation may be more likely.

Geographical variations

Numerous studies have documented large differences in both the use of health services and the type of treatment offered according to geographic location. Three alternative hypotheses have been advanced to explain such variations (Chassin, 1993). The first is that variations are caused by inappropriate overuse of services in high-use areas. However, there is evidence that procedures are used inappropriately to the same extent in both high- and low-use areas (Chassin et al., 1987). The second hypothesis, the 'uncertainty hypothesis', maintains that the lack of data on effectiveness permits reasonable doctors to come to different conclusions on when to use various procedures (Wennberg, 1987), particularly in the 'grey area' between clearly appropriate and clearly inappropriate procedures. However, there is no evidence that there are more cases falling within the 'grey area' in high-use areas (Chassin et al., 1987). A third hypothesis suggested by Chassin (1993) is that the differences are caused by variations in the enthusiasm doctors have for particular procedures. In reviewing the evidence relating to variations in surgical rates, Hulka and Wheat (1985) comment that:

> taken together, these studies provide strong evidence that surgical rates do not correlate with need, but do relate to demand for surgery whether that be physician or patient initiated. (p. 444)

As noted, medical decisions undertaken by the practitioner are as likely to be based upon habit or convenience as upon any clear medical rationale. Many practitioners may also be more likely to refer an articulate and demanding patient for specified treatments.

Patients' gender

It has been suggested that gender stereotypes held by professionals influence decisions made on behalf of patients, with men's problems being taken more seriously and defined in organic terms, while women's problems are interpreted in psychosomatic terms (Nathanson, 1977). As a result, women are prescribed more psychotropic drugs and tend to seek additional sources of support in order to satisfy their health needs (Bernstein and Kane, 1981). Vague or poorly defined complaints presented by women may be more likely to be regarded as hypochondriacal in nature. In a study of colorectal cancer patients, Marshall and Funch (1986) found that, subsequent to having consulted a doctor, women with cancer of the colon experienced more delay than men in securing a definitive diagnosis.

In a further study, Tobin *et al.* (1987) noted a differential rate of referral for catheterisation amongst men and women suspected of having ischemic heart disease. A referral for catheterisation indicates that patient and doctor are considering the option of cardiac surgery or angioplasty. Slightly more than 40 per cent of men were referred compared with 4 per cent of the women. This variability was only partially explained by factors such as previous heart disease or angina. The authors suggest that the differences may relate to the widely held belief that coronary artery bypass surgery is less effective for women, although long-term rates of survival are in fact similar for men and women. They conclude by asking whether there should in fact be any gender difference in referral rates.

Clearly medical decisions are multifactorial in nature, influenced not only be medical parameters but by a host of personal characteristics and social and economic considerations. As Sox *et al.* (1988) note:

> medical care is often said to be the art of making decisions without adequate information. Physicians must frequently choose treatment long before they know which disease is present. Even when the illness is known, one must usually select from among several treatment options, and the consequences of each cannot be foretold with certainty. Indeed, uncertainty is intrinsic in the practice of medicine.

Summary

In the context of biomedical health care, communication between health care provider and patient plays a vital role. Some have gone as far as to argue that:

> communication promotes health and illness within society, makes the system run at optimal or marginal effectiveness, and can facilitate efforts to treat illness and prevent its recurrence. Communication is also pervasively taken for granted. (Pettegrew and Logan, 1987, p. 676)

However, patient–provider interactions within a health care context are based upon the premise that both parties share similar assumptions about the encounter. Yet the 'culture' of medicine and the 'culture' of the patient may be quite distinct. The parties concerned may think quite differently about health and illness, having differing communication styles and approaches towards health-related issues. It is thus not surprising that medical encounters can be problematic.

However, evaluating the research literature relating to patient–provider interaction is not facilitated by the fact that, for the most part, research is not theoretically cohesive, while research methods used are highly variable between studies (Roter, Hall and Katz, 1988). Nevertheless, numerous studies have attempted to delineate factors influencing both the pattern of communication in doctor–patient interactions and problems in health care consultations. These have tended to focus upon either characteristics of the patient and provider or the interaction between them. In relation to patient characteristics there is some evidence that female patients have a more positive experience with their doctor, not only receiving more information than their male counterparts, but also receiving a more empathic reaction from their doctor who interrupts them less and who provides them with more comprehensible information. There is also evidence that patients of higher social class, who also tend to be better educated and have longer consultations with their doctors, receive more information from their doctors. Findings from research studies investigating the effect of patient age upon doctor–patient communication tend to be contradictory.

In relation to provider characteristics a number of studies suggest that female doctors tend to be more empathic than their male counterparts, conduct longer, more communicative medical visits, reflect more partnership orientation and are more positive, are more sensitive to the doctor–patient relationship, and are more accepting of the patient's feelings and more open to psychosocial factors in patient care.

While many factors inevitably influence the nature of medical encounters the search for either provider-related or patient-related factors, which give rise to problematic encounters, is misplaced. Given the different agenda for doctors and their patients, it is perhaps not surprising that when a doctor's expectations and explanations differ from that repeatedly sought by a patient, the doctor experiences some degree of frustration. It is also not surprising, given the power imbalance in medical encounters and the desire of many practitioners to maintain this imbalance, facilitated by the use of medical rather than everyday language, that the exchange of information in medical encounters is often unsatisfactory; information provided to patients is frequently misunderstood by them, while patients are often not involved in decisions about their own health care. While such factors are frequently assessed as outcome measures in relation to medical encounters, actual health status is rarely monitored.

There is a general assumption that improving medical communication would serve to enhance not only satisfaction and medical adherence but also, related to such factors, health outcome. There is little evidence that this is actually the case. Medical communication is also an intrinsic element in medical decision making, although the latter is influenced by a range of non-medical factors such as the patient's age, gender, socio-economic status and lifestyle factors as well as broader social and economic parameters. In an increasingly cost conscious health system, issues of rationing health care inevitably form part of the decision-making process, introducing ethical and moral considerations into the equation.

FURTHER READING

J. A. Hall and M. C. Dornan (1988). What patients like about their medical care and how often they are asked: A meta-analysis of the satisfaction literature. *Social Science and Medicine*, **27**, 935–939.

J. A. Hall, D. L. Roter and N. R. Katz (1988). Meta-analysis of correlates of provider behavior in medical encounters. *Medical Care*, **26**, 657–675.

D. L. Roter and J. A. Hall (1989). Studies of doctor–patient interaction. *Annual Review of Public Health*, **10**, 163–180.

D. L. Roter and J. A. Hall (1992). *Doctors Talking with Patients/Patients Talking with Doctors*. Westport, CT: Auburn House.

H. R. Winefield (1992). Doctor–patient communication: An interpersonal helping process. In S. Maes, H. Leventhal and M. Johnston (eds), *International Review of Health Psychology*. Vol. I. Chichester: Wiley.

CHAPTER 6

Adhering to treatment advice

CHAPTER OVERVIEW

This chapter examines the question of adherence/non-adherence to medical advice. After reviewing the extent and potential dangers of non-adherence the difficulty of measuring adherence is addressed. Various methods involving self-reports, others' judgements, pill counts, mechanical devices and blood or urine analyses are reviewed. The main body of the chapter then reviews the various factors which are thought to influence adherence to treatment advice. These include various patient, treatment and disease and provider characteristics, the interaction between patient and health care provider, patient understanding and recall, past behaviour and patient beliefs and expectations. The final part of the chapter reviews various attempts to improve adherence through the use of memory aids, effective communication, social support, patient education and various behavioural interventions.

This chapter covers:

Measuring adherence
Adherence and treatment outcome
Factors influencing adherence to treatment advice
Improving adherence

Introduction

Adherence to medical advice is frequently assessed as an outcome measure in relation to health care provider–patient interactions. In this context medical advice usually refers to medication regimens. As Turk and Meichenbaum (1991) point out:

> With the availability of expanded scientific knowledge and the advancement of pharmacological knowledge, adherence became, and continues to be, a major concern in the provision of health care. (p. 249)

However, adherence relates to a far broader range of parameters than just medication and includes adherence to appointments for preventive programmes, participation in various lifestyle change programmes and psychosocial interventions. The questions of adherence to exercise and dietary regimens and adherence to requests to participate in screening programmes has been discussed previously. The focus of the present chapter is adherence to treatment advice which includes advice relating to medication.

Patient adherence with medical instructions has been the focus of a vast body of research. Donovan and Blake (1992) note that 4,000 English language articles had been published on the topic up to 1985 with a further 4,000 listed on Medline up to 1990. In the past five years a further 4,500 articles have been published in this area (Myers and Midence, 1998).

Adherence to any aspect of health care advice assumes that provider and patient share a common set of assumptions about symptoms and illness which, as has been noted previously, is not necessarily the case. This needs to be kept in mind in relation to the material reviewed here.

Adherence defined

Patient non-compliance or non-adherence involves the patient not carrying out the treatment regime as the practitioner intended (Meichenbaum and Turk, 1987).

> Patient non-compliance refers to patients' lack of adherence to or co-operation with specific behavioural recommendations made by their physician or other health professional ... such as non-adherence to a restricted (e.g. low-sodium) diet, taking only one of three prescribed pills per day, and not returning for a follow-up appointment. (Hays and DiMatteo, 1987, p. 38)

The term adherence is currently more widely used than the term compliance. The latter term implies one-way communication from health care provider to patient and hence refers to the extent to which the patient obediently and faithfully follows health care advice. Adherence emphasises co-operation between doctor or other health care provider and patient in a mutually acceptable course of behaviour (Turk and Meichenbaum, 1991). However, until recently, the term compliance predominated, particularly within the medical literature, being closely tied to the dominance of Western medicine and implying that failure to comply was the fault of the patient or caused by problems with the doctor–patient relationship (Waitzkin, 1989). As Donovan and Blake (1992) note:

> Compliance is, itself, a value-laden term, closely entangled with issues surrounding the dominance of medicine and concerns about costs. (p. 507)

Leventhal (1993) has argued that:

> the conceptual shift from compliance to adherence represents an important first step in moving away from roles emphasising obedience to instructions toward models emphasising the independence, or self-regulatory activity of the patient.

Adherence then refers to a range of behaviours such as following dietary or exercise recommendations, self-monitoring, medication use or attending for scheduled appointments. With regard to medication it may refer to the patient not collecting their prescribed medication, not taking it, or not completing the full course, not taking it frequently enough, not accurately following the dosage and timing instructions or taking additional non-prescribed medication (Ley, 1988; Ley and Llewelyn, 1995). With regard to lifestyle change, adherence may refer to advice to reduce alcohol intake, to increase physical activity or exercise, to alter one's diet or lose weight or to avoid stress. With regard to other aspects of preventive behaviour, adherence can refer to recommendations to attend for mammography or other screening programmes or to undertake breast, skin or testicular self-examination. Given the variety of activities covered by the label adherence, it is doubtful if there are many instances when patients actually adhere precisely to instructions.

How widespread is non-adherence?

Numerous authors have made the point that non-adherence is not a trivial issue. Published figures suggest that rates of non-adherence vary from a low of 15 per cent to a high of 93 per cent depending upon the patient population studied and the definition of non-adherence used (Kaplan and Simon, 1990). Problems with non-adherence seem to be least marked within the context of short-term interventions and most problematic when lifestyle change is involved. Estimates suggest that 70–80 per cent of patients consistently adhere to short-term medication regimens for an acute problem, while fewer than 60 per cent adhere to preventive programmes and less than 50 per cent adhere to recommendations for lifestyle change (DiMatteo and DiNicola, 1982). Even for adherence to an appointment schedule, estimates suggest that between 15 per cent and 60 per cent of appointments are missed (Deyo and Inui, 1980).

With regard to medication, research suggests that one-half to three-quarters of patients fail to follow instructions properly, over a half discontinue the medication before they are supposed to and one-quarter to one-third make medication errors in ways that may endanger their health (Haynes, Taylor and Sackett, 1979). Non-adherence to medication also increases with number of concurrent medications prescribed and the length of time that treatment is required. Stone (1979) found that, for patients who took one medication, non-adherence due to errors alone was 15 per cent; when two or three medications were prescribed the rate of non-adherence due to errors increased to 25 per cent and when five or more medications were prescribed non-adherence due to error was 35 per cent. Turk and Speirs (1984) note that the longer it is necessary for the patient to take prescribed medications the more likely it is that non-adherence will occur. Thus, in one study, as many as a quarter of a group of hypertensive patients on a medication regimen were lost to follow up within the first two years (Luscher and Vetter, 1990).

With regard to lifestyle change, 75–80 per cent of those who give up smoking or take up exercise and dietary modification programmes may fail to adhere to the programme (Dunbar and Agras, 1980). Well-documented statistics consistently indicate that the attrition rates from exercise programmes approximate 50 per cent in the first six months (Oldridge, 1982).

Non-adherence is also greater when schedules involve a complex set of factors including both medication and lifestyle change. Rates of adherence can be worryingly low for people with chronic conditions such as diabetes, where a combination of lifestyle change and self-monitoring of intake and bodily state may be required, or for some elderly populations for whom complex medication schedules are necessary. In one of the first published studies documenting the extent of non-adherence in adults with diabetes, Watkins et al. (1967) found that more than 50 per cent were making insulin dosage errors, 66 per cent were testing incorrectly and 75 per cent were judged unacceptable in terms of quality, quantity and timing of meals. In relation to the elderly it has been estimated that under adherence (that is taking less medication than prescribed) occurs in 40 per cent of cases (Kiernan and Isaacs, 1981).

It is of interest to note that adherence among doctors to treatment or prescription protocols is no better than adherence to instructions by patients in general (Blackwell, 1973). For example, Schleifer et al. (1991) found that, for a sample of patients receiving chemotherapy treatment for breast cancer, 56 per cent received unjustified changes to at least one of their medications. In a further study, Yoong et al. (1992) found that for a sample of pregnant women less than a quarter of the prescribed actions referred to in departmental protocols were adhered to by the examining obstetrician.

Potential dangers of non-adherence

In many instances failure to adhere to instructions or to a treatment regime can have dire consequences. For example, errors in the management of medication accounts for 5 per cent to 15 per cent of hospitalisation among the elderly (Gryfe and Gryfe, 1984). Abram, Moore and Westervelt (1971) note that non-adherence to the recommended diet was the direct cause of death in 4 per cent of their end-stage renal disease patients undergoing hemodialysis. End-stage renal disease is a chronic, life-threatening condition. Upon the cessation of kidney function patients must undergo lifelong medical therapy to stay alive. A variety of treatments are available including renal transplantation and several forms of renal dialysis. One of the criteria for success in relation to hemodialysis treatment is patient adherence to strict dietary and fluid-intake regimens. Yet, in spite of the fact that non-adherence is linked to diminished life expectancy, rates of non-adherence tend to be high. For example, Brown and Fitzpatrick (1988) found that clinical criteria of dietary abuse indicated problems in over half their sample of forty one dialysis patients; similar figures have been reported in other studies (Poll and Kaplan De-Nour, 1980).

It is worth bearing in mind, however, that in many instances, even absolute adherence does not necessarily assure symptom relief or full recovery. For example, good diabetic control may not guarantee future health although it may help to prevent serious complications (Cahill, Etzwiler and Freinkel, 1976). This issue is discussed later in the chapter.

Measuring adherence

Numerous authors have noted that studying non-adherence is hampered by the lack of adequate measures. Inevitably the question of what to measure varies according to whether adherence is being assessed in relation to medical regimens or with regard to health behaviour interventions. The former usually refers to participation adherence: that is, how well a patient follows a prescribed regimen such as pills correctly taken. In contrast, adherence to health behaviour interventions usually involves not only participation adherence, for example attendance at a smoking cessation clinic, but also some measure of actual behaviour change: for example, any decrease in the number of cigarettes smoked or the number of participants who stop smoking.

A number of both indirect and direct methods have been used to assess adherence to medication regimens (see box 6.1).

Box 6.1 Measuring adherence

Indirect methods

Patient self-reports
Second-hand reports from health care professionals, family members or friends
Pill counts
Mechanical or electronic methods for monitoring dose dispensed

Direct methods

Urine or blood tests
Observation

(See Hays and DiMatteo, 1987; O'Brien, Petrie and Raeburn, 1992; Turk and Meichenbaum, 1991.)

Self-report

Patient self-reports are the most easily obtained and most frequently used measure of adherence. However, the inaccuracy of self-reports of health-related behaviours is well established; with particular regard to medication, difficulty recalling information and misunderstanding treatment recommendations may bias reports regardless of the intent on the part of the patient to provide accurate information. In summarising several studies with a variety of patient groups, Roth (1987) concludes that self-reports of medication adherence were not corroborated by other objective indicators of adherence. In spite of this general evidence for the lack of reliability of self-reports there is some indication that, as long as efforts are made to ensure that questioning is simple and direct, then accurate information about the likelihood that a patient will adhere to treatment can be obtained (Kaplan and Simon, 1990). Indeed, certain changes in lifestyle, such as adherence to dietary or exercise regimens, can only be assessed by self-reports (Carmody, Matarazzo and Istvan, 1987).

Others' judgements

The accuracy of second-hand reports from doctors, nurses or other health professionals, friends or family members will inevitably depend upon their familiarity with the patient. In general, doctors' assessments of their patients' adherence tends to be poor (Hays and DiMatteo, 1987). For example, in one study comparing primary health care providers' predictions of parents' adherence to their children's short-term antibiotic regimen (assessed by amount of medication used) and scheduled follow-up appointment, providers greatly overestimated the percentage of parents who would adhere (Finney *et al.*, 1993). However, accuracy of reports from family members also tends to be poor (Hays and DiMatteo, 1987). Although patient reports are generally more accurate than estimates obtained from either doctors or family members, all self-reports tend to overestimate true levels of adherence (Orme and Binik, 1989). Ley (1988) reports that estimates of non-adherence from patient reports average 22 per cent. This contrasts with average rates of non-adherence of 54 per cent when more reliable methods such as urine analysis or mechanical devices are used to estimate medication use. Certain behaviours, such as keeping scheduled appointments or obtaining a subsequent prescription, are more readily subject to accurate monitoring by others.

Pill counts

Other indirect indices involve monitoring medication via various checking methods or pill counting: for example, the number of pills left after a certain time (Putnum *et al.*, 1994). Although more objective than self-reports, measures such as pill counts rely on patients not seeking to deceive (for example, by throwing pills away). In addition, pill counting does not reveal incorrect self-medication due to factors such as forgetting and then doubling subsequent intake. Comparison of pill counts with other measures, such as blood or urine levels of the drug given, suggest that pill counts are not totally reliable (Ley, 1988; Roth, 1987).

Mechanical devices

More recent methods of monitoring medication adherence include techniques such as radioactive material, photographic film, mechanical devices or the use of portable bar code readers (Leirer *et al.*, 1991) or electronic measurement devices (Cramer and Spilker, 1991). While such devices may monitor whether a dose has been dispensed, this does not necessarily mean it has been taken. Reviews suggest that such methods of measuring adherence are more reliable than pill counts (Roth, 1987; Rudd and Marshall, 1987). This is substantiated by one recent study which found that both self-reports and pill counts suggested significantly higher adherence than the event monitoring system, indicating that electronic methods may be the more accurate measure (Walterhouse *et al.*, 1993).

Direct methods

Direct measures, such as blood or urine tests, are of high cost, of limited use in clinical practice and invasive (Turk and Meichenbaum, 1991). In addition, while biochemical markers of medication intake derived from blood or urine tests are more objective than other methods, they may be affected by variations in metabolism; they are also only sensitive to pill taking two or three days before the test.

A number of studies suggest there is often little relationship between the different methods used to assess adherence. Thus, in a study of three methods of adherence assessment (self-report, reports from others and objective measures), for three types of adherence (taking medication, diet and fluid intake), with hemodialysis patients, Cummings *et al.* (1984) found very little correspondence between the different sources of adherence information. Of interest is the finding that self-reports tend to be enhanced when the patient is led to believe that other sources of information will be used to verify their reports (Stacy *et al.*, 1985). Given that each method of measuring adherence has its limitations, several authors have suggested the use of multiple measures determined in part by resources available and the question to be investigated (Ley, 1988; Meichenbaum and Turk, 1987).

The relationship between adherence and treatment outcome

Often patients adhere to the treatment but fail to gain the desired health outcome, while non-adherent patients may improve clinically (Becker, 1985). For example, Inui, Carter and Pecoraro (1981) found that, on the basis of pill counts, 40 per cent of well-controlled hypertensives were in fact non-adherent. In relation to diabetes, while some studies suggest a positive relationship between patient adherence and diabetic control (e.g. Webb *et al.*, 1984), especially with regard to adherence to diet (Hays *et al.*, 1994), many others do not (e.g. Bond, Aiken and Somerville, 1992; Brownlee-Duffeck *et al.*, 1987; Connell *et al.*, 1988; Glasgow, McCaul and Schafer, 1987). The results of a recent large-scale study (Hays *et al.*, 1994) suggest there is little better than chance relationship between adherence and health outcome and that, in some instances, adherence is associated with diminished physical health (see box 6.2).

Inevitably the relationship between adherence and heath outcome is complicated by a range of other factors. For example, with regard to health behaviour change, knowledge of adherence is derived from those who choose to attend intervention programmes; many people choose not to attend formal programmes and self-change may be common (Schachter, 1982). Little is known about those who attempt to change their own behaviour. In addition, in some instances, such as with antihypertension medication, the effects of non-adherence may only become apparent for a minority of patients or for those failing to adhere for extended periods of time.

Health outcome is also affected by a range of other factors related to both one's inherited characteristics and one's environmental circumstances. For example, metabolic control in diabetes is a function of the appropriateness of the prescribed regimen, duration of disease, presence of other illness conditions, heredity and, particularly in the case of adolescents, changes in hormone level and stress (Jonhson, 1992). As Glasgow, McCaul and Schafer (1987) suggest:

> patient initiative in responding to changing environmental and biological conditions may be more strongly related to good control than is adherence to a fixed regimen prescription. (p. 411)

In addition, adherence does not necessarily have specific effects. In relation to medication adherence, a number of studies have found better outcomes for adherers compared

Box 6.2 The Medical Outcome Study and the relationship between adherence and treatment outcome (Hays *et al.*, 1994)

The Medical Outcome Study (MOS) is a four year longitudinal observational study designed to examine the influence of specific characteristics of providers, patients, and health systems to outcomes of care. Hays *et al.* report the relationship between self-reported adherence and health outcomes over time for 2,125 patients with four chronic conditions – diabetes, hypertension, congestive heart failure and recent myocardial infarction. Depressive symptoms were also assessed at the beginning of the study.

The **measure of adherence** consisted of two lists:
  list one – recommendations made by the provider: for example, to exercise, follow a low-salt diet
  list two – how often the patient actually carried out these activities

Health outcomes

  Physical functioning
  Role limitations due to physical health problems
  Role limitations due to emotional health problems
  Social functioning
  Pain
  Energy/fatigue
  Emotional well-being
  General health perceptions

Results

  Little better than a chance association between reported adherence and health outcomes.
  Insulin using and depressed patients who adhered to medication actually exhibited diminished physical health.

to non-adherers even when the drug was a placebo (Horwitz and Horwitz, 1993). This does not seem to be because non-adherers are more chronically ill. It is more likely to be due to differences in personal characteristics or because adherers are more likely to engage in additional health-enhancing behaviours.

Given such issues it is perhaps unfortunate that many studies use health indicators to assess patient adherence. In the absence of additional information about what the patient is actually doing, health outcome may provide misleading information. In addition, the fact that adherence is not necessarily related to health outcome raises questions about the search for factors predictive of non-adherence and studies seeking to enhance adherence. The question of adherence cannot be fully addressed without reference to people's beliefs about health and illness and their expectations about health care or without a consideration of these and other factors in relation to health outcome.

Factors influencing adherence to treatment advice

Although there have been hundreds of empirical studies and several comprehensive reviews of the adherence literature, conclusive evidence about what factors determine adherence remains elusive. In evaluating the research evidence DiMatteo and DiNicola (1982) conclude that five major explanatory areas consistently demonstrate value in explaining adherence. These involve past behaviour, health perception, individual characteristics, social support and the doctor–patient relationship. However, patients choose to comply with or ignore health care advice, based on a complex set of factors including both personal and situational variables. While certain variables may be predictive of certain behaviours in relation to certain illnesses in certain circumstances, the same factors may not be central in other instances. Initial research, based upon the concept of compliance, focused upon identifying characteristics of the patient, the regimen, the disease or the provider as predictors of adherence (see box 6.3). More recently social cognition models and Leventhal's self-regulatory theory have been presented as explanatory paradigms in the study of patient beliefs and expectations in relation to adherence (Dunbar-Jacob, 1993; Horn and Weinman, 1998).

Patient characteristics

With regard to patient-related variables there seems to be little evidence for any association between adherence and either patient personality characteristics (Meichenbaum and Turk, 1987) or demographic factors, such as age, gender, education, socio-demographic status, marital status, religion or ethnic background (Gabbard-Alley, 1995; Haynes, Taylor and Sackett, 1979; Kaplan and Simon, 1990). The one exception with regard to individual characteristics seems to be coping style. The use of denial has been related to long-term resistance to adherence (Croog, Shapiro and Levine, 1971). Those reporting avoidance-coping strategies such as 'hoping for a miracle' tend to be less likely to adhere to medical advice and recommendations (Sherbourne et al., 1992).

In relation to socio-demographic characteristics, age has been most frequently investigated with some investigators suggesting that non-adherence is associated with extremes of age. Meichenbaum and Turk (1987) suggest this may be because the very young are averse to taking bad-tasting medicine while the very old are more susceptible to forgetfulness or self-neglect. However, of eighty nine studies investigating the effects of age on adherence which are cited by Haynes and his colleagues, only eighteen revealed a positive effect of age on adherence, seven a negative effect and sixty four no relationship between age and adherence (Haynes, Taylor and Sackett, 1979). Contradictory evidence is also provided by more recent research. For example, Lorenc and Branthwaite (1993) report that age is unrelated to adherence while Bosley et al. (1995) suggest that younger patients may be less adherent. In spite of such findings, reviews still misleadingly refer to adherence among older adults as a greater care problem than is the case for younger adults (Griffith, 1990). This is in part due to the fact that other potentially age-related factors, such as living with a relative, do influence adherence. Older adults also suffer more chronic diseases than their younger counterparts and use more prescribed and non-prescribed medication. They therefore have more opportunity for non-adherence even though average rates of adherence for older and younger adults may not differ.

Box 6.3 Factors related to nonadherence to treatment advice

Patient characteristics

Use of coping styles involving avoidance or denial
Being young or old
Lack of patient understanding of information given to them
Failure to adhere on previous occasions
Lack of availability of social support
Family conflict
Negative beliefs relating to medication

Disease-related variables

Illness severity
A perception that one's health is poor
Perceived lack of likely improvement

Treatment variables

Complexity of treatment
Long duration of treatment
Treatment side effects
Small perceived benefits of treatment
Degree of behaviour change required

Provider characteristics

Doctor insensitivity
Health care provider's lack of satisfaction with their job

Provider–patient interaction

Lack of a sufficiently clear explanation provided to the patient
Provider unwillingness to answer questions
Use of technical or information seeking questions
Negative attitude to patient
Lack of interest in patient
Failure of provider to be empathic
Failure of provider to be understanding
Low patient satisfaction with the consultation
Lack of patient involvement in decision making

(DiMatteo and DiNicola, 1982; Haynes, Taylor and Sackett, 1979; O'Brien, Petrie and Raeburn, 1992; Meichenbaum and Turk, 1987.)

It is also worth bearing in mind that, while socio-demographic factors are generally not related to adherence, such findings do not necessarily apply to all patient groups. Thus, male hypertensives, who are younger, obese at entry, cigarette smoking, not currently taking antihypertensive medication, with moderate hypertension and of low socio-economic status are more likely to drop out of treatment (Luscher and Vetter, 1990). For hemodialysis patients, having family problems and being younger and male has been found to be associated with poorer fluid compliance (Boyer *et al.*, 1990;

Cummings *et al.*, 1982) as has time on dialysis (Boyer *et al.*, 1990). A number of studies with adolescents with diabetes have found that as age increases, adherence to the exercise, injection, and eating and glucose testing frequency components of the regimen decrease (Bond, Aiken and Somerville, 1992; Johnson *et al.*, 1986).

In general, however, as Horne (1998) notes, the search for socio-demographic or personality characteristics as sole determinants of adherence is a rather fruitless exercise as adherence may vary not only over time and between different aspects of the treatment regimen but also between and within individuals with the same disease and condition.

Treatment and disease characteristics

With regard to regimen and disease-related factors, a number of studies suggest that the complexity of the treatment regimen, side effects of the treatment and the characteristics of the disease, such as symptom severity and perceived chance of improvement, are of potential relevance to adherence (Becker and Maiman, 1975; Haynes, 1979). Such factors are frequently incorporated into studies evaluating cost-barrier aspects in relation to the health belief model, as will be discussed later in the chapter.

Provider characteristics

Studies have also investigated the relationship between patients' self-reported adherence and characteristics of the doctor concerned. For example, DiMatteo, Hays and Prince (1986) found that doctors' sensitivity to (accuracy at decoding) audio-tape non-verbal cues was associated with fewer cancelled and unrescheduled appointments. Health care providers' job satisfaction has also been found to be positively related to actual and self-reported patient behaviour (Weisman and Nathanson, 1985) and adherence to medication (DiMatteo *et al.*, 1993).

Provider–patient interaction

A number of studies suggest that the quality of the doctor–patient relationship and resulting patient satisfaction with medical care is related to adherence (Nagy and Wolfe, 1984; Noble, 1998; Sherbourne *et al.*, 1992). Indeed, adherence has been widely used as an outcome measure for assessing the effectiveness of health care provider communication. Thus, patients are less likely to adhere to treatment recommendations when their doctor has not provided a sufficiently clear explanation (Armstrong *et al.*, 1990) and are more willing to adhere when their doctor is willing to answer all their questions regardless of the time required to do so (DiMatteo *et al.*, 1993). The doctor's attitude and interest in the patient also appears to increase adherence to a given regimen (Becker and Maiman, 1975), in addition to an empathic and understanding manner. In a qualitative review of the literature relating to provider–patient interaction and adherence Squier (1990) argues that there is a:

> positive relationship between practitioners' ability to make empathic, affective contact with the patient, the patient's satisfaction with the consultation, release of tension during the interview, commitment to a treatment plan and adherence to the therapeutic regime. (p. 331)

He further argues that patients' expectations for factual information, involvement in decision making and agreement about treatment plans relate to the notion of empathic understanding.

A useful summary of specific aspects of health care provider–patient relationships, which are of importance in relation to adherence, is provided by Hall, Roter and Katz in their review of studies published between 1967 and 1986. They conclude that adherence is related to the amount of information provided, more provider positive talk (reassurance, support and encouragement) and less negative talk (anger and anxiety). Adherence decreases when doctors ask technical or information-seeking questions and is enhanced when they question patients about their opinions or understanding, or make requests for suggestions.

In sum, a participatory relationship between doctor and patient seems to be the most successful in promoting adherence (Hall, Roter and Karz, 1988): that is, the patient has a feeling of active participation in their treatment programme (Kaplan, Greenfield and Ware, 1989). However, adherence also increases when providers take a more dominant role, suggesting that many patients prefer to be told what to do just as many prefer to be involved in decisions relating to their health care. Although a variety of aspects of the provider–patient interaction contribute to adherence it is worth noting that, in their review, Hall, Roter and Katz (1988) conclude that, overall, provider behaviour is relatively weakly related to adherence.

Patient understanding and recall

Patients frequently misunderstand or forget what they have been told during interactions with their doctor or other health care provider. Indeed, even within the context of seemingly straightforward information – that is, whether a further appointment was either possibly needed or judged to be unnecessary – one study reported little agreement between doctors and patients about what had actually been recommended (Armstrong et al., 1990). Given that up to 50 per cent of doctors' advice and statements are forgotten almost immediately (Ley, 1979), it is perhaps not surprising that instructions relating to the timing of, or rationale for, medication is also frequently not recalled. Forgetfulness, either about the correct way to take the medication, or when to take it, can be a particular problem for the elderly (Leirer et al., 1991). In one study of people over sixty five, Kiernan and Isaacs (1981) found that incorrect recall of dosage increased from 6 per cent for one tablet a day to 75 per cent for three tablets a day. Similarly, forgetting to take the medication at all increased with the number of different prescriptions the patient needed. There is also some evidence to suggest that impaired cognitive functioning is predictive of poor adherence, although there is also contradictory evidence for this (Leirer et al., 1991).

The relationship between understanding, memory, recall and adherence has been investigated in a number of studies. Although there seems to be a relationship between understanding and adherence (Ley, 1983), adherence is not necessarily enhanced by increased recall. This is highlighted by results from a study by Kravitz and colleagues (1993). While the majority of patients with a chronic medical condition recalled information about medication (more that 90 per cent), fewer patients recalled being told about dietary restrictions or the need for exercise. Yet, even amongst those who recalled the information, adherence varied between 90 per cent adhering to medication advice and only 20 per cent adhering to advice to exercise. Thus, adherence is affected by the regimen to be adhered to rather than patients' recall of information about it.

Past behaviour

As discussed previously, numerous studies suggest that past behaviour is the best predictor of future action. Similar findings have been reported with regard to adherence. Thus, Sherbourne et al. (1992) found that, regardless of disease condition or type of adherence outcome, the strongest predictor of adherence was whether or not the patient had adhered in the past. In their longitudinal investigation of adherence, one of the best predictors of adherence at two years was initial baseline adherence (DiMatteo et al., 1993).

Social support

A number of studies suggest that perceived availability and quality of social support are important correlates of adherence to treatment. Thus, the presence of social support has been found to predict adherence for patients with diabetes (Sherbourne et al., 1992), while, conversely, poor social support and psychological stress are associated with poor self-management (Goodall and Halford, 1991). Social support has also been found to be predictive of adherence with antihypertensive medication regimens (Stanton, 1987). In addition, living with a spouse or relative has been found to be related to better adherence in patients across a broad age spectrum (Lorenc and Branthwaite, 1993).

Several studies also provide evidence which suggests that a family environment characterised by higher levels of perceived cohesion and expressiveness and lower levels of conflict is associated with greater adherence to health care advice. Thus, while adherence in children with insulin-dependent diabetes has been shown in both cross-sectional and prospective studies to be related to various aspects of family functioning (e.g. Hanson, Henggeler and Burghen, 1987; Hauser et al., 1990; Jacobson et al., 1987), increased family conflict is the one aspect of family relations most consistently linked to poor adherence (Miller-Johnson et al., 1994). In relation to hemodialysis patients, low conflict, high cohesion and expressiveness among family members has been found to be associated with more positive psychological adjustment and more favourable adherence to fluid intake restrictions (Christensen et al., 1989, 1992). There is also evidence from some studies that the beneficial effect of support is more pronounced for patients with a greater degree of illness-related physical impairment (Christensen et al., 1989; Littlefield et al., 1990) although this has not been found in other studies (Christensen et al., 1992).

Patient beliefs and expectations

A number of studies suggest that patients hold complex beliefs about medication and that these might influence adherence (Britten, 1994; Conrad, 1985). A negative view of medication is not uncommon. For example, 'natural' remedies are seen as being safer than 'unnatural' medicines, the dangerous aspect of medication being linked to their chemical origin (Conrad, 1985). The need to take medication in the context of chronic illness may also be perceived as a 'threat to self reliance' (Conrad, 1985). More recently

Horn and Weinman (see Horn, 1997) have examined the extent to which beliefs about medicines in general can be differentiated from beliefs about specific medicines prescribed for their illness. Their ongoing research suggests that it is specific beliefs which influence medication adherence.

The health belief model has also provided a framework for research in relation to adherence. Patients' beliefs about susceptibility to a disease or illness, severity of the illness, belief in the efficacy of treatment, barriers and costs related to treatment and cues to action have all been shown to influence the extent to which patients will or will not adhere to treatment (Christensen-Szlanski and Northcraft, 1985; O'Brien, Petrie and Raeburn, 1992). A tendency to perceive one's health as poor has also been shown to be related to poor adherence (Sherbourne et al., 1992).

The most frequently investigated health belief model variable relates to perceived costs and barriers. Kaplan and Simon (1990) have argued that patients will comply with treatment when they perceive a net health benefit from doing so. If both the potential treatment and emotional costs are high then non-adherence is more likely to occur (Turk, Salovey and Litt, 1985). For example, a significant relationship has been found between perceived barriers to adherence and compliance in adolescents with diabetes (Glasgow, McCaul and Schafer, 1986). People are less likely to adhere when the consequences of adherence, for example current side effects, outweigh the expected benefits, for example long-term health gain (Haynes, Taylor and Sackett, 1979; Ley, 1988; Meichenbaum and Turk, 1987). It is somewhat ironic that in many instances adherence can increase the probability of side effects (Kaplan and Simon, 1990).

In the case of most chronic illnesses a delay of the inevitable fatal outcome or an amelioration of symptoms is the best which can be expected. In such instances the small benefits of adherence may not justify the inconvenience and discomfort. There may thus be instances when 'non-adherence is the most logical, rational response to professional instruction' (Turk and Meichenbaum, 1991, p. 258). This is illustrated by a study of paediatric asthma and non-adherence (Deaton, 1985) which investigated reasons for adherence and non-adherence. When parents took a decision not to adhere to prescribed medication based upon their knowledge of their child's disease, seasonal variability in asthma symptoms, concern about side effects and limited utility of the medication, this was related to better asthma control than when they decided to adhere passively to the medical regime. Thus, patients carry out their own cost–benefit analysis for each treatment they are offered (Kaplan, 1991). They weigh up the expected benefits (usually symptom relief) against the severity of their symptoms and the perceived risks of treatment (dependence, side effects, time and effort involved) according to their lay beliefs and information at their disposal. As a result, some people actually choose not to comply (Donovan and Blake, 1992).

A number of studies have examined the capacity of the health belief model to predict adherence to a medical regimen on the part of those suffering from such chronic illnesses as diabetes or end-stage renal disease. In relation to diabetes, Brownlee-Duffeck et al., (1987) used a thirty five item questionnaire administered to fifty four older adolescent and younger adult outpatients with insulin dependent diabetes mellitus to measure perceived severity, perceived susceptibility, perceived benefits, perceived barriers and perceived cues. Health belief model variables accounted for 52 per cent of the variance in self-reported adherence. In a more recent study Bond, Aiken and Somerville (1992) extended Brownlee-

Duffeck *et al.*'s study to younger adolescents with diabetes and reported that health belief model components predicted 25 per cent of variance on questionnaire measures of compliance and only 9 per cent and 13 per cent of the variance in interview-based measures of injection and eating and glucose testing frequency. Of further interest in this study, cues, measured by questions such as 'if you experienced cold sweats would you be likely to seek help?', were most closely associated with adherence. However, contrary to health belief model predictions, although high threat (high perceived susceptibility and severity) was related to adherence with low perceived benefits–costs, with high benefits–costs perceived threat was negatively related to adherence. Threat in the case of chronic disease is ever present, and high threat may reduce the impact of perceived benefits of the recommended medical regimen (Bond, Aiken and Sommerville, 1992). Thus, while health belief model variables may be valuable in identifying those who have already adhered, it has disappointing prospective value (O'Brien, Petrie and Raeburn, 1992).

In relation to fluid compliance in end-stage renal disease Schneider *et al.* (1991) found that cognitions mediated past and future adherence through the attribution of success, effort and self-efficacy. In a further study of end-stage renal disease patients, Christensen *et al.* (1990) found that dietary adherence was better when mode of treatment (home versus in-centre dialysis) was consistent with their preferred level of behavioural involvement in health care. That is, home self-care dialysis patients with a preference for behavioural involvement and in-centre patients with a low preference for involvement showed better adherence to dietary restriction.

In studying diabetes control in adolescents in a special summer camp for diabetics, an inverse 'U' relationship was found between knowledge and adherence (Hamburg and Inoff, 1982). Adolescents who knew very little about their regimens and illness were found to be poor adherers, those whose knowledge was adequate to understand the nature of their regimens and how to administer them properly, adhered best, while those whose knowledge extended beyond their regimens into life-long consequences, outcomes and prognosis actually exhibited the lowest adherence. When faced with the complete reality of one's condition the person may feel too discouraged, frightened or depressed about the prospect of life-long adherence to a complex regimen.

A number of psychosocial factors have also been found to influence adherence with diet in dialysis patients. For example, both Poll and Kaplan De-Nour (1980) and Brown and Fitzpatrick (1988) report that patients with an internal locus of control tended to be more accepting of their disability which in turn was associated with dietary control.

In sum, adherence to health care advice is inevitably influenced in a complex manner by multiple factors. As Donovan and Blake (1992) note, patients are not:

> 'blank sheets' when they arrive at clinics. They have many beliefs and theories which suggest courses of action, and these are moderated by information from others, particularly family members, medical staff and the media. (p. 512)

In order to understand non-adherence it is necessary to take into account patients' needs, expectations, perceptions and beliefs about health and illness, as well as their decision-making abilities. In this context even the term adherence, while more appropriate than the term compliance, still conveys an impression of a correct professional view and a incorrect lay view and hence undervalues the patient's view of health and illness. This also needs to be borne in mind in any discussion of attempts to improve adherence.

Improving adherence

As recently as 1982 Epstein and Cluss noted that:

> the overwhelming majority of clinical-compliance research is atheoretical, with the major goal being the technological solving of specific compliance problems. Few individual studies have had a psychological rationale for the development of their treatments. (p. 967)

Reviews of the literature suggest a number of factors that are likely to be effective in enhancing adherence in a range of settings (see box 6.4).

Box 6.4 Strategies for improving adherence

Memory aids – charts, diary records, telephoned or written reminders.

Improving provider–patient interaction.

Involving family or friends in the treatment regimen.

Patient education.

Behavioural interventions:
  Self-monitoring
  Behavioural contracting
  Reinforcement
  Goal-setting

(See Camaron and Best, 1987; Carmody, Matorazzo and Istvan, 1987; Haynes, McKibbon and Kanaki, 1996; Haynes, Wang and de Mota Gomes, 1987.)

A number of models for adherence research can be identified from the literature (Horn and Weinman, 1998; Leventhal and Cameron, 1987), including social cognition models and Leventhal's self-regulatory model (Leventhal, Meyer and Nerenz, 1980). A number of specific intervention strategies for longer-term medication and lifestyle change have been derived from these, particularly within the last decade. Strategies derived from the health belief model emphasise cognitive tactics to produce attitude and behaviour change through persuasive communication.

With particular regard to chronic illness, specific interventions used in isolation have been found to have limited efficacy in enhancing adherence. In such instances treatment combinations including self-monitoring, contingency contracting, enhancing social support, rewards and reinforcement for adherence and supervised self-management tend to be more effective. However, there is evidence that for medication adherence at least, patients may not agree to participate in time-consuming and complex psychological interventions and, of those that do, many will drop out of the programme (Haynes, Wang and de Mota Gomes, 1987). Hence, even interventions which both have a clear psychological rationale and are successful in improving adherence may only do so for a restricted number of patients. In a recent systematic review of the literature Haynes, McKibbon and Kanani (1996) comment that the majority of interventions are limited in scope and that controlled studies suggest they are not particularly effective in spite of the amount of effort and resources invested.

Memory aids

Memory aids include charts or diary records or, more recently, computer generated telephone reminders (Leirer *et al.*, 1991). Letter prompts have also been used as a method of increasing adherence to scheduled appointments (Gates and Colborn, 1976). With short-term medication treatments the provision of special instructions emphasising the need to take the medication, or the provision of tablet diary cards, have been found to be effective in enhancing adherence as has the provision of medication in less frequent doses (Haynes, Wang and de Mota Gomes, 1987).

Effective communication

Appropriate information conveyed in an empathic and sympathetic manner can serve to enhance adherence. As noted earlier, a number of studies have found that patient involvement in their health care relates to increased patient satisfaction and enhanced adherence (Hall, Roter and Katz, 1988; Ley, 1988). In this regard research suggests that training patients to gain a sense of control during a medical consultation results in higher levels of patient satisfaction, participation, information recall and adherence as well as improved health outcome (Greenfield, Kaplan and Ware, 1985; Kaplan, Greenfield and Ware, 1989; Thompson, Nanni and Schwankovsky, 1990). Donovan and Blake (1992) argue that the key to improving adherence is:

> the development of active, co-operative relationships between patients and doctors. For this to be successful doctors need to recognise patients' decision making abilities ... patients will need to make more explicit their needs and expectations. (p. 512)

Social support

A number of studies suggest that social support from friends or family as well as interpersonal support from health care professionals is effective in enhancing adherence in a variety of contexts. Patients are influenced by the approval or disapproval of others such as close friends or relations as well as by the social and cultural group to which they belong. Thus, in the case of chronic illnesses such as diabetes and hypertension, where there is a need to adhere to dietary regimens, research suggests that the patient's family may play a crucial role in supporting adherence (Edelstein and Linn, 1985; Levy, 1983), with broader social support also of importance. In one intervention study of medication adherence in a group of hypertensive patients, the patients were assigned to permutations and combinations of three tactics, involving either counselling by a health educator or group discussion or home visits designed to engender social support. Patients assigned to treatments involving encouragement or social support were more likely to have survived at five-year follow up (Morisky, 1983).

Patient education

Patient education programmes have played a particularly important role in relation to diabetes management. The underlying assumption of such programmes has been that people with diabetes do not manage their condition effectively because they lack the necessary knowledge. Although a range of such education studies report improvements in knowledge about diabetes, this does not necessarily translate into better long-term glycaemic control or to decreased hospitalisation (Goodall and Halford, 1991; Shillitoe, 1988). A small number of studies have provided skills training and feedback in addition to basic information. For example, McCulloch *et al.* (1983) required patients to make choices from a menu, recognising and selecting appropriate quantities of permitted food from those available, receiving immediate appropriate feedback from a dietician. This intervention was compared with education or information provision alone. After seven days, self-report food records showed improved dietary management for the feedback group in relation to the two comparison groups.

Behavioural interventions

A number of studies have evaluated behavioural interventions in relation to health behaviour change programmes, including weight loss, smoking cessation and exercise, and in relation to chronic illness: for example, to improve diabetes management in children, adolescents and adults and to improve fluid restriction and diet in dialysis patients. Issues relating to exercise and diet have been alluded to in an earlier chapter; the following will be restricted to a brief comment on behavioural interventions relating to diabetes and end-stage renal disease.

Management of diabetes

The treatment goal for diabetes is to keep blood sugar at normal levels. This is accomplished through insulin injections, weight control, exercise, dietary control, such as reduced sugar and carbohydrate intake, and stress management. The regime is made more complex by the need to modify each of these factors over time, depending upon the level of activity of the patients and their self-monitored blood glucose level. Inevitably, such a self-regulation programme, involving voluntary restriction of diet, engaging in exercise and the accurate monitoring of blood-glucose levels, is no easy matter. Indeed, patients often fail to monitor their blood glucose level adequately (Wysocki, Green and Huxtable, 1989), relying upon what it 'feels like' (Hampson, Glasgow and Toobert, 1990). In addition, diet and exercise are difficult aspects of diabetic treatment to manage. In order to improve self-regulation of diabetes a variety of behaviourally based interventions have been applied.

Diabetes management programmes involving adults have primarily been aimed at weight loss, although the focus of some has been upon helping patients engage in appropriate self-injection or effective monitoring of blood sugar levels (Diamond, Massey and Covey, 1989). Results from such studies have not been encouraging, leading one group of researchers (Wing *et al.*, 1986) to suggest that the most effective self-regulation treatment programme might involve a multiple intervention package teaching patients to monitor blood sugar accurately, and use this information as a basis for making changes in behaviour through self-injection, reinforcing themselves for efforts to improve blood sugar control, managing stress, controlling diet and exercising.

Psychological interventions aimed at children and adolescents include systematic goal setting, self-monitoring, behavioural contracting, supervised exercise programmes and skills training. For example, Carney, Schechter and Davis (1983) evaluated a token reinforcement programme where points were given for appropriately and accurately testing glucose levels. In addition, parental praise was contingent upon the test being performed without prompting within ten minutes of the appropriate time. Although improved self-management and glycaemic control were achieved, the small sample (three children) and limited follow up (four months) limit conclusions. Unfortunately these are common criticisms of many studies in this area.

Of particular relevance to diabetic adolescents is the part played by peer pressure in causing deviation from management regimes. This has led some to evaluate social skills training to promote assertive resistance to such pressure, although results have not necessarily been positive. For example, Gross et al. (1983) found an improved level of social skills in the nine to twelve year old children who participated in their study, but no improvements in glycaemic control.

Management of end-stage renal disease

Patients with end-stage renal disease must limit their intake of fluid and other elements of their diet such as protein, potassium and phosphorous. The few studies which have evaluated behavioural interventions for increasing adherence in dialysis patients have generally produced favourable results. For example, Keane, Prue and Collins (1981) suggest improved adherence as a result of positive reinforcement. In a further study Hegel et al. (1992) compared a behavioural intervention, consisting of positive reinforcement, shaping and self-monitoring, with a counselling intervention, designed to modify health beliefs as methods of improving adherence to fluid restrictions in eight male hemodialysis patients. While both interventions produced strong and immediate effects the behavioural intervention was superior in producing and maintaining optimal adherence levels.

In sum, interventions to enhance adherence have been directed at behaviours ranging from medication intake to lifestyle change. With regard to the former, research has tended to be atheoretical, aimed at solving a specific 'problem'. With regard to longer-term medication and lifestyle change, research has been guided by a number of theories from which specific intervention strategies have been derived. With complex treatment regimens, such as for diabetes, organised programmes of self-regulation seem to be most effective in enhancing adherence (Glasgow et al., 1989). Common to many successful adherence enhancement programmes is the encouragement of active patient participation in their own health care.

Summary

Patient non-adherence involves the patient not carrying out instructions or treatment recommendations as the health care practitioner intended. Adherence, which implies a degree of co-operation between patient and health care provider on a mutually acceptable course of action, is now more widely used than the term compliance, which tends to imply an obedient patient following instructions from an omnipotent practitioner. Nevertheless, the term adherence itself is value laden, resting as it does upon the assumption that both provider and patient share a common set of assumptions about symptoms and illness and hence that the former will naturally attempt to adhere to the latter's instructions. Given that lay and practitioner beliefs do not necessarily coincide it is perhaps not surprising that non-adherence is widespread. Rates of non-adherence vary from a low of 15 per cent for short-term regimens in relation to acute illness to a high of 93 per cent for longer-term, complex regimens involving lifestyle change. Although a number of authors have highlighted the fact that failure to adhere to instructions or to a treatment regime can have dire consequences, others have pointed out that patients who adhere to the treatment may fail to gain the desired health outcome, while non-adherent patients may improve clinically.

Numerous studies have sought to establish factors predictive of non-adherence, initially searching for identifying characteristics of the patient, the regimen, disease or provider. While there is little evidence of a relationship between adherence and patient characteristics, a number of studies suggest that various aspects of the treatment regimen, such as its complexity or side effects, as well as the quality of the patient–provider interaction are of potential relevance to adherence. A number of studies also suggest that perceived availability and quality of social support are important correlates of adherence to treatment. More recently the utility of both social cognition models and self-regulation theory in predicting adherence has been evaluated. The most important component seems to relate to the costs and benefits; patients weigh up the expected benefits against the perceived costs according to their lay beliefs and information at their disposal and, as a result, choose whether to adhere or not to adhere to advice. As Leventhal and Cameron (1987) point out, it is important to recognise the:

> separate contributions of automatic (habitual) and deliberate (reasoned) determinants of compliance; and the possibility of taking into account the uniqueness of individual understanding of illness and individual patterns of coping with illness. (p. 117)

Individuals may make quite rational decisions not to adhere to advice as a function of their needs, expectations, perceptions and beliefs about health and illness. Until recently such factors have often been ignored in research both in relation to factors predictive of adherence as well as in studies evaluating interventions designed to enhance adherence. Interventions have been directed at a broad spectrum of behaviours ranging from medication intake to lifestyle change. The former have tended to adopt a practical, problem-solving approach focusing upon memory aids or aspects of the relationship between patients and doctors. With regard to lifestyle change, specific intervention strategies have been derived from a number of theories. The general consensus from research is that patients benefit greatly from taking an active role in their own health care (Kaplan, 1991).

FURTHER READING

J. L. Donovan and D. R. Blake (1992). Patient non-compliance: Deviance or reasoned decision making? *Social Science and Medicine*, **34**, 507–513.

D. H. Meichenbaum and D. C. Turk (1987). *Facilitating Treatment Adherence: A practitioner's Guidebook*. New York: Plenum Press.

L. B. Myers and K. Midence (eds) (1998). *Adherence to Treatment in Medical Conditions*. Amsterdam: Harwood Academic Publishers.

M. K. O'Brien, K. Petrie and J. Raeburn (1992). Adherence to medication regimens: Updating a complex medical issue. *Medical Care Review*, **49**, 435–454.

CHAPTER 7

Hospitalisation and medical care

CHAPTER OVERVIEW

This chapter examines issues raised by hospitalisation. Although the hospital is a place of recovery, hospitalisation is inevitably anxiety provoking both because of natural concerns about surgery and treatment and also because of the loss of personal and physical privacy it entails and the restrictions it imposes. Issues relating to recovery from surgery and the impact of hospitalisation upon children are addressed and studies evaluating the various ways in which people can be psychologically prepared for surgery are reviewed. These involve the provision of information, relaxation and behavioural coping techniques, modelling and cognitive approaches. Finally this chapter examines the issue of coping with unpleasant treatments, focusing specifically upon anticipatory nausea and vomiting in relation to cancer chemotherapy.

This chapter covers:

Being hospitalised
Recovery in hospital
The hospitalised child
Preparation for surgery
Coping with unpleasant treatment

Introduction

Hospitals are places to recover from both illness and surgery; hospitals can also provide respite care in allowing the usual caregiver an opportunity to replenish their resources and energy. Yet, anxiety is often a natural response to hospitalisation which is rarely acknowledged or addressed within the research literature. Nichols (1987) refers to hospital-induced distress, which he distinguishes from illness-induced distress, and which he suggests results from a combination of the lack of attention given to the personal, emotional needs of the person and the lack of useful information with which they are provided. This discrepancy between medical provision and patients' emotional needs is illustrated in a study by Johnston (1982). She compared hospital patients' worries with nursing staff estimates of what they assumed would be major concerns of patients. Patients tended to be more concerned with their lives beyond the ward while nursing staff thought that patients would be more concerned about aspects of medical care. Given the role of hospitals in relation to biomedical health care it is perhaps not surprising that medical issues are the central focus of concern for professionals, while patients may have interpersonal or emotional concerns which are often neither recognised nor addressed.

Not only does the hospitalised person have to contend with their illness, they also have to contend with a strange environment in which they are expected to entrust their care to strangers. As Parsons (1951) has argued, the patient is expected to be co-operative, dependent and helpful and to place themselves totally in the care of the medical authorities. Although attempts have been made to humanise certain ward environments, particularly in relation to paediatric care and the care of the dying, the experience of hospitalisation remains a potentially distressing experience.

Surgery and treatment can also be stressful for a number of reasons, including not only the ward routine, but also the physical trauma involved in the procedure itself, peripheral aspects of surgical or anaesthetic procedures, the fear that surgery might reveal other diseases, anxiety about treatment involved and about the course of recovery and a feeling that one is unable to control events (Salmon, 1992; Weinman and Johnston, 1988).

Being hospitalised

Hospitalisation is a step taken in the interests of a person's health, and yet it is often associated with adverse consequences in terms of increased distress and problems of adaptation. (Hall, 1987)

Although the primary purpose of hospitalisation is to care for the person's health and well-being, hospitalisation also involves loss of both personal and physical privacy and the imposition of a number of restrictions. Patients are often in close proximity to each other, while intimate contact between health care provider and patient is unavoidable. In such contexts patients are frequently depersonalised, being treated as conditions rather than people.

Parrott and his colleagues (1989) have documented a number of violations of patients' physical privacy perpetrated by health professionals in the course of their work. These include watching a patient get ready for a physical examination, touching the patient unexpectedly or overhearing intimate conversation or activities. Such instances inevitably create dissatisfaction with care. In contrast, taking care to establish privacy during an examination, sitting down while talking to the patient, using their first name and discussing with them plans for treatment or discharge, are factors associated with patient satisfaction with hospital treatment (Blanchard *et al.*, 1988).

Hospitalisation inevitably restricts normal activity. Some restrictions, such as those imposed by bed rest or traction, may be therapeutically desirable, while others, such as visiting times, may be related more to organisational than therapeutic concerns. Patients react in many different ways to such restrictions. Those who view them as unnecessary, feeling that they are being excessively controlled or that their freedom is being curtailed, may become increasingly angry at their situation. Taylor (1979) notes that patients may sometimes relieve such anger by:

> petty acts of mutiny such as making passes at nurses, drinking in one's room, smoking against medical advice and wandering up and down the halls. (p. 172)

In contrast, other patients may perceive their apparent loss of control as freedom from responsibility, giving them the opportunity to devote their energy to the process of recovery. Both patients and health professionals have expectations about their respective roles which may not necessarily be shared.

Sick role behaviour

As noted previously, Parsons (1951) has argued that patients are expected to take a passive role, one in which they are quiet, pleasant and co-operative. Hence, the 'good' patient has a simple medical problem, is uncomplaining and docile, takes up little time and has an uncomplicated recovery. 'Average' patients are very like good patients except that they have some minor complaint that can be handled routinely. 'Bad' patients are of two types: firstly, those who are seriously ill and complain and, secondly, those who are not seriously ill but complain anyway (Taylor, 1979). The 'good' patient role, rather than resulting from a calm acceptance of available care, may be adopted as a result of anxiety. Thus, Tagliacozzo and Mauksch (1972) note that patients frequently feel unable to express their concerns for fear that some necessary service may be withheld from them; hence they remain quiet and uncomplaining while not necessarily being satisfied with the care received. Interestingly, Karmel (1972) reports higher morale and fewer instances of depression among a group of patients he labelled 'intransigent': that is, those who challenged staff and the hospital routine. It is clearly important for health care professionals to seek to understand apparently 'difficult' patient behaviour and to recognise that there may be a discrepancy between their expectations of how patients may react to hospitalisation and actual patient behaviour.

Factors influencing recovery in hospital

There is an extensive literature examining the efficacy of psychological preparation for surgery in reducing post-surgical distress. This is often measured not only in terms of anxiety, medication, pain, comfort and well-being but also in relation to length of hospital stay. There is evidence that, subsequent to surgery, support from family, friends, medical personnel and even from other patients facilitates hospital recovery. For example, Kulik and Mahler (1989) found that frequent visits from spouses predicted faster recovery, assessed by amount of analgesic medication and length of post-operative stay, subsequent to cardiac surgery. However, there were exceptions to this general finding. Partly due to their own distress occasioned by their partner's surgery, many spouses were unable to provide adequate support.

Support from medical personnel can also be important. Thus Schulze and his colleagues (1988) report that medical in-patients' perceptions of their doctor's supportiveness was associated with lower levels of depression. In a further study, Levy *et al.* (1990), in an assessment of breast cancer patients two weeks after surgery, found that greater perceived emotional support from spouse and doctor, in addition to patients' use of social support as a coping strategy, was related to natural killer cell activity which was used as a measure of immune function.

In line with the social support literature in general, adequate and appropriate social support can have a beneficial effect both upon the process of recovery from surgery and in response to treatment. Conversely, part of the stress occasioned by hospitalisation is that it inevitably moves the person from a familiar and supportive environment. This is a particular concern in the context of child health.

The hospitalised child

A large body of research has been directed towards the question of the impact of hospitalisation on children and conversely programmes aimed at preparing children for hospitalisation. The major thrust of the latter has been to help acutely ill children cope with painful medical procedures. More recently, attention has been directed towards questions of paediatric ward design, staff training and psychological consultation (Salmon, 1992). Although there have been many improvements in hospital care for children (see box 7.1), being admitted to hospital remains a potentially stressful experience.

Box 7.1 Improvements in hospital care for children

Day surgery or outpatient treatment when feasible.

Preparation for hospitalisation – information leaflets, audio or video presentation or prior visits and familiarisation with hospital equipment.

Provision of education facilities in an environment distinct from the hospital.

Play as a recreation, as an education and as therapy.

Unrestricted parental visits; parents accommodated overnight.

Nursing staff supporting and educating parents to care for their child in hospital.

Case assignment to reduce the number of nursing staff dealing with a particular child.

For children, hospitalisation means not just a strange environment with multiple care-givers, but also separation from family and home. The latter is a major concern for children under the age of five, while for older children and adolescents, concerns are more likely to focus upon enforced dependence, and loss of bodily control or competence (Brunnquell and Kohen, 1991). There is some evidence that, when interviewed, girls report more anxiety then boys about the experience of hospitalisation, although there are no gender differences in actual behaviour (Saylor et al., 1987).

Early research indicated that children displayed negative emotional and behavioural reactions both during and after hospitalisation (Prugh and Eckhardt, 1980); indeed, most studies indicate that negative behaviour increases for about a two week period after discharge from hospital, regardless of age or medical condition (Thompson and Vernon, 1993). However, few studies have demonstrated a direct relationship between children's anxiety to a hospital stressor and later behaviour changes, and recent work suggests that very few children actually develop such problems (Brophy and Erickson, 1990; Eiser and Eiser, 1990). Thus Eiser and Eiser report little difference between children with and without experience of hospitalisation in terms of subsequent illness behaviour or social and personal consequences. These authors suggest that, as a result of improvements in paediatric care, it is no longer inevitable that hospitalisation will be associated with long-term disadvantage for the majority of children. However, in this study, no account was taken of length of hospitalisation, with the majority of children who had been in hospital having been there for less than one week.

Although the very experience of hospitalisation can be distressing, the impact may well vary according to whether the admission is for an extended period due to serious injury or chronic disease, whether it is for a brief period for minor surgery or whether it is for repeated outpatient attendance for investigation and monitoring. However, one recent study suggests that chronically ill and acutely ill/injured children describe similar stressors associated with hospitalisation, focusing particularly upon lack of privacy and disrupted sleep (Spirito, Stark and Tyc, 1994).

In the case of both hospitalisation and surgery, studies have examined the extent to which distress experienced by children can be modified. For example, research has evaluated psychological preparation of children for hospitalisation and operative procedures with information leaflets, films about hospitalisation or prior visits to enable familiarisation with the hospital environment (Stenbak, 1982). Positive results for each technique have generally been obtained. Other studies suggest that distress can be reduced by reducing the length of stay in hospital or by allowing parents to stay in hospital with their child (Taylor and O'Connor, 1989). The general thrust of psychological research, however, has been towards the question of coping with painful and/or stressful medical procedures. This is reviewed in the following sections in relation to adults as well as children.

Preparation for surgery

The prospect of undergoing an unpleasant medical procedure may be anxiety provoking for a number of reasons: patients might be concerned about the pain and discomfort they expect to experience; they may be unfamiliar with the procedure; and they may have concerns about the diagnosis and prognosis. Janis (1958) was one of the first to examine systematically the link between preoperative anxiety and post-surgical adjustment, suggesting a curvilinear relationship. He argued that patients with a moderate amount of preoperative anxiety would show best adjustment, whereas patients with low or high presurgical anxiety, or fear, would show the poorest adjustment. He argued that moderate levels of preoperative fear motivated the patients to do the necessary 'work of worry'. Rather than finding a curvilinear relationship subsequent research using broader samples and more varied outcome measures has tended to find a small but significant linear relationship between anticipatory fear and subsequent recovery, with high fear patients showing the least favourable outcome (Sime, 1976). The basic focus of this research was that anxiety was a reflection of the trauma of surgery. In support of this contention a number of studies suggest that anxiety increases immediately prior to surgery and declines rapidly following surgery (e.g. Salmon, Evans and Humphrey, 1986). However, with more traumatic forms of surgery, anxiety may reach its maximum post-operatively and remain elevated until after discharge from hospital (Vogele and Steptoe, 1986).

Within the past three decades there has been an accumulating research literature concerning psychological techniques designed to prepare patients, both adults and children, for invasive surgical procedures. Numerous reviews of this work have appeared within the past decade (e.g. Contrada, Leventhal and Anderson, 1994; Edelmann, 1992; Johnston and Vogele, 1993; Ludwick-Rosenthal and Neufeld, 1988; Saile, Burgmeier and Schmidt, 1988; Salmon, 1992; Schultheis, Peterson and Selby, 1987; Weinman and Johnston, 1988; Whelan and Kirkby, 1998). Intervention studies have employed a range of techniques including informative, psychotherapeutic, modelling, behavioural, cognitive-behavioural and/or hypnotic procedures, the aim of which is to reduce one of more of the following: preoperative anxiety, complications during surgery, postoperative distress and recovery time. In general this research suggests that these techniques can be effective, although variations in sample characteristics and outcome measures mitigate against uncritical generalisations of results.

A central feature of current theorising relating to interventions designed to reduce psychological distress involves perceptions of control. Providing coping techniques via behavioural methods, such as relaxation training or breathing exercises, or via cognitive strategies, such as calming self-talk or distraction, could serve to generate perceptions of control. Information provision could operate in a similar manner by enabling the person to generate their own ways of controlling events, although this was not the initial rationale for providing patients with information.

Research in this area is not without its difficulties. One issue relates to which measures are most appropriate as indices of outcome. For example, length of postoperative recovery and amount of analgesic medication, although widely used measures, may reflect the patient's readiness to complain, medical personnel's perception of the patient, or ward or hospital policy, rather than providing a true reflection of the patient's psychological state. In addition, the various indices of outcome used often show very little relationship to each other (Salmon, 1992).

Information provision

The notion that information will reduce distress was based upon Janis's (1958) conceptualisation that preparatory communication results in a moderate level of anticipatory fear, which in turn leads to the constructive 'work of worrying'. Too much or too little fear was thought to be detrimental. A number of studies have evaluated the efficacy of procedural information (describing the medical event) and/or sensory information (sensations likely to be felt during and/or after the procedure) either compared with each other or in relation to other preparatory interventions in reducing the stress of surgery.

Procedural or sensory information

In their review of the literature, Anderson and Masur (1983) refer to five studies, while Taylor and Clark (1986) refer to ten studies which have examined the effects of procedural information alone. Taylor and Clark conclude that eight of the ten studies indicate at least some positive impact on some indices of adjustment while only two studies found virtually no effects. However, the effects were in general small and procedural information provision had little effect on many variables examined. Other studies by Johnson and her colleagues (see Johnson, 1984) have compared the relative impact of procedural or sensory information, although the results of such studies tend to be contradictory. This is no doubt due in part to the fact that patient groups differ across studies in terms of both the severity of the complaint and the gender of the sample, but also due to the fact that sample sizes are highly variable. In addition, any attempt to compare sensory and procedural information is clouded by the fact that provision of the former inevitably involves some degree of provision of the latter. A number of studies have thus specifically investigated the combined effects of procedural and sensory information.

Combined procedural and sensory information

The efficacy of sensory plus procedural information has been investigated either in relation to low information or alternative information, or in comparison to alternative interventions. These studies have used a variety of modes of presenting information, including videotape (Anderson, 1987) and audiotape (Wilson, 1981), detailed information booklets (Wallace, 1984) or verbal presentation of information (Langer et al., 1975). In addition, studies have employed a variety of outcome measures, including days to discharge and number of post-operative medications (Andrew, 1970), attitude, mood and ward adjustment (Vernon and Bigelow, 1974), anxiety, self-report, state anxiety, self-statement, adjustment and attitude (Kendall et al., 1979). Some studies have compared treatment groups with control groups receiving routine hospital care (Vernon and Bigelow, 1974) or have assessed an attention placebo control group (Langer et al., 1975).

Given such between-study variations it is perhaps not surprising that different reviews arrive at different conclusions. Thus, some reviews conclude that preoperative information alone can have beneficial effects on outcome (Anderson and Masur, 1983; Taylor and Clarke, 1986) with a combination of procedural and sensory information being most effective (Anderson and Masur, 1983), whilst others suggest that there is only moderate support for the efficacy of information provision (Ludwick-Rosenthal and Neufeld, 1988). In their meta-analytic review of twenty one studies published between 1967 and 1984 Suls and Wan (1989) conclude that sensory information, but not procedural information, has significant benefits over no instruction, but that combined sensory-procedural information preparation yields the strongest and most consistent benefits in terms of reduced negative affect, pain reports and other-rated distress. Only studies which specifically compared sensory, procedural, combined sensory/procedural and/or no instruction were included in their comparison, with studies providing information in conjunction with other techniques or multicomponent packages excluded.

Individual differences and information provision

A number of studies suggest that individual difference variables, in particular coping style, predict response to information provision (see box 7.2).

Box 7.2 Individual differences in response to information provision

A number of studies have evaluated the efficacy of information provision in reducing operative distress in relation to individual differences in coping style, particularly information seekers compared with avoiders.

Miller and Mangan (1983) divided gynaecological patients at risk from cervical cancer and about to undergo a diagnostic procedure (colposcopy) into information-seekers (monitors) and information avoiders (blunters). Half of each group were provided with voluminous information (a twenty minute visual and verbal presentation about both procedural and sensory details), the other half were provided with low-level information. Overall, low-information patients expressed less subjective tension/anxiety than high-information patients, and blunters showed less subjective and behavioural anxiety than monitors. In addition, blunters showed less physiological arousal with low information and monitors less physiological arousal with high information.

Martelli *et al.* (1987) provided prosthetic oral surgery patients, classified into high- or low-information preference groups, with either a problem-focused, emotion-focused or mixed-focused stress management intervention. The problem-focused intervention was largely information-based with instructions to facilitate rational analysis of this information. Better adjustment and satisfaction and lower self-reported pain were obtained when high-information preference subjects were given a problem-focused intervention.

Ludwick-Rosenthal and Neufeld (1993) assigned first-time cardiac catheterisation patients, classified into high- or low-information preference groups, to either a high- or low-information preparation. The high-information group heard an eight minute audiotape providing procedural and sensory information, while the low information group heard a three and a half minute audiotape which provided a general description of the procedure. There was less behavioural anxiety during catheterisation when coping disposition and information provision level were matched.

It seems blunters/avoiders prefer to attempt to cope with threat by not taking direct problem-solving action, hence the absence of information or the provision of general non-threatening information is most effective for this group. In contrast, monitors/sensitisers seek information, and hence information provision is likely to be more effective for this group. Intervention strategies are likely to be maximally effective when individual coping styles are considered and when the intervention and individual styles are congruent.

The general finding is that information is most effective when its provision is congruent with coping style.

Most reviews conclude that preoperative information provision in general provides benefits to individuals undergoing stressful medical procedures, with sensory or combined sensory and procedural information having the most beneficial effects (Suls and Wan, 1989; Taylor and Clarke, 1986). While the most consistent finding is that successful interventions should mesh with and reinforce the patient's own coping style, some studies have not found the expected interaction between individual difference variables and treatment (Ludwick-Rosenthal and Neufeld, 1988). Indeed, the latter authors sound a rather more cautionary note than is the case with other reviews, commenting that:

> the overall clinical significance of information provision as a preparatory intervention may be open to question. (p. 331)

This is due to the fact that effectiveness is partly dependent upon the patient acting upon the information received in a way which enhances their perceptions of control. Thus effectiveness is dependent upon the patient rather that the psychological preparation.

Relaxation and behavioural coping preparations

Relaxation has been used both as a behavioural preparatory approach aimed at anxiety reduction and as a coping preparation to provide training in a specific skill or behaviour to facilitate recovery. Deep-breathing or coughing exercises have also been used in conjunction with relaxation. Several studies suggest that relaxation as a preparatory procedure has generally positive results.

In a study which pioneered the use of psychological preparations (Egbert, Barrit and Welch, 1964), the intervention consisted of a combination of information regarding pain during recovery and instruction in a breathing training relaxation technique for use as a coping strategy. Patients who received the intervention required significantly fewer analgesics and had significantly shorter post-operative hospitalisation relative to a control group given only procedural information by an anaesthetist. Given the treatment combination used it is not possible to judge the relative efficacy of the relaxation procedure. However, a number of studies have investigated relaxation procedures as coping strategies either using relaxation alone or in conjunction with breathing or movement exercises or cognitively based strategies.

In one study, Anderson (1987) compared information-only and information plus coping preparations with a contact control group. The coping preparation consisted of a sound/slide show outlining a post-operative exercise regime which showed a therapist guiding a patient through coughing, deep-breathing and leg exercises, and other movements designed to reduce muscle stiffness. Both preparations were equally successful in reducing distress and improving recovery relative to the control group. Similar deep-breathing and relaxation exercises have been shown to reduce anxiety, discomfort and physiological measures of arousal in children undergoing dental surgery (e.g. Siegel and Peterson, 1980).

Individual differences and relaxation effectiveness

As with information provision, there is some evidence that relaxation effectiveness is dependent on the degree of congruence with the individual's preferred coping style.

Wilson (1981) examined the relative effectiveness of relaxation, information provision or a combination of these treatments in relation to routine hospital care for elective surgery patients. The relaxation preparation consisted of a twenty minute taped exercise in autogenic relaxation, which was used once before and as often after surgery as desired. The relaxation and combined groups used less medication and had shorter hospital stays in comparison to the control group. However, this was only the case for low-fear subjects; relaxation was not sufficient for initially high-fear patients. The extent to which patients complied with relaxation instructions is unclear as it is reported that only 45 per cent used the tape at least once a day.

In a further study by Martelli *et al.* (1987), referred to previously, their emotion-focused intervention involved instruction in the use of brief relaxation procedures and cognitive techniques aimed at enhancing their use. In comparison to their problem-focused and mixed-focus stress management procedure the emotion-focused intervention produced the lowest overall adjustment in response to surgery. Better adjustment and satisfaction and lower self-reported pain were obtained when low-information preference subjects were given an emotion-focused intervention.

Although relatively few studies have employed relaxation training without additional procedures, it does seem that relaxation is effective in reducing anxiety and improving adjustment. Whether the observed effects are due solely to relaxation training, or to some other non-specific factors, such as distraction, which provide the patient with additional coping resources is unclear.

Modelling approaches

A large body of research suggests that exposure to a coping model, demonstrating initial fear and stress followed by successful coping, can help to reduce patients', particularly children's, distress (Klingman *et al.*, 1984; Peterson *et al.*, 1984; Pinto and Hollandsworth, 1989) (see box 7.3). In general a coping model is likely to produce more beneficial effects than either a masterful or fearful model (Anderson and Masur, 1983). However, a review by Saile, Burgmeier and Schmidt (1988) suggests that modelling techniques may not be as effective in preparing children for hospitalisation as this research tends to suggest (see the commentary and critique of this review paper by Eiser, 1988).

Bandura (1969) outlines three processes by which modelling might facilitate one's capacity to cope with stressful circumstances. First, the person may acquire new coping strategies through observational learning. Second, strategies already available to the individual may be enhanced by response facilitation. Third, behaviours which promote positive consequences are encouraged while those resulting in negative consequences are discouraged or inhibited. More recently Bandura (1977) has argued that modelling alters people's expectations about their ability to perform certain actions and their expectations regarding the likely consequences of performing such actions: that is, their self-efficacy beliefs.

Studies involving children

In their review of psychological preparation of children for invasive medical procedures Saile, Burgmeier and Schmidt (1988) identify fifty six treatment comparisons involving modelling procedures out of a total of 125 treatments carried out in seventy five studies. In 80 per cent of these cases the model was presented by film, in 9 per cent by dolls and in 2 per cent by live models. In 41 per cent of cases the film showed the model in a setting comparable to that experienced by the children. On average the modelling was presented forty five minutes prior to the medical procedure and lasted for approximately nineteen minutes. In the majority of cases (70 per cent) the intervention was directed towards the child, although in a number of cases (20 per cent) both mother and child were present (see box 7.3).

Box 7.3 Surgical preparation through modelling

A typical participant modelling procedure is described by Faust *et al.* (1991) in their evaluation of behavioural stress exhibited by children during recovery from surgery. In their study children were divided into three groups, one of whom saw a participant modelling slide-tape display alone, another of whom saw the same slide-tape display with their mothers present and a third who were provided with standard procedural information.

Children in the modelling groups were shown a ten minute audio-slide presentation of a five year old girl (the model) undergoing surgery procedures. Both procedural and sensory information were presented. Periodically during the presentation the five year old model displayed appropriate anxiety accompanied by the relevant coping skills. These included breathing deeply and imagining floating calmly on a cloud. The model encouraged the watching children to practise these during the audio-slide presentation. Although not specifically asked to do so, mothers, when present, encouraged their children to participate during the presentation.

Both participant modelling groups exhibited significantly fewer behavioural signs of distress during recovery in comparison to the information provision group.

In summarising the outcome effects for different treatments and methods used to prepare children for surgery Saile, Burgmeier and Schmidt (1988) comment that:

> among the preparation method classified as behaviour therapy, techniques based on the modelling paradigm were below the average of all preparation methods evaluated in this study. (p. 116)

They further note, when commenting upon non-specific effects, that:

> preparations using coping modelling films ... result in only minimal effects when ... non-specific factors are controlled by placebo-attention control groups. (p. 124)

However, as Eiser (1988) points out, Saile, Burgmeier and Schmidt (1988) included all available studies, regardless of methodological adequacy, in their meta-analysis. As a number of authors have noted (e.g. Elkins and Roberts, 1983), many of the early studies evaluating preparation of children for hospitalisation suffer from methodological limitations; including these in a review inevitably limits the conclusions which can then be drawn.

In addition, studies suggest that the effectiveness of modelling is dependent upon a number of factors, such as the degree of initial fear of and experience with the medical procedure and degree of involvement in the modelling intervention. Thus, Elkins and Roberts (1985) found that viewing an audio-visual peer-modelling procedure reduced medical fears for highly fearful non-patient children but produced no change for low-fearful non-patient children. In a further study Klorman *et al.* (1980) found that modelling reduced uncooperative behaviour in inexperienced paediatric dental patients, but had little effect on children with prior restorative dental treatment. Further, modelling has been found to increase arousal and self-reported medical concerns in young, experienced paediatric surgery patients (Faust and Melamed, 1984). It is possible that, for the experienced children, the modelling serves as a reminder of prior aversive experiences, while inexperienced patients may focus more on the coping efforts of the model. In relation to the degree of involvement in the modelling procedure, Klingman *et al.* (1984) found that participant modelling, in which the children were encouraged to practise the techniques as they watched them modelled, was more effective (though not significantly) than merely watching a videotaped model, in reducing disruptive behaviour and physiological arousal during dental treatment.

While a number of studies suggest that modelling procedures are effective in preparing children for hospitalisation, a number of studies suggest less-positive results and highlight the fact that outcome is influenced by a number of moderating variables. As with any procedure it is important to consider the conditions under which they are optimally effective. In addition, many unprepared children appear to undergo surgical procedures with limited subsequent distress, making extensive preparation of limited value in such cases (Beeby and Morgan-Hughs, 1980). The efficient use of preparatory interventions may be achieved by targeting children most at risk of adverse reactions.

Studies involving adults

There have been relatively few studies evaluating modelling as preparation for adults undergoing surgery. In one of the first such studies Shipley *et al.* (1978) examined the effect of viewing an explicit preparation videotape either zero, one or three times for endoscopy patients, classified as repressors or sensitisers. Subjects also received procedural and sensory information independently. The stress of the endoscopy was reduced as a function of the number of viewings of the videotape for sensitisers, while repressors showed an inverted-U-shaped function with one viewing producing the highest heart rate change. Employing a similar procedure, Shipley, Butt and Horwitz (1979) report that when coping style was ignored the intervention had no effect, but when subjects' coping style was taken into account a significant reduction in anxiety was found for the sensitisers. In the absence of an information-only comparison group, it is not possible to say whether these effects are due to exposure to the model rather than the receipt of information.

In a further study of eleven patients referred for hyperbaric oxygen therapy, those assigned to a videotaped coping model intervention were more relaxed and completed significantly more of the prescribed treatment sessions than a standard hospital care comparison group (Allen, Danforth and Drabman, 1989). The small sample size, however, necessitates caution in interpreting the results. Also, as the model specifically described several strategies involving relaxation, cognitive coping statements and imagery, it is not possible to say whether there was one specifically salient component or whether it was the combination of strategies which was effective.

In a more recent study Burish, Snyder and Jenkins (1991) randomly assigned sixty cancer chemotherapy patients to one of four treatments: relaxation training with guided imagery, a general coping package, relaxation plus coping or a routine clinical control treatment. The coping preparation included information booklets and a tour of the department, an opportunity for discussion and a twenty minute videotaped presentation about chemotherapy showing a coping model. The coping preparation group were superior to the relaxation and control patients on a number of outcome measures, including knowledge about their disease and treatment; they were less depressed before all their chemotherapy treatments and had less volatile hostility levels, less disruption in their daily lives in general and less impairment in their work. Again, however, given that the coping preparation was multifaceted it is not possible to discern whether one or more aspects or a combination of them were the effective components. The authors themselves emphasise the provision of clear and accurate information to enhance the patient's understanding and perceived control.

In general then, while modelling procedures seem to be effective, results are not uniformly positive and are influenced by a range of variables. In addition, it is worth bearing in mind that information relating to the medical procedure is likely to be conveyed by any modelling procedure, hence it is not possible to ascertain whether treatment effects are due to modelling or information provision although some studies have attempted to separate these effects. Thus Melamed *et al.* (1978) exposed groups of children to different combinations of modelling and procedural information. Those exposed to the model showed less self-reported fear and less disruptive behaviour than those viewing the demonstration in the absence of a model. This may, however, illustrate the beneficial effects of modelling in enhancing the effects of information provision per se and does not rule out the possibility that the information component inherent in modelling procedures plays a role in reducing distress.

Cognitive approaches

The rationale for cognitive interventions is that the patient's perception and appraisal of the invasive event help to determine the degree of the anxiety and distress they experience. Thus distraction, attention focusing and the use of positive self-statements, as well as multiple strategy packages have been used in an attempt to alter the patient's perception and appraisal of the situation. The efficacy of such techniques as preparation for adults has been evaluated in relation to relaxation (Pickett and Clum, 1982), information provision (Ridgeway and Mathews, 1982) and standard hospital care (Wells, Howard, Nowlin and Vargas, 1986). Cognitive interventions have also been used with varying degrees of success with children (e.g. Siegel and Peterson, 1980; Peterson and Shigetomi, 1981; Dahlquist *et al.*, 1986; Whelan and Kirkby, 1998).

In the Pickett and Clum (1982) study, a group of gallbladder surgery patients trained in cognitive distraction showed significantly reduced anxiety relative to groups receiving relaxation training and relaxation instructions and a no-treatment control. Ridgeway and Mathews (1982) found that a group trained in calming self-talk and distraction tended to show better post-operative adjustment than groups receiving procedural information or routine care. In a study of preparation for elective surgery patients, Wells *et al.* (1986) evaluated a cognitive intervention which consisted of an information phase, a skills acquisition phase (monitoring cognitive cues, deep breathing, relaxation, induction of pleasant images, use of coping and reinforcing self-statements) and an application phase involving rehearsing and applying the procedure. In relation to a standard hospital care group the treated group showed reduced levels of self-reported anxiety and pain, reduced medication use and faster recovery. However, given the small sample size (twelve subjects per group) and the fact that the treatment group received more attention, it is difficult to ascertain the true extent of any treatment effects. Also, it is not possible to say whether any one aspect of the treatment was particularly important or whether the components had an additive impact.

In an evaluation of cognitive interventions with children, Siegel and Peterson (1980) randomly assigned forty two children attending for dental treatment to one of three conditions: self-control coping skills (relaxation, deep and regular breathing, imagery and calming self-talk), sensory information or a no-treatment control. Although both treatments were effective in reducing disruptive behaviour, ratings of anxiety and discomfort and physiological arousal, there were no differences in effectiveness between the two treatment groups. In a study with children scheduled for tonsillectomies Peterson and Shigetomi (1981) compared the efficacy of coping skills provision (relaxation, imagery and self-talk) with information provision, a filmed model or a combination of coping skills and modelling. Although, on the basis of parental reports, both the coping skills groups showed less distress, there were no between group differences on any measures obtained from the children themselves.

In a further report Dahlquist et al. (1986) compared training in coping skills (deep breathing and positive self-talk) with provision of sensory information, combined sensory information and coping skills training, an attention control (discussing a non-medical topic with an adult) and a no-treatment control. In general, children with neutral or positive past medical experience were unaffected by the preparation they received, while children with previous negative medical experience became more distressed as a result of discussing a non-medical topic.

In general then, cognitive-behavioural interventions seem to be effective with adults but less effective with children. However, the cognitive interventions evaluated have differed in nature across studies, making between study comparisons difficult. Multiple component treatments have also been used, consisting of some combination of relaxation, self-talk, breathing and imagery. It is not possible to say whether one component or some combination of treatments is essential.

Methodological issues

It seems then, on the basis of the evidence available from a variety of studies and reviews, that several types of intervention technique, most notably informational, modelling and cognitive-behavioural, are effective to varying degrees in reducing the stress occasioned by hospitalisation. However, as every review makes clear, the numerous variations between studies mean that conclusions drawn must of necessity be treated with caution (see box 7.4).

A further difficulty relates to the inclusion of a suitable control group. Some studies have assigned patients to a routine hospital care group although this fails to control for the effect of attention such patients will receive. In addition, Auerbach (1989) has suggested that an attention placebo condition, rather than being inert, is likely to stimulate emotion-focused coping. He thus agues in favour of studies comparing the relative efficacy of operationally and theoretically distinctive psychological treatments.

A further issue relates to individual variations in response to preparation for surgery. Anxiety, prior experience with the medical procedure and coping style seem to influence

Box 7.4 Studies evaluating preparation for surgery – methodological issues

Differing population groups across studies.

Patients undergoing various medical procedures are often included in the same group.

Within a given category of invasive procedure little attempt is made to control for variations in the severity of the patient's medical condition.

Problems of a suitable 'control' group – studies often use 'routine hospital care' without specifying what this entails.

Preparations of the same 'type' vary greatly between studies.

Various psychological preparations are often used in combination, making it difficult to ascertain the efficacy of any one treatment component.

Process measures are frequently ignored – it is thus not clear whether patients trained in a particular skill actually use it.

A wide variety of outcome measures have been used, making it difficult to compare across studies.

outcome. For example, Boeke *et al.* (1991), in a study of fifty eight cholecystectomy patients, found longer periods of hospitalisation for patients with high state anxiety measured on the third day post-operatively, particularly if the patients were male, had undergone more previous operations and had post-operative complications. In addition, as noted, a number of studies have found an interaction between preparation and coping style, with, in general, information seekers responding more positively to information provision prior to surgery in comparison to avoiders. In general then, although there is evidence that information provision, relaxation, modelling and cognitive-preparatory interventions all have some beneficial effects in reducing distress associated with noxious medical procedures, methodological deficiencies in studies often preclude any firm conclusions from being drawn.

Coping with unpleasant treatment

It is now possible to cure or prolong the life of many patients with life threatening illnesses. However, treatments themselves can be physically and psychologically aversive. For example, side effects of cancer chemotherapy, one of the most common cancer treatments, include loss of appetite, hair loss, tiredness and negative mood. As a result such treatments have received particular attention within the psychological literature. Psychological interventions have been targeted at the specific psychological factors associated with cancer chemotherapy: that is, nausea and vomiting. Other studies have targeted psychological distress – that is, vomiting, anxiety and panic – associated with dialysis treatment of end-stage renal disease. In the latter case relaxation has been shown to be effective in reducing anxiety and panic while, in conjunction with systematic desensitisation and contingency management, relaxation has also been found to be effective in reducing frequency of vomiting behaviours accompanying dialysis (see Long, 1989). The largest body of psychological research in relation to aversive treatments has been directed towards the question of anticipatory nausea and vomiting associated with cancer chemotherapy.

Anticipatory nausea and vomiting

Pharmacologically induced nausea and vomiting are among the most common side effects of chemotherapeutic agents used in the treatment of cancer. With repeated chemotherapy treatments many patients develop nausea and vomiting prior to drug administration: for example, at the sight of the nurse administering the chemotherapy or the smell of the drugs. Such anticipatory nausea and vomiting (ANV) is experienced by between 25 and 30 per cent of patients by the time of their fourth infusion (Morrow and Dobkin, 1988). One explanation for the development of ANV is based upon the classical conditioning paradigm. Thus conditioned stimuli (smells, tastes and sights) occurring in proximity to an unconditioned stimuli (drug infusion) will elicit an unconditioned response (post-infusion nausea and vomiting). This model implies that the number of learning trials (i.e. number of treatment sessions) and the intensity of the unconditioned response (i.e. severity of post-infusion nausea and vomiting) would be the two main predictors for the development of ANV. Thus, in one study, only patients who experienced post-infusion nausea and vomiting developed ANV (Kvale et al., 1991). A number of studies reviewed by Morrow and Dobkin (1988) confirm the suppositions of the conditioning model. In some instances it is the occurrence of post-treatment side effects following initial infusion that is considered a primary causal factor (Morrow, Lindke and Black, 1991).

There are also wide individual variations in the development of ANV. Factors associated with ANV include severity of post-treatment nausea and vomiting and anxiety. For example, retrospective studies suggest that self-reported anxiety is related to the development of ANV (Carey and Burish, 1985). However, prospective studies have shown either no relationship between self-reported anxiety and the development of ANV (Kvale et al., 1991) or that self-reported anxiety only accounts for a very small amount of the variance (Andrykowski, Redd and Hatfield, 1985). Kvale and colleagues note that autonomic reactivity rather than self-reported anxiety was a more accurate marker of ANV susceptibility. Indeed, in reviewing the evidence, Andrykowski (1990) argues that anxiety does not cause ANV but may instead potentiate the conditioned effect. A number of mechanisms by which this process may operate have been suggested by Burish and Cary (1986). One possibility is that anxious people might condition more easily or that highly anxious people may be more vigilant of their environment, thereby becoming more sensitive to the clinical stimuli surrounding chemotherapy, which can then, by classical conditioning, develop into a conditioned stimulus.

Younger patients are also more likely to develop ANV (Morrow, Lindke and Black, 1991; Watson and Marvell, 1992), although the mechanism by which age influences reaction remains unclear. The prevalence of ANV may also be influenced by situational factors: for example, chemotherapy administered in the presence of similarly treated patients tends to increase prevalence (van Komen and Redd, 1985; Cohen *et al.*, 1986). Explanations for this are based upon principles of modelling – that is, the sight of others being sick disinhibits one's own control – although as Watson (1993) points out, sickness in others may also provide cognitive cues causing the person to focus on their own discomfort.

Psychological intervention and ANV

ANV seems to be particularly resistant to medication so that considerable attention has been focused upon psychological interventions (see Black and Morrow, 1991; Carey and Burish, 1988; and Morrow and Dobkin, 1988 for reviews). These include relaxation training (e.g. Burish and Lyles, 1981), systematic desensitisation (Morrow, 1986), relaxation training with guided imagery (e.g. Burish *et al.*, 1987), cognitive/attentional distraction (e.g. Redd *et al.*, 1987) and information provision/modelling (Burish, Snyder and Jenkins, 1991) (see box 7.5).

Box 7.5 Psychological interventions used to treat anticipatory nausea and vomiting

Relaxation – The basic procedure for progressive muscular relaxation is to tense each muscle group in turn, holding the tension on each occasion for a few seconds before releasing it and allowing that muscle and the body generally to relax. The relaxation procedure working round each muscle group in the body takes about twenty minutes.

Systematic desensitisation – The basic principle behind this technique is counter conditioning of an incompatible response (relaxation) to stimuli or events that elicit maladaptive responses (nausea and vomiting). The patient constructs a hierarchy of situations in which they experience increasingly intense anticipatory side effects. When deeply relaxed the patient imagines each of the scenes in their hierarchy – only moving on to the next scene when they are able to report remaining relaxed while imaging the previous one.

Information provision – This might involve written information, video- or audio-taped presentations about chemotherapy or tours of the oncology unit and discussions about the steps involved in a typical clinic visit.

Distraction techniques – A variety of strategies have been used including the use of video games played during chemotherapy sessions.

Cognitive-behaviour therapy – Involves the patient identifying problems and working with the therapist, through homework assignments, to find methods for coping with the problems. The importance of thoughts as directly causal to levels of distress and the link between thoughts and emotions is discussed during therapy.

Relaxation training has proved to be effective in a number of intervention studies. Thus, Burish and Lyles (1981) found that patients taught relaxation immediately prior to chemotherapy, allied with guided mastery used when relaxed and while drugs were administered, showed lower levels of both patient- and nurse-reported distress, in addition to less nausea and anxiety in comparison with a no-relaxation control group. In a further report, Burish et al. (1987) taught one group of patients relaxation and guided mastery prior to their first cycle of chemotherapy. During the fourth and fifth cycles of chemotherapy, when ANV might be expected to occur, the incidence of ANV was significantly lower for the treated group than for the no-treatment control. In another study, Morrow (1986) found that systematic desensitisation was superior to relaxation, counselling or a no-treatment control in reducing ANV. In view of this Morrow suggests that relaxation is a necessary but not sufficient treatment for ANV and that attending to cognitive cues inherent in systematic sensitisation is an important element of treatment. This is illustrated in a number of intervention studies.

Burish, Snyder and Jenkins (1991) found that a coping preparation group, who received information and a videotaped presentation of a coping model, in comparison to a relaxation group and a group of control patients, were less nauseated before chemotherapy treatments and were the only patients who did not show an increase in immediate post-treatment vomiting with successive chemotherapy treatments and reported less vomiting at home during the first day after each chemotherapy. In a study with paediatric chemotherapy patients, Redd et al. (1987) found that video game distraction reduced nausea and vomiting.

More recently, the research group at the Royal Marsden Hospital, London, UK have developed an Adjuvant Psychological Therapy based upon Beck's (1976) cognitive therapy, the aim being to reduce anxiety and engender a fighting spirit and sense of control over the disease and its treatments (Watson, 1993). Patients are encouraged to be more aware of negative patterns of thinking and to explore strategies such as distraction, cognitive rehearsal, self-instruction and cognitive restructuring to deal with problems. Initial findings suggest that the treatment would appear to be effective in the reduction of anxiety (Greer et al., 1992).

There are several possible explanations for how and why psychological interventions are effective (Carey and Burish, 1988; Morrow and Dobkin, 1988). One possibility is that these techniques distract patients sufficiently to divert their attention away from the chemotherapy treatments, such that conditioning no longer occurs. Certainly this may be the case in those studies using relaxation, guided imagery or cognitive distraction where attention is diverted to either pleasant bodily sensations or pleasant images, but would seem less likely to apply in the case of systematic desensitisation which specifically focuses attention on to the aversive stimuli associated with chemotherapy. A second possibility is that relaxation is the effective component. Certainly research suggests that relaxation as a treatment for ANV reduces physiological arousal (Burish et al., 1987) and may also reduce the subjective anxiety component that may serve as a conditioned stimulus for ANV. Relaxation may also decrease muscular contractions in the gastro-intestinal tract, thus having a direct effect of reducing the likelihood of nausea and vomiting. Few studies exist comparing different interventions for ANV; such studies could perhaps clarify the mechanism by which psychological therapies operate.

Summary

The present chapter has examined the issues associated with hospitalisation, the stress of surgery and treatment and the efficacy of psychological interventions in reducing this stress. Although the primary purpose of hospitalisation is to care for the person's health and well-being it is also associated with a number of aversive consequences. As well as loss of privacy and the imposition of restrictions resulting from the need to adhere to ward routine, the hospitalised person may suffer the physical trauma of surgical procedures or distressing treatments. Although there is an extensive literature examining the efficacy of psychological interventions as preparation for surgery and for reducing psychological problems associated with medical treatment, less attention has been paid to the experience of hospitalisation itself.

With regard to preparation for surgery, there is evidence that information provision, relaxation, modelling and cognitive-preparatory procedures all have some beneficial effects in reducing distress associated with noxious medical procedures. Modelling has yielded the widest range of positive effects on a range of indices, particularly with children. However, Saile, Burgmeier and Schmidt (1988) in reviewing the evidence paint a somewhat less positive picture, although this review is not without its critics (Eiser, 1988). Cognitive-behavioural preparations seem to offer promise, but there are fewer evaluative studies of this approach. Most recent studies have used multicomponent packages involving information provision, relaxation and cognitive self-control strategies to some effect, although it is not possible to evaluate the effective ingredients of such programmes.

The many reviews of the research literature relating to psychological preparation for surgery which have appeared within the past decade have all drawn attention to methodological deficiencies which prevent any firm conclusions from being drawn. Problems include the use of idiosyncratic measures, heterogeneous subject populations in terms of medical conditions, frequent failure to include an adequate control group and the lack of process measures to indicate whether the intervention has actually been used by the patients concerned.

Treatments not involving surgical procedures can also be physically and psychologically aversive. In this regard a large body of psychological research has been directed towards the question of anticipatory nausea and vomiting associated with cancer chemotherapy. Such anticipatory nausea and vomiting (ANV) which develops prior to drug administration, for example in response to the smell of the drugs, is experienced by between 25 and 30 per cent of patients by the time of their fourth infusion. ANV seems to be particularly resistant to medication and, as a result, considerable attention has been focused upon psychological interventions. These include relaxation training, systematic desensitisation, relaxation training with guided imagery, cognitive/attentional distraction and information provision/modelling, all of which seem to be effective in reducing ANV. Although there are several explanations for how such interventions operate, the precise mechanism remains to be determined.

FURTHER READING

R. J. Contrada, E. A. Leventhal and J. R. Anderson (1994). Psychological preparation for surgery: Marshalling individual and social resources to optimise self-regulation. *International Review of Health Psychology*, **3**, 219–266.

M. Johnston and C. Vogele (1993). Benefits of psychological preparation for surgery: A meta-analysis. *Annals of Behavioral Medicine*, **15**, 245–256.

P. Salmon (1992). Psychological factors in surgical stress: Implications for management. *Clinical Psychology Review*, **12**, 681–704.

M. Watson and C. Marvell (1992). Anticipatory nausea and vomiting among cancer patients: A review. *Psychology and Health*, **6**, 97–106.

T. A. Whelan and R. J. Kirkby (1998). Advantages for children and their families of psychological preparation for hospitalisation and surgery. *Journal of Family Studies*, **4**, 35–51.

CHAPTER 8

Chronic illness

CHAPTER OVERVIEW

This chapter examines the impact of chronic illness upon psychological
functioning and factors influencing coping and adjustment. Chronic illness can
produce a variety of adverse outcomes including pain and disability, anxiety and
depression. Chronic illness also impacts upon relationships in a number of
different ways. How people adapt to chronic health problems is influenced to a
considerable degree by their evaluation, perception and reaction to their illness;
attributions of causality and perceptions of control are important factors in this
regard as is the availability of social support. Such factors have served to shape
psychological interventions designed to enhance the quality of life of those
suffering a chronic illness.

This chapter covers:

> The impact of chronic illness on psychological functioning
> Social support
> Causal attributions
> Control and adjustment to chronic illness
> Coping with chronic illness
> Psychological interventions

Introduction

Chronic illness refers to any condition which involves some disability, caused by non-reversible pathological change, and which requires training or motivation on the part of the patient to care for themselves. Such conditions can range from the relatively minor, such as partial hearing loss, to the severe and life threatening, such as cancer, coronary heart disease and diabetes. In the Western world chronic health problems have largely replaced infectious diseases as the leading causes of death (Satariano and Syme, 1981).

Chronic illness is increasing, particularly in the Western world, for two main reasons. Firstly, improved treatment means that more people survive, both during the initial critical stages of acute illness or trauma (e.g. stroke, myocardial infarction) and for conditions which previously had an early childhood mortality, and hence have to live with the longer-term consequences of such illness. For example, approximately one in ten children are born with chronic or disabling conditions and, in the Western world, 85 per cent of them survive until at least twenty years of age (Blum, 1992). The most common chronic diseases in childhood are asthma, with a survival rate similar to that of well children, congenital heart disease and chronic kidney disease (Gortmaker, 1985). It has been estimated that as many as 31.5 per cent of adolescents in the United States have one or more chronic conditions (Newacheck, McManus and Fox, 1991). Secondly, also within the Western world, the relative proportion of elderly people is increasing and such a population is more prone to develop chronic illnesses (Coyne and Fiske, 1992).

Chronic illness presents the individual with a range of challenges (see box 8.1). Particular problems can be encountered with progressive illnesses, such as motor neurone

---

Box 8.1 Potential physical and psychosocial impact of chronic illness

Physical effects
  Pain
  Disability
  Physical deterioration
  Disfigurement

Psychosocial effects
  Uncertainty
  Perceived loss of control

  Social problems
  Dependency on others
  Disruption to family and social life

  Emotional problems
  Anxiety
  Depression

  Lowered self-esteem

  Sexual dysfunction

disease, multiple sclerosis or rheumatoid arthritis, where the prognosis is variable, the course of the illness being marked by intermittent periods of disease flare and remission. In one study of patients with rheumatoid arthritis, uncertainty about the course of the disease was the major stressor associated with their illness (Wiener, 1975). Similarly, with regard to multiple sclerosis, Devins and Seland (1987) have noted that the unpredictable course of disabling symptoms and lack of control over symptom course are two of the more stressful aspects of the condition.

Sexual dysfunction as a result of illness is also common: for example, research indicates that such difficulties may be associated with diabetes, hypertension, myocardial infarction and cancer (Anderson, Anderson and deProsse, 1989; Harland and Huws, 1997; Plaud *et al.*, 1996).

There is, however, wide individual variation in both the physical and the psychosocial impact of chronic illness which cannot be explained purely on the basis of medical factors such as the severity, prognosis or stage of the disease. Functioning is affected by a range of non-medical factors, including how the individual appraises and copes with their illness and the social support they receive (Holroyd and Lazarus, 1982; Cohen and Syme, 1985). For example, there is evidence that some people spontaneously generate feelings of control, so improving adjustment. In order to discuss these issues in context, physical and emotional aspects of illness, in addition to the influence of the person's cognitive evaluations and social support resources as factors moderating the impact of chronic illness, will be briefly reviewed.

Given the multifaceted nature of the psychological impact of chronic illness, psychological interventions can be appropriately targeted at a range of issues with the aim of improving the person's quality life. These include cognitive-behavioural interventions for pain management, cognitive-behavioural interventions designed to help people cope with the psychological effects of illness, maximising support or working with families, cognitive-behavioural interventions designed to enhance self-management of illness in addition to psychosexual counselling, or counselling to assist the process of adjustment to disfigurement or disability. These issues will be discussed in the final section of this chapter.

The impact of chronic illness

Chronic illness can produce a variety of adverse outcomes including pain and disability, anxiety and depression. While the latter reactions may be a natural response to physical symptoms they may also be associated with other indirect factors, such as the person's uncertainty about their future. Psychological distress, as with physical symptoms, may impede the person's ability to work or engage in social activities, hence further undermining that person's quality of life.

It is widely recognised that those diagnosed with a chronic illness pass through a series of stages akin to the bereavement process (Shontz, 1975) (see box 8.1). In this regard, anxiety, depression and denial are common reactions to a diagnosis of chronic illness. For example, Derogatis *et al.* (1983) found that the rate of psychological disorder in 215 newly admitted cancer patients was approximately three times that of the general population and twice that of other medical patients, with 85 per cent receiving a diagnosis of depression or anxiety as central symptoms.

Box 8.2 Chronic illness – stages of reaction to diagnosis

Stage 1   *Immediately after diagnosis*
A state of crisis marked by physical, social and psychological disequilibrium which people attempt to cope with by drawing upon a range of coping resources (Moos, 1977; Moos and Schaefer, 1984). Characterised by a state of shock, feeling stunned and bewildered.

Stage 2   *The encounter reaction*
Characterised by a sense of loss, grief, helplessness and despair.

Stage 3   *Retreat phase*
Characterised by denial or retreat.

Stage 4   *Facing up to reality*
Characterised by adjustment and acceptance.

(See Shontz, 1975.)

While denial might be usual, and even beneficial at certain stages of adjustment to chronic illness, it may also impede recovery or treatment. Shontz argues that it is important for a person to face up to the reality of their situation, a process which, he suggests, begins during the retreat phase. Moos and Schaefer (1987) argue that individuals are motivated to re-establish a sense of equilibrium, although this can result in a maladaptive response rather than necessarily healthy adaptation. A further view, advanced by Taylor (1983), is that individuals cope with chronic illness by searching for meaning, mastery and developing self-esteem. Even though such beliefs in one's ability to master the situation, to find meaning in it and to feel positive about oneself may be illusory they nevertheless promote adjustment to illness. It is thus important to identify adaptive and maladaptive reactions and to offer psychological treatment as appropriate.

Physical problems and chronic illness

Physical problems associated with illness include pain, such as chest pain experienced by cardiovascular patients or unpredictable painful episodes in relation to sickle cell disease, loss of breath associated with respiratory disorders, metabolic changes associated with cancer, or physical disability associated with rheumatoid arthritis, multiple sclerosis or spinal cord injury. In the case of rheumatoid arthritis, the combination of pain, stiffness, disability and social restrictions with which it is associated are significant predictors of depression (Anderson *et al.*, 1985). In addition, patients whose physical appearance is affected by illness, such as those who have suffered severe burns or undergone a mastectomy, may face a major crisis concerning their sense of self as a result of their altered appearance.

In addition to the physical problems associated with chronic illness, the medical treatment involved can itself present the patient with innumerable difficulties. Indeed, the medical treatment for disease is often more debilitating that the disease itself. As noted previously, cancer patients receiving chemotherapy often face nausea, vomiting, hair loss and skin discoloration (Burish *et al.*, 1987). Cancer patients receiving radiation therapy have to cope with burning of the skin and gastrointestinal problems (Nail, King and Johnson, 1986).

Anxiety

Anxiety is commonly experienced in relation to chronic illness. Particular points of anxiety include waiting for test results, the diagnosis, subsequent lifestyle alterations and fear of recurrence. Anxiety at various points during the rehabilitation phase is also commonly experienced. For example, serial measurements of anxiety in coronary patients admitted to hospital suggest that anxiety is highest on admission to the coronary care unit and immediately after transfer to the ward. It then falls rapidly over the following weeks, rising just prior to discharge and falling to the lowest level at four months post-discharge, although returning to work is associated with a further increase in anxiety (Thompson *et al.*, 1987). Subsequently, every episode of angina pectoris, which may occur for many months or even years post-discharge, is likely to provoke further anxiety for both patients and their families (Langosch, 1984). Uncertainty associated with the initial outcome from illness and subsequent change in life almost inevitably prompts an increase in anxiety; similar increases in anxiety are associated with medical tests or treatment.

While anxiety in such circumstances is not unusual, sustained high levels of anxiety can be problematic because they interfere with good adjustment. For example, research suggests that highly anxious patients cope poorly with radiotherapy for cancer (Graydon, 1988) and show poorer recovery from myocardial infarction, including a reduced subsequent return to work (Maeland and Havik, 1987).

Depression

Depression is also a common reaction to chronic illness, with as many as one-third of such inpatients reporting at least moderate symptoms of depression (Rodin, Craven and Littlefield, 1991; Rodin and Voshart, 1986). However, depression associated with chronic illness seems to be marked by low positive affect rather than the negative cognitions typical of psychiatric patients (Clark, Cook and Snow, 1998).

Several research studies have documented the point of diagnosis as being particularly distressing (e.g. Manuel *et al.*, 1987) both for patients and their relatives. For example, depression has been reported amongst parents at the diagnosis of insulin dependent diabetes mellitus in their children (Kovacs *et al.*, 1990).

The extent of depression in both patients and family members during the course of their relative's illness is determined in part by the extent of depression at the time of diagnosis. Thus, in two studies of patients with rheumatoid arthritis, the best predictor of subsequent depression, assessed either six or twenty two months after admission, was level of depression at the time of admission (Brown, Nicassio and Wallston, 1989; Skevington, 1993). Degree of distress and depression exhibited by mothers shortly after their children were diagnosed with insulin dependent diabetes mellitus was a strong predictor of their later symptomatology (Kovacs *et al.*, 1990).

Depression is not only evident at diagnosis but is also a reaction to the ongoing stress association with the illness itself. Increased depression has been found to be associated with chronic respiratory disease (Williams, 1989), MS (Joffe *et al.*, 1987; Minden, Oran and Reich, 1987; Schubert and Folliart, 1993), end-stage renal disease (Smith, Hong and Robson, 1985) and coronary artery disease (Carney *et al.*, 1987). Other studies suggest that increased depression is associated with illness severity in the case of Parkinson's disease (Dakof and Mendelsohn, 1986); the amount of pain, the extent of disability and the belief that the pain would continue and be uncontrollable in relation to rheumatoid arthritis (Anderson *et al.*, 1985; Hawley and Wolfe, 1988; Fitzpatrick *et al.*, 1988; Skevington 1993); degree of physical impairment in relation to diabetes (Littlefield *et al.*, 1990) and motor neurone disease (Hogg, Goldstein and Leigh, 1994); and with lack of social support or negative life events in cancer patients (Bukberg, Penman and Holland, 1984). In a review of sixty studies of children and adolescents with a chronic medical problem, Bennett (1994) suggests that such children are at a slightly elevated risk for depressive symptoms, although most are not clinically depressed.

Unlike anxiety, which appears to be episodic, depression can be a long-term reaction to chronic illness (Taylor and Aspinwall, 1990). Although depression can occur at any phase of the adjustment process, it is likely to occur at a somewhat later stage than anxiety as it tends to be associated with a realisation by the patient of the implications of their condition.

As with anxiety, depression similarly impedes rehabilitation and recovery. For example, depressed, in comparison to non-depressed stroke patients, are likely to remain in hospital for a longer period of time (Cushman, 1986). This is no doubt due in part to the fact that depressed stroke patients tend to be less motivated to undergo rehabilitation and are hence less likely to improve as a result of such interventions (Thompson *et al.*, 1989). Myocardial infarction patients who are depressed are less likely to return to work one year later and are more likely to be re-hospitalised (Stern, Pascale and Ackerman, 1977). Increased depression has also been found to predict early death from complications of end-stage renal disease (Burton *et al.*, 1986). Unfortunately, because many of the symptoms of depression, such as loss of appetite, weight loss and sleeplessness, are also symptoms of disease, depression is not always diagnosed and treated. However, recent research suggesting differences between the presentation of depressive symptoms in medically ill and depressed psychiatric patients may facilitate the assessment of depression in medically ill populations (Clark, Cook and Snow, 1998).

The impact on relationships

Chronic illness can serve as a threat to social resources (Lyons, Sullivan and Ritvo, 1995). Disruption in the life of one family member inevitably effects the lives of others. As Patterson and Garwick (1994) note:

> Chronic illness happens to a family ... not just to an individual ... it affects them emotionally, cognitively, and behaviorally, often changing day-to-day routines, plans for the future, feelings and meanings about the self, others, and even life itself. (p. 131)

Spouses, in particular, can experience multiple difficulties related to their partner's illness. In addition to coping with their partner's own emotional distress, difficulties include the burden of providing care to the sick partner, and disruption to social, sexual and recreational activities. Thus, the distress of spouses of medical patients correlates with the patients' own distress. For example, Coyne and Smith (1991) found that the distress experienced by wives was at least as great as that experienced by their husbands six months after an uncomplicated myocardial infarction. Soskoline and De-Nour (1989) found similar levels of distress for patients undergoing dialysis and their spouses, while Baider, Perez and De-Nour (1989) found that the emotional impact of colon cancer was as great on spouses as on the patient. Other studies with cancer patients report as much if not more stress in close family members as for the patients themselves (Gotay, 1984). In families where a child has a chronic illness, marital conflict and strain are more common (Johnson, 1985), although some parents report improvements in the quality of their relationship and in the closeness of the family as a result of having a chronically ill child (Midence, Fuggle and Davies, 1993).

Reduced social contact is also frequently reported by those with chronic illness (Berkman and Syme, 1979). Withdrawal from the work role due to illness inevitably results in less opportunities for supportive interaction (Bloom and Seigel, 1984). In addition, social isolation may result from the withdrawal of family and friends who normally provide social support either because they may feel unable to deal with the ill person or because of the sick person's special needs and demands which place restrictions upon their interaction (Wortman and Dunkel-Schetter, 1979). Thus, Cobb (1976) has argued that the loss of supportive relationships following cancer diagnosis is due to the fact that people feel uncomfortable in the presence of someone with cancer due to its stigma. They do not know what to say, how to interact or when to help, resulting in discomfort and tension, which is reduced by avoiding the patient (Albrecht, Walker and Levy, 1982).

However, empirical evaluations of social support changes following a diagnosis of cancer do not necessarily support such a stigma hypothesis. Thus, Tempelaar *et al.* (1989) found that cancer patients assessed initially soon after surgical treatment and again at the beginning of chemotherapy treatment had more positive social experiences and fewer negative ones than a random population sample. In fact, those with the poorest prognosis reported the most positive experiences. Similar increases in emotional support following cancer diagnosis are reported by Bloom and Kessler (1994). In a longitudinal evaluation, cancer patients reported receiving more emotional support than women experiencing other types of surgery in the three months following surgery (Bloom and Kessler, 1994).

Clearly chronic illness impacts upon relationships in a number of different ways. In some instances the number of social contacts may decline as a direct result of restricted activity and opportunities to interact with others. It also seems inevitable that family life will face a number of challenges and pressures as a result of chronic illness (Altschuler, 1997). However, social support is important in mitigating the negative influence of chronic illness and in this regard it is the quality of relationships with regard to the emotional and personal support they provide rather than the quantity of relationships which is important.

Coping and adjustment to chronic illness

Causal attributions and adjustment

Chronic illness is almost inevitably associated with life change. This may involve dietary control, vigilance for symptom recurrence, alteration in daily activities or a more generally restricted lifestyle. How people adapt to chronic health problems is influenced to a considerable degree by their evaluation, perception and reaction to their illness; in this context, people often search for causal explanations (Wong and Weiner, 1981). Attribution theory is concerned with the way in which people seek to explain events and, within the health context, the relationship between attributions about illness and adjustment. Estimates of the occurrence of causal attributions about illness among patients range from 69 to 95 per cent with attributions varying as a result of the nature of the illness, disease severity and length of time since diagnosis (Turnquist, Harvey and Anderson, 1988). For example, in a survey of breast cancer patients, while 28 per cent reported that what caused their cancer was important at the time of diagnosis, the figure had increased to 41 per cent during recovery (Taylor, Lichtman and Wood, 1984).

Research investigating the content of attributions made by people with life-threatening illness has tended to classify them according to whether they refer to 'other', 'self', 'environment' or 'chance'. The type of attribution tends to vary according to the illness or injury experienced. Thus, accident victims frequently attribute the outcome to chance (Kiecolt-Glaser and Williams, 1987), while heart attack victims frequently attribute their illness to 'stress' (Affleck et al., 1987).

The assumption is that by identifying causes, we are able to give meaning to the event and hence make our social world more stable, predictable and controllable (Heider, 1958). But, are particular explanations about the cause of the illness (e.g. self-blame, blaming others, environmental factors or chance events) and its perceived controllability related to adjustment or response to treatment? The evidence relating to causal attributions would seem to be equivocal.

There seems to be no clear relationship between luck or environmental factors and adjustment (Affleck et al., 1987). Some studies suggest that self-blame relates to poor adjustment. For example, Bombardier, D'Amico and Jordon (1990) found that self-blame was related to greater depression in a heterogeneous group of chronically ill patients. In a further study, Kiecolt-Glaser and Williams (1987) found that self-blame in burn patients resulted in guilt and depression while Schiaffino, Shawaryn and Blum (1998) found that rheumatoid arthritis patients who saw themselves as responsible for their illness reported significant increases in depression over time. However, other studies suggest that self-blame is neither adaptive nor maladaptive (Taylor, Lichtman and Wood, 1984), while others suggest beneficial effects of self-blame (Tennen et al., 1984).

In contrast, blaming another person for one's difficulties seems to be more consistently maladaptive (Affleck et al., 1987; Taylor, Lichtman and Wood, 1984). One of the initial studies in this area was conducted by Bulman and Wortman (1977) who examined patients with spinal cord injuries (paraplegics and quadriplegics). Level of adjustment was judged by the patient's social worker. Attributions of blame to others was the best predictor of poor coping while self-blame was positively correlated with effective coping. In a further study with a sample of patients with genital herpes, Manne and Sandler (1984) found that attributing blame to the person who gave herpes to the subject was related to greater difficulty adjusting to their condition. However, characterological self-blame (inherent traits of the person), but not behavioural self-blame (controllable, modifiable behaviours) was also related to poor adjustment. In one study blaming others was found to be associated with a greater likelihood of reinfarction in relation to recovery from coronary heart disease (Affleck, Tennen and Croog, 1987).

In their review of illness attributions and adjustment, Turnquist, Harvey and Anderson (1988) comment that patients who report any implicit or explicit causal explanation for their illness seem to have more positive physical or emotional outcomes than patients who fail to report a causal explanation. They add, however, that 'the association between particular attributional characteristics and adjustment is unclear' (p. 63). They do though offer three possible mechanisms by which attributions might contribute to good or poor adjustment. These involve preservation of self-esteem, maintenance of a perception of justice and achievement of control as mediating factors. The significance of the explanation relates more to outcome than to the assumed cause of the illness.

In a similar vein, Thompson (1991) has argued that it is important to distinguish between three types of attribution: causal attributions, selective incidence attributions (why me instead of someone else?), and responsibility attributions (is the person personally responsible for the event?). In a sample of stroke patients she found that 'both patients and caregivers were better adjusted if they reported finding meaning in the experience, if they did not ask themselves "Why me?", if they did not hold themselves responsible, and if they had identified a cause of the stroke' (p. 92). Seeking to understand the nature of illness gives that illness some meaning. Meaning in turn contributes to the person's ability to adapt to and cope with the illness.

Control and adjustment

As with attributions, there is marked disagreement concerning the relationship of locus of control or control beliefs to adjustment. Some studies suggest that external locus of control is related to positive adjustment (Burish et al., 1984), while others do not (Taylor et al., 1991). Thus Taylor et al. report that a belief that there are others, most usually medical personnel, who can control the disease is associated with poor adjustment.

There is some consensus amongst studies suggesting that patients who believe they can control their illness show better psychological adjustment than patients without such beliefs. The relationship between internal locus of control and adjustment has been reported for patients with cancer (Taylor, Lichtman and Wood, 1984), rheumatoid arthritis (Affleck et al., 1987), stroke (Partridge and Johnston, 1989) and patients with spinal cord injuries (Schulz and Decker, 1985). Among mothers of infants with perinatal complications, perceived control was related to adaptation (Tennen, Affleck and Greshman, 1986). In a further study, coronary heart disease patients who attributed their heart disease to factors which they could subsequently control – that is, eating, drinking and smoking behaviour – were more likely to believe that future attacks could be avoided (Affleck et al., 1987).

Conversely, patients who seek control but who do not have control opportunities are likely to experience distress. Thus, Michela (1986) found that MI (myocardial infarction) patients, who reported feelings of helplessness and lack of control were more likely to be depressed. In a questionnaire study with arthritis patients, Nicassio et al. (1985) found that perceptions of helplessness or diminished control were associated with reduced self-esteem, greater anxiety and depression, personal perceptions of poorer clinical status and greater impairments in daily living. Similarly, patients who believe they must hold back from doing what they want are prone to greater depressive symptoms and poorer psychosocial adjustment (Bombardier, D'Amico and Jordon, 1990). In this regard, a belief in personal control over aspects of illness can lead to poor adjustment when control beliefs are undermined: for example, by irrefutable discordant evidence, such as an increase in disease severity or poor outcome from treatment (Affleck *et al.*, 1987; Burish *et al.*, 1984; Christensen *et al.*, 1991; Taylor *et al.*, 1991) (see box 8.3).

Box 8.3 Beliefs in personal control and adjustment to illness

A belief in personal control tends to be associated with better adjustment in relation to chronic illness. However, if such beliefs in controllability are challenged, for example by an increase in disease severity or by a poor outcome from treatment, then strong beliefs in personal control can lead to poor adjustment. This is illustrated in the following two studies:

Affleck *et al.* (1987)
   The sample consisted of 92 patients with rheumatoid arthritis.
   In the context of an interview patients were asked to rate the degree of personal control they felt they had over day-to-day symptoms, the course of the disease and their medical care and treatment.
   For all patients a belief in personal control over medical care and treatment was associated with positive mood and psychosocial adjustment.
   Perceived control over symptoms was unrelated to mood in patients with mild symptoms, but was significantly associated with positive mood in patients who had moderate or severe symptoms.
   Perceived personal control over the course of their illness was marginally associated with positive mood in patients with mild disease, but negatively associated with mood for moderately and severely diseased rheumatoid arthritis patients.

Christensen *et al.* (1991)
   The sample population consisted of 96 hemodialysis patients, 66 of whom had not undergone renal transplant and 30 of whom had undergone an unsuccessful transplant. Participants completed a range of questionnaires to assess locus of control, depression and disease severity.
   A belief that one's health is controllable was associated with less depression among hemodialysis patients who had not previously experienced a failed renal transplant. This same belief was associated with greater depression for patients who had returned to dialysis following an unsuccessful transplant.
   This relationship between beliefs and depression occurred among severely ill patients, but for those with less severe disease, control beliefs were unrelated to depression.
   The link between control and depression was true for both control perceptions related to the patient's own beliefs and for beliefs about the health care provider's ability to influence health outcome.

The experience associated with illness serves to challenge the person's belief in their control over their health. At Taylor *et al.* (1991) note:

> when the situation gets beyond a point where control is likely to have any impact on the course or consequence of the aversive events, believing such control exists may be maladaptive. (p. 106)

It seems then that the role of health-related cognitions is constrained by the physical realities of disease. Dakof and Mendelsohn (1989) found that for patients with mild to moderate impairment from Parkinson's disease a sense of control, a belief that things could be worse and an ability to put negative thoughts out of their mind were related to positive psychological adjustment. Patients with severe impairment, however, reported elevated passivity or depression regardless of their beliefs. Similar findings have been reported by Rosenbaum and Palmon (1984) for patients with epilepsy. For patients with low to moderate seizure frequency, lower anxiety and depression was associated with a belief that their seizures could be controlled. Patients with high frequency of seizures reported negative effects, irrespective of beliefs about controllability of seizures.

However, illusions of control do seem to some extent to be a necessary component of cognitive adaptation (Taylor, Lichtman and Wood, 1984; Thompson, Armstrong and Thomas, 1998) while reality may be detrimental to adjustment. Maintaining a sense of belief in one's ability to shape the course of the illness may serve to maintain psychological well-being. It may be necessary to maintain and adjust one's illusions in the face of changes in illness which challenge control beliefs in order to maintain one's ability to cope with chronic illness.

Coping with chronic illness

Coping refers to cognitive and behavioural efforts to manage demands appraised as taxing or exceeding available resources (Lazarus and Folkman, 1984). A number of factors including situational, socio-environmental and personal resources are known to influence coping behaviour (Folkman and Lazarus, 1980). Although chronic illnesses vary widely, with regard to both diagnosis and its effect upon the individual, the person concerned is faced with demands as with any other stressful life event. How such demands are dealt with affects emotional well-being and the person's adaptation to the illness. Case studies and reports have identified a number of typical coping strategies adopted by people in response to the stress of a chronic illness. These include denial, selective ignoring, information seeking, avoidance and reminiscing about former good times (Cohen and Lazarus, 1979). Similar patterns of coping have emerged from factor analytic studies of psychometric instruments such as the Ways of Coping Checklist (Folkman and Lazarus, 1980).

Denial

As noted, denial or avoidance of the implications of illness seems to be a common reaction to diagnosis. In the short term, such reactions can save the patient from having to face immediately the full range of problems posed by their illness, possibly providing them with time to mobilise other coping strategies. Hence it serves a protective function. For example, myocardial infarction patients with high levels of denial of impact of the condition while hospitalised show least short-term emotional upset (Havik and Maeland, 1990). In a further study, breast cancer patients who showed an initial attitude towards their illness of 'fighting spirit' or 'denial' were more likely to survive five to ten years later than those who displayed 'stoic acceptance' or a 'helpless/hopeless' attitude (Pettingale et al., 1985). Although it is likely that coping responses change over time, few studies have monitored different stages of reaction to diagnosis and illness.

One such study found that patients with 'denial' or 'fighting' characteristics initially, displayed 'stoicism' over the next two years (Morris, Greer and White, 1977)

In the longer term, however, denial may impede the process of recovery as patients may fail to monitor their condition, fail to follow medication regimes or fail to change their lifestyle in a way which would enhance their quality of life. Thus, Bracken and Bernstein (1980) found that, for patients with a spinal cord injury, those who continued to deny their disability one year after injury had become more anxious and depressed and were coping less well. In a study of patients with motor neurone disease, those who were more accepting of their illness showed less anxiety and depression (Hogg, Goldstein and Leigh, 1994). Bloom and his colleagues have also found that avoidance coping predicts depression, poorer outlook on life and poorer social functioning in patients with both early and advanced breast cancer and long-term survivors of Hodgkin's Disease (Bloom, 1982; Bloom and Spiegel, 1984; Bloom et al., 1991). It seems then that, in the longer term, denial or avoidance coping may be a risk factor for adverse response to illness (Felton, Revenson and Hinrichsen, 1984).

There is also some evidence that denial is associated with the ill person's desire to hide their illness from others. Thus, Walsh and Walsh (1989), in a study of people with multiple sclerosis, found that denying or resisting the disease was more likely in those social situations in which the disease may become embarrassingly apparent. Many people with disabling and life-threatening conditions live life to the full in spite of their ill health. However, denial of the limitations imposed by chronic illness in the presence of others impedes the capacity of friends and relatives to provide appropriate support. Social support, as discussed later, serves a protective function in relation to adaptation to chronic illness.

Avoidance coping

There is evidence that emotion-focused strategies, involving an element of avoidance, self-blame or wishful thinking, are also related to poorer adjustment. Thus, Felton and Revenson (1984), in an investigation of subsequent psychological adjustment among patients with four types of chronic illness, found that regardless of the diagnosis or the controllability of the illness, emotion-focused coping (wishful thinking) had a negative effect on adjustment while problem-focused coping (information seeking) had a positive effect. A similar finding is reported by Bombardier, D'Amico and Jordan (1990) for a heterogeneous group of chronically ill patients. In a further report, escape-avoidance coping was associated with more emotional distress for cancer patients, 72 per cent of whom had been diagnosed with initial cancers in the previous five years (Dunkel-Schetter et al., 1992). In two studies of adults with sickle cell disease, pain coping strategies characterised by negative thinking and passive adherence (catastrophising, fear self-statements, resting, taking fluids) were associated with more severe pain episodes, less activity during painful episodes, more frequent hospitalisations and emergency room visits and higher levels of psychological distress (Gill et al., 1989) including depression and anxiety (Thompson et al., 1992). Finally, passive coping was one of the variables associated with worse outcome on disease specific measures of functioning and social function for three groups of chronically ill patients (Scharloo et al., 1998).

Confrontive coping

In contrast, patients who have a confrontative response, who seek advice, information or support, who focus on the positive and who believe they can personally control their illness, tend to show less psychological distress (e.g. Affleck *et al.*, 1987; Burgess, Morris and Pettingale, 1988; Dunkel-Schetter *et al.*, 1992; Felton, Revenson and Hinrichsen, 1984). Other studies suggest that rather than necessarily employing active problem-focused strategies, avoiding the use of negative coping strategies is positively related to functional status (Bombardier, D'Amico and Jordan, 1990; Keefe *et al.*, 1987).

Effective management may thus depend upon identifying which strategies facilitate recovery at which stages of illness and for which particular patients. Such knowledge could subsequently be used to assist patients in the process of developing effective coping strategies. As Baum, Herberman and Cohen (1995) note, sharpening coping skills holds great promise in reducing the personal cost of chronic illness and enhancing patients' quality of life.

Social support

Adapting to chronic illness is also enhanced by having an effective system of interpersonal or social support (Burman and Margolin, 1992; Coyne and Downey, 1991; Wallston *et al.*, 1983): that is, support which is perceived as being useful rather than merely being available. The relationship between good social relationships and positive adjustment to illness has been reported for a wide variety of patient groups including cancer patients (Bloom, 1982; Bloom and Spiegel, 1984; Bloom *et al.*, 1991; Neuling and Winefield, 1988), rheumatoid arthritis patients (Brown, Wallston and Nicassio, 1989; Fitzpatrick *et al.*, 1988; Fitzpatrick *et al.*, 1991; Goodenow, Reisine and Grady, 1990; Manne and Zautra, 1989; Revenson *et al.*, 1991), chronic pain patients (Kerns and Turk, 1984), persons with diabetes (Littlefield *et al.*, 1990), people with genital herpes (Manne and Sandler, 1984), patients with spinal cord injuries (Schulz and Decker, 1985) and patients with multiple sclerosis (McIvor, Riklan and Reznikoff, 1984). Other studies suggest that family function-ing characterised by high levels of support and low levels of conflict and control is associated with better psychological adjustment in adults with sickle cell disease (Thompson *et al.*, 1992). Patients with AIDS, who perceive themselves as having more available social support, experience less depression and helplessness (Zich and Temoshok, 1987). Studies also suggest that a high intimacy marriage is related to less depressed mood in men three years after a heart attack (Waltz *et al.*, 1988), and that a supportive marriage is associated with better diabetes control (Marteau, Bloch and Baum, 1987). In addition, studies have found that social support from family and friends reduces distress during recovery from coronary heart disease (Fontana *et al.*, 1989). Other studies have found that emotional and instrumental support from family and friends is related to better social functioning in long-term cancer survivors regardless of time since diagnosis, the stage at which the cancer is diagnosed and the type of treatment needed to control the disease (Bloom *et al.*, 1991).

One possibility is that the 'right kind' of support assists the individual's coping efforts. Thus, effective social support depends upon a match between what one needs and what one receives from those within one's social network. Dakof and Taylor (1990) suggest that different people within a social network are valued for providing different types of support. Emotional support is valued from those we are closer to at a personal level, while information and advice are valued from experts. Evidence for the relationship between emotional support and psychological well-being tends to be relatively consistent (Cohen and Wills, 1985).

In relation to chronic illness, while most studies find relatively low levels of negative social interactions, not all interactions with family and friends are supportive. There are occasions when close relationships not only fail to provide needed social support but can themselves serve as a potential source of stress (Coyne and DeLongis, 1986; Revenson *et al.*, 1991). Wortman and Lehman (1985) have identified a number of unsupportive reactions to people with chronic illness including well-intentioned efforts at problem minimisation and enforced cheerfulness, as well as more negative reactions such as avoiding the individual or avoiding discussion of the troublesome event. Just as good support can be beneficial, non-supportive interactions may have detrimental effects on psychological well being. Just as emotionally close and gratifying marriages are likely to facilitate coping attempts so a lack of coherence and social stress in marriage may hinder effective coping behaviour (Manne and Zautra, 1989; Pagel, Erdly and Becker, 1987; Revenson *et al.*, 1991). Thus, Manne and Zautra found that spousal criticism of their partner with rheumatoid arthritis was related to maladaptive coping behaviour and had an indirect effect upon the psychological adjustment of the patient. Pagel, Erdly and Becker (1987) found that criticism, unhelpful actions and the absence of expected support were stronger predictors of mental health outcomes than the receipt of (helpful) support.

It is also possible to be too supportive and hence to interfere with the patient's adaptive coping. In the case of chronic pain, for example, supportive responses from family members often act to reinforce the patient's pain behaviours such as grimacing and rubbing (Gil *et al.*, 1987) and hence contribute to greater functional impairment. Studies show that reinforcements from family members/spouse can maintain the patient in the sick role (Bebbington and Delemos, 1996).

As a result of decreasing energy, mobility or the need to manage medication regimes, chronic illness may lead to a concentration of energy on essential day-to-day tasks, with visiting or being visited by friends decreasing accordingly. Studies with rheumatoid arthritis patients (Fitzpatrick *et al.*, 1990) and those with chronic respiratory illness (Williams and Bury, 1989) have noted that their inability to get out and about as much results in difficulty maintaining social contacts. A number of studies indicate that a reduction in the size of a patient's social network seems to be related to a corresponding reduction in availability of emotional support (Bloom and Kessler, 1994; Bloom and Spiegel, 1984).

Psychological interventions for chronic illness could thus usefully address issues relating to social support. Increasing the effectiveness of existing support resources, facilitating support groups, involving families of the chronically ill in treatment, as well as helping the families themselves to cope, are all areas where psychology can contribute. Indeed, studies that have evaluated the efficacy of social support or self-help groups have generally found beneficial results for such patients when compared with waiting list controls or non-participants (Telch and Telch, 1986; Waltz, 1986).

Psychological interventions

Given the physical and emotional aspects of chronic illness and its treatment, and the fact that adverse effects can, to some extent, be ameliorated by both cognitive appraisal and social resources, these are areas where rehabilitation efforts can usefully be directed. At the physical level, cognitive-behavioural interventions for pain control are likely to have an increasingly important role to play, as is the psychological management of adverse emotional reactions to chronic illness.

Although counselling has been advocated and discussed for a range of chronic conditions (Davis and Fallowfield, 1991) there is a surprising lack of published evaluations of intervention studies in this area (Baum, Herberman and Cohen, 1995). Two specific aspects of psychological intervention with chronic illness will be briefly reviewed in this final section: strategies for achieving pain reduction and strategies for modifying negative emotional reactions.

Coping with pain

The control of pain remains a serious problem for many patients with chronic illness. For example, Dalton and Feuerstein (1988) estimate that 25 per cent of cancer patients do not find relief from pain. Although medication remains the primary method for treating cancer-related pain, behavioural methods (Davis et al., 1987) are now also being used.

Although psychologists have contributed extensively to the study and management of chronic pain, this has generally been in relation to muscle or joint pain, especially low back pain, vascular pain, especially migraine headaches, and phantom limb pain. A number of such studies suggest that programmes involving education and cognitive-behavioural interventions are effective in helping people to manage their chronic pain (Flor, Fydrich and Turk, 1992). Less attention has been paid to pain associated with chronic illnesses such as cancer or rheumatoid arthritis. Not only might psychological interventions help in pain control, they could also help to limit the consequences of pain, such as sleep disturbance, irritability and other behavioural difficulties.

Patient education programmes and cognitive-behavioural interventions for pain have also been explored in relation to rheumatoid arthritis (Lorig et al., 1989; O'Leary et al., 1988; Parker et al., 1988). For example, O'Leary et al. randomly assigned patients to either a cognitive-behavioural programme where they were taught skills in managing stress, pain and symptoms of the disease, or an arthritis information group where they received a self-help book giving details of arthritis self-management. Results indicated that those in the cognitive-behavioural group experienced reduced pain and joint inflammation and improved psychosocial functioning.

Coping with emotions

A number of studies have investigated the utility of psychological interventions for helping patients to cope with anxiety and/or depression in chronic illness. Interventions have been evaluated both in regard to the acute phase of illness, for example immediately post-myocardial infarction or subsequent to the diagnosis of a potentially life-threatening disease, as well as during the course of chronic disease, for example in relation to asthma.

In the former case, there is some evidence that psychological intervention during the acute coronary care phase can have a beneficial outcome on both psychological and medical parameters (Gruen, 1975; Thompson and Meddis, 1990). In one of the earliest studies, Gruen (1975) randomly assigned seventy myocardial infarction patients to either a control group receiving standard hospital care or a treatment group receiving support, reinforcement and reassurance. Those receiving the intervention fared better on a number of measures including days hospitalised and anxiety both in hospital and at four month follow up. In a more recent report, Thompson and Meddis (1990) randomly assigned sixty male myocardial infarction patients admitted to a coronary care unit with a first-time acute myocardial infarction to either a treatment group receiving in-hospital counselling in addition to routine care, or a control group which received routine care only. The counselled group reported significantly less anxiety and depression in comparison to the routine care group both in hospital and at six month follow up. Taken together with other findings this led Thompson and Meddis to comment that:

> such simple intervention in the acute phase is therapeutically beneficial, efficient and economic, and should be offered routinely to patients who have suffered a first MI. (p. 247)

In relation to newly diagnosed cancer patients, Worden and Weisman (1984) evaluated the efficacy of two different four-session psychotherapeutic interventions for lowering emotional distress and improving coping skills in relation to a no-treatment control group. In the first, patient-centred treatment, the therapist's role was to help the patient identify and explore ways of solving problems they were experiencing. In the second, problem-focused intervention, patients were provided with a specific step-by-step approach to problem solving. Both treatment groups had significantly lower emotional distress at each of a series of follow-up assessments and resolved problems more effectively in comparison to the control group. There were no differences between the two intervention groups. However, until the last decade there were few well-controlled studies evaluating psychosocial interventions with cancer patients (Telch and Telch, 1985). In one such study Telch and Telch (1986) compared group coping skills training to supportive group therapy to no treatment for highly distressed cancer patients. At six weeks the coping skills group showed less emotional distress, fewer problems, more vigour and heightened self-efficacy in comparison to the support or no-treatment groups. Such findings appear to be related to the fact that patients in the coping group reported enhanced perceptions of control.

With the course of any disease, patients understandably experience varying emotional reactions. Determining the relationship of psychological factors to the course of a disease and developing effective intervention programmes is of particular importance. A number of studies have evaluated psychological interventions in coronary heart disease subsequent to hospital discharge. For example, Burgess et al. (1987) randomly assigned 180 post-MI patients to either a cardiac rehabilitation programme, consisting of cognitive-behavioural counselling, or standard cardiological aftercare. At three months the cardiac rehabilitation group reported less distress, anxiety and depression than the control group, although at thirteen months follow up none of the between group differences was significant. However, in reviewing the evidence from a range of studies evaluating psychological interventions post-MI, Bundy (1989) comments that 'most have been successful on some outcome measures' (p. 170).

A range of interventions including hypnosis, relaxation, systematic desensitisation and contingency management have also been used as treatment for asthma (Yorkston *et al.*, 1974). Although the aim of such treatments has generally been to improve lung function, there is little evidence for their efficacy in this regard. Such treatments are, however, meaningful when tension or anxiety are secondarily associated with asthma.

Psychological interventions have also been used to help patients and their spouses cope with the psychological consequences of a range of other chronic illnesses, including diabetes (Shillitoe, 1988) and stroke (Krantz and Deckel, 1983). More general counselling has also been advocated across a range of conditions (Davis and Fallowfield, 1991). Such interventions have a clear role to play in improving the person's ability to cope with a disease once it has been diagnosed. However, it is not always clear what outcome measures should be used to assess counselling and hence it can be difficult to determine whether those who receive such interventions actually derive therapeutic benefit.

Summary

The present chapter has examined the range of challenges presented by chronic illness and those psychosocial factors likely to modify its impact. The challenges include pain and disability, anxiety and depression and disruption to social relationships. While anxiety and depression in relation to both the diagnosis and treatment of chronic illness may not be unusual, sustained high levels of such reactions can be problematic because they interfere with good adjustment. Depression is also a common reaction amongst relatives of the chronically ill. A number of authors have noted that the lives of all family members, not just the patient's, are disrupted by chronic illness. Distress experienced by family members or spouses is often as great as that experienced by the patient themselves.

However, the psychosocial impact of chronic illness is modified by a range of non-medical factors, including how the individual appraises and copes with their illness and the social support they receive. Particular research interest has focused upon attributions; a number of studies indicate that people search for causal explanations for their illness. However, the association between specific attributions and adjustment is far from clear; it seems that patients who report any implicit or explicit causal explanation for their illness have more positive physical or emotional outcomes than patients who fail to report a causal explanation. There is also marked disagreement concerning the relation of locus of control or control beliefs to adjustment; however, personal control seems to enhance adjustment unless the realities of the illness challenge such beliefs.

A number of studies have also investigated the relationship between coping and adjustment to chronic illness. Denial or avoidance of the implications of illness is a common reaction to diagnosis and, in the short term, seems to serve a protective function. In the longer term, however, such denial may result in the patient failing to monitor their condition and hence may be detrimental to health. There is also evidence that emotion-focused coping is negatively related to adjustment while problem-focused coping, involving seeking advice, information or support, is related to positive adjustment. In addition, a number of studies have found a relationship between good social relationships and positive adjustment to illness. As a result, a number of studies have evaluated the efficacy of modifying a person's social resources as a strategy for enhancing adjustment to chronic illness. In addition, an increasing number of studies have evaluated the efficacy of cognitive-behavioural interventions for chronic pain and emotional difficulties associated with chronic illness. Although counselling has been widely advocated in relation to chronic illness, and specific psychological interventions have a clear role to play in improving the person's ability to cope with disease, relatively few well-controlled evaluative studies have been conducted. While a variety of psychosocial interventions are applied in the context of chronic illness there is an increasing need for further evaluative research.

FURTHER READING

A. Baum, H. Herberman and L. Cohen (1995). Managing stress and managing illness: Survival and quality of life in chronic disease. *Journal of Clinical Psychology in Medical Settings*, **2**, 309–333.

R. F. Lyons, M. J. L. Sullivan and P. G. Ritvo (1995). *Relationships in Chronic Illness and Disability*. London: Sage.

P. M. Nicassio and T. W. Smith (eds) (1995) *Managing Chronic Illness*: *A biopsychosocial perspective*. Washington, DC: American Psychological Association.

J. J. Sweet, R. H. Rozensky and S. M. Tovian (eds) (1991) *Handbook of Clinical Psychology in Medical Settings*. New York: Plenum Press.

S. E. Taylor and L. G. Aspinwall (1990). Psychosocial aspects of chronic illness. In P. T. Costa and G. R. VandenBos (eds), *Psychological Aspects of Serious Illness*: *Chronic conditions, fatal diseases and clinical care*. Washington, DC: American Psychological Association.

D. C. Turnquist, J. H. Harvey and B. Anderson (1988). Attributions and adjustment to life threatening illness. *British Journal of Clinical Psychology*, **27**, 55–65.

CHAPTER 9

Terminal care

CHAPTER OVERVIEW

This chapter examines issue relating to care of the terminally ill. The first issue addressed is the question of continuing with medical care, the aim of which is to cure the patient, when the patient's disease or condition can no longer be altered. In this context questions of euthanasia, living wills and the need to inform the terminally ill patient are addressed. Emotional reactions and adjustment during the course of terminal illness are examined. Also addressed is the question of caring for the dying with home care compared with hospital and hospice care. Finally issues relating to bereavement and grief are discussed and, in this context, psychological support available to the bereaved.

This chapter covers:

The issue of prolonging life
Informing the terminally ill
Adjustment to dying
Caring for the dying
Bereavement and grief

Prolonging life

The medical aim is to cure even when the patient's disease or condition can no longer be altered. Indeed, with technological advances many more medical procedures are available to prolong life. Maddi (1990) refers to these as 'heroic measures' which are:

> aggressive procedures for prolonging life when someone is at risk of imminent death or for reinstating life when death can be regarded as actually having occurred. These procedures are considered heroic in the sense that they are a radical departure from what might be termed *natural* or *conventional* care. (p. 156, italics in original)

Such life support includes emergency resuscitation and intensive care procedures (Wanzer *et al.*, 1984), intravenous feeding, and organ transplants coupled with immuno-suppressive therapy to reduce the chances of organ rejection. In a Canadian survey of deaths in acute care facilities and continuing care facilities, almost every in-patient died with one or more technologies in continuous operation (Wilson, 1997).

As Maddi (1990) notes, the major issues raised by such measures become apparent when one explores the implications of trying to save everyone regardless of the 'patient's age, condition, or whether the confronting condition was curable'. If the patient is in extreme pain or makes a request to be allowed to die in peace or if their resulting quality of life is severely impaired, should life-sustaining measures still be pursued? As Maddi further notes, while there are a number of problems inherent in trying to save everyone, not trying to do so probably raises even more dilemmas. If selective treatment is an option, who decides and using what criteria? Within any health care system the inevitable questions of cost and availability of biomedical care become difficult to disentangle from the complex issue of quality of life.

However, quality of life is itself a difficult concept to define and assess and even if this were the sole treatment determinant how much weight should be attached to the patient's or relative's views as opposed to those of the health care practitioner concerned? As Kaplan (1991) notes, when given the opportunity for control and involvement, patients may well decline services which do not help them achieve improved health outcomes. However, questions of when not to attempt resuscitation or when to withdraw water and food from dying, suffering or permanently unconscious patients raise complex moral and ethical concerns and frequently involve court action invoked by the dying patient's relatives who wish to end the life-support system (Wanzer *et al.*, 1989). The frequency of such actions is unknown but unlikely to be low (Wanzer *et al.*, 1989).

Euthanasia

Passive euthanasia – that is, the withdrawing or non-performance of a procedure which is required to sustain life – is a generally accepted part of medicine. The Institute of Medical Ethics Working Party on the Ethics of Prolonging Life and Assisting Death (1990) notes that:

> A doctor, acting in good conscience, is ethically justified in assisting death if the need to relieve intense and unceasing pain or distress caused by an incurable illness greatly outweighs the benefits to the patient of further prolonging his life. This conclusion applies to patients whose sustained wishes on this matter are known to the doctor and should thus be respected as outweighing any contrary opinions expressed by others. (p. 613)

The question of active euthanasia – that is, the performing of a procedure with the express purpose of ending a person's life – although sanctioned in a few countries, such as the Netherlands, is inevitably an even more contentious issue. A number of authors have addressed the problem of the misuse and abuse which can arise from the legalising of active euthanasia, which has also been referred to as doctor-assisted suicide (Hendin and Klerman, 1993). With medicine increasingly able to prolong 'life' when there is no hope that the person concerned will ever be able to lead any form of meaningful existence, there are clearly many moral and ethical issues which will continue to be raised and debated.

With the focus on prolonging the process of dying, inadequate attention is all too frequently paid to preparing the patient and his or her family for this eventuality. Curative care frequently conflicts with the actual needs of those who are dying (Geyman, 1983). This conflict is partly responsible for changes in the management of and expectations relating to terminal care which have taken place during the past three decades. One such change has been the development of home nursing care and the hospice movement with the emphasis on palliative care and patient autonomy and the right to die in as comfortable a manner as possible (Saunders and Baines, 1983). The second change, becoming more common, particularly in the United States but also supported by a number of groups within the UK (Gallagher, 1993), is the development of advance directives such as 'living wills'.

Advance directives

Advance directives are instructions to doctors concerning the extent of care the patient would wish to receive in relation to the process of dying (Ezekiel and Ezekiel, 1990; Levy, 1990). Living wills are not at present recognised legal documents in the UK. This is justified by the fact that, although the patient has a right either to refuse or to accept treatment, where the patient is *in extremis* and incapable of giving consent, a constructive consent is assumed by law: that is, that patients would always consent to measures to save their lives. The living will is a direct challenge to such an assumption of consent (Gallagher, 1993). Moves to secure the legal status of such directives would seem to be gathering momentum. However, a recent survey suggests that most directives specify simply that the person wishes to forgo life-sustaining treatment without providing specific instructions about what care would or would not be acceptable. Even when instructions were present, care was potentially inconsistent with the patient's wishes in half the cases (Teno *et al.*, 1997).

Informing the terminally ill

The extent to which terminally ill patients are aware of their impending death will clearly influence the way other people interact with them. Glaser and Strauss (1965) have described four awareness contexts (see box 9.1).

While 'closed awareness' may be determined by the patient who does not wish to know, it is more likely to be determined by health care professionals involved or the patient's relatives. It is often the case that family members are initially informed of their relative's terminal illness but that they then choose to keep from the patient the knowledge that he or she is dying. Such 'closed awareness' seems more common when the

---

Box 9.1 Awareness contexts and terminal illness

Glaser and Strauss (1965) have described four contexts to reflect the extent to which the terminally ill and others close to them are aware of and acknowledge the person's impending death:

'**Open awareness**' – when both the dying person and others are aware of and acknowledge the existence of the terminal illness.

'**Suspected awareness**' – when the dying person suspects what is wrong but maintains silence about it.

'**Mutual pretence awareness**' – where each party is aware that the other knows but both parties maintain silence about it.

'**Closed awareness**' – where the dying person does not know what is wrong with him or her while others are party to knowledge about the patient's condition.

---

terminally ill person is suffering mental confusion (Seale, 1991b).

In the past two decades there has been a general move towards telling terminally ill patients their diagnosis. For example, while Oken *et al.*, reporting in 1962, found that only 12 per cent of doctors expressed a preference for informing cancer patients of their diagnosis, Novack *et al.*, reporting in 1979, found that 98 per cent of doctors expressed such a preference. Similar moves towards greater openness between doctors and dying patients and their families are reported in a more recent paper by Seale (1991b). He found that, while in 1969 37 per cent of people dying from cancer knew certainly or probably that they were dying, the comparable figure in 1987 was 67 per cent. For other terminal illnesses the move to openness was less marked with 38 per cent knowing about their impending death in 1969 compared with 42 per cent in 1987.

As Seale (1991b) notes, most people prefer to know the truth. Indeed, Seale also reports findings which suggest that practitioners find it easier to care for people who are dying if the person is actually aware that they are dying. He adds that doctors generally wait to be asked and tend to proceed cautiously, appearing to be good at identifying the minority of patients who prefer not to know. As Zisook *et al.* (1995) conclude:

> the appropriate question is not whether to inform the patient, but rather when and how to do so. (p. 359)

Adjustment to dying

A number of different models have been proposed for the process of change in the person's level of awareness and degree of acceptance of their impending death which occurs during the course of terminal illness. In a landmark publication, Kubler-Ross (1969) argued that five stages preceded death: denial and isolation, anger, bargaining, depression and acceptance (box 9.2).

Box 9.2 Stages of adjustment to dying (Kubler-Ross, 1969)

Kubler-Ross (1969) suggested, on the basis of her observations of 200 terminally ill people, that the dying person progresses through a particular pattern of emotional responses. She argued that there were the following five stages preceding death:

(i) **Denial and isolation** – Denial is a common reaction to the initial diagnosis of terminal illness; some people may never admit to either themselves or anyone else that they are dying.

(ii) **Anger** – After a relatively short period of time denial may be replaced by anger which the person may direct inwardly towards themselves, towards family and friends, caregivers, fate or God or towards the world in general (the 'why me?' phase).

(iii) **Bargaining** – The replacement of anger with bargaining is seen as being an attempt to trade good actions for good health. According to Kubler-Ross:

Bargaining is really an attempt to postpone; it usually includes a prize for good behaviour, a self-imposed deadline and a promise that the patient will not ask for more if the postponement is granted. (p. 83–84)

(iv) **Depression** – Once the person realises that there is little they can do to control the course of their illness, a realisation which may be associated with a worsening of physical symptoms, then depression may occur.

(v) **Acceptance** – The final stage of acceptance occurs when the person is resigned to the prospect of death.

In the early stages after diagnosis denial may serve a protective function, allowing the person to mobilise their resources to enable them to cope more effectively with the implications of their impending death (Lazarus, 1983). The following stage of anger can be very difficult for family and friends to cope with as every encounter with the patient can be distressing. As a result social contact with the patient can decrease, which only serves to increase the patient's distress.

Kubler-Ross regarded the fourth stage, depression, as setting the scene for 'anticipatory grief' to occur, during which the person mourns the prospect of their own impending death. This stage may be associated with a worsening of physical symptoms although the range of such symptoms will obviously depend upon the disease and its management. Severe distressing pain is the most frequent physical symptom experienced by the terminally ill, but breathing difficulties, loss of bowel or bladder control, vomiting and sleeplessness may also present as problems (Cartwright, Hockey and Anderson, 1973). As noted previously, anxiety and depression are frequently experienced in relation to chronic illness and are thus, perhaps not surprisingly, also commonly reported reactions among the terminally ill (Wilson, 1989).

While being a landmark publication, providing rich descriptions of the experience of death and dying and raising a range of issues relating to counselling the terminally ill,

Kubler-Ross's model has not been without its critics. Although Kubler-Ross noted that patients might not progress through the stages in an orderly sequence, and that some stages might be omitted or returned to, the notion of discrete stages has been the main focus of criticism of the theory. The terminally ill fluctuate markedly in their reactions to their impending death, so that the feelings associated with the five stages may be experienced by some patients on an alternating basis (Hinton, 1984) and people may experience feelings other than those she identified. Guilt, fear, anxiety and confusion are common psychological reactions of dying people. Anxiety in particular is not fully acknowledged by Kubler-Ross and may be more prominent than feelings of depression: for example, in response to symptoms or separation from family and friends in hospitalised patients. Critics have also pointed out that the final stage described by Kubler-Ross, that of acceptance, which is assumed to represent the end of the struggle, may not actually be attained by terminally ill patients (Schneidman, 1978).

Others have noted both the disease-specific aspects and cultural specificity of the model (Kastenbaum, 1975). The person's cultural and religious background play an important role in determining beliefs about death and hence coping strategies used; methods of dealing with death and dying are extremely varied (Firth, 1993). For many religious or spiritual groups, death is viewed as a transition from one stage to another and hence death has a positive element; it is in more secular societies that death is viewed with finality.

Also within the model, little account is taken of likely age and gender differences, the type of illness and hence associated difficulties such as disability and pain. Reaction to impending death may be very different for a very disabled elderly person in extreme pain whose health has deteriorated over many years and a young person stricken with a terminal illness, the progression of which has been relatively rapid.

In addition to such issues there is also a surprising lack of systematic empirical research evaluating the model. In one of the few studies, Shulz and Aderman (1974) found little evidence for the presence of systematic stages with only depression uniformly present in the dying. As these same authors argue, it is unlikely that any stage model would adequately describe the process of dying which involves a range of behavioural complexities; rather it provides a general framework (Zisook et al., 1995). Thus, while Kubler-Ross's work is largely responsible for the increase in public awareness of death and the more sensitive and humane treatment of terminally ill patients which has occurred within the past two decades, no stage model can embrace the full emotional and behavioural complexities involved in the process of dying.

Care of the dying

In spite of the many changes which have occurred within the past two decades in the care of the dying, the majority of deaths in Britain, about 60 per cent, still take place in hospital (Victor, 1993), while 25 per cent take place in the person's home. In contrast, most of the care of dying patients takes place either at home or in non-hospital contexts, such as nursing homes (Cartwright and Seale, 1990). The decision to admit terminally ill patients to hospital is due to a combination of factors other than the fact that death is approaching. These are an inability to control symptoms, an inability of family and friends to continue caring for the person at home, or in many cases their non-availability to provide care, as well as lack of support from health care workers. In fact, most people would prefer not to die in hospital; in their study of terminally ill cancer patients, Townsend, Phillimore and Beattie (1988) found that only 20 per cent reported that they would choose hospital as their preferred place of terminal care.

Studies during the 1960s suggested extreme shortcomings of institutional care of the dying (e.g. Sudnow, 1965), in which imposing order and impersonal routines dominated over the provision of personalised care. Weisman has argued that an essential goal in the treatment of dying patients is to help them achieve an 'appropriate death' (Weisman, 1972, 1974). The patient should be as pain free as possible, functioning as effectively as possible within the constraints imposed by their condition and able to recognise and resolve any residual conflicts. Geyman (1983) suggests that dying patients have four basic requirements: as much independence as possible, dignity, acceptance by others and relief from symptoms, most usually pain. These are the goals of palliative care which aims to relieve unpleasant symptoms and improve the quality of life for all those with non-curable conditions. At least during the 1960s, hospitals largely ignored some of these requirements of care and even today many hospital wards are not geared towards caring for the terminally ill. Staff may not have had specific training in either the care of the dying or pain control. Ward routines are not necessarily appropriate to the needs of dying people and with the medical emphasis upon cure, death may be seen by many care staff as the ultimate failure.

Such inadequacies influenced the foundation of the modern hospice movement. However, hospital care of the dying has greatly changed since the 1960s so that it may have become closer to the hospice approach in recent years. A different approach does not necessarily imply a different institution so that many hospitals have continuing care units or special care teams for the terminally ill (Lunt and Hillier, 1981). There is also some evidence that hospices have become more like hospitals in terms of both organisation and patient care so that differences between them are now less marked (Seale, 1989). It is also worth noting that, as Seale (1989) points out, there are few studies, particularly from the UK, which examine actual care procedures involved in hospices and hence it is difficult to know how they actually differ one from another or from hospital care.

Home care

As noted, most of the care of dying patients takes place at home or in other non-hospital contexts; many dying patients would in fact prefer to be cared for at home. Thus, Mor and Hiris (1983) report that 50 per cent of their sample of terminally ill patients would have preferred home care. In contrast to the depersonalised environment of the hospital the person's home environment is clearly a familiar place where they will be surrounded by personal items. Bowling (1983) has argued that the trend towards hospitalisation at the time of death has adverse consequences: more people die alone or without their relatives or friends, and this means that the pain of bereavement for those unable to say 'goodbye' is worse. Bowling and Cartwright (1982) found that, of a sample of married people, 74 per cent of those who died in hospital did so without a relative present compared with only 15 per cent of those who died at home. However, there is evidence that the incidence of dying alone either in one's home or in hospital varies considerably depending upon the sample studied. Thus Seale (1990) found that only 22 per cent of those dying in hospital died without anyone else present compared with 31 per cent of those dying at home. These figures were influenced by the fact that many elderly people live alone. Dying at home may thus be more psychologically appropriate for some patients but clearly this will depend upon the patient's circumstances at the time of death.

In this context, it is also worth noting that, as Hinton (1984) points out, caring for a terminally ill person at home can be physically and emotionally exhausting. The possible impact of the burden of such care is discussed in the following chapter. There is also some evidence that, in certain instances, the death of a loved one at home can be more distressing than if the death occurs in hospital. Thus, Birenbaum and Robinson (1991) note that, in the case of terminal care for children dying of cancer, families who received home care were less expressive and cohesive and had more conflict than families whose child received care in the hospital. At follow up, after the child's death, parents whose child received hospital care were more cohesive and expressive and expressed less conflict than parents whose child was cared for at home.

Varying amounts of professional support are available for family members caring for dying relatives at home; the hospice movement has facilitated the provision of such support. In Britain, the majority of home nursing services for the terminally ill are provided by district nurses. With regard to cancer care, the Macmillan Fund, as well as the hospice movement, has led to the rapid expansion of nursing care available for the dying at home (Seale, 1989). However, this care is generally 'hands off', supportive and educational in nature rather than involving practical nursing tasks (Seale, 1992). A number of authors have also noted that there is insufficient professional support available to enable a person to die at home even if they and their relatives wish this to occur (Naysmith and O'Neill, 1989). These same authors argue that lack of suitable professional support is the main reason for the high proportion of deaths occurring in hospital.

The hospice movement

In 1960, in the United Kingdom and Ireland, specialist facilities for terminal care were restricted to a small number of long-established Catholic hospices, ten Marie Curie homes and a small number of allocated beds at the Royal Cancer Hospital, London (James and Field, 1992). The opening of St Christopher's Hospice in London in 1967 foreshadowed the growth of the hospice movement in the United Kingdom in the 1970s and 1980s. By 1991 there were 430 different hospice services in the United Kingdom and Republic of Ireland. Among the services, 159 offered in-patient care, there were 321 home care teams working from community units, hospitals or hospices, 151 day care units and 140 hospitals with support teams or support nurses (Clark, 1991). Similar developments have occurred in the United States and Canada, so that by 1986 there were over 1,500 hospice programmes in existence (Paradis and Cummings, 1986). The hospice movement developed partly as a result of new therapeutic techniques available at that time, such as chemotherapy, palliative radiotherapy and pain control and partly due to increased understanding of the psychosocial aspects of death, dying and bereavement (Zimmerman, 1981) (see box 9.3).

It is difficult to gauge the proportion of people who die in hospices in comparison to hospitals in the United Kingdom as Government statistics do not make such a distinction.

> ### Box 9.3 The hospice approach
>
> Key elements in the hospice approach:
>
> Openness about illness and death.
>
> Prolonging life at the expense of unnecessary suffering should be avoided where possible.
>
> Symptom relief, particularly pain, is of prime importance.
>
> The family should be involved in the care of their dying relatives with hospices providing a welcoming atmosphere for visitors.
>
> (Saunders and Baines, 1983.)

In addition, most hospice care has been for cancer patients rather than any other condition. In one study, out of a total sample of 1,400 randomly selected death registration forms, forty one people or 2.9 per cent died in a hospice. Of the 217 people in the sample who died of cancer 14 per cent died in a hospice (Seale, 1991a). As noted previously, the majority of terminal care, both prior to and since the development of the hospice movement, takes place in the person's home, although over half of all deaths occur in hospitals.

Hospice versus hospital

A key issue is whether hospices differ from hospitals not only in their philosophical intent but also in their actual care of patients and the way in which patients experience the care they receive. A number of studies both in Britain and the United States have compared hospice with hospital experience by assessing recollections of relatives several months after the death (for example, Parkes and Parkes, 1984; Seale, 1991a; Wallston *et al.*, 1988 and also a review by Seale, 1989). Some such studies have found little by way of difference for patients receiving hospice compared with hospital care (Parkes and Parkes, 1984), while others report only modest differences. However, measures used and issues evaluated have varied markedly between studies.

With regard to awareness of their illness and impending death, although patients in both contexts are likely to know what is wrong with them, hospice patients may be more aware of the fact they are dying. Seale (1991a) reports that, in a sample of forty-five hospice service cancer patients compared to 126 other cancer patients, relatives reported retrospectively that 95 per cent of hospice patients were 'certainly' or probably aware they were dying compared with 65 per cent of patients in conventional care. Such retrospective reports may reflect differences in the communicative atmosphere of the environment concerned (talking about death is facilitated in the hospice context) rather than differences in the patient's factual awareness. However, openness about death and the opportunity to be with other dying people may be important. Thus, there would seem to be some benefit to patients in observing another person die in the hospice. Honeybun, Johnston and Tookman (1992) report that, in a small sample ($N = 11$) of hospice patients, those who had observed a death were less depressed.

Other studies have specifically assessed the terminally ill patient's experiences just prior to their death. In developing their study, Wallston *et al.* (1988) argued that previous outcome measures were not sensitive enough to detect differences between hospital and hospice care. They thus developed a specific quality of death measure. Quality of death was defined as the patient experiencing, in the last three days of life, feelings and events that terminally ill people reported they desired. The authors conclude that hospice care, both at home and in a hospital setting, optimises the quality of death. However, not only is there an absence of available data to indicate whether Wallston *et al.*'s quality of death measure is a reliable or valid instrument, it could be argued that hospice patients, perceiving themselves as receiving 'special' care, would feel obliged to report they were obtaining what they desired.

The fact that patients and their relatives in hospices may be more aware of the imminence of death is argued by some to permit the expression of 'anticipatory grief' (Sweeting and Gilhooly, 1990), which, it is argued, facilitates greater calm and acceptance of the ensuing death (Ransford and Smith, 1991). In the light of this a number of studies have evaluated grief resolution of bereaved relatives in hospice and traditional hospital settings (Cameron and Parkes, 1983; Kane *et al.*, 1986; Ransford and Smith, 1991). Cameron and Parkes (1983), in a comparison of twenty close relatives of patients who had died in a palliative care unit, with twenty relatives of patients who had died of cancer in other wards in the same hospital, found less psychological distress in the former group one year after the death. In a further comparison of the spouses of thirty six patients who had died in a hospice with the spouses of thirty five patients who had died in a hospital, Ransford and Smith (1991) found lower levels of depression and a more orderly appearance in the former at six month follow up with further differences in the direction of better adjustment for the hospice group emerging at twelve months follow up. This contrasts with earlier findings reported by Kane *et al.* (1986) who obtained no significant difference between the bereaved of hospice patients and hospital patients on measures of depression, anxiety and social participation at six, twelve or eighteen months follow up. Ransford and Smith suggest that the differing findings between their own study and that of Kane *et al.* could be explained by the fact that, while they studied bereaved spouses, half of Kane *et al.*'s sample consisted of first degree relatives and others rather than spouses. Kane *et al.*'s study has also been criticised because the hospice in the study was located in the hospital in which the control group patients were treated (although the same is true of the Cameron and Parkes, 1983 study) with patients receiving comparable therapeutic and invasive procedures, hence there was not a real separation of groups in the study (Seale, 1989). However, Seale and Kelly (1997) report no differences between the spouses of patients who had died in hospital and those who had died in hospices on outcome measures including adjustment to bereavement and anxiety.

In his review, Seale (1989) concludes by noting that it is still far from clear how hospice care compares to that provided in other settings. Overall, research has identified few measurable differences between hospices and conventional hospitals in the care provided to patients and their families, although hospice recipients frequently express a higher level of satisfaction with the care they receive (Dawson, 1991). However, care for the terminally ill has clearly changed and the hospice movement has played an influential role in prompting change. As James and Field (1992) note, although hospices may have been largely integrated into mainstream services and have tended to be re-medicalised:

This is not to imply that the hospices have changed nothing, nor that they have been unsuccessful in achieving their initial goal of transforming terminal care provision. The process of social change has meant that the hospices affected and were affected by the structures of terminal care to which they were, and continue to be, a response. (p. 1373)

Psychological management of the terminally ill

There are a number of descriptive and anecdotal accounts but few empirical investigations of the application of psychological techniques to the management of physical and emotional problems experienced by the terminally ill. Many of the therapies used are not clearly specified although therapeutic interventions referred to include individual therapy, group support and family therapy (Levy, 1990). Psychological techniques developed for the management of chronic pain, anxiety and depression are also likely to be appropriate with the terminally ill (Wilson, 1989). With regard to psychotherapeutic interventions, Levy (1990) argues that the goal of such therapy:

is not to change the individual's personality, life-style or fundamental values, but to build on strengths within the patient and his or her family that can assist adaptive strategies and that are already at least a nascent part of the patient's repertoire of adaptive behaviours. (p. 205)

Most of the limited empirical research has focused on group support. In one such evaluation, Spiegel, Bloom and Yalom (1981) conducted a one year randomised prospective outcome study with eighty six women with metastatic carcinoma to examine the efficacy of weekly support group meetings and self-hypnosis for pain relief. Issues explored in the group involved the problems of terminal illness such as relationships between the patient and their family and the ability to live as full a life as possible in the face of death. Patients were evaluated at four month intervals. The treatment group in comparison to the control group were found to have significantly lower mood disturbance scores, fewer maladaptive coping strategies and less phobic symptoms. In a subsequent ten year follow up Spiegel *et al.* (1989) report that the intervention group actually had longer survival times – 36.6 months compared with 18.9 months for the control group. Support groups, at the very least, provide their members with significant mutual support in the face of death (Levy, 1990). Whether they provide more than this and if so the mechanism by which this might operate is an intriguing question for future research.

Bereavement and grief

Bereavement is associated with an increase in the prevalence of morbidity and mortality in surviving family members (Helsing and Szklo, 1981). Widow(er)hood in particular is associated with a higher mortality for both sexes, but the excess risk is much higher for men (Bowling, 1987). Most of the research seems to indicate that men are at most risk during the first six months of bereavement. Parkes (1986) found that the mortality rate for widowers after the death of their spouse was 40 per cent higher than the expected rate for men of the same age who were married.

The mechanisms by which grief affects health are unclear. Indirect mechanisms may be implicated: for example, poor self-care such as inadequate diet, disturbed sleep patterns and increased alcohol consumption. Thus, Gass (1989) reports greater alcohol, tobacco and tranquillizer use among a widowed group than among a group of matched, non-widowed controls. This difference persisted for up to thirteen months after the death of the spouse. It is possible that bereaved men in particular may use alcohol to excess; thus, Stroebe and Stroebe (1983) reported higher rates of mortality from cirrhosis of the liver among widowers than among widows. It is possible that direct mechanisms may also account for the increased health risk due to bereavement. Several studies have found impaired immunological function in bereaved individuals (Schleifer *et al.*, 1983; Zisook, 1994).

Grief

A number of descriptions of uncomplicated grief and bereavement have appeared in the literature, several investigators proposing stages or phases which people pass through. For example, Parkes (1972) refers to four phases of mourning (see box 9.4.)

Box 9.4 Stages of grief and bereavement

Parkes (1972) refers to the following four phases of mourning:

(i)   numbness following the loss.
(ii) yearning for the loved one and denial of the permanence of the loss.
(iii) disorganisation and despair.
(iv) reorganisation when the bereaved person begins to reshape and rebuild their lives.

Bowlby (1981), whose early work clearly influenced Parkes, refers to four similar stages. The criticisms which were advanced in relation to stages of dying models referred to earlier can similarly be applied to stages of grief models. While the models provide a useful descriptive framework it is inevitable that people may oscillate between stages, which may not be time limited and some of which may be omitted.

Others have argued that identifying the tasks of mourning is more appropriate and more useful clinically than attempting to define phases or stages (Worden, 1991). An additional issue underlying the stage model is an assumption that one can identify typical and untypical reactions and that the latter reactions, which do not follow the stages in the expected manner, are 'pathological'. The fact that this assumption may often not be warranted is discussed in the following sections.

Morbid or pathological patterns of grief

Pathological grief may be associated either with complications of the process of grief itself or with reactions to bereavement unrelated to the grief process (Zisook *et al.*, 1995). The latter includes depression (Clayton, 1990) and anxiety (Jacobs *et al.*, 1990). In relation to the grief process, pathological grief is associated with either too little grief (delayed grief) or too much grief: that is, grief that is too long (chronic grief) or too intense (hypertrophic grief) (Parkes and Weiss, 1983; Rynearson, 1990). Unfortunately, there is no empirical data to document how much is too much or how little is too little.

The idea that the absence of grief results in later pathological problems has also not been confirmed empirically. Indeed, Wortman and Silver (1989) point out a basic paradox in the notion. The basic assumption is that the bereaved person should experience certain feelings and that failure to do so represents denial and repression of those feelings. This failure is judged as a sign of pathology. If this is so, then those who do show signs of deep distress initially, should adapt more successfully. However, the evidence suggests the opposite – those who are most distressed initially are also likely to be depressed later. Wortman and Silver conclude that:

> the bulk of research to date provides little support for the widely held view that those who fail to exhibit early distress will show subsequent difficulties. The data clearly suggest that 'absent grief' is not necessarily problematic, and at least as it is assessed in the studies conducted to date, 'delayed grief' is far less common than clinical lore would suggest. (p. 351)

In contrast, several investigators have found that intense or hypertrophied grief may be the precursor of chronic or enduring anxiety or depression (Parkes and Weiss, 1983; Worden, 1991), while chronic grief is perhaps the best validated pathological variant of grieving. However, there is no clear consensus about the timescale required to reach a normal resolution of one's grief. As Wortman and Silver (1989) note, notions about length of the recovery process are highly variant, ranging from four to six weeks to four to seven years.

Rather than assuming that pathology is associated with complications of the process of grief itself, a number of authors have identified 'risk factors' which make bereavement more difficult (Sanders, 1988). There is, for example, some evidence that younger widows suffer more in the short term but that older widows suffer more in the longer term. There is also some evidence that lower socio-economic status makes bereavement more difficult, partly due to reduced income which makes it difficult to maintain social contacts. There is also some evidence that those experiencing a sudden, unexpected bereavement have more difficulty adjusting to their loss (Parkes, 1975), suicide placing a particular burden on survivors (Osterweiss, Solomon and Green, 1984).

Rather than assume that grief is 'normal' or 'pathological' there are clearly factors which can serve to make bereavement more or less difficult. As Worden (1991) notes:

> there is more of a continuous relationship between normal and abnormal grief reactions, between the complicated and the uncomplicated, and that pathology is more related to the intensity of a reaction or the duration of a reaction rather than to the simple presence or absence of a specific behaviour. (p. 71)

Anticipatory grief

The term anticipatory grief was first introduced by Lindemann (1944) to describe grief occurring prior to a loss. Sweeting and Gilhooly (1990) note that there is evidence from a variety of studies that family members of the terminally ill experience a range of reactions prior to the death which resemble those associated with bereavement. A number of authors have additionally argued that those gaining the emotional preparation provided by such anticipatory grief, experience less grief after the death. There are clearly limits to this process, however, as anticipation of death for more than six months has been associated with greater post-death grief (Gerber, Rusalem and Hannon, 1975). In reviewing the literature, Sweeting and Gilhooly (1990) note that there is conflicting evidence for the value of anticipatory grief in mitigating post-bereavement grief. They argue that this is partly due to the differing definitions of anticipatory grief used in various studies, differing study designs and varied subject groups.

For example, in many studies, anticipatory grief is evaluated by comparing expected with unexpected death (Parkes, 1975). As noted, unexpected death is more difficult to adjust to. It is clearly questionable whether this is merely due to the denied opportunity for anticipatory grief. In the case of a prolonged terminal illness, family members can still hope for a cure no matter how unrealistic this is and can begin to understand the cause of the person's illness and hence their subsequent death.

Support for the survivors

Various psychological therapies are available to bereaved individuals including self-help groups, voluntary organisations and group psychotherapy (Parkes, 1981), family therapy involving the dying person (Acworth and Bruggen, 1985) and counselling (Speck, 1985). Within the hospice setting, emphasis is often placed on helping families of the dying cope with the impending death and their life after the death. A number of studies have documented the importance of intra-familial support for coping with a death as well as more formal support groups for survivors (Koocher, 1986). Support groups enable people to provide each other with mutual help as well as interpersonal contact and closeness (Dimond, Lund and Caserta, 1987). In reviewing the efficacy of professional support, voluntary and self-help services, Parkes (1980) concluded that such 'services were capable of reducing the risk of psychiatric and psychosomatic disorder resulting from bereavement' (p. 9).

In relation to grief counselling a number of authors have talked about the need to 'work through' the phases or stages of grief. Worden (1991) refers to a series of four stages, each with its attendant tasks. The task of the first stage is to accept the reality of the loss; the task of the second stage is to experience the pain of grief; the task of the third stage is to adjust to an environment from which the deceased is missing; while the task of the fourth stage involves emotionally relocating the deceased person (i.e. finding an appropriate place for the dead in the bereaved person's emotional life) and so moving on with life. The notion of 'grief work' derives from Freud's (1917) essay on 'Mourning and Melancholia'. The goals of grief counselling, which correspond with the four tasks of grieving are: to increase the reality of the loss; to help the person deal with both expressed and latent affect; to help the person overcome various impediments to readjustment after the loss; and to encourage them to say an appropriate goodbye and to feel comfortable reinvesting back in life (Humphrey and Zimpfer, 1996; Worden, 1991).

There is some evidence that intervention in the early stages after loss can be helpful for people at high risk – for example, in relation to losses associated with traumatic incidents – but that for the general bereaved population such immediate intervention will have little impact (Rynearson, 1990). However, not all bereaved people need or want formal intervention and, for many, available support from family and friends is sufficient. In addition, the lack of outcome data relating to the efficacy of interventions makes it difficult to determine which treatments are appropriate for whom and when (Zisook et al., 1995). As these authors note:

> A variety of treatments are available for bereaved individuals; however, no one form of treatment has been proven superior to another, and there is no standard to be used for all patients (p. 373)

Summary

This chapter has examined a range of issues relating to death, dying and bereavement. Within a biomedical context the focus is upon curing the disease rather than caring for the person and many advanced life support or 'heroic measures' can be taken to prolong life. Indeed, people may be kept alive even though they may be unable to lead any form of meaningful existence. Many have argued that such measures and care of the dying conflict with the actual needs of the dying and their families. This conflict is partly responsible for changes in the management of, and expectations relating to, terminal care which have taken place during the past three decades. One such change becoming more common is the development of advance directives such as 'living wills'. Such a will details the amount of care the patient would wish to receive in relation to the process of dying, although it is not at present a recognised legal document in the UK. A further change has been the development of home nursing care and the hospice movement with its emphasis upon palliative care.

The majority of terminal care, both prior to and since the development of the hospice movement, takes place in the person's home or in other non-hospital contexts and many dying patients would prefer to be cared for at home. However, over half of all deaths occur in hospitals. Until the 1960s, hospital care available for the terminally ill was not really geared towards their needs; the same is no doubt true of many hospital environments even today. Such inadequacies influenced the foundation of the modern hospice movement with its emphasis upon palliative care, which aims to relieve unpleasant symptoms and improve the quality of life for all those with non-curable conditions rather than seeking to cure the non-curable. However, of the many studies, both in Britain and the United States, which have compared hospice and hospital care most report little by way of difference in patient experiences while a few report just modest differences. However, care for the terminally ill has clearly changed, with the hospice movement playing an influential role in prompting such change; many hospitals are now closer to the hospice approach while many hospices have become medicalised.

The fact that bereavement is associated with an increase in the prevalence of morbidity and mortality in surviving family members is well documented in the literature, although the mechanisms by which grief affects health are unclear. Several investigators have proposed stages or phases which people pass through in the process of mourning with an assumption that reactions not following the stages in the expected manner are 'pathological'. However, the stage model has not been without its critics. Indeed, it has been argued that identifying the tasks of mourning is more appropriate than attempting to define phases.

A number of different areas of study have provided information about, and added to our knowledge and understanding of, the experiences associated with death, dying and bereavement. Psychology clearly has an important but often under-represented role to play. As Zisook et al. (1995) point out, many of us will experience apprehension and fear about the prospect of our own demise and will have to deal with the death of those we hold dear. While various psychological therapies are available for the dying and bereaved, further research is required to evaluate the appropriateness and efficacy of such interventions.

FURTHER READING

D. Dickenson and M. Johnson (eds) (1993) *Death, Dying and Bereavement*. London: Sage .

S. E. Maddi (1990). Prolonging life by heroic measures: A humanistic existential measure. In P. T. Costa and G. R. VandenBos (eds), *Psychological Aspects of Serious Illness: Chronic conditions, fatal diseases, and clinical care*. Washington, DC: American Psychological Association.

C. M. Parkes, M. Relf and A. Couldrick (1996). *Counselling in Terminal Care and Bereavement*. Leicester: British Psychological Society.

C. Seale (1989). What happens in hospices: A review of research evidence. *Social Science and Medicine*, **28**, 551–559.

J. W. Worden (1991). *Grief Counseling and Grief Therapy: A handbook for the mental health practitioner* (2nd edn). New York: Springer.

S. Zisook, J. J. Peterkin, S. R. Shuchter and A. Bardone (1995). Death, dying and bereavement. In P. M. Nicassio and T. W. Smith (eds), *Managing Chronic Illness. A biopsychosocial perspective*. Washington, DC: American Psychological Association.

CHAPTER 10

The cost of caring

This chapter examines the impact, both negative and positive, of caring for a chronically ill person for both family and friends and professional health care providers. The first issue addressed is the problem of drawing conclusions from the research conducted given wide variations in definitions of caregiving across studies, variations in the carer who is the focus of research and a range of methodological problems identified in studies conducted. The chapter also addresses the potential stress of caring and factors moderating the psychological impact of fulfilling a caring role. The influence of the person's appraisal of their role and the potentially positive aspects of caring are also discussed. The final section of this chapter addresses the issue of the impact of caring upon professional health care providers.

This chapter covers:

> Definitions of caregiving
> The stress of caring
> Positive aspects of caring
> Stress in health care professionals

Introduction

There are numerous ways in which a chronic illness in one person can impinge upon the lives of those who are close to, or who are likely to care for, that person. As well as placing demands upon the caregiver's time, caring can be both physically and emotionally demanding. In the case of family or friends who act as carers a range of emotional reactions may be experienced. Initially fear and distress at the time of diagnosis are a common response. As Wortman and Dunkel-Schetter (1979) note, in relation to cancer, a diagnosis in a loved one creates fear and aversion to the illness, while at the same time creating a realisation of the need to provide support. Other common reactions amongst family and friends who provide care are feelings of isolation and depression, as the multiple demands of long-term caring become apparent. Indeed, such carers are often faced with conflicting emotions, a wish to look after a friend or loved one and yet a fear that they will not be able to cope with the demands of doing so, particularly if the illness concerned is physically or mentally debilitating. In this context, Light and Lebowitz (1989) have described the process of caregiving as a kind of living bereavement.

It is perhaps then not surprising that research evidence suggests that caregiving affects the psychological and physical well-being of many carers. Indeed, many authors have referred to the demands of looking after an ill relative or friend as imposing a 'burden of care'. This term highlights the fact that 'caring' involves tasks additional to the practical aspects of caregiving and that personal limitations are imposed upon the carer by their caring role. Caregiving is likely to impose demands upon both the time and energy of the carer as well as restricting their opportunity for engaging in social activities (Miller and Montgomery, 1990). Whether it is necessary to have a specific term, such as 'burden of care' or 'care giver burden', to highlight these issues is, however, open to question. Indeed, some have argued that more generic terms, such as stress or effects upon well-being, are equally if not more appropriate (Montgomery, 1989).

While caring for the chronically ill is predominantly undertaken by nursing staff, an increasing role in care is being taken by relatives and friends, the so-called informal or unpaid carers. In one report, one adult in seven of the population within the United Kingdom indicated they were providing care to a sick, handicapped or elderly person. Although the majority of carers are women, when the differential sex ratio is taken into account only a slightly higher proportion of women in comparison to men act as carers. However, even when men are the primary caregivers they are less likely to provide intensive, personal care and are more likely to continue pursuing additional activities outside the home (Green, 1988). Broadly similar findings are reported for the United States (Stone, Cafferata and Sangl, 1987). This may explain the findings from some studies that, in relation to caring for family members or friends with brain injury (Allen et al., 1994), stroke (Barusch and Spaid, 1989) and dementia, female caregivers experience a higher level of burden then male caregivers (Morris, R. G. et al., 1991).

However, while caregiving is undoubtedly a demanding activity and while many studies have found that prolonged caregiving can have a detrimental effect upon both mental and physical health, many studies have found no such negative effects. Indeed the results of some studies suggest positive reactions to caregiving. While such differences are due, in part, to variations in the attributes of both the caregiver and the illness concerned, they are also a function of the differing definitions of caregiving used in the literature.

Defining caregiving

The literature illustrates a lack of consensus about how caregiving should be defined. As Barer and Johnson (1990) comment:

> definitions [of caregiver] are almost as broad as the number of journal articles represented and range from great specificity to varied and flexible categories. (p. 26)

Care provided can be classified according to its relative importance, the degree of personal involvement required from the caregiver or the needs of the recipient.

'Care', defined from the perspective of the caregiver's involvement, can range from one instance of assistance to prolonged periods of full-time involvement; it can involve telephone contact, companionship, household assistance or full physical care and can be provided by a range of individuals or agencies (see box 10.1).

Box 10.1 Forms of caregiver involvement

Stone, Cafferata and Sangl (1987) distinguish between primary and secondary caregivers.

Primary caregivers – have total responsibility for the provision of care, although they may also have formal (paid) or informal help
Secondary caregivers – do not assume the main responsibility for caring.

Cicirelli (1983) describes primary and secondary care not according to the degree of involvement required per se but on the basis of the tasks of caregiving involved.

Primary care involves help with:
homemaking
housing
income
maintenance
personal care
some health care

Secondary care involves:
transportation
psychological support
social and recreational activities
spiritual support
protection
bureaucratic mediation

'Care' defined on the basis of the need, either actual or perceived, of the recipient of care can also reveal considerable individual variation. Someone requiring continuous personal care will clearly place a greater 'burden' upon a carer than someone who requires in-home assistance while being relatively independent.

As well as defining care from the perspective of the caregiver's involvement, or the perceived need of the recipient, studies have also defined care in terms of the degree of impairment of the recipient of care. Hence, care-related stress is inferred from the characteristics of the recipient rather than being based upon any measurement of the actual demands experienced by individual carers. For example, in relation to caregiving of individuals with brain injury, McKinlay *et al.* (1981) define the objective burden as the total of those problems encountered by the person with the head injury. This includes their physical, cognitive and emotional functioning, and their degree of dependence and behavioural disturbance. Subjective burden is the amount of psychological strain on relatives that is attributable to changes in the person who lives with the consequences of brain injury. Chwalisz (1992), in his review of the literature pertaining to burden of care in relation to brain injury, extended this distinction. He conceptualised objective burden as not only involving observable changes in the person with brain injury, but also environmental changes for the caregiver: that is financial strain, changes in employment status or role. He further argues that subjective burden should include the caregiver's negative reaction to the presence of objective burden. In this regard Livingstone and Brooks (1988) suggest that burden may be thought of as a composite of caregivers' complaints, such as increased frustration, perceived lack of support and being prevented from achieving one's goals (subjective burden), measurable effect of stress on the caregiver (objective burden) and the effect of the injury on family interaction. Numerous studies have assessed burden of care in family members caring for an individual with brain injury, in relation to perceived personality changes, such as loss of temper and anger, finding that the burden actually intensifies in magnitude over time (e.g. Brooks *et al.*, 1987).

Which carer to study

In addition to variations across studies in definitions of care, studies also differ according to which family member(s) or friend(s) is studied in relation to burden of care. The most frequent focus is upon family relations including both parents and spouses (e.g. Allen *et al.*, 1994; Brooks *et al.* 1987; Livingston, Brooks and Bond, 1985), the spouse (e.g. Barusch and Spaid, 1989; Zarit, Todd and Zarit, 1986), adult children (e.g. Matthews and Rosner, 1988) or parents (e.g. Bauma and Schweitzer, 1990; Holroyd and Guthrie, 1986). Taking this particular approach a number of studies have investigated the possibility of differences in reports pertaining to burden of care according to whether the carer is the parent, spouse, sibling, son or daughter of the recipient of care. For example, Allen *et al.* (1994), Livingston, Brooks and Bond (1985) and Brooks *et al.* (1987) compared parents and spouses caring for an individual with a brain injury. In Allen *et al.*'s study, although there were few differences between parents and spouses overall, in comparison to parents, spouses reported that they lived more isolated lives, while the definition of burden conveyed by spouses was more emotional in nature than that conveyed by parents. In contrast, Livingstone *et al.* found no difference in depression, anxiety or social adjustment of mothers and wives, while Brooks *et al.* found no difference in reported subjective burden. Other studies have argued that families caring for children with chronic illness are likely to face specific stressors, such as the impact upon the dynamics of the family and concern about the inadequate attention that might be paid to other siblings (Sherman, 1995).

Clearly the issue is a complex one and it is not merely the type of familial relationship between carer and care recipient which will affect reported caregiver burden. Many other factors including the nature of their prior relationship, living arrangements, personal disposition and additional support available are likely to influence the carer's reaction to their new role.

Thus, in contrast to the caregiver with limited social support, a carer with a supportive network of family and friends will not only be in a position to share the caring role but may well have the opportunity to take some respite from continuous care. It seems reasonable to suppose that a married daughter living in her own home while caring for her elderly widowed mother who lives locally and who receives additional support from other family members will have a very different set of experiences to an unmarried daughter living with, and being the sole carer of, her elderly widowed mother.

Other methodological problems

In addition to variations in definitions of caregiving across studies and variations in the carer studied, a range of methodological problems have been identified within the caregiving literature (Barer and Johnson, 1990). These include the fact that samples cited in studies are frequently unrepresentative of caregivers in general, being recruited from branches of carers' associations, through responses to advertisements or through formal social or health care agencies. Those who are coping adequately may not be linked into any such contact routes and hence samples studied may provide distorted results, caregiver burden being less marked than many studies suggest.

A further problem relates to measures of caregiver burden used across studies which are often specific to particular disability types. For example, Livingston, Brooks and Bond (1985) derived their Perceived Burden Scale specifically for studying burden in relation to caring for an individual with brain injury. Such specifically constructed scales may produce results pertinent to one population group but they prevent meaningful comparisons from being made across disabilities.

In their review, Barer and Johnson (1990) conclude by arguing that:

> because of predominantly arbitrary definitions of caregiver in the literature; usually a vague consideration of needs; largely self-selected samples; and scant mention of the care recipient and his or her total social support network, it is possible that researchers and practitioners do not have a very clear conception of the caregiving process. (p. 28)

The stress of caring

A number of studies have highlighted the potential stress imposed by caring for a chronically ill relative or friend and the potential psychological and physical impact this may have. In an attempt to provide a framework for this research, Pearlin *et al.* (1990) have argued that caregiving is marked by two types of stressor (see box 10.2).

A particular demand may be placed on the carer as a result of the changing relationship between carer and care recipient. Caregiver and recipient may remain husband and wife or parent and child, yet the adoption of the caregiving role means that new role-related expectations and obligations evolve which are often at odds with the expectations of the primary relationship, which may now exist in name only. Indeed, the

Box 10.2 Stress imposed by caring

It has been argued that caregiving is marked by the following two types of stressor:

Primary stressors – these relate to the tasks and demands involved in daily care:
   Supervising the person
   Restraining them from potentially harmful actions
   Performing bodily maintenance tasks, such as bathing, dressing and feeding
   Performing instrumental tasks such as paying bills

Secondary stressors then develop or intensify as caregiving continues over time and include:
   Economic hardship
   Family conflict
   The changing relationship between carer and care recipient
   An inability to maintain social contacts, leisure pursuits or paid employment

(Pearlin *et al.*, 1990; Scharlach, Sobel and Roberts, 1991; Stone, Cafferata and Sangl, 1987.)

carer may feel trapped in their new role which has developed from their pre-existing relationship. While they entered the initial relationship willingly they may now feel an obligation to remain with the care recipient who is no longer the person they once were, the carer additionally feeling guilty about any desire they may experience not to care for their loved one.

In this regard, Pearlin *et al.* (1990) refer to perceived stress as a major dimension of caregiver stress; of particular importance in relation to this is the feeling of being captive in an unwanted role. Caregiving is frequently characterised by high levels of demand combined with limited discretion on the caregiver's part about whether to perform a caregiving role, the very characteristics which research has shown to be related to high levels of strain and dissatisfaction (Orbell and Gillies, 1993). Key markers of such strain are psychological morbidity and physical health problems, indices which have been frequently assessed in the context of caregiving.

Psychological impact of caring

That caregiving is stressful is evident from psychological morbidity documented in carers; in reviewing the literature, Schulz, Visintainer and Williamson (1990) concluded that the available studies document an increase in self-reported psychiatric symptoms and psychiatric illness among most caregivers when compared to population norms or control groups. Feelings of depression, stress, low morale, poor self-esteem and reduced life satisfaction are commonly reported by caregivers, as are sleep problems, severe fatigue, anxiety and feelings of hopelessness about the future (Haley *et al.*, 1987a; Kiecolt-Glaser *et al.*, 1987, 1991).

The high risk of depression in particular has been documented in numerous studies of caregivers (Cohen and Eisdorfer, 1988; Coppel *et al.*, 1985; Kiecolt-Glaser *et al.*, 1987; Morris, R. G., Morris and Britton, 1988; Schulz, Tompkins and Rau, 1988; Thompson and Haran, 1985; Wade, Leigh-Smith and Hewer, 1986). Thus, Thompson and Haran

(1985) found evidence for psychiatric symptomatology in 40 per cent of carers of patients who had undergone a leg amputation. Schulz, Tompkins and Rau (1988) found that caregivers of stroke patients had two to three times the level of depression compared with non-caregiving adults, while Wade, Leigh-Smith and Hewer (1986) found that 13 per cent of their stroke carers were clinically depressed. Studies also report a marked incidence of depression in dementia caregivers although disorder rates are highly variable across studies, ranging from 14 per cent to 81 per cent (Coppel *et al.*, 1985; Morris, R. G., Morris and Britton, 1988).

Such variation is no doubt explained in part by the method used for assessing depression (self-report measures versus diagnostic interviews) and samples studied (spouse versus other carer). For example, Coppel *et al.* (1985), using a diagnostic interview schedule in their study of spousal caregivers of Alzheimer's patients, found that 41 per cent of their sixty eight carers were currently depressed and that an additional 40 per cent had been previously depressed during care giving. However, they included mild depression within their diagnostic group rather than more stringent criteria, which may have led to an overestimate of the incidence.

The problems posed by depression for caregivers of spouses with dementia are illustrated in one of the few longitudinal studies conducted to date. In this study eighty six spousal carers of dementia sufferers were compared with eighty six matched controls not involved in any caregiving activity (Dura, Stukenberg and Kiecolt-Glaser, 1990; Kiecolt-Glaser *et al.*, 1987). The authors report that spousal caregivers in comparison to a matched control group did not differ in frequency of depressive disorder in the year prior to caregiving. However, after a year of providing care, 30 per cent of spousal caregivers had experienced a depressive disorder compared with only 1 per cent of the matched controls.

Risk of depression is dependent on a number of factors including the caregiver's past psychiatric state, personality and social support network, the nature of the illness and the degree of impairment of the care recipient and the nature of the relationship between carer and care recipient. For example, Tompkins, Schulz and Rau (1988) found that caregivers of stroke patients most at risk for depression were those who were less optimistic, more concerned about future care for the patient and in a closer relationship with, that is married to, the patient.

Physical impact of caring

There is also some evidence from questionnaire and interview studies that those involved in caring for a chronically ill relative or friend also suffer increased physical health problems. Caregivers report higher rates of anaemia, arthritis, back pain, cancers, cardiovascular disorders and diabetes either in comparison with their non-caregiving peers or than would be expected on the basis of population norms (e.g. Haley *et al.*, 1987a; Pruchno and Potashnik, 1987). Indeed, Pruchno and Potashnik report that only a quarter of their sample of caregivers rated their own health as better than that of those for whom they were caring. However, as Hart (1994) notes, many such studies rely on subjective ratings of health status and one can clearly question the reliability of such data. Longitudinal studies by Kiecolt-Glaser and her colleagues involving direct measures of health status (Kiecolt-Glaser *et al.*, 1987, 1991) do, though, provide confirmatory evidence of impaired physical health in carers. They found that carers relative to controls exhibited decrements on three measures of cellular immunity, as well as having higher rates of infectious illness, primarily upper respiratory tract infections.

Factors affecting caregiver stress

A number of factors moderate the potential impact of caring. The most frequently investigated in the literature are the carer's age and gender, the quality of the prior relationship between the carer and care recipient, the illness of the care recipient, the carer's wider social support network and coping resources.

Age

There are a number of inconsistent findings relating age to impact of caring. Some studies indicate that younger carers are more adversely affected (e.g. Haley *et al.*, 1987b), other studies suggest no relationship between caregiver age and the psychological impact of caring (Pratt *et al.*, 1985), while other studies suggest that younger caregivers report more positive aspects of caring (Kinney *et al.*, 1995). Inevitably a range of other factors, such as social support and prior relationship, are likely to interact with age to influence the impact of caring.

Gender

A number of studies suggest that the impact of caring is greater for women than for men. For example, Lieberman and Fisher (1995) found that women carers in comparison to male carers of a family member with Alzheimer's disease or vascular dementia reported more anxiety and depression. Indeed, in their review, Dwyer and Coward (1991) suggest that the available literature indicates that gender is a crucial variable influencing caregiver stress. However, other studies suggest little by way of any gender difference in this regard (Kiecolt-Glaser *et al.*, 1991). Such differing results no doubt reflect, in part, the various methodologies used and the failure, in some studies, to take into account the general tendency for women to be more likely than men to report emotions. In addition, any gender differences which do exist may be attributable to the fact that female caregivers in contrast to their male counterparts provide the most care, are more likely to assume an intensive, personal role and are less likely to maintain outside interests. They are thus more likely to perceive their caring role as being a high demand task over which they have limited discretion and hence one involving strain and dissatisfaction (Orbell and Gillies, 1993).

Illness of care recipient

It seems reasonable to assume that the level of demand placed upon the caregiver will vary according to the severity of the care recipient's illness. Illness severity has been variously conceptualised as involving functional impairment and/or cognitive impairment. With regard to the former, a number of studies have found only relatively weak or non-significant relationships with carer well-being (Gilhooly, 1984; Pruchno and Resch, 1989). In contrast, a number of studies have found a positive relationship between degree of cognitive impairment and caregiver stress (Allen *et al.*, 1994; Barusch and

Spaid, 1989; Lieberman and Fisher, 1995; Pratt *et al.*, 1985) although this is far from being a universal finding.

In the context of cognitive impairment, a number of studies have highlighted the particular burden posed for those who care for individuals with Alzheimer's disease or other progressive dementias, or those with cognitive impairment following stroke; others have highlighted the burden of caring for those who exhibit personality change subsequent to brain injury. The course of Alzheimer's disease is unpredictable, as is the rapidity of decline, with survival after onset varying from eight to over twenty years. In many such instances the recipient of care may not even be aware they are being cared for and hence not empathise with, or appreciate, the caregiver's efforts. Patients also may become delusional or develop other psychotic symptoms. Thus a number of studies with carers of those with Alzheimer's disease, other progressive dementias, stroke and brain injury have found that variations in the severity of disease or degree of cognitive impairment are related to variations in health or well-being of spouse and adult children (e.g. Allen *et al.*, 1994; Barusch and Spaid, 1989; Lieberman and Fisher, 1995; Pratt *et al.*, 1985). Indeed, Lieberman and Fisher (1995) found that illness severity (which included elements of both cognitive and functional impairment) was related to impaired physical health not only in the spouse, who was the primary caregiver, but also in the children of the ill person and their own husbands and wives. However, other studies suggest that caregiver well-being is either unaffected or only slightly affected by the severity of cognitive impairment in care recipients (Eagles *et al.*, 1987; Gilhooly, 1984; Zarit, Reever and Bach-Peterson, 1980).

Such differing findings are due in part to differing methodologies and measuring instruments used, but are also due to the fact that behavioural correlates of cognitive decline are more important markers of caregiver stress than cognitive impairment per se (Zarit, Todd and Zarit, 1986) and that type and level of behavioural disturbance shown by the care recipient is associated with carer stress (Hinchliffe, Hyman and Blizzard, 1992). Indeed, there is not a linear relationship between cognitive impairment and behavioural disturbance. As Orbell and Gillies (1993) note, with moderate levels of cognitive impairment the person may be more active and hence more of a potential risk while with more extreme impairment the person may be more passive and, although they may need to be fed, bathed, toileted and clothed, require less vigilant attention. Thus, behavioural problems perceived by the caregiver are more likely to be related to poor carer well-being than degree of cognitive impairment per se (Gilleard *et al.*, 1984; O'Connor *et al.*, 1990; Orbell and Gillies, 1993; Zarit, Todd and Zarit, 1986). Allen *et al.* (1994) found that cognitive and behavioural problems of the brain injured individual were associated with a greater degree of burden than other aspects of injury severity or physical disability.

Quality of prior relationship

There are a number of inconsistent findings relating quality of prior relationship to impact of caring. For example, while Gilhooly (1984) found no relationship between quality of relationship prior to illness between carer and recipient of care on impact of caring, Morris, L. W., Morris and Britton (1988) found that a positive relationship lessened the impact of caring. Such findings are inevitably based upon retrospective recall and such judgements are unlikely to be perfectly reliable. It also seems reasonable to conclude that someone in a poor relationship prior to a partner or friend's illness developing may avoid taking on a caring role. Hence, study samples are likely to be restricted to those who were in at least a reasonably good relationship prior to the illness developing. It is also likely that many other variables will interact with the quality of prior relationship to influence the impact of caring.

Social support

As noted, caregiving can inevitably restrict the carer's opportunities for social contacts. In a comparison of caregivers with matched controls, Kiecolt-Glaser *et al.* (1991) found that caregivers reported fewer important personal relationships and saw members of their network less frequently. Caregivers also gave lower ratings to both the closeness and helpfulness of the relationships they had in comparison to the controls. Yet, the importance of social support as a buffer against stress has been well documented in the literature (Cohen and Wills, 1985). While not all caregiver studies report beneficial effects of social support (e.g. Pratt *et al.*, 1985) most studies suggest that social support is an important moderating variable in relation to the potential psychological impact of caregiving. Thus, caregivers who report receiving more informal social support also report that they feel less burdened (e.g. Zarit, Reever and Bach-Peterson, 1980) and rate their health as better (Haley *et al.*, 1987b). Support from one's wider network of family and friends as well as from service agencies, when assessed as useful, reduces the negative consequences of caring (Chiriboga, Weiler and Nielsen, 1989) and enhances the carer's ability to cope. As Silliman *et al.* (1987) note, the family caregivers of the elderly stroke patients in their study were able to cope with the stress because of extensive involvement and support from other family members and friends.

In one of the few studies measuring immune function rather than relying on self-reported measures, Kiecolt-Glaser *et al.* (1991) found that caregivers with lower levels of social support had poorer immune function assessed between nine and twenty four months later. On the basis of available research evidence it seems reasonable to conclude that social support enhances both the mental and physical health of caregivers and enables them to cope more effectively with the stress of caring.

Although informal carers often receive additional formal support from visiting nurses and physical therapists, a number of studies suggest that such formal services play a relatively less important supportive role than that played by family members or friends of the carer (Silliman *et al.*, 1987). In contrast, a number of studies have also emphasised the utility of respite care, or short-term relief for primary caregivers in maintaining psychological well-being. Respite care can involve any service, treatment or activity the intended purpose of which is temporarily to relieve primary caregivers, from caregiving responsibilities. This might involve periodic nursing help at the carer's home or a brief period of hospitalisation for the care recipient. In relation to home-based paediatric respite care for parents caring for a chronically ill child, Sherman (1995) reports improved quality of life and reduced somatic complaints for primary caregivers. While family and friends may be most highly valued as providers of secondary support, formal, supportive care also plays an important role in providing temporary relief from caring and hence in maintaining psychological well-being.

Appraisal and coping

As with stress in general, there is evidence from the caregiving literature that perception of events as stressful or pleasurable is more important in determining health and well-being than the type or quantity of objective events performed per se (Kinney and Stephens, 1989; Zarit, Reever and Bach-Peterson, 1980). Thus, there is evidence that not all caring is perceived as stressful and that many people perceive and document positive aspects to caregiving.

The stress of caregiving also seems to be moderated by coping style. Thus, there is evidence that depression, anxiety and burden in caregivers is associated with the adoption of passive, non-confronting or avoidance coping strategies (Matson, 1994; Pratt *et al.*, 1985), while problem-solving coping has a relatively modest impact in terms of reducing carer stress (Wright *et al.*, 1991). Adopting a stress-coping framework to guide research in this area may provide more meaningful results than merely examining demographic and illness-related variables.

In sum, a number of studies attest to the fact that caregiving can be stressful, impinging upon both the physical and mental health of the carer. Indeed, according to Zarit (1989), who refers to the numerous descriptive studies which exist documenting how much stress caregivers experience, the fact that caregiving is stressful has been well established. However, as discussed above, there is clearly variability in the responses of caregivers to the challenge of caregiving and the negative impact of caring is moderated by a number of variables. These include the severity and type of illness, availability of social support, coping resources and quality of prior relationships. Unfortunately, the literature relating to factors determining the impact of caregiving upon caregivers is replete with inconsistent findings. This is no doubt due in part to the variety of outcome measures employed, the range of variables likely to influence outcome and differing sample characteristics, as well as the varying definitions of caregiving employed and as a consequence the number and intensity of caregiving demands faced by study participants. While carer stress has been most frequently defined in relation to degree of caregiver involvement or recipient need, less attention has been paid to the carer's perception and appraisal of their role and hence the likelihood that there may be positive as well as negative aspects to caregiving has all too often been overlooked.

Positive aspects of caring

Although Zarit (1989) asserts that 'the fact that caregiving is stressful has been well established', not all studies report high levels of psychological distress amongst carers. For example, Silliman *et al.* (1987), in a study of family caregivers of elderly stroke patients, note that although there were emotional and social consequences for caregivers most were 'content and committed to their roles' (p. 369). Others have also highlighted the various positive aspects of caregiving (see box 10.3).

As with negative aspects of caring, positive aspects will be influenced by a range of factors, most notably the carer's appraisal and perception of the situation, their social support network and the nature of the care recipient's illness. With regard to the latter, Kinney *et al.* (1995) report that participants in their study who were caring for a relative who had experienced a stroke within the past two years reported more positive aspects of caring

> ### Box 10.3 Positive aspects of caring
>
> The following positive aspects of caring have been documented:
> Satisfaction and a sense of fulfilment for the caregiver
> Pride in one's ability to manage problems and deal with crisis
> An opportunity to learn more about the care recipient
> An increased feeling of closeness between the caregiver and their relative
> Pleasures resulting from day-to-day interactions with the care-recipient
>
> (Kinney and Stephens, 1989; Kinney et al., 1995; Stephens, Franks and Townsend, 1994.)

than an earlier sample they had studied who were caring for relatives with Alzheimer's disease. One reason they suggest for this is that stroke is a medical crisis that has the potential for stability, if not recovery, while, in marked contrast, Alzheimer's disease is characterised by progressive deterioration. A similar point in relation to caring for elderly stroke patients is made by Silliman *et al.* (1987) who suggest that watching a sick older person improve is satisfying and may enhance caregiver morale.

In sum then it seems reasonable to conclude that caregiving is stressful as Zarit (1989) asserts but, as with any stressor, the impact is moderated by a range of factors. It is also important not to overlook the potentially positive aspects of caring for a relative. Rather than merely seeking to delineate the psychological or physical impact of caring, a goal for future research might be to determine factors predictive of vulnerability to adverse reactions amongst carers. In this way appropriate support could be targeted at those who are most in need of respite.

Health care professionals

Just as caring can be stressful for informal carers there is a large body of research indicating that work stress, demoralisation and a sense of frustration are common among professional health care workers (Moos and Schaefer, 1987). The term burnout has often been used in such contexts. Burnout in nursing staff in particular has received considerable attention in the literature (e.g. Moos and Schaefer, 1987) but has also been documented in other groups of health care professionals including general practitioners (Kirwan and Armstrong, 1995), hospital consultants (Ramirez *et al.*, 1996), social workers (Koeske and Kelly, 1995) and psychotherapists (Myers, 1996). Indeed, one writer has even referred to burnout as 'a health care professional's occupational disease' (Felton, 1998, p. 237).

The concept and phenomenon of burnout first received serious attention when Freudenberger (1974) used the term to denote a state of physical and emotional depletion resulting from conditions of work. The concept was popularised in the 1970s and 1980s by Maslach (1976, 1982) who investigated the prolonged effects of stress in a variety of professional groups (see box 10.4).

Just as with stress in general, burnout contributes to emotional and physical problems, absenteeism, employee turnover, poor staff morale and performance and strained relationships outside the work context as well as adversely affecting the quality of patient care (Felton, 1998). Thus, in relation to health care workers, Jones (1981)

Box 10.4 Components of burnout

Maslach has argued that burnout is marked by three components:
  emotional exhaustion or energy depletion
  the development of negative, cynical attitudes about recipients (depersonalisation
    of the patient)
  a tendency to evaluate oneself negatively, especially with regard to a reduced sense
    of accomplishment in one's job

(Maslach, 1976; Maslach and Jackson, 1982.)

reports an association between burnout in nurses and unauthorised extensions of work breaks, while Firth and Britton (1989) report an association between burnout and absence and departure from the job.

The prevalence of such problems related to burnout is attested to by a recent UK national survey of over seven and a half thousand National Health Service employees including doctors, nurses and professionals allied to medicine (Hardy, Shapiro and Borrill, 1997). The results indicated that levels of fatigue amongst health care workers were higher than for the general population. Highest levels of general fatigue were experienced by doctors, especially female doctors and professions allied to medicine, while highest levels of fatigability were experienced by ancillary and nursing staff. Both general fatigue and fatigability were associated with high levels of psychological distress.

In an effort to conceptualise the interplay of forces inherent in burnout at work, Moos and Schaefer (1987) have drawn on the stress and coping literature. They argue that determinants of stress at work include environmental factors (i.e. organisational and contextual) and personal factors (encompassing types of job as well as background characteristics of the person). These are affected by the individual's cognitive appraisal and coping resources which feed into outcome in terms of staff morale and quality of care. As with stress in general, two dimensions in particular seem to be predictive of high levels of stress at work: that is, an increasingly heavy workload combined with a lack of control or choice about how or when to perform a particular task or set of tasks (i.e. high levels of demand combined with limited discretion). As in any other work context, role ambiguity and perceived lack of influence over decision making are related to poor morale and detachment (Maslach and Jackson, 1982). A healthy work environment is one characterised by a workload which is perceived to be manageable, a sense of participation in the organisation, a positive view of leadership and satisfactory support with work-related problems (Thomsen *et al.*, 1998). There is some evidence that such factors may not be readily evident in many health care contexts.

Thus, Moos and Schaefer (1987) note that, in comparison to employees in business settings, health care workers report less job involvement and less co-worker cohesion and supervisor support. Landsbergis (1988) found that job satisfaction, burnout, depression and psychosomatic symptoms among hospital and nursing home employees were related to high workload and low perceived discretion over tasks, even after controlling for hours worked. In support of this Parkes (1982) found that a move to a ward with greater job discretion and work support was associated with an increase in work satisfaction and improved performance as well as a decrease in emotional difficulties in a group of student nurses. Similarly, Decker (1985) reports an association between increased job satisfaction and increased independence and decision-making power for nurses. These general factors also emerge in a review of stress research in the nursing profession reported by Hingley and Cooper (1986). These authors refer to five general sources of stress; these were qualitative and quantitative workload, organisational support and involvement in decision making, home–work conflict, dealing with patients and relatives, and role confidence and competence.

Burnout and specific work environments

Numerous studies have sought to investigate particular aspects of the working environment which are stressful for a variety of health care professionals. In one study of 150 student nurses the six most frequently cited sources of stress were care of dying patients cited by 30 per cent of the sample, interpersonal conflict with other nurses (18 per cent), insecurity about professional competence and fear of failure (19 per cent), interpersonal problems with patients (10 per cent), work overload (8 per cent) and concerns about nursing care (3 per cent) (Parkes, 1985). The stress of working in specifically demanding environments, dealing with personal care, death and dying, is obviously an important issue for many health care workers.

Dealing with death and dying

Moos and Schaefer (1987) report particularly high rates of burnout in staff working in intensive care, emergency or terminal care. As noted above, in one study, care of dying patients was the stressor most frequently reported by student nurses (Parkes, 1985). In a further study of a sample of ninety two community nurses, who had provided home nursing care during the last twelve months of a patient's life, half the nurses interviewed said they found it difficult coping with the emotional distress of terminally ill patients and their relatives. In addition, one-third found it difficult to cope with their own reactions to death and dying and nearly three quarters found it more difficult caring for people who were dying than caring for other patients (Seale, 1992). Seale notes that a substantial amount of stress was associated with feelings of lack of control over important determinants of the patient's distress, such as drug doses, or telling the prognosis, or arriving early enough in the course of the disease. In a study of doctors and nurses working with AIDS and in oncology, Catalan et al. (1996) report levels of psychological distress comparable for medical in-patients and out-patients, while about one-fifth of the staff concerned had significant levels of work-related stress. Situations staff found particularly difficult involved caring for people in deteriorating health, those in terminal stages, young patients, dealing with psychological problems and the families of the patients. Similar issues have been reported in other studies (Woolley et al., 1989; Cull, 1991).

Given the natural difficulties experienced by health care staff working with terminally ill patients, it is of interest to evaluate whether staff working only in specifically designated terminal care environments, such as provided by hospices, experience more stress than nursing staff working in other environments. Indeed, given the ethos of the hospice movement and the expectations of staff support, one might anticipate greater staff satisfaction and morale and less stress in such environments. In one such comparison of heath care staff reactions in hospice and hospital settings, Cooper and Mitchell (1990) reported that hospital staff had lower job satisfaction than hospice nurses, but that hospice nurses had more anxiety and psychosomatic complaints. Contrary results are reported in a later study comparing palliative care nurses with nurses from medical oncology units (Plante and Bouchard, 1995). The palliative care nurses reported less occupational stress and burnout and significantly more professional support than their colleagues working in medical oncology units. In a comprehensive review of staff stress in hospice/palliative care environments, Vachon (1995) concludes that, although stress was a problem early in the development of the hospice movement, much of the current literature suggests that staff in palliative care have less burnout than professionals in mental health, oncology or emergency care and less anxiety than established norms and less difficulty in dealing with issues of death and dying than their hospital based colleagues. She concludes by noting that:

> while stress exists in hospice/palliative care, it is by no means a universal phenomenon ... this ... may be due to ... staff support programmes and team development ... the stress that currently exists in palliative care is due in large measure to organisational issues, but there is still some difficulty in dealing with issues of death and dying. (p. 109)

Factors moderating burnout

As with stress in general several studies report that a range of factors including social support, personality and coping resources moderate the effects of burnout. Thus, Hare and Pratt (1988) found that nurses who received social support from outside the work setting were less likely to experience burnout than those who received less informal support (Hare and Pratt, 1988). Indeed, informal support is widely used given the general lack of provision of formal support networks in many environments (Catalan et al., 1996). There is also evidence that higher levels of supervisor support and peer cohesion are associated with lower levels of burnout amongst nursing staff (Eastburg et al., 1994). Eastburg et al. additionally found that extroverts in particular required social support in order to reduce burnout. They also report that when nurse supervisors were trained in giving positive feedback to staff the latter's level of emotional exhaustion declined. Also, as with stress in general, research suggests that a strong personality, involving commitment, control and challenge, is associated with significantly less burnout, such findings having been reported both for general hospital nurses (McCranie, Lambert and Lambert, 1987) and for nurses working in oncology and AIDS wards (Constantini et al., 1997).

In sum, workers in health care contexts inevitably face demands additional to those faced by many other professionals. Particular stress is likely to be experienced by those having to deal with death and dying on a regular basis (Catalan et al., 1996; Cull, 1991; Woolley et al., 1989; Silverman, 1993). Drawing a balance between involvement but not overinvolvement and detachment while not appearing to be disinterested in the person is difficult to achieve (Koeske and Kelly, 1995). There is evidence that informal support (Hare and Pratt, 1988), supervisor support and peer cohesion (Eastburg et al., 1994) and formal structured staff support (Cull, 1991) can all be of value in helping staff cope with the emotional aspects of caring for patients with terminal illness.

Clearly, early identification of, and assistance with, emotional difficulties among staff members should be a central feature of any environment placing a heavy emotional emand upon its workforce. Unfortunately, such difficulties are often overlooked or assumed to be a normal hazard of the job. Prevention is clearly desirable and could be facilitated with limited, targeted changes to the work environment. Providing the individual worker with greater perceived job control, improving communication, introducing flexible working hours and facilitating support meetings would all help to limit the development of problems. Supervisor and staff support can be important in relation to both prevention and treatment although the latter would be more appropriately provided via the various employee assistance programmes promoted in the USA and now increasingly available in the UK. Unfortunately these are often restricted to business employees rather than being available to health care professionals.

Summary

The present chapter has examined the impact of caring for the chronically ill upon both relatives and friends, the so-called informal carers, and upon professional health care staff. A number of studies attest to the fact that caring can be stressful, impinging upon both the physical and mental health of the carer. The high risk of depression in particular has been documented in numerous studies. However, the potentially negative impact of caring is moderated by a range of variables. Thus, a number of studies suggest that conditions resulting in cognitive impairment, such as is the case with Alzheimer's disease or other progressive dementias, or following stroke, pose a particular burden for carers. Factors ameliorating the burden of caring include availability of social support and use of problem-focused coping.

However, the literature relating to factors determining the impact of caregiving upon carers is replete with inconsistent findings. This is due in part to the variety of outcome measures employed, which are often designed specifically for the study in question, and varying definitions of caregiving used. Caring has been defined according to its relative importance, the degree of personal involvement required from the caregiver or the needs of the recipient. Inevitably carers' involvement can be highly varied, ranging from minimal but regular telephone contact to prolonged periods of full-time involvement providing full physical care. Inevitably the burden of care will vary dramatically in such different instances. Although the majority of studies evaluating the burden of care have focused upon family members, studies also differ according to which family member(s) or friend(s) form the focus of research. In addition, samples cited in studies are frequently unrepresentative of caregivers in general, being recruited from branches of carers' associations, through responses to advertisements or through formal social or health care agencies.

While caring is undoubtedly stressful little attention has been paid to the potentially positive aspects of caring. Studies have documented feelings of fulfilment and pride on the part of caregivers in spite of the undoubted demands they face.

Just as caring can be stressful for informal carers there is a large body of research indicating that caring can be stressful for professional health care workers. The term burnout is frequently used in such contexts. Staff working in intensive care, emergency or terminal care clearly have a demanding role. Particular difficulties relate to caring for people in deteriorating health, those in terminal stages, young patients, patients with psychological problems and the families of the patients. As with stress in general, several studies report that a range of factors, including social support, moderates the effects of burnout.

The majority of care for the sick, handicapped and elderly is undertaken by family and friends; almost 15 per cent of the adult population in the UK is involved in such care. This figure may well increase given the decreasing availability of hospital care. Although positive aspects of caring have been noted, caring is undoubtedly demanding. Carers, both informal and formal, need adequate support; in the latter instance this may involve staff groups or peer support. In the case of informal carers, temporary relief from caring provided either by formal, nursing backup or from family and friends can be essential in maintaining psychological well-being.

FURTHER READING

B. M. Barer and C. L. Johnson (1990). A critique of the caregiving literature. *The Gerontologist*, 30, 26–29.

R. J. V. Montgomery (1989). Investigating caregiver burden. In K. S. Markides and C. L. Cooper (eds), *Aging, Stress and Health*. Chichester: Wiley.

R. H. Moos and J. A. Schaefer (1987). Evaluating health care work settings: A holistic conceptual framework. *Psychology and Health*, 1, 97–122.

L. I. Pearlin, J. T. Mullan, S. J. Semple and M. M. Skaff (1990). Caregiving and the stress process: An overview of concepts and their measures. *The Gerontologist*, 30, 583–594.

R. Schulz, P. Visintainer and G. Williamson (1990). Psychiatric and physical morbidity effects of caregiving. *Journal of Gerontology: Psychological Sciences*, 45, P181–P191.

REFERENCES

Abram, H. S., Moore, G. L. and Westervelt, F. B. (1971). Suicidal behavior in chronic dialysis patients. *American Journal of Psychiatry*, 127, 1199–1204.

Acworth, A. and Bruggen, P. (1985). Family therapy when one member is on the death bed. *Journal of Family Therapy*, 7, 379–385.

Adam, S. A., Horner, J. K. and Vessey, M. P. (1980). Delay in treatment for breast cancer. *Community Medicine*, 2, 195–201.

Affleck, G., Tennen, H. and Croog, S. (1987). Causal attribution, perceived benefits and morbidity after a heart attack: An eight year study. *Journal of Consulting and Clinical Psychology*, 55, 29–35.

Affleck, G., Tennen, H., Croog, S. and Levine, S. (1987). Causal attribution, perceived control, and recovery from a heart attack. *Journal of Social and Clinical Psychology*, 5, 339–355.

Affleck, G., Tennen, H., Pfeiffer, C. and Fifield, C. (1987). Appraisals of control and predictability in adapting to chronic disease. *Journal of Personality and Social Psychology*, 53, 273–279.

Aiken, L. S., West, S. G., Woodward, C. K. and Reno, R. R. (1994a). Health beliefs and compliance with mammography-screening recommendations in asymptomatic women. *Health Psychology*, 13, 122–129.

Aiken, L. S., West, S. G., Woodward, C. K., Reno, R. and Reynolds, K. D. (1994b). Increasing screening mammography in asymptomatic women: Evaluation of a second generation, theory based program. *Health Psychology*, 13, 526–538.

Ajzen, I. (1988). *Attitudes, Personality and Behavior*. Chicago, IL: Dorsey Press.

Ajzen, I. (1991).The theory of planned behavior. *Organizational Behavior and Human Decision Processes*, 50, 179–211.

Albrecht, G., Walker, V. and Levy, J. (1982). Distance from the stigmatized: A test of two theories. *Social Science and Medicine*, 16, 1319–1327.

Alen, K. D., Danforth, J. S. and Drabman, R. S. (1989). Videotaped modelling and film distraction for fear reduction in adults undergoing hyperbaric oxygen therapy. *Journal of Consulting and Clinical Psychology*, 57, 554–558.

Alexander, R. W. and Fedoruk, M. J. (1986). Epidemic psychogenic illness in a telephone operators' building. *Journal of Occupational Medicine*, 28, 42–45.

Allen, K., Linn, R. T., Gutierrez, H. and Willer, B. S. (1994). Family burden following traumatic brain injury. *Rehabilitation Psychology*, 39, 28–48.

Alonzo, A. (1984). An illness behavior paradigm: A conceptual exploration of a situational-adaptation perspective. *Social Science and Medicine*, 19, 499–510.

Alonzo, A. (1986). The impact of the family and lay others on care-seeking during life-threatening episodes of suspected coronary artery disease. *Social Science and Medicine*, 22, 1297–1304.

Altschuler, J. (1997). *Working with Chronic Illness*. Basingstoke, Hampshire: Macmillan Press.

American Cancer Society (1987). Special touch: A personal plan of action for breast health. 87–IMM–No. 2095–LE.

Andersen, R. and Newman, F. (1973). Societal and individual determinants of medical care utilization in the United States. *Milbank Memorial Fund Quarterly*, 51, 95– 107.

Anderson, B. L., Anderson, B. and deProsse, C. (1989). Controlled prospective longitudinal study of women with cancer: 1. Sexual functioning outcomes. *Journal of Consulting and Clinical Psychology*, 57, 683–691.

Anderson, E. and Anderson, P. (1987). General practitioners and alternative medicine. *Journal of the Royal College of General Practitioners*, **37**, 52–55.

Anderson, E. A. (1987). Preoperative preparation for cardiac surgery facilitates recovery, reduces psychological distress, and reduces the influence of acute postoperative hypertension. *Journal of Consulting and Clinical Psychology*, **55**, 513–520.

Anderson, K. O., Bradley, L. A., Young, L. D. and McDaniel, L. K. (1985). Rheumatoid arthritis: Review of psychological factors related to etiology, effects and treatment. *Psychological Bulletin*, **98**, 358–387.

Anderson, K. O. and Masur, F. T. (1983). Psychological preparation for invasive medical and dental procedures. *Journal of Behavioral Medicine*, **6**, 1–40.

Andrew, J. M. (1970). Recovery from surgery, with and without preparatory instructions, for three coping styles. *Journal of Personality and Social Psychology*, **40**, 264–271.

Andrykowski, M. A. (1990). The role of anxiety in the development of anticipatory nausea in cancer chemotherapy: A review and synthesis. *Psychosomatic Medicine*, **52**, 458–475.

Andrykowski, M. A., Redd, W. H. and Hatfield, A. K. (1985). Development of anticipatory nasuea: A prospective analysis. *Journal of Consulting and Clinical Psychology*, **53**, 447–454.

Angel, R. and Thoits, P. (1987). The impact of culture on the cognitive structure of illness. *Culture, Medicine and Psychiatry*, **11**, 465–494.

Anson, O., Carmel, S. and Levin, M. (1991). Gender differences in the utilization of emergency department services. *Women and Health*, **17**, 91–104.

Antonovsky, A. and Hartman, H. (1974). Delay in the detection of cancer: A review. *Health Education Monographs*, **2**, 98–128.

Arber, S. (1987). Social class, non-employment, and chronic illness: Continuing the inequalities in health debate. *British Medical Journal*, **294**, 1069–1073.

Armelagos, G. J., Leatherman, T., Ryan. M. and Sibley, L. (1992). Biocultural synthesis in medical anthropology. *Medical Anthropology*, **14**, 35–52.

Armstrong, D., Glanville, T., Bailey, E. and O'Keefe, G. (1990). Doctor-initiated consultations: A study of communication between general practitioners and patients about the need for reattendance. *British Journal of General Practice*, **40**, 241–242.

Astin, J. A. (1998). Why patients use alternative medicine: Results of a national study. *Journal of the American Medical Association*, **279**, 1548–1553.

Atkins, E., Solomon, L. J., Worden, J. K. and Foster, R. S. Jr. (1991). Relative effectiveness of methods of breast self-examination. *Journal of Behavioral Medicine*, **14**, 357–367.

AuBuchon, P. G. and Calhoun, K. S. (1985). Menstrual cycle symptomatology: The role of social expectancy and experimental demand characteristics. *Psychosomatic Medicine*, **47**, 35–45.

Auerbach, S. M. (1989). Stress management and coping research in a healthcare setting: An overview and methodological commentary. *Journal of Consulting and Clinical Psychology*, **57**, 388–385.

Baer, H. A., Singer, M. and Johnsen, J. H. (1986). Toward a critical medical anthropology. *Social Science and Medicine*, **23**, 95–98.

Baider, L., Perez, T. and De-Nour, A. (1989). Gender and adjustment to chronic disease: A study of couples with colon cancer. *General Hospital Psychiatry*, **11**, 1–8.

Baker, B. and Mersky, H. (1983). Classification and association of hypochondriasis in patients from a psychiatric hospital. *Canadian Journal of Psychiatry*, **28**, 629–634.

Bandura, A. (1969). *Principles of Behavior Modification*. New York: Holt, Rinehart & Winston.

Bandura, A. (1977). Self-efficacy: Toward a unifying theory of behavior change. *Psychological Review*, **84**, 191–215.

Bandura, A. (1986). *Social Foundations of Thought and Action: A social cognitive theory*. Englewood Cliffs, NJ: Prentice Hall.

Barer, B. M. and Johnson, C. L. (1990). A critique of the caregiving literature. *The Gerontologist*, 30, 26–29.

Barondess, J. (1979). Disease and illness – A crucial distinction. *American Journal of Medicine*, 66, 375–376.

Barsky, A. and Klerman, G. (1983). Overview: Hypochondriasis, bodily complaints, and somatic style. *American Journal of Psychiatry*, 140, 273–283.

Barsky, A., Wychak, G. and Klerman, G. (1986). Medical and psychiatric determinants of outpatient medical utilization. *Medical Care*, 24, 548–560.

Barusch, A. and Spaid, W. (1989). Gender differences in caregiving: Why do wives report greater burden? *The Gerontologist*, 19, 667–676.

Bass, L. W. and Cohen, R. L. (1982). Ostensible versus actual reasons for seeking pediatric attention: Another look at parental ticket of admission. *Pediatrics*, 70, 870–874.

Bass, M. J., Buck, C., Turner, L., Dickie, P., Pratt, G. and Robinson, H. C. (1986). The physician's actions and the outcome of illness in family practice. *Journal of Family Practice*, 23, 43–47.

Bastani, R., Marcus, A. C. and Hollatz–Brown, A. (1991). Screening mammography rates and barriers to use: A Los Angeles county survey. *Preventive Medicine*, 20, 350–363.

Bastani, R., Marcus, A. C., Maxwell, A. E., Prabhu, I. and Yan, K. X. (1994). Evaluation of an intervention to increase mammography screening in Los Angeles. *Preventive Medicine*, 23, 83–90.

Battistella, R. M. (1971). Factors associated with delay in the initiation of physicians' care among late adulthood persons. *American Journal of Public Health*, 61, 1348–1361.

Baum, A., Herberman, H. and Cohen, L. (1995). Managing stress and managing illness: Survival and quality of life in chronic disease. *Journal of Clinical Psychology in Medical Settings*, 2, 309–333.

Bauma, R. and Schweitzer, R. (1990). The impact of chronic illness on family stress: A comparison between autism and cystic fibrosis. *Journal of Clinical Psychology*, 45, 722–730.

Baumann, L. J. and Leventhal, H. (1985). I can tell when my blood pressure is up, can't I ? *Health Psychology*, 4, 203–218.

Baumann, L. J., Brown, R. L., Fontana, S. A. and Cameron, L. (1993). Testing a model of mammography intention. *Journal of Applied Social Psychology*, 23, 1733–1756.

Baumann, L. J., Cameron, L. D., Zimmerman, R. S. and Leventhal, H. (1989). Illness representations and matching labels with symptoms. *Health Psychology*, 8, 449–469.

Bebbington, P. and Delemos, I. (1996). Pain in the family. *Journal of Psychosomatic Research*, 40, 451–456.

Beck, A. T. (1976). *Cognitive Therapy and the Emotional Disorders*. New York: International Universities Press.

Becker, M. H. (1985). Patient adherence to prescribed therapies. *Medical Care*, 23, 539–555.

Becker, M. H. and Maiman, L. A. (1975). Sociobehavioral determinants of compliance with health and medical care recommendations. *Health Care*, 13, 10–24.

Beckman, H. B. and Frankel, R. M. (1984). The effect of physician behavior on the collection of data. *Annals of Internal Medicine*, 101, 692–696.

Beckman, H. B., Kaplan, S. H. and Frankel, R. (1989). Outcome based research on doctor–patient communication: A review. In M. Stewart and D. Roter (eds), *Communicating with Medical Patients*. Newbury Park, CA: Sage.

Beeby, D. G. and Morgan-Hughs, J. O. (1980). Behaviour of nonsedated children in the anaesthetic room. *British Journal of Anaesthesia*, 52, 279–281.

Benbassat, J., Pilpel, D. and Tidhar, M. (1998). Patients' preferences for participation in clinical decision making: A review of published surveys. *Behavioral Medicine*, 24, 81–88.

Bennett, D. S. (1994). Depression among children with chronic medical problems: A meta-analysis. *Journal of Pedriatric Psychology*, 19, 149–169.

Bennett, S. E., Lawrence, R. S., Fleischmann, K. H., Gifford, C. S. and Slack, W. V. (1983). Profile of women practicing breast self-examination. *Journal of the American Medical Association*, 249, 488–491.

Bentler, P. M. and Speckart, G. (1981). Attitudes 'cause' behaviors: A structural equation analysis. *Journal of Personality and Social Psychology*, **40**, 226–238.

Berkanovic, E., Hurwicz, M. and Landsverk, J. (1988). Psychological distress and the decision to seek medical care. *Social Science and Medicine*, **11**, 1215–1221.

Berkanovic, E. and Telesky, C. (1982). Social networks, beliefs, and the decision to seek medical care: An analysis of congruent and incongruent patterns. *Medical Care*, **20**, 1018–1026.

Berkanovic, E., Telesky, C. and Reeder, S. (1981). Structural and social psychological factors in the decision to seek medical care for symptoms. *Medical Care*, **19**, 693–709.

Berkman, L. F. and Syme, S. L. (1979). Social networks, host resistance and mortality: A nine year follow-up of Alameda County residents. *American Journal of Epidemiology*, **109**, 186–204.

Berman, P., Hogan, D. B. and Fox, R. A. (1987). The atypical presentation of infection in old age. *Age and Ageing*, **16**, 201–208.

Bernstein, B. and Kane, R. (1981). Physicians' attitudes towards female patients. *Medical Care*, **19**, 600–608.

Beunderman, R. and Duyvis, D. J. (1990). Cardiac phobia. In A. A. Kaptein, H. M. van der Ploeg, B. Garssen, P. J. G. Schreurs and R. Beunderman (eds), *Behavioural Medicine: Psychological treatments of somatic disorders*. Chichester: Wiley.

Bianchi, G. N. (1971). The origins of disease phobia. *Australian and New Zealand Journal of Psychiatry*, **5**, 241–257.

Birenbaum, L. K. and Robinson, M. A. (1991). Family relationships in two types of terminal care. *Social Science and Medicine*, **32**, 95–102.

Bishop, G. D. (1984). Gender, role and illness behaviour in a military population. *Health Psychology*, **3**, 519–534.

Bishop, G. D. (1987). Lay conceptions of physical symptoms. *Journal of Applied Social Psychology*, **17**, 127–146.

Bishop, G. D. (1991). Understanding the understanding of illness: Lay disease representations. In J. A. Skelton and R. T. Croyle (eds), *Mental Representation in Health and Illness*. New York: Springer.

Bishop, G. D. and Converse, S. A. (1986). Illness representations: A prototype approach. *Health Psychology*, **5**, 95–114.

Bishop, G. D., Briede, C., Cavazos, L., Grotzinger, R. and McMahon, S. (1987). Processing illness information: The role of disease proptotype. *Basic and Applied Social Psychology*, **8**, 21–43.

Black, D. (1980). Inequalities in health: Report of a Research Woring Group chaired by Sir Douglas Black. London: DHSS.

Black, P. M. and Morrow, G. R. (1991). Anticipatory nausea and emesis: Behavioural interventions. In M. Watson (ed.), *Cancer Patient Care: Psychosocial treatment methods*. BPS/Cambridge University Press.

Blackwell, B. (1973). Drug therapy: Patient compliance. *New England Journal of Medicine*, **289**, 249–253.

Blair, S. N., Goodyear, N. N., Gibbons, L. W. and Cooper, K. H. (1984). Physical fitness and incidence of hypertension in healthy normotensive men and women. *Journal of the American Medical Association*, **252**, 487–490.

Blair, S. N., Kohl, H. W. III, Paffenbarger, R. S., Clark, D. G., Cooper, K. H. and Gibbons, L. W. (1989). Physical fitness and all-cause mortality. *Journal of the American Medical Association*, **262**, 2395–2401.

Blanchard, C. G., Labrecque, M. S., Ruckdeschel, J. C. and Blanchard, E. B. (1988). Information and decision-making preferences of hospitalized cancer patients. *Social Science and Medicine*, **27**, 1139–1148.

Blanchard, E. B., Martin, J. E. and Dubbert, P. M. (1988). *Non-drug Treatments for Essential Hypertension*. Elmsford, NY: Pergamon Press.

Blaney, P. H. (1986). Affect and memory: A review. *Psychological Bulletin*, **99**, 29–246.

Blaxter, M. (1983). The causes of disease: Women talking. *Social Science and Medicine*, **17**, 59–69.

Blaxter, M. (1990). *Health and Lifestyles*. London: Routledge.

Blaxter, M. and Paterson, E. (1982). *Mothers and Daughters: A three generational study of health attitudes and behaviour*. London: Heinemann.

Bloom, J. R. (1982). Social support, accomodation to stress, and adaptation to breast cancer. *Social Science and Medicine*, **16**, 1329–1338.

Bloom, J. R. and Kessler, L. (1994). Emotional support following cancer: A test of the stigma and social activity hypothesis. *Journal of Health and Social Behavior*, **35**, 118–133.

Bloom, J. R. and Spiegel, D. (1984). The effect of two dimensions of social support on the social functioning and psychological well-being of women with advanced breast cancer. *Social Science and Medicine*, **59**, 831–837.

Bloom, J. R., Fobair, P., Spiegel, D., Cox, R. S., Varghese, A. and Hoppe, R. (1991). Social supports and the social well-being of cancer survivors. *Advances in Medical Sociology*, **2**, 95–114.

Bloor, M., Samphier, M. and Prior, L. (1987). Artifact explanations of inequalities in health: An assessment of the evidence. *Sociology of Health and Illness*, **9**, 231–264.

Blum, R. W. M. (1992). Chronic illness and disability in adolescence. *Journal of Adolescent Health*, **13**, 364–368.

Blumenthal, J. A. and McCubbin, J. A. (1987). Physical exercise as stress management. In A. Baum and J. E. Singer (eds), *Handbook of Health Psychology*, Vol. V. Stress. Hillsdale, NJ: Lawrence Erlbaum Associates.

Blumenthal, J. A., Williams, R. S., Williams, R. B. and Wallace, A. G. (1980). Effects of of exercise on the type A (coronary-prone) behavior pattern. *Psychosomatic Medicine*, **42**, 289–296.

Bodegard, G., Fyro, K. and Larsson, A. (1982). Psychological reactions in 102 families with a newborn who has a falsely positive screening test for congenital hypothyroidism. *Acta Paediatrica Scandinavica*, Suppl 304, 1–21.

Boeke, S., Stronks, D., Verhage, F. and Zwaveling, A. (1991). Psychological variables as predictors of the length of post-operative hospitalization. *Journal of Psychosomatic Research*, **35**, 281–288.

Bombardier, C. H., D'Amico, C. and Jordan, J. S. (1990). The relationship of appraisal and coping to chronic illness adjustment. *Behaviour Research and Therapy*, **28**, 297–304.

Bond, G. G., Aiken, L. S. and Somerville, S. C. (1992). The health belief model and adolescents with insulin-dependent diabetes mellitus. *Health Psychology*, **11**, 190–198.

Bond, J., Coleman, P. and Peace, S. (eds) (1993). *Ageing in Society: An introduction to social gerontology*. London: Sage.

Bosley, C.M., Fosburg, J.A. and Cochrane, G.M. (1995). The psychological factors associated with poor compliance with treatment in asthma. *European Respiratory Journal*, **8**, 899–904.

Bostick, R. M., Sprafka, J. M., Virnig, B. A. and Potter, J. D. (1994). Predictors of cancer prevention attitudes and participation in cancer screening examinations. *Preventive Medicine*, **23**, 816–826.

Bouchard, C., Shepherd, R. J., Stephens, T., Sutton, J. R. and McPherson, B. D. (eds). (1990). *Exercise, Fitness and Health: A consensus of current knowledge*. Champaign, IL: Human Kinetics.

Bouma, R. and Schweitzer, R. (1990). The impact of chronic childhood illness on family stress: A comparison between autism and cyctic fibrosis. *Journal of Clinical Psychology*, **45**, 722–730.

Bourhis, R. Y., Roth, S. and MacQueen, G. (1989). Communication in the hospital setting: A survey of medical and everyday language use amongst patients, nurses and doctors. *Social Science and Medicine*, **28**, 339–345.

Bowlby, J. (1961). Processess of mourning. *International Journal of Psychoanalysis*, **42**, 317–330.

Bowling, A. (1983). The hospitalisation of death: Should more people die at home? *Journal of Medical Ethics*, **9**, 158–161.

Bowling, A. (1987). Mortality after bereavement: A review of the literature on survival periods and factors affecting survival. *Social Science and Medicine*, **24**, 117–124.

Bowling, A. and Cartwright, A. (1982). *Life After A Death: A study of the elderly widowed*. London: Tavistock.

Bowman, M. A., Herndon, A., Sharp, P. C. and Digman, M. B. (1992). Assessment of the patient–doctor interaction scale for measuring patient satisfaction. *Patient Education and Counselling*, **19**, 75–80.

Boxer, P. A. (1985). Occupational mass psychogenic illness. *Journal of Occupational Medicine*, **27**, 867–872.

Boyer, C. B., Friend, R., Chlouverakis, G. and Kaloyanides, G. (1990). Social support and demographic factors influencing compliance of hemodialysis patients. *Journal of Applied Social Psychology*, **20**, 1902–1918.

Bracken, M. B. and Bernstein, M. (1980). Adaptation to and coping with disability one year after spinal cord injury: An epidemiological study. *Social Psychiatry*, **15**, 33–41.

Brandt-Rauf, P. W., Andrews, L. R. and Schwarz-Miller, J. (1991). Sick-hospital syndrome. *Journal of Occupational Medicine*, **33**, 737–739.

Bray, G. A. (1986). Effects of obesity on health and happiness. In K. D. Brownell and J. P. Foreyt (eds), *Handbook of Eating Disorders: Physiology, psychology and treatment of obesity, anorexia and bulimia*. New York: Basic Books.

Britten, N. (1994). Patients' ideas about medicines: A qualitiative study in a general practice population. *British Journal of General Practice*, **44**, 465–468.

Brody, D. S. (1980). The patient's role in clinical decision making. *Annals of Internal Medicine*, **93**, 718–722.

Brody, E. and Kleban, M. H. (1983). Day-to-day mental and physical health symptoms of older people: A report on health logs. *The Gerontologist*, **23**, 75–85.

Brody, E. M., Kleban, M. H. and Moles, E. (1983). What older people do about their day-to-day mental and physical health symptoms. *Journal of the American Geriatrics Society*, **31**, 489–498.

Brooks, N., Campsie, L., Symington, C., Beattie, A. and McKinlay, W. (1987). The effects of severe-head injury on patient and relative within seven years of injury. *Journal of Head Trauma Rehabilitation*, **2**, 1–13.

Brooks-Gunn, J. (1986). Differentiating premenstrual symptoms and syndromes. *Psychosomatic Medicine*, **48**, 385–387.

Brooks-Gunn, J. and Ruble, D. N. (1986). Men's and women's attitudes and beliefs about the menstrual cycle. *Sex Roles*, **14**, 287–299.

Brophy, C. and Erickson, M. (1990). Children's self-statements and adjustment to elective outpatient surgery. *Journal of Developmental and Behavioral Pediatrics*, **11**, 13–16.

Brown, G. K., Nicassio, P. M. and Wallston, K. A. (1989). Pain coping strategies and depression in rheumatoid arthritis. *Journal of Consulting and Clinical Psychology*, **57**, 652–657.

Brown, G. K., Wallston, K. A. and Nicassio, P. M. (1989). Social support and depression in rheumatoid arthritis: A one-year prospective study. *Journal of Applied Social Psychology*, **19**, 1164–1181.

Brown, J. and Fitzpatrick, R. (1988). Factors influencing compliance with dietary restrictions in dialysis patients. *Journal of Psychosomatic Research*, **32**, 191–196.

Brownell, K. D. and Wadden, T. A. (1992). Etiology and treatment of obesity: Understanding a serious, prevalent and refractory disorder. *Journal of Consulting and Clinical Psychology*, **60**, 435–442.

Brownlee-Duffeck, M., Peterson, L., Simonds, J. F., Goldstein, D., Kile, C. and Hoette, S. (1987). The role of health beliefs in the regimen adherence and metabolic control of adolescents and adults with diabetes mellitus. *Journal of Consulting and Clinical Psychology*, **55**, 139–144.

Brubaker, R. and Wickersham, D. (1990). Encouraging the practice of testicular self-examination: A field application of the theory of reasoned action. *Health Psychology*, 9, 154–163.

Brunnquell, D. and Kohen, D. P. (1991). Emotions in pediatric emergencies: What we know, what we can do. *Children's Health Care*, 20, 240–247.

Bukberg, J., Penman, D. and Holland, J. C. (1984). Depression in hospitalized cancer patients. *Psychosomatic Medicine*, 46, 199–212.

Buller, M. K. and Buller, D. B. (1987). Physicians' communication style and patient satisfaction. *Journal of Health and Social Behavior*, 28, 375–388.

Bullough, B. (1972). Poverty, ethnic identity and preventive health care. *Journal of Health and Social Behavior*, 13, 359–374.

Bulman, J. R. and Wortman, C. B. (1977). Attributions of blame and coping in the 'real world': Severe accident victims react to their lot. *Journal of Personality and Social Psychology*, 35, 351–363.

Bundek, N. I., Marks, G. and Richardson, J. L. (1993). The role of health locus of control beliefs in cancer screening of elderly Hispanic women. *Health Psychology*, 12, 193–199.

Bundy, C. (1989). Cardiac disorders. In A. Broome (ed.), *Health Psychology: Process and applications*. London: Chapman and Hall.

Burgess, C., Morris, T. and Pettingale, K. W. (1988). Psychological response to cancer diagnosis – II. Evidence for coping styles (coping styles and cancer diagnosis). *Journal of Psychosomatic Research*, 32, 263–272.

Burgess, I. S., Lerner, D. J., D'Agostino, R. B., Vokanas, P. S., Hartman, C.R. and Gaccione, P. (1987). A randomised control trial of cardiac rehabilitation. *Social Science and Medicine*, 24, 359–370.

Burish, T. G. and Carey, M. P. (1986). Conditioned aversive responses in cancer chemotherapy patients: Theoretical and developmental analysis. *Journal of Consulting and Clinical Psychology*, 54, 593–600.

Burish, T. G. and Lyles, J. N. (1981). Effectiveness of relaxation training in reducing aversive reactions to cancer chemotherapy. *Journal of Behavioral Medicine*, 4, 65–78.

Burish, T. G., Carey, M. P., Krozely, M. G. and Greco, F. A. (1987). Conditioned side effects induced by cancer chemotherapy: Prevention through behavioral treatment. *Journal of Consulting and Clinical Psychology*, 55, 42–48.

Burish, T., Carey, M., Wallston, K., Stein, M., Jamison, R. and Lyles, J. (1984). Health locus of control and chronic disease: An external locus of control may be advantageous. *Journal of Social and Clinical Psychology*, 2, 326–332.

Burish, T., Snyder, S. and Jenkins, R. (1991). Preparing patients for cancer chemotherapy: Effect of coping preparation and relaxation interventions. *Journal of Consulting and Clinical Psychology*, 59, 5, 18–525.

Burman, B. and Margolin, G. (1992). Analysis of the association between marital relationships and health problems: An interactional perspective. *Psychological Bulletin*, 112, 39–63.

Burnam, M. A., Timbers, D. M. and Hough, R. L. (1984). Two measures of psychological distress among Mexican Americans, Mexicans and Anglos. *Journal of Health and Social Behaviour*, 25, 24–33.

Burton, H. J., Kline, S. A., Lindsay, R. M. and Heidenheim, A. P. (1986). The relationship of depression to survival in chronic renal failure. *Psychosomatic Medicine*, 48, 261–269.

Bury, M. (1987). *Health and Illness in a Changing Society*. London: Routledge.

Byles, J. E., Redman, S., Hennrikus, D. and Sanson-Fisher, R. W. (1992). Delay in consulting a medical practitioner about rectal bleeding. *Journal of Epidemiology and Community Health*, 46, 241–244.

Byrne, P. and Long, B. (1976). *Doctors Talking to Patients: A study of the verbal behaviour of general practitioners consulting in their surgeries*. London: HMSO.

Cacioppo, J. T. and Petty, R. E. (1982). *Perspectives in Cardiovascular Psychophysiology*. New York: Guildford Press.

Cacioppo, J. T., Andersen, B. L., Turnquist, D. C. and Petty, R. E. (1986) Psychophysiological comparison processes: Interpreting cancer symptoms. In B. L. Andersen (ed.), *Women with Cancer: Psychological perspectives*. New York: Springer-Verlag.

Cacioppo, J. T., Andersen, B. L., Turnquist, D. C. and Tassinary, L. G. (1989). Psychophysiological comparison theory: On the experience, description, and assessment of signs and symptoms. *Patient Education and Counselling*, **13**, 257–270.

Caggiula, A. W., Christakis, G., Farrand, M., Hulley, S. B., Johnson, R., Lasser, N. L., Stamler, J. and Widdowson, G. (1981). The multiple risk factor intervention trial (MRFIT): IV. Intervention on blood lipids. *Preventive Medicine*, **10**, 443–475.

Cahill, G. F. Jr., Etzwiler, D. D. and Freinkel, N. (1976). 'Control' and diabetes. *New England Journal of Medicine*, **294**, 1004–1005.

Calabrese, L. H. (1990). Exercise, immunity, cancer, and infection. In C. Bouchard, R. J. Shepherd, T. Stephens, J. R. Sutton, and B. D. McPherson (eds), *Exercise, Fitness and Health: A consensus of current knowledge*. Champaign, IL: Human Kinetics.

Calle, E. E., Flanders, D., Thun, M. J. and Martin, L. M. (1993). Demographic predictors of mammography and Pap smear screening in US women, *American Journal of Public Health*, **83**, 53–60.

Calnan, M. (1987). *Health and Illness: The lay perspective*. London: Tavistock.

Calnan, M. and Johnson, B. (1985). Health, health risks and inequalities: An exploratory study of women's perceptions. *Sociology of Health and Illness*, **7**, 54–75.

Calnan, M. and Rutter, D. R. (1986). Do health beliefs predict health behaviour? An analysis of breast self-examination. *Social Science and Medicine*, **22**, 673–678.

Cameron, J. and Parkes, C. M. (1983). Terminal care: Evaluation of effects on surviving care before and after bereavement. *Post-graduate Medical Journal*, **59**, 73–78.

Cameron, L., Leventhal, E. A. and Leventhal, H. (1993). Symptom representation and affect as determinants of care seeking in a community-dwelling, adult sample population. *Health Psychology*, **12**, 171–179.

Cameron, L., Leventhal, E. A. and Leventhal, H. (1995). Seeking medical care in response to symptoms and life stress. *Psychosomatic Medicine*, **57**, 37–47.

Cameron, R. and Best, J. A. (1987). Promoting adherence to health behavior change interventions: Recent findings from behavioral research. *Patient Education and Counselling*, **10**, 139–154.

Campbell, J. D., Mauksch, H. O., Neikirk, H. J. and Hosokawa, M. C. (1990). Collaborative practice and provider styles of delivering health care. *Social Science and Medicine*, **30**, 1359–1365.

Carey, M. P. and Burish, T. G. (1985). Anxiety as a predictor of behavior therapy outcome for cancer chemotherapy patients. *Journal of Consulting and Clinical Psychology*, **53**, 860–865.

Carey, M. P. and Burish, T. G. (1988). Etiology and treatment of the psychological side effects associated with cancer chemotherapy: A critical review and discussion. *Psychological Bulletin*, **104**, 307–325.

Carmody, T. P., Fey, S. G., Pierce, D. K., Connor, W. E. and Matarazzo, J. D. (1982). Behavioral treatment of hyperlipidemia: Techniques, results and future directions. *Journal of Behavioral Medicine*, **5**, 91–116.

Carmody, T. P., Istvan, J., Matarazzo, J. D., Connor, S. L. and Connor, W. E. (1986). Applications of social learning theory in the promotion of heart-healthy diets: The Family Heart Study dietary intervention model. *Health Education Research*, **1**, 13–27.

Carmody, T. P., Matarazzo, J. D. and Istvan, J. A. (1987). Promoting adherence to heart-healthy diets: A review of the literature. *The Journal of Compliance in Health Care*, **3**, 105–124.

Carney, R. M., Rich, M. W., teVelde, A., Saini, J., Clark, K. and Jaffe, A. S. (1987). Major depressive disorder in coronary artery disease. *American Journal of Cardiology*, **60**, 1273–1275.

Carney, R. M., Schechter, K. and Davis, T. (1983). Improving adherence to blood glucose testing in insulin-dependent diabetic children. *Behavior Therapy*, **14**, 247–254.

Carroll, D., Bennett, P. and Davey Smith, G. (1993). Socio-economic health inequalities: Their origins and implications. *Psychology and Health*, **8**, 295–316.

Cartwright, A. and Seale, C. F. (1990). *The Natural History of a Survey: An account of the methodological issues encountered in a stduy of life before death*. London: King's Fund.

Cartwright, A., Hockey, L. and Anderson, J. (1973). *Life before Death*. London: Routledge.

Catalan, J., Burgess, A., Pergami, A., Hulme, N., Gazzard, B. and Phillips, R. (1996). The psychological impact on staff of caring for people with serious diseases: The case of HIV infection and oncology. *Journal of Psychosomatic Research*, **40**, 425–435.

Celentano, D., Linet, M. S. and Stewart, W. F. (1990). Gender differences in the experience of headache. *Social Science and Medicine*, **30**, 1289–1295.

Chaitchik, S., Kreitler, S., Shaked, S., Schwartz, I. and Rosin, R. (1992). Doctor–patient communication in a cancer ward. *Journal of Cancer Education*, **7**, 41–54.

Champion, V. L. (1985). Use of the health belief model in determining frequency of breast self-examination. *Research in Nursing and Health*, **8**, 373–379.

Champion, V. L. (1990). Breast self-examination in women 35 and older: A prospective study. *Journal of Behavioral Medicine*, **13**, 523–538.

Champion, V. L. (1992). Relationship of age to factors influencing breast self-examination practice. *Health Care for Women International*, **13**, 1–9.

Champion, V. L. and Miller, T. K. (1992). Variables related to breast self-examination. *Psychology of Women Quarterly*, **16**, 81–96.

Chassin, M. R. (1993). Explaining geographic variation: The enthusiasm hypothesis. *Medical Care*, **31**, YS37–YS44.

Chassin, M. R., Kosecoff, J., Park, R. E. *et al.* (1987). Does inappropriate use explain geographic variations in the use of health care services? *Journal of the American Medical Association*, **258**, 2533.

Chiriboga, D., Weiler, P. G. and Nielsen, K. (1989). Stress of caregivers. *Journal of Applied Social Sciences*, **13**, 118–141.

Chrisman, N. J. and Kleinman, A. (1983). Popular health care, social networks, and cultural meanings: The orientation of medical anthropology. In D. Mechanic (ed.), *Handbook of Health, Health Care, and the Health Professions*. New York: Free Press.

Christensen, A. J., Smith, T. W., Turner, C. W., Holman, J. M. Jr. and Gregory, M. C. (1990). Type of hemodialysis and preference for behavioral involvement: Interactive effects of adherence in end-stage renal disease. *Health Psychology*, **9**, 225–236.

Christensen, A. J., Smith, T. W., Turner, C. W., Holman, J. M. Jr., Gregory, M. C. and Rich, M. A. (1992). Family support, physical impairment, and adherence in hemodialysis: An investigation of main and buffering effects. *Journal of Behavioral Medicine*, **15**, 313–325.

Christensen, A. J., Turner, C. W., Slaughter, J. M. and Holman, J. M. (1989). Perceived family support as a moderator of psychological well-being in end-stage renal disease. *Journal of Behavioral Medicine*, **12**, 249–265.

Christensen, A. J., Turner, C. W., Smith, T. W., Holman, J. M. Jr. and Gregory, M. C. (1991). Health locus of control and depression in end-stage renal disease. *Journal of Consulting and Clinical Psychology*, **59**, 419–424.

Christensen-Szlanski, J. J. J. and Northcraft, G. B. (1985). Patient compliance behavior: The effects of time on patients' values of treatment regimens. *Social Science and Medicine*, **21**, 263–273.

Chwalisz, K. (1992). Perceived stress and caregiver burden after brain injury: A theoretical integration. *Rehabilitation Psychology*, 37, 189–203.

Cicirelli, V. G. (1983). A comparison of helping behavior to elderly parents of adult children with intact and disrupted marriages. *The Gerontologist*, 23, 619–625.

Cioffi, D. (1991). Beyond attentional strategies: A cognitive-perceptual model of somatic interpretation. *Psychological Bulletin*, 109, 25–41.

Clark, D. (1991). Contradictions in the development of new hospices: A case study. *Social Science and Medicine*, 33, 995–1004.

Clark, D. A., Cook, A. and Snow, D. (1998). Depressive symptom differences in hospitalized, medically ill, depressed psychiatric inpatients and nonmedical controls. *Journal of Abnormal Psychology*, 107, 38–48.

Clayton, P. J. (1990). Bereavement and depression. *Journal of Clinical Psychiatry*, 51, 34.

Cleary, P. D., Mechanic, D. and Greenley, J. R. (1982). Sex differences in medical care utilization: An empirical investigation. *Journal of Health and Social Behavior*, 23, 106–119.

Cobb, S. (1976). Social support as a moderator of life stress. *Psychosomatic Medicine*, 38, 300–314.

Cockerham, W. C., Kunz, G. and Lueschen, G. (1988). Psychological distress, perceived health status, and physician utilization in America and West Germany. *Social Science and Medicine*, 26, 829–838.

Cody, R. and Lee, C. (1990). Behaviors, beliefs, and intentions in skin cancer prevention. *Journal of Behavioral Medicine*, 13, 373–389.

Cohen, D. and Eisdorfer, C. (1988). Depression in family members caring for a relative with Alzheimer's disease. *Journal of the American Geriatric Society*, 36, 885–889.

Cohen, F. and Lazarus, R. S. (1979). Coping with the stresses of illness. In G. S. Stone, F. Cohen and N. E. Alder (eds), *Health Psychology*. San Francisco: Jossey-Bass.

Cohen, R. E., Blanchard, E. B., Ruckdeschel, J. C. and Smolen, C. (1986). Prevalence and correlates of post-treatment and anticipatory nausea and vomiting in cancer chemotherapy. *Journal of Psychosomatic Research*, 30, 643–654.

Cohen, S. and Syme, S. L. (eds) (1985) *Social Support and Health*. New York: Academic Press.

Cohen, S. and Williamson, G. W. (1991). Stress and infectious disease in humans. *Psychological Bulletin*, 109, 5–24.

Cohen, S. and Wills, T. A. (1985). Stress, social support and the buffering hypothesis. *Psychological Bulletin*, 98, 310–357.

Colligan, M., Pennebaker, J. and Murphy, L. (eds) (1982). *Mass Psychogenic Illness: A social psychological analysis*. Hillsdale, NJ: Erlbaum.

Connell, C. M., O'Sullivan, J. J., Fisher, E. B. and Storandt, M. (1988). Variables predicting adherence and metabolic control among retirement community residents with non-insulin dependent diabetes mellitus. *Journal of Compliance in Health Care*, 3, 135–149.

Conner, M. and Norman, P. (eds) (1996). *Predicting Health Behaviour*. Buckingham: Open University Press.

Conrad, P. (1985). The meaning of medications: Another look at compliance. *Social Science and Medicine*, 20, 29–37.

Constantini, A., Solano, L., DiNapoli, R. and Bosco, A. (1997). Relationship between hardiness and risk of burnout in a sample of 92 nurses working in oncology and AIDS wards. *Psychotherapy and Psychosomatics*, 66, 78–82.

Contrada, R. J., Leventhal, E. A. and Anderson, J. R. (1994). Psychological preparation for surgery: Marshalling individual and social resources to optimize self-regulation. *International Review of Health Psychology*, 3, 219–266.

Cooper, C. L. and Mitchell, S. J. (1990). Nursing the critically ill and dying. *Human Relations*, 43, 297–311.

Coppel, D. B., Burton, C., Becker, J. and Fiore, J.(1985). Relationships of cognitions associated with coping reactions to depression in spousal caregivers of Alzheimer's disease patients. *Cognitive Therapy and Research*, **9**, 253–266.

Corney, R. H. (1990). Sex differences in general practice attendance and help seeking for minor illness. *Journal of Psychosomatic Research*, **34**, 525–534.

Costa, P. T. and McCrae, R. R. (1980). Somatic complaints in males as a function of age and neuroticism: A longitudinal analysis. *Journal of Behavioral Medicine*, **3**, 245–257.

Costa, P. T. and McCrae, R. R. (1985). Hypochondriasis, neuroticism, and aging: When are somatic complaints unfounded? *American Psychologist*, **40**, 19–28.

Costa, P. T. and McCrae, R. R. (1987). Neuroticism, somatic complaints, and disease. Is the bark worse than the bite? *Journal of Personality*, **55**, 299–316.

Cott, A. (1986). The disease–illness distinction: A model for effective and practical integration of behavioural and medical science. In S. McHugh and T. M. Vallis (eds), *Illness Behavior: A multidisciplinary model*. New York: Plenum Press.

Coulton, C. and Frost, A. (1982). Use of social and health services by the elderly. *Journal of Health and Social Behavior*, **23**, 330–339.

Cox, D. B. (1987). *The Health and Lifestyle Survey: Preliminary Report*. London: The Health Promotion Research Trust.

Coyne, J. C. and DeLongis, A. (1986). Going beyond social support: The role of social relationships in adaptation. *Journal of Consulting and Clinical Psychology*, **54**, 454–460.

Coyne, J. C. and Downey, G. (1991). Social factors and psychopathology: Stress, social support and coping processes. *Annual Review of Psychology*, **42**, 410–425.

Coyne, J. C. and Fiske, V. (1992). Couples coping with chronic illness. In T. J. Akamatsu, J. C. Crowther, S. C. Hobfoll and M. A. P. Stevens (eds), *Family Health Psychology*. Washington, DC: Hemisphere.

Coyne, J. C. and Smith, D. A. F. (1991). Couples coping with a myocardial infarction: A contextual perspective on wife's distress. *Journal of Personality and Social Psychology*, **61**, 404–412.

Cramer, J. A. and Spilker, B. (eds) (1991). *Patient Compliance in Medical Practice and Clinical Trials*. New York: Raven Press.

Crandall, L. A. and Duncan, R. P. (1981). Attitudinal and situational factors in the use of physician services by low-income persons. *Journal of Health and Social Behavior*, **22**, 64–77.

Croog, S. H., Shapiro, D. S. and Levine, S. (1971). Denial among male heart patients. *Psychosomatic Medicine*, **33**, 385–397.

Croyle, R. T. and Barger, S. D. (1993). Illness cognition. In S. Maes, H. Leventhal and M. Johnston (eds), *International Review of Health Psychology*. Vol. II. Chichester: Wiley.

Croyle, R. T. and Ditto, P. M. (1990). Illness cognition and behavior: An experimental approach. *Journal of Behavioral Medicine*, **13**, 31–52.

Croyle, R.T. and Jemmott, J. B. III (1991). Psychological reactions to risk factor testing. In J. A. Skelton and R. T (eds.), *Mental Representation in Health and Illness*. New York: Springer-Verlag.

Croyle, R. T. and Sande, G. N. (1988). Denial and confirmatory search: Paradoxical consequences of medical diagnosis. *Journal of Applied Social Psychology*, **18**, 473–490.

Croyle, R. T. and Uretsky, M. B. (1987). Effects of mood on self-appraisal of health status. *Health Psychology*, **6**, 239–253.

Cull, A. (1991). Staff support in medical oncology: A problem-solving approach. *Psychology and Health*, **5**, 129–136.

Cummings, K. M., Becker, M. H., Kirscht, J. P. and Levin, N. W. (1982). Psychosocial factors affecting adherence to medical regimens in a group of hemodialysis patients. *Medical Care*, **20**, 567–580.

Cummings, K. M., Kirscht, J. P., Becker, M. H. and Levin, N. W. (1984). Construct validity comparisons of three methods for measuring patient compliance. *Health Services Research*, **19**, 103–116.

Cummings, K. M., Lampone, D., Mettlin, C. and Pontes, J. E. (1983). What young men know about testicular cancer. *Preventive Medicine*, **12**, 326–330.

Cushman, L. A. (1986). Secondary neuropsychiatric complications in stroke: Implications for acute care. *Archives of Physical Medicine and Rehabilitation*, **69**, 877–879.

d'Houtaud, A. and Field, M. G. (1984). The image of health: Variations in perception by social class in a French population. *Sociology of Health and Illness*, **6**, 30–60.

Dahlquist, L. M., Gil, K. M., Armstrong, F. D., DeLawyer, D. D., Greene, P. and Wuori, D. (1986). Preparing children for medical examinations: The importance of previous medical experience. *Health Psychology*, **5**, 249–259.

Dakof, G. A. and Mendelsohn, G. A. (1986). Parkinson's disease: The psychological aspects of a chronic illness. *Psychological Bulletin*, **99**, 375–387.

Dakof, G. A. and Mendelsohn, G. A. (1989). Patterns of adaption to Parkinson's disease. *Health Psychology*, **8**, 355–372.

Dakof, G. A. and Taylor, S. E. (1990). Victims' perceptions of social support: What is helpful to whom? *Journal of Personality and Social Psychology*, **58**, 80–89.

Dalton, J.A. and Feuerstein, M. (1988). Biobehavioural factors in cancer pain. *Pain*, 33, 137–147.

Davey Smith, G., Bartley, M. and Bane, D. (1990). The Black Report on socioeconomic inequalities in health – ten years on. *British Medical Journal*, **301**, 373–377.

Davis, H. and Fallowfield, L. (eds) (1991). *Counselling and Communication in Health Care*. Chichester: Wiley.

Davis, M. (1968). Variations in patients' compliance with doctors' advice. *American Journal of Public Health*, **54**, 274–288.

Davis, M., Vasterling, J., Bransfield, D. and Burish, T. G. (1987). Behavioral interventions in coping with cancer-related pain. *British Journal of Guidance and Counselling*, **15**, 17–28.

Davis, M. A. (1981). Sex differences in reporting osteoarthritic symptoms: A sociomedical approach. *Journal of Health and Social Behaviour*, **22**, 289–310.

Dawson, N. J. (1991). Need satisfaction in terminal care settings. *Social Science and Medicine*, **32**, 83–87.

Day, J. J., Bayer, A. A., Pathy, M. S. J. and Chadha, J. S. (1987). Acute myocardial infarction: Diagnostic difficulties and outcome in advanced old age. *Age and Ageing*, **16**, 239–247.

Dean, K. (1981). Self-care responses to illness: A selective review. *Social Science and Medicine*, **15A**, 673–685.

Dean, K. (1986). Lay care in illness. *Social Science and Medicine*, **22**, 275–284.

Deaton, A. V. (1985). Adaptive noncompliance in pediatric asthma: The patient as expert. *Journal of Pediatric Psychology*, **10**, 1–14.

Decker, F. H. (1985). Socialisation and interpersonal environment in nurses' affective reactions to work. *Social Science and Medicine*, **20**, 499–509.

DeFriese, G. and Woomert, A. (1983). Self-care among the US elderly. *Research on Aging*, **5**, 3–23.

Demers, R. Y., Altamore, R., Mustin, H., Kleinman, A. and Leonard, D. (1980). An exploration of the dimensions of illness behavior. *Journal of Family Practice*, **11**, 1085–1092.

Denney, D., Kole, D. and Matarazzo, R. (1965). The relationship between age and number of symptoms reported by patients. *Journal of Gerontology*, **20**, 50–53.

Department of Health (1992). *Health of the Nation*. London: HMSO.

Derogatis, L. R., Morrow, G. R., Fetting, J., Penman, D., Piasetsky, S., Schmale, A. M., Henrichs, R. and Carnickle, C. L. M. (1983). The prevalence of psychiatric disorders among cancer patients. *Journal of the American Medical Association*, **249**, 751–757.

DeVellis, B. M., Blalock, S. J. and Sandler, R. S. (1990). Predicting participation in cancer screening: Perceived behavioural control. *Journal of Applied Social Psychology*, 20, 639–660.

Devins, G. M. and Seland, T. P. (1987). Emotional impact of multiple sclerosis: Recent findings and suggestions for future research. *Psychological Bulletin*, 101, 363–375.

Deyo, R. A. and Inui, T. S. (1980). Dropouts and broken appointments: A literature review and agenda for future research. *Medical Care*, 18, 1146–1157.

Diamond, J., Massey, K. L. and Covey, D. (1989). Symptom awareness and blood glucose estimation in diabetic adults. *Health Psychology*, 8, 15–26.

DiClemente, C. C., Prochaska, J. O., Fairhurst, S. K., Velicer, W. F., Veleasquez, M. M. and Rossi, J. S. (1991). The process of smoking cessation: An analysis of precontemplation, contemplation, and preparation stages of change. *Journal of Consulting and Clinical Psychology*, 59, 295–304.

DiMatteo, M. R. and DiNicola, D. D. (1982). *Acheiving Patient Compliance*. Elmsford, NY: Pergamon Press.

DiMatteo, M. R., Hays, R. D. and Prince, L. M. (1986). Relationship of physicians' nonverbal communication skills to patient satisfaction, appointment noncompliance, and physician workload. *Health Psychology*, 5, 581–594.

DiMatteo, M. R., Sherbourne, C. D., Hays, R. D., Ordway, L., Kravitz, R. L., McGlynn, E. A., Kaplan, S. and Rogers, W. H. (1993). Physicians' characteristics influence patients' adherence to medical treatment: Results from the Medical Outcomes Study. *Health Psychology*, 12, 93–102.

Dimond, M. F., Lund, D. A. and Caserta, M. S. (1987). The role of social supports in the first two years of bereavement in an elderly sample. *Gerontologist*, 27, 599–604.

Dingwall, R. (1976). *Aspects of Illness*. London: Martin Robertson.

Dishman, R. K. (1982). Compliance/adherence in health-related exercise. *Health Psychology*, 1, 237–267.

Dishman, R. K. (1991). Increasing and maintaining exercise and physical activity. *Behavior Therapy*, 22, 345–378.

Dishman, R. K. and Ickes, W. (1981). Self-motivation and adherence to therapeutic exercise. *Journal of Behavioral Medicine*, 4, 421–438.

Dishman, R. K., Sallis, J. F. and Orenstein, D. R. (1985). The determinants of physical activity and exercise. *Public Health Reports*, 100, 158–171.

Ditto, T. T. and Jemmott, J. B. III (1989). From rarity to evaluative extremity: Effects of prevalence information on evaluations of positive and negative characteristics. *Journal of Personality and Social Psychology*, 57, 16–26.

Doll, J. and Orth, B. (1993). The Fishbein and Ajzen theory of reasoned action applied to contraceptive behavior: Model variants and meaningfulness. *Journal of Applied Social Psychology*, 23, 395–410.

Donovan, J. L. and Blake, D. R. (1992). Patient non-compliance: Deviance or reasoned decision-making? *Social Science and Medicine*, 34, 507–513.

Dracup, I. K., Moser, D. K., Eisenberg, M., Meischke, H., Alonzo, A. and Braslow, A. (1995). Causes of delay in seeking treatment for heart attack symptoms. *Social Science and Medicine*, 40, 379–392.

Dubbert, P. M. (1992). Exercise in behavioral medicine. *Journal of Consulting and Clinical Psychology*, 60, 613–618.

Dunbar, J. M. and Agras, W.S. (1980). Compliance with medical instructions. In J. M. Ferguson and C. B. Taylor (eds), *Comprehensive Handbook of Behavioral Medicine*, Vol. III. New York: Spectrum.

Dunbar-Jacob, J. (1993). Contributions to patient adherence: Is it time to share the blame? *Health Psychology*, 12, 91–92.

Duncan, T. E. and McAuley, E. (1993). Social support and efficacy cognitions in exercise adherence: A latent growth curve analysis. *Journal of Behavioral Medicine*, **16**, 199–218.

Dunkel-Schetter, C., Feinstein, L. G., Taylor, S. E. and Falke, R. L. (1992). Patterns of coping with cancer. *Health Psychology*, **11**, 79–87.

Dura, J. R., Stukenberg, K. W. and Kiecolt-Glaser, J. K. (1990). Chronic stress and depressive disorders in older adults. *Journal of Abnormal Psychology*, **99**, 284–290.

Duval, S. and Wicklund, R. (1972). *A Theory of Self-Awareness*. New York: Academic Press.

Dwyer, J. W. and Coward, R. T. (1991). A multivariate comparison of the involvement of adult sons versus daughters in the care of impaired parents. *Journal of Gerontology, Social Sciences*, **46**, S259–S269.

Eagles, J. M., Beattie, J. A. G., Blackwood, G. W., Restall, D. B. and Ashcroft, G. W. (1987). The mental health of elderly couples: 1. The effects of a cognitively impaired spouse. *British Journal of Psychiatry*, **150**, 299–303.

Eagly, A. H. and Chaiken, S. (1993). *The Psychology of Attitudes*. Fort Worth, TX: Harcourt Brace Jovanovich.

Eastburg, M. C., Williamson, M., Gorsuch, R. and Ridley, C. (1994). Social support, personality, and burnout in nurses. *Journal of Applied Social Psychology*, **24**, 1233–1250.

Edelmann, R. J. (1992). *Anxiety: Theory, research and intervention in clinical and health psychology*. Chichester: Wiley.

Edelstein, J. and Linn, M. (1985). The influence of the family on control of diabetes. *Social Science and Medicine*, 21, 541–544.

Edwards, W. (1954). The theory of decision making. *Psychological Bulletin*, **51**, 380–417.

Egbert, L. D., Barrit, G. E. and Welch, C. E. (1964). Reduction of postoperative pain by encouragement and instruction of patients. *New England Journal of Medicine*, **270**, 825–827.

Eisenberg, D., Kessler, R. C. and Foster, C. (1993). Unconventional medicine in the United States. *New England Journal of Medicine*, **328**, 246–252.

Eisenberg, J. M. (1970). Sociologic influences on decision making by clinicians. *Annals of Internal Medicine*, **90**, 957–964.

Eisenberg, L. (1977). Disease and illness: Distinction between professional and popular ideas of illness. *Culture, Medicine and Society*, **1**, 9–23.

Eiser, C. (1988). Do children benefit from psychological preparation for hospitalization? *Psychology and Health*, **2**, 133–138.

Eiser, C. and Eiser, J. R. (1990). The effects of personal and family hospital experience on children's health beliefs, concerns and behaviour. *Social Behaviour*, **5**, 307–314.

Elkins, G. R., Gamino, L. A. and Rynearson, R. R. (1988). Mass psychogenic illness, trance states, and suggestion. *American Journal of Clinical Hypnosis*, **30**, 267–275.

Elkins, P. D. and Roberts, M. C. (1983). Psychological preparation for pediatric hospitalization. *Clinical Psychology Review*, **3**, 275–295.

Elkins, P. D. and Roberts, M. C. (1985). Reducing medical fears in a general population of children: A comparison of three audio-visual modeling procedures. *Journal of Pediatric Psychology*, **10**, 67–75.

Elliott-Binns, C. (1973). An analysis of lay medicine. *Journal of the Royal College of General Practitioners*, **23**, 255–57.

Ende, J., Kazis, L., Ash, A. and Moskowitz, M. A. (1989). Measuring patients' desire for autonomy: Decision making and information-seeking preferences among medical patients. *Journal of General Internal Medicine*, **4**, 23–30.

Engel, G. L. (1977). The need for a new medical model: A challenge for biomedicine. *Science*, **196**, 129–136.

Engel, G. L. (1980). The clinical application of the biopsychosocial model. *American Journal of Psychiatry*, **137**, 535–544.

Epstein, L. H. and Cluss, P. A. (1982). A behavioral medicine perspective on adherence to long-term medical regimens. *Journal of Consulting and Clinical Psychology*, **50**, 950–971.

Epstein, L. H., Koeske, R. and Wing, R. R. (1984). Adherence to exercise in obese children. *Journal of Cardiac Rehabilitation*, **4**, 185–195.

Ezekiel, E. and Ezekiel, L. (1990). Living wills: Past, present and future. *Journal of Clinical Ethics*, **1**, 9–19.

Fabrega, H. (1974). *Disease and Social Behavior: An interdisciplinary perspective*. Cambridge, MA: MIT Press.

Fabrega, H. (1975). The need for an ethnomedical science. *Science*, **189**, 969–975.

Fabrega, H. and Van Egeren, L. (1976). A behavioral framework for the study of disease. *Annals of Internal Medicine*, **84**, 200–208.

Facione, N. C. (1993). Delay versus help seeking for breast cancer symptoms: A critical review of the literature on patient and provider delay. *Social Science and Medicine*, **12**, 1521–1534.

Falkner, B. and Light, K. C. (1986). The interactive effects of stress and dietary sodium on cardio-vascular reactivity. In K. A. Matthews, S. M. Weiss, T. Detre, T. M. Dembroski, B. Falkner, S. B. Manuck and R. B. Williams (eds), *Handbook of Stress, Reactivity, and Cardiovascular Disease*. New York: Wiley.

Fallowfield, L. J., Rodway, A. and Baum, M. (1990). What are the psychological factors influencing attendance, non-attendance and re-attendance at a breast screening centre? *Journal of the Royal Society of Medicine*, **83**, 547–551.

Falvo, D. R. and Smith, J. K. (1983). Assessing residents' behavioral science skills: Patients' views of physician-patient interaction. *Journal of Family Practice*, **17**, 479–483.

Farmer, P. (1990). Sending sickness: Sorcery, politics, and changing concepts of AIDS in rural Haiti. *Medical Anthropology Quarterly*, **4**, 6–27.

Faust, J. and Melamed, B. G. (1984). Influence of arousal, previous experience, and age on surgery preparation of same day surgery and in-hospital pediatric patients. *Journal of Consulting and Clinical Psychology*, **52**, 359–365.

Faust, J., Olson, R. and Roderiquez, H. (1991). Same-day surgery preparation: Reduction of pediatric patient arousal and distress through participant modelling. *Journal of Consulting and Clinical Psychology*, **59**, 475–478.

Felton, B. J. and Revenson, T. A. (1984). Coping with chronic illness: A study of illness controllability and the influence of coping strategies on psychological adjustment. *Journal of Consulting and Clinical Psychology*, **52**, 343–353.

Felton, B. J., Revenson, T. A. and Hinrichsen, G. A. (1984). Stress and coping in the explanation of psychological adjustment among chronically ill adults. *Social Science and Medicine*, **18**, 889–898.

Felton, J. S. (1998). Burnout as a clinical entity – its importance in health care workers. *Occupational Medicine*, **48**, 237–250.

Fillingim, R. B. and Fine, M. A. (1986). The effects of internal vs external information processing on symptom perception in an exercise setting. *Health Psychology*, **5**, 115–123.

Finney, J. W., Hook, R. J., Friman, P. C., Rapoff, M. A. and Christophersen, E. R. (1993). The overestimation of adherence to pediatric medical regimens. *Children's Health Care*, **22**, 297–304.

Finney, J. W., Weist, M. D. and Friman, P. C. (1995). Evaluation of two health-education strategies for testicular self-examination. *Journal of Applied Behavior Analysis*, **28**, 39–46.

Firth, H. and Britton, P. (1989). 'Burnout', absence, and turnover amongst British nursing staff. *Journal of Occupational Psychology*, **62**, 55–59.

Firth, S. (1993). Cross-cultural perspectives on bereavement. In D. Dickenson and M. Johnson (eds), *Death, Dying and Bereavement*. London: Sage.

Fischhoff, B., Goitein, B. and Shapira, Z. (1982). The experienced utility of expected utility approaches. In N. T. Feather (ed.), *Expectations and Actions: Expectancy-value models in psychology*. Hillsdale, NJ: Lawrence Erlbaum Associates.

Fishbein, M. and Ajzen, I. (1975). *Belief, Attitude, Intention and Behavior*. Reading, MA: Addison-Wesley.

Fitzpatrick, R., Newman, S., Archer, R. and Shipley, M. (1991). Social support, disability and depression: A longitudinal study of rheumatoid arthritis. *Social Science and Medicine*, 33, 605–611.

Fitzpatrick, R., Newman, S., Lamb, R. and Shipley, M. (1988). Social relationships and psychological well-being in rheumatoid arthritis. *Social Science and Medicine*, 27, 399–403.

Fitzpatrick, R., Newman, S., Lamb, R. and Shipley, M. (1990). Patterns of coping in rheumatoid arthritis. *Psychology and Health*, 4, 187–200.

Flor, H., Fydrich, T. and Turk, D. C. (1992). Efficacy of multidisciplinary pain treatment centres: A meta-analytic review. *Pain*, 49, 221–230.

Folkman, S. and Lazarus, R. S. (1980). An analysis of coping in a middle-aged community sample. *Journal of Health and Social Behavior*, 21, 219–239.

Fontana, A. F., Kerns, R. D., Rosenberg, R. L. and Colonese, K. L. (1989). Support, stress, and recovery from coronary heart disease: A longitudinal causal model. *Health Psychology*, 8, 175–193.

Forrest, A.P.M. (1986). Breast cancer screening: Report of a Working Group to the Health Ministers of England, Wales, Scotland and Northern Ireland. London: HMSO.

Fox, S. A., Murata, P. J. and Stein, J. A. (1991). The impact of physician compliance on screening mammography for older women. *Archives of Internal Medicine*, 151, 50–56.

Frankel, R. and Beckman, H. (1989). Evaluating the patient's primary problem(s). In M. Stewart and D. Roter (eds), *Communication with Medical Patients*. Newbury Park, CA: Sage.

Freedman, J. L. (1982). Theories of contagion as they relate to mass psychogenic illness. In M.J. Colligan, J.W. Pennebaker and L.R. Murphy (eds), *Mass Psychogenic Illness*. Hillsdale, NJ: Lawrence Erlbaum Associates.

Freer, C. B. (1980). Health diaries: An efficient but under-used method for collecting of whole person health information. *Journal of the Royal College of General Practitioners*, 30, 279.

Freidson, E. (1960). Client control and medical practice. *American Journal of Sociology*, 65, 374–382.

Freidson, E. (1961). *Patients' View of Medical Practice*. New York: Russell Sage Foundation.

Freidson, E. (1970). *Professional Dominance: The social structure of medical care*. Chicago: Aldine.

Freud, S. (1957). *Mourning and Melancholia* (1917), standard edition, Vol. XIV. London: Hogarth.

Freudenberger, H. (1974). Staff burnout. *Journal of Social Issues*, 30, 17–29.

Friedman, L. C., Bruce, S., Webb, J. A., Weinberg, A. D. and Cooper, H. P. (1993). Skin self-examination in a population at increased risk for skin cancer. *American Journal of Preventive Medicine*, 9, 359–364.

Friedman, L. C., Nelson, D. V., Webb, J. A., Hoffman, L. P. and Baer, P. E. (1994). Dispositional optimism, self-efficacy, and health beliefs as predictors of breast self-examination. *American Journal of Preventive Medicine*, 10, 130–135.

Froelicher, V. F. and Oberman, A. (1977) Analysis of epidemiologic studies of physical inactivity as a risk factor for coronary artery disease. In E. H. Sonnenblisk and M. Lesch (eds), *Exercise and Heart Disease*. New York: Grune and Stratton.

Frost, R. O., Morgenthau, J. E., Riessman, C. K. and Whalen, M. (1986). Somatic response to stress, physical symptoms and health service use. *Behaviour Research and Therapy*, 24, 569–576.

Funch, D. P. (1985). Diagnostic delay in symptomatic colorectal cancer. *Cancer*, 56, 2120–2124.

Funch, D. P. (1988). Predictors and consequences of symptom reporting behaviors in colorecatal cancer patients. *Medical Care*, 26, 1000–1008.

Furnham, A. and Bhagrath, R. (1993). A comparison of health and behaviours of clients of ortho-dox and complementary medicine. *British Journal of Clinical Psychology*, **32**, 237–246.

Furnham, A. and Forey, J. (1994). The attitudes, behaviours and beliefs of patients of conventional vs. alternative (complementary) medicine. *Journal of Clinical Psychology*, **50**, 458–469.

Furnham, A. and Smith, C. (1988). Choosing alternative medicine: A comparison of the beliefs of patients visiting a GP and a homeopath. *Social Science and Medicine*, **26**, 685–687.

Fyro, K. and Bodegard, G. (1987). Four-year follow-up of psychological reactions to false positive screening tests for congenital hypothyroidism. *Acta Paediatrica Scandinavica*, **76**, 107–114.

Gabbard-Alley, A. S. (1995). Health communication and gender: A review and critique. *Health Communication*, **7**, 35–54.

Gallagher, U. (1993). The living will in clinical practice. In D. Dickenson and M. Johnson (eds), *Death, Dying and Bereavement*. London: Sage.

Gamino, L. A., Elkins, G. R. and Hackney, K. U. (1989). Emergency management of mass psychogenic illness. *Psychosomatics*, **30**, 446–449.

Garfield, S. R., Collen, M. F., Feldman, R., Soghikian, K., Richart, H. and Duncan, J. H. (1976). Evaluation of an ambulatory medical care delivery system. *New England Journal of Medicine*, **294**, 426–431.

Garner, D. M. and Wooley, S. C. (1991). Confronting the failure of behavioral and dietary treatments for obesity. *Clinical Psychology Review*, **11**, 729–780.

Gass, K. A. (1989). Appraisal, coping and resources: Markers associated with the health of aged widows and widowers. In D. A. Lund (ed.), *Older Bereaved Spouses*. New York: Hemisphere Publishing Corp.

Gates, S. J. and Colborn, D. K. (1976). Lowering appointment failures in a neighbourhood health center. *Medical Care*, **14**, 263–267.

Gelfand, S., Ullman, L. P. and Krasner, L. (1963). The placebo-response – an experimental approach. *Journal of Nervous and Mental Disease*, **136**, 379–387.

George, V. and Howards, I. (1991). *Poverty amidst Affluence*. Cheltenham: Edward Elgar.

Gerber, L., Rusalem, R. and Hannon, N. (1975). Anticipatory grief and aged widows and widowers. *Journal of Gerontology*, **30**, 225–229.

Gerbert, B. (1984). Perceived likeability and competence of simulated patients: Influence on physicians' management plans. *Social Science and Medicine*, **18**, 1053–1060.

Gerson, E. M. (1976). The social character of illness: Deviance or politics? *Social Science and Medicine*, **10**, 219–224.

Geyman, J. P. (1983). Problems in family practice: Dying and death of a family member. *The Journal of Family Practice*, **17**, 125–134.

Gil, K. M., Abrams, M. R., Phillips, G. and Keefe, F. J. (1989). Sickle cell disease pain: Relation of coping strategies to adjustment. *Journal of Consulting and Clinical Psychology*, **57**, 725–731.

Gil, K. M., Keefe, F. J., Crisson, J. E. and Van Dalfsen, P. J. (1987). Social support and pain behavior. *Pain*, **29**, 209–217.

Gilhooly, M. L. M. (1984). The impact of caregiving on caregivers: Factors associated with the psychological well-being of people supporting a dementing relative in the community. *British Journal of Medical Psychology*, **57**, 35–44.

Gilleard, C. J., Gilleard, E., Gledhill, K. and Whittick, J. (1984). Caring for the elderly mentally infirm at home: A survey of supporters. *Journal of Epidemiology and Community Health*, **38**, 319–325.

Glaser, B. G. and Strauss, A. L. (1965). *Awareness of Dying*. Chicago: Aldine.

Glasgow, R. E., McCaul, K. D. and Schafer, L. C. (1986). Barriers to regimen adherence among persons with insulin-dependent diabetes. *Journal of Behavioral Medicine*, **9**, 65–77.

Glasgow, R. E., McCaul, K. D. and Schafer, L. C. (1987). Self-care behaviors and glycemic control in Type 1 diabetes. *Journal of Chronic Disease*, 40, 399–417.

Glasgow, R. E., Toobert, D. J., Riddle, M., Donnelly, J., Mitchell, D. K. and Calder, D. (1989). Diabetes-specific social learning variables and self-care behaviors among persons with Type II diabetes. *Health Psychology*, 8, 285–303.

Godin, G., Valois, P. and Lepage, L. (1993). The pattern of influence of perceived behavioral control upon exercising behavior: An application of Ajzen's Theory of Planned Behavior. *Journal of Behavioral Medicine*, 16, 81–101.

Goldman, S. L., Whitney-Saltiel, D., Granger, J. and Rodin, J. (1991). Children's representations of 'everyday' aspects of health and illness. *Journal of Pedriatric Psychology*, 16, 747–766.

Good, M. D., Good, B. J. and Nassi, A. J. (1983). Patient requests in primary health care settings: Development and validation of a research instrument. *Journal of Behavioral Medicine*, 6, 151–168.

Goodall, T. A. and Halford, W. K. (1991). Self-management of diabetes mellitus: A critical review. *Health Psychology*, 10, 1–8.

Goodenow, C., Reisine, S. T. and Gragy, K. E. (1990). Quality of social support and associated social and psychological functioning in women with rheumatoid arthritis. *Health Psychology*, 9, 266–284.

Gortmaker, S. L. (1985). Demography of chronic childhood diseases. In N. Hobbs and J. M. Perrin (eds), *Issues in the Care of Children with Chronic Illness*. San Fransisco: Jossey-Bass.

Gortmaker, S. L., Eckenrode, J. and Gore, S. (1982). Stress and the utilisation of health services: A time series and cross-sectional analysis. *Journal of Health and Social Behavior*, 23, 25–38.

Gotay, C. C. (1984). The experience of cancer during early and advanced stages: The views of patients and their mates. *Social Science and Medicine*, 18, 605–613.

Gove, W. R. (1984). Gender differences in mental and physical illness: The effects of fixed roles and nurturant roles. *Social Science and Medicine*, 19, 77–91.

Graydon, J. E. (1988). Factors that predict patients' functioning following treatment for cancer. *International Journal of Nursing Studies*, 25, 117–124.

Green, H. (1988). *Informal Carers: General Household Survey 1985*, Supplement A. London: HMSO.

Greene, M. G., Adelman, R., Charon, R. and Hoffman, S. (1986). Ageism in the medical encounter: An exploratory study of the language and behavior of doctors with their old and young patients. *Language and Communication*, 6, 113–124.

Greenfield, S., Kaplan, S. and Ware, L. E. (1985). Expanding patient involvement in care. *Annals of Internal Medicine*, 102, 520–528.

Greer, S., Moorey, S., Baruch, J., Watson, M., Robertson, B., Mason, A., Rowden, L., Law, M. and Bliss, J. M. (1992). Adjuvant psychological therapy for patients with cancer: A prospective randomised trial. *British Medical Journal*, 304, 675–680.

Grembowski, D., Patrick, D., Diehn, P., Durham, M., Beresford, S., Kay, E. and Hecht, J. (1993). Self-efficacy and health behavior among older adults. *Journal of Health and Social Behaviour*, 34, 89–104.

Griffith, S. (1990). A review of factors associated with patient compliance and the taking of prescribed medicines. *British Journal of General Practice*, 40, 114–116.

Gross, A. M., Heimann, L., Shapiro, R. and Schultz, R. M. (1983). Children with diabetes: Social skills training and hemoglobin A-sub-1c levels. *Behavior Modification*, 7, 151–164.

Groves, J. E. (1978). Taking care of the hateful patient. *New England Journal of Medicine*, 298, 883–887.

Gruen, W. (1975). Effects of brief psychotherapy during the hospitalization period on the recovery process in heart attacks. *Journal of Consulting and Clinical Psychology*, 43, 223–232.

Gryfe, C. I. and Gryfe, B. (1984). Drug therapy of the aged: The problem of compliance and the rules of physicians and pharmacists. *Journal of the American Geriatrics Society*, **32**, 301–307.

Guadagnoli, E. and Ward, P. (1998). Patient participation in decision-making. *Social Science and Medicine*, **47**, 329–339.

Hackett, T. P. and Cassem, N. H. (1969). Factors contributing to delay in responding to the signs and symptoms of myocardial infarction. *The American Journal of Cardiology*, **24**, 651–658.

Hackett, T. P., Cassem, N. H. and Raker, J. W. (1973). Patient delay in cancer. *New England Journal of Medicine*, **289**, 14–20.

Hadlow, J. and Pitts, M. (1991). The understanding of common health terms by doctors, nurses and patients. *Social Science and Medicine*, **32**, 193–196.

Haley, W. E., Levine, E. G., Brown, S. L. and Bartolucci, A. A. (1987b). Stress, appraisal, coping and social support as predictors of adaptational outcome among dementia caregivers. *Psychology and Aging*, **2**, 323–330.

Haley, W. E., Levine, E. G., Brown, S. L., Berry, J. W. and Hughes, G. H. (1987a). Psychological, social, and health consequences of caring for a relative with senile dementia. *Journal of the American Geriatrics Society*, **35**, 405–411.

Hall, D. (1987). Social and psychological care before and during hospitalisation. *Social Science and Medicine*, **25**, 721–732.

Hall, E. M. and Johnson, J. V. (1989). A case study of stress and mass psychogenic illness in industrial workers. *Journal of Occupational Medicine*, **31**, 243–250.

Hall, J. A. and Dornan, M.C. (1988a). Meta-analysis of satisfaction with medical care: Description of research domain and analysis of overall satisfaction levels. *Social Science and Medicine*, **27**, 737–644.

Hall, J. A. and Dornan, M. C. (1988b). What patients like about their medical care and how often they are asked: A meta-analysis of the satisfaction literature. *Social Science and Medicine*, **27**, 935–939.

Hall, J. A. and Dornan, M. C. (1990). Patient sociodemographic characteristics as predictors of satisfaction with medical care: A meta-analysis. *Social Science and Medicine*, **30**, 811–818.

Hall, J. A., Epstein, A. M., DeCiantis, M. L. and McNeil, B. J. (1993). Physicians' liking for their patients: More evidence for the role of affect in medical care. *Health Psychology*, **12**, 140–146.

Hall, J. A., Irish, J. T., Roter, D. L., Ehrlich, C. M. and Miller, L. H. (1994). Gender in medical encounters: An analysis of physician and patient communication in a primary care setting. *Health Psychology*, **13**, 384–392.

Hall, J. A., Milburn, M. A., Roter, D. L. and Daltroy, L. H. (1998). Why are sicker patients less satisfied with their medical care? Tests of two explanatory models. *Health Psychology*, **17**, 70–75.

Hall, J. A., Roter, D. L. and Katz, N. R. (1988). Meta-analysis of correlates of provider behavior in medical encounters. *Medical Care*, **26**, 657–675.

Hamburg, B. A. and Inoff, G. E. (1982). Relationship between behavioral factors and diabetic control in children and adolescents: A camp study. *Psychosomatic Medicine*, **44**, 321–329.

Hamm, P., Shekelle, R. B. and Stamler, J. (1989). Large fluctuations in bodyweight during young adulthood and twenty-five year risk of coronary death in men. *American Journal of Epidemiology*, **129**, 312–318.

Hampson, S. E., Glasgow, R. E. and Toobert, D. J. (1990). Personal models of diabetes and their relation to self-care activities. *Health Psychology*, **9**, 632–646.

Hampson, S. E., Glasgow, R. E. and Zeiss, A. (1994). Personal models of osteoarthritis and their relation to self-management and quality of life. *Journal of Behavioral Medicine*, **17**, 143–158.

Hansell, S. and Mechanic, D. (1984). Introspectiveness and adolescent symptom reporting. *Journal of Human Stress*, **11**, 165–176.

Hanson, C. L., Henggeler, S. W. and Burghen G. A. (1987). Social competence and parental support as mediators of the link between stress and metabolic control in adolescents with insulin-dependent diabetes mellitus. *Journal of Consulting and Clinical Psychology*, 55, 529–533.

Hardy, G. E., Shapiro, D. A. and Borrill, C. S. (1997). Fatigue in the workforce of national health service trusts: Levels of symptomatology and links with minor psychiatric disorder, demographic, occupational and work role factors. *Journal of Psychosomatic Research*, 43, 83–92.

Hare, J. and Pratt, C. C. (1988). Burnout: Differences between professional and paraprofessional nursing staff in acute care and long-term health facilities. *Journal of Applied Gerontology*, 7, 60–72.

Harland, R. and Huws, R. (1997). Sexual problems in diabetes and the role of psychological intervention. *Sexual and Marital Therapy*, 12, 147–157.

Harrison, J. A., Mullen, P. D. and Green, L. W. (1992). A meta-analysis of studies of the health belief model with adults. *Health Education Research*, 7, 107–116.

Hart, S. (1994). The costs of caring for elderly people. In G. N. Penny, P. Bennett and M. Herbert (eds), *Health Psychology: A lifespan perspective*. Chur, Switzerland: Harwood Academic Publishers.

Haskett, R. F. and Abplanalp, J. M. (1983). Premenstrual Tension Syndrome: Diagnostic criteria and selection of research subjects. *Psychiatric Research*, 9, 125–138.

Haug, M. (1981). Age and medical care utilization patterns. *Journal of Gerontology*, 36, 103–109.

Haug, M., Wykle, M. and Namazi, K. (1989). Self-care among older adults. *Social Science and Medicine*, 29, 171–183.

Haug, M. R. and Lavin, B. (1981). Practitioner or patient: who's in charge? *Journal of Health and Social Behavior*, 22, 212–229.

Hauser, S. T., Jacobson, A. M., Lavori, P., Wolfsdorf, J. I., Herksowitz, R. D., Wertlieb, D. and Stein, J. (1990). Adherence among children and adolescents with insulin-dependent diabetes mellitus over a four-year longitudinal follow-up: II. Immediate and long-term linkages with the family milieu. *Journal of Pediatric Psychology*, 15, 527–542.

Havik, O. E. and Maeland, J. G. (1990). Patterns of emotional reactions after myocardial infarction. *Journal of Psychosomatic Research*, 34, 271–285.

Hawley, D. J. and Wolfe, F. (1988). Anxiety and depression in patients with reumatoid arthritis: A prospective study of 400 patients. *Journal of Rheumatology*, 15, 932–941.

Hayes-Bautista, D. E. (1976). Modifying the treatment: Patient compliance, and medical care. *Social Science and Medicine*, 10, 233–238.

Hayley, W. E., Levine, E. G., Browen, S. L., Berry, J. W. and Hughes, G. H. (1987). Psychological, social, and health consequences of caring for a relative with senile dementia. *Journal of the American Geriatrics Society*, 35, 405–411.

Haynes, R. B. (1979). Strategies to improve compliance with referrals, appointments and prescribed medical regimens. In R. B. Haynes, D. W. Taylor and D. L. Sackett (eds), *Compliance in Health Care*. Baltimore: Johns Hopkins University Press.

Haynes, R. B., McKibbon, K. A. and Kanani, R, (1996). Systematic review of randomised clinical trials of interventions to assist patients follow prescriptions for medications. *Lancet*, 348, 383–296.

Haynes, R. B., Taylor, D. W. and Sackett, D. L. (1979). *Compliance in Health Care*. Baltimore, MD: Johns Hopkins University Press.

Haynes, R. B., Wang, E. and de Mota Gomes, M. (1987). A critical review of interventions to improve compliance with prescribed medication. *Patient Education and Counselling*, 10, 155–166.

Hays, R. D. and DiMatteo, M. R. (1987). Key issues and suggestions for patient compliance assessment: Sources of information, focus of measures, and nature of response options. *The Journal of Compliance in Health Care*, 2, 37–53.

Hays, R. D., Kravitz, R. L., Mazel, R. M., Sherbourne, C. D., DiMatteo, M. R., Rogers, W. H. and Greenfield, S. (1994). The impact of patient adherence on health outcomes for patients with chronic disease in the Medical Outcomes Study. *Journal of Behavioral Medicine*, **17**, 347–360.

Hayward, R. A., Shapiro, M. F., Freeman, H. E. and Corey, C. R. (1988). Who gets screened for cervical and breast cancer? Results from a new national survey. *Archives of Internal Medicine*, **148**, 1177–1181.

Hegel, M. T., Ayllon, T., Thiel, G. and Oulton, B. (1992). Improving adherence to fluid restrictions in male hemodialysis patients: A comparison of cognitive and behavioral approaches. *Health Psychology*, **11**, 324–330.

Heggenhougen, H. K. and Shore, L. (1986). Cultural components of behavioural epidemiology: Implications for primary health care. *Social Science and Medicine*, **22**, 1235–1245.

Heider, F. (1958). *The Psychology of Interpersonal Relations*. New York: Wiley.

Heinrich, R. L. and Schag, C. C. (1985). Stress and activity management: Group training for cancer patients and spouses. *Journal of Consulting and Clinical Psychology*, **53**, 439–446.

Helman, C. (1985). Disease and pseudo-disease: A case history of pseudo-angina. In R. A. Hahn and A. D. Gaines (eds), *Physicians of Western Medicine: Anthropological approaches to theory and practice*. Dordrecht: D. Reidel.

Helman, C. G. (1990). *Culture, Health and Illness* (2nd edn). London: Wright.

Helsing, K. J. and Szklo, M. (1981). Mortality after bereavement. *American Journal of Epidemiology*, **114**, 41–52.

Hendin, J. and Klerman, G. (1993). Physician-assisted suicide: The dangers of legalization. *American Journal of Psychiatry*, **150**, 143–145.

Hennig, P. and Knowles, A. (1990). Factors influencing women over 40 years to take precautions against cervical cancer. *Journal of Applied Social Psychology*, **20**, 1612–1621.

Herbert, T. B. and Cohen, S. (1993). Depression and immunity: A meta-analytic review. *Psychological Bulletin*, **113**, 1–15.

Herzlich, C. (1973). *Health and Illness: A social psychological analysis*. London: Academic Press.

Hibbard, J. H. and Pope, C. R. (1983). Gender roles, illness orientation and use of medical services. *Social Science and Medicine*, **17**, 129–137.

Hickey, T. (1988). Self-care behavior of older adults. *Family and Community Health*, **11**, 23–32.

Hill, D., Gardner, C. and Rassaby, J. (1985). Factors predisposing women to take precautions against breast and cervical cancer. *Journal of Applied Social Psychology*, **15**, 59–79.

Hinchliffe, A. C., Hyman, I. and Blizzard, B. (1992). The impact on carers of behavioural difficulties in dementia: A pilot study on management. *International Journal of Geriatric Psychiatry*, **7**, 579–583.

Hingley, P. and Cooper, C. L. (1986) *Stress and the Nurse Manager*. Chichester: Wiley.

Hinton, J. (1977). Bearing cancer. In R. H. Moos (ed.), *Coping with Physical Illness*. New York: Plenum Medical Books.

Hinton, J. M. (1984). Coping with terminal illness. In R. Fitzpatrick, J. M. Hinton and S. Newman (eds), *The Experience of Illness*. London: Tavistock Publications.

Hogbin, B. and Fallowfield, L. J. (1989). Getting it taped: The 'bad news' consultation with cancer patients. *British Journal of Hospital Medicine*, **31**, 330–334.

Hogg, K. E., Goldstein, L. H. and Leigh, P. N. (1994). The psychological impact of motor neurone disease. *Psychological Medicine*, **24**, 625–632.

Holland, W. W. and Stewart, S. (1990). *Screening in Health Care*. London: Nuffield.

Holroyd, J. and Guthrie, D. (1986). Family stress with chronic childhood illness: Cystic fibrosis, neuromuscular disease, and renal disease. *Journal of Clinical Psychology*, **42**, 552–561.

Holroyd, K. A. and Coyne, J. (1987). Personality and health in the 1980s: Psychosomatic medicine revisited? *Journal of Personality*, **55**, 359–375.

Holroyd, K. A. and Lazarus, R. S. (1982). Stress, coping and somatic adaption. In L. Goldberger and S. Breznitz (eds), *Handbook of Stress*. New York: Free Press.

Holtzman, D. and Celentano, D. (1983). The practice and efficacy of breast self-examination: A critical review. *American Journal of Public Health*, **73**, 1324–1326.

Honeybun, J., Johnston, M. and Tookman, A. (1992). The impact of a death on fellow hospice patients. *British Journal of Medical Psychology*, **65**, 67–72.

Hooper, E. M., Comstock, L. M., Goodwin, J. M. and Goodwin, J. S. (1982). Patient characteristics that influence physician behavior. *Medical Care*, **20**, 630–638.

Horn, R. (1997). Representations of medication and treatment: Advances in theory and measurement. In K. J. Petrie and J. A. Weinman (eds), *Perceptions of Health and Illness*. Amsterdam: Harwood Academic Publishers.

Horn, R. (1998). Adherence to medication: A review of the existing research. In L. Myers, and K. Midence (eds), *Adherence to Treatment in Medical Conditions*. Amsterdam: Harwood Academic Publishers.

Horn, R. and Weinman, J. (1998). Predicting treatment adherence: An overview of theoretical models. In L. Myers and K. Midence (eds), *Adherence to Treatment in Medical Conditions*. Amsterdam: Harwood Academic Publishers.

Horwitz, R. I. and Horwitz, S. M. (1993). Adherence to treatment and health outcomes. *Archives of Internal Medicine*, **153**, 1863–1868.

Hulka, B. S. and Wheat, J. R. (1985). Patterns of utilization: The patient perspective. *Medical Care*, **23**, 438–460.

Humphrey, M. and Zimpfer, D. G. (1996). *Counselling for Grief and Bereavement*. London: Sage.

Illich, I. (1976). *Limits to Medicine: Medical Nemesis: The expropriation of health*. London: Marion Boyars.

I-Min, L., Paffenbarger, R. S. Jr. and Hsoeh, C. (1991). Physical activity and risk of developing colorectal cancer among college alumni. *Journal of the National Cancer Institute*, **83**, 1324–1329.

Ingram, R. E. (1990). Self-focused attention in clinical disorders: Review and a conceptual model. *Psychological Bulletin*, **107**, 156–176.

Ingstad, B. (1989). Healer, witch, prophet or modern health worker?: The changing role of Ngaka ya Setswana. In A. Jacobson-Widding and D. Westerlund (eds), *Culture, Experience and Pluralism: Essays on African ideas of illness and healing*. Stockholm: Almqvist & Wiksell International.

Institute of Medical Ethics Working Party on the Ethics of Prolonging Life and Assisting Death (1990). Viewpoint. *Lancet*, 610–613.

Inui, T. S. and Carter, W. B. (1985). Problems and prospects for health services on patient–provider communication. *Medical Care*, **23**, 521–538.

Inui, T. S., Carter, W. B. and Pecoraro, R. E. (1981). Screening for non compliance among patients with hypertension: Is self-report the best available measure? *Medical Care*, **19**, 1061–1064.

Jacob, R. G., Wing, R. and Shapiro, A. P. (1987). The behavioral treatment of hypertension: Long–term effects. *Behavior Therapy*, **18**, 325–352.

Jacobs, S. C., Hansen, F., Kasl, S., Ostfeld, A., Berkman, L. and Kim, K. (1990). Anxiety disorders during acute bereavement: Risk and risk factors. *Journal of Clinical Psychiatry*, **7**, 269–274.

Jacobson, A. M., Hauser, S. T., Wolfsdorf, J. L., Noulihan, J. H., Milley, J. E., Herskowitz, R. D., Wertlieb, D. and Watt, E. (1987). Psychologic predictors of compliance in children with recent onset of diabetes mellitus. *Journal of Pediatrics*, **110**, 805–811.

Jacobson, B., Smith, A. and Whitehead, M. (1991). *The Nation's Health: A stategy for the 1990s*. (2nd edn) London: King's Fund.

James, N. and Field, D. (1992). The routinization of hospice: Charisma and bureaucratization. *Social Science and Medicine*, **34**, 1363–1375.

Janis, I. L. (1958). *Psychological Stress: Psychoanalytic and behavioral studies of surgical patients*. New York: Wiley.

Janz, N. K. and Becker, M. H. (1984). The health belief model: A decade later. *Health Education Quarterly*, **11**, 1–47.

Jensen, M. P. and Karoly, P. (1991). Motivation and expectancy factors in symptom perception: A laboratory study of the placebo effect. *Psychosomatic Medicine*, **53**, 144–152.

Jewett, J. J., Hibbard, J. H. and Weeks, E. C. (1991/92). Predictors of health care utilization for the young-old and the old-old: A structural modeling approach. *Behavior, Health, and Aging*, **2**, 29–41.

Joffe, R. T., Lippert, G. P., Gray, T. A., Sawa, G. and Horvath, Z. (1987). Mood disorder and multiple sclerosis. *Archives of Neurology*, **44**, 376–378.

Johnson, J. E. (1984). Psychological interventions and coping with surgery. In A. Baum, S. E. Taylor and J. E. Singer (eds), *Handbook of Health Psychology, Vol. IV: Social psychological aspects of health*. Hillsdale, NJ: Erlbaum.

Johnson, S. B. (1985). The family and the child with chronic illness. In D. C. Turk and R. D. (eds), *Health, Illness, and Families: A lifespan perspective*. New York: Wiley.

Johnson, S. B. (1992). Methodological issues in diabetes research. Measuring adherence. *Diabetes Care*, **15**, 1658–1667.

Johnson, S. B., Silverstein, T., Rosenbloom, A., Carter, R. and Cunningham, W. (1986). Assessing daily management in childhood diabetes. *Health Psychology*, **5**, 545–564.

Johnston, M. (1982). Recognition of patients' worries by nurses and by other patients. *British Journal of Clinical Psychology*, **21**, 255–261.

Johnston, M. and Vogele, C. (1993). Benefits of psychological preparation for surgery: A meta-analysis. *Annals of Behavioral Medicine*, **15**, 245– 256.

Jones, J. A., Eckhardt, L. E., Mayer, J. A., Bartholomew, S., Malcarne, V. L., Hovell, M. F. and Elder, J. P. (1993). The effects of an instructional audiotape on breast self-examination proficiency. *Journal of Behavioral Medicine*, **16**, 225–235.

Jones, J. L. (1994). *The Social Context of Health and Health Work*. Basingstoke, Hampshire: Macmillan.

Jones, J. W. (1981). Dishonesty, burnout and unauthorised work break extensions. *Personality and Social Psychology Bulletin*, 7, 406–409.

Jones, R. A. (1990). Expectations and delay in seeking medical care. *Journal of Social Issues*, **46**, 81–95.

Jones, R. A., Weise, H. J., Moore, R. W. and Haley, J. V. (1981). On the perceived meaning of symptoms. *Medical Care*, **19**, 710–717.

Judge, K. and Benzeval, M. (1993). Health inequalities: new concerns about the children of single mothers. *British Medical Journal*, **306**, 677–680.

Kane, R. L., Klein, S. J., Bernstein, L. and Rothenberg, R. (1986). The role of hospice in reducing the impact of bereavement. *Journal of Chronic Disease*, **39**, 735–742.

Kannel, W. B. and Gordon, T. (1979). Physiological and medical concomitants of obesity: The Framingham study. In G. A. Bray (ed.), *Obesity in America*. Washington DC: NIH Publication No. 79–359.

Kaplan, R. M. (1991). Health-related quality of life in patient decision making. *Journal of Social Issues*, **47**, 69–90.

Kaplan, R. M. and Simon, H. J. (1990). Compliance in medical care: Reconsideration of self-predictions. *Annals of Behavioral Medicine*, **12**, 66–71.

Kaplan, S. H., Greenfield, S. and Ware, J. E. (1989). Impact of the doctor–patient relationship on the outcomes of chronic disease. In M. Stewart and D. Roter (eds), *Communicating with Medical Patients*. Newbury Park, CA: Sage.

Karmel, M. (1972). Total institutions and models of adaptation. *Journal of Clinical Psychology*, 28, 574–576.

Kart, C. (1981). Experiencing symptoms: Attribution and misattribution of illness among the aged. In M. Haug (ed.), *Elderly Patients and Their Doctors*. New York: Springer.

Kasl, S. V. and Cobb, S. (1966). Health behavior, illness behavior and sick role behavior. *Archives of Environmental Health*, 12, 246–266.

Kastenbaum, R. (1975). Is death a life crisis? On the confrontation with death in theory and practice. In N. Datan and L. H. Eisenberg (eds), *Life-span Development Psychology Normative Life Crisis*. New York: Academic Press.

Kay, M. A. (1993). Fallen fontanelle: Culture-bound or cross-cultural. *Medical Anthropology*, 15, 137–156.

Keane, T. M., Prue, D. M. and Collins, F. L. (1981). Behavioral contracting to improve dietary compliance in chronic renal dialysis patients. *Journal of Behavior Therapy and Experimental Psychiatry*, 12, 63–67.

Keefe, F. J., Caldwell, D. S., Queen, K. T., Gil, K. M., Martinez, S., Crisson, J. E., Ogden, W. and Nunley, J. (1987). Pain coping strategies in osteoarthritis patients. *Journal of Consulting and Clinical Psychology*, 55, 208–212.

Keinan, G., Carml, D. and Rieck, M. (1991–2). Predicting women's delay in seeking medical care after discovery of a lump in the breast: The role of personality and behavior patterns. *Behavioral Medicine*, 17, 177–183.

Kellert, S. P. (1976). A sociocultural concept of health and illness. *Journal of Medical Philosophy*, 1, 222–228.

Kellner, R. (1985). Functional somatic symptoms and hypochondriasis. *Archives of General Psychiatry*, 42, 821–833.

Kellner, R., Abbott, P., Winslow, W. W. and Pathak, D. (1987). Fears, beliefs and attitudes in DSM–III hypochondriasis. *Journal of Nervous and Mental Disease*, 175, 20–25.

Kellner, R., Slocumb, J. C., Wiggins, R. J., Abbott, P., Romanik, R. and Winslow, W. W. (1986). The relationship of hypochondriacal fears and beliefs to anxiety and depression. *Psychiatric Medicine*, 4, 15–24.

Kendall, P. C., Williams, L., Pechacek, T. F., Graham, L. E., Sisslak, C. and Herzoff, N. (1979). Cognitive-behavioral and patient education interventions in cardiac catheterization procedures: The Palo Alto Medical Psychology Project. *Journal of Consulting and Clinical Psychology*, 47, 49–58.

Kerns, R. D. and Turk, D. C. (1984). Depression and chronic pain: The mediating role of the spouse. *Journal of Marriage and the Family*, 46, 845–852.

Kessler, R. (1986). Sex differences in the use of health services. In S. McHugh and T. M. Vallis (eds), *Illness Behavior: A multidisciplinary model*. New York: Plenum Press.

Kiecolt-Glaser, J. K. and Williams, D. A. (1987). Self-blame, compliance, and distress among burn patients. *Journal of Personality and Social Psychology*, 53, 187–193.

Kiecolt-Glaser, J. K., Dura, J. R., Speicher, C. E., Trask, O. J. and Glaser, R. (1991). Spousal caregivers of dementia victims: Longitudinal changes in immunity and health. *Psychosomatic Medicine*, 53, 345–362.

Keicolt-Glaser, J. K., Glaser, R., Shuttleworth, E. C., Dyer, C. S., Ogrocki, P. and Speicher, C. E. (1987). Chronic stress and immunity in family caregivers of Alzheimer's disease victims. *Psychosomatic Medicine*, 49, 523–535.

Kiernan, P. J. and Isaacs, J. B. (1981). Use of drugs by the elderly. *Journal of the Royal Society of Medicine*, 74, 196–200.

Kindelan, K. and Kent, G. (1987). Concordance between patients' information preferences and general practitioners' perceptions. *Psychology and Health*, 1, 339–409.

Kinney, J. M. and Stephens, M. A. P. (1989). Hassles and uplifts of giving care to a family member with dementia. *Psychology and Aging*, **4**, 402–408.

Kinney, J. M., Stephens, M. A. P., Franks, M. M. and Norris, V. K. (1995). Stresses and satisfactions of family caregivers to older stroke patients. *The Journal of Applied Gerontology*, **14**, 3–21.

Kirscht, J. P. (1983). Preventive health behavior: A review of research and issues. *Health Psychology*, **2**, 277–301.

Kirwan, M. and Armstrong, D. (1995). Investigation of burnout in a sample of British general practitioners. *British Journal of General Practice*, **45**, 259–260.

Klebanov, P. K. and Jemmott, J. B. III (1992). Effects of expectations and bodily sensations on self-reports of premenstrual symptoms. *Psychology of Women Quarterly*, **16**, 289–310.

Klein, P. (1988). *Psychology Exposed: Or the Emporor's New Clothes*. London: Routledge.

Kleinknecht, R. A. and Lenz, J. (1989). Blood/injury fear, fainting and avoidance of medically related situations: A family correspondence study. *Behaviour Research and Therapy*, **28**, 429–437.

Kleinman, A. (1980). *Patients and Healers in the Context of Culture*. Berkeley: University of California Press.

Kleinman, A. (1982). Neurasthenia and depression. *Culture, Medicine and Psychiatry*, **6**, 117–189.

Kleinman, A. (1988). *The Illness Narratives: Suffering, healing and the human condition*. New York: Basic Books.

Kleinman, A., Eisenberg, L. and Good, B. (1978). Culture, illness, and care: Clinical lessons from anthropologic and cross-cultural research. *Annals of Internal Medicine*, **88**, 251–258.

Klingman, A., Melamed, B. G., Cuthbert, M. I. and Hermecz, D. A. (1984). Effects of participant modelling on information acquisition and skills utilisation. *Journal of Consulting and Clinical Psychology*, **52**, 414–422.

Klorman, R., Hilpert, P. L., Michael, R., LaGana, C. and Sveen, O. B. (1980). Effects of coping and mastery modeling on experienced and inexperienced pedodontic patients' disruptiveness. *Behavior Therapy*, **11**, 156–268.

Koeske, G. F. and Kelly, T. (1995). The impact of over involvement on burnout and job-satisfaction. *American Journal of Orthopsychiatry*, **65**, 282–292.

Kohl, H. W., LaPorte, R. E. and Blair, S. N. (1988). Physical activity and cancer: An epidemiological perspective. *Sports Medicine*, **6**, 222–237.

Komen, R. W. van and Redd, W. H. (1985). Personality factors associated with anticipatory nausea/vomiting in patients receiving cancer chemotherapy. *Health Psychology*, **4**, 189–202.

Koocher, G. P. (1986). Coping with a death from cancer. *Journal of Consulting and Clinical Psychology*, **54**, 623–631.

Kovacs, M., Iyengar, S., Goldston, D., Obrosky, D. S., Stewart, J. and Marsh, J. (1990). Psychological functioning among mothers of children with insulin dependent diabetes mellitus: A longitudinal study. *Journal of Consulting and Clinical Psychology*, **58**, 189–195.

Krantz, D. S. and Deckel, A. W. (1983). Coping with coronary heart disease and stroke. In T. G. Burish and L. A. Bradley (eds), *Coping with Chronic Disease: Research and applications*. New York: Academic Press.

Kravitz, R. L., Hays, R. D., Sherbourne, C. D., DiMatteo, R., Rogers, W. H., Ordway, L. and Greenfield, S. (1993). Recall of recommendations and adherence to advice among patients with chronic medical conditions. *Archives of Internal Medicine*, **153**, 1869–1878.

Kreitler, S., Chaitchik, S. and Kreitler, H. (1990). The psychological profile of women attending breast screening tests. *Social Science and Medicine*, **31**, 1177–1185.

Kristiansen, C. M. (1987). Social learning theory and preventive health behavior: Some neglected variables. *Social Behaviour*, **2**, 73–86.

Kroeger, A. (1983). Anthropological and socio-medical health care research in developing countries. *Social Science and Medicine*, 17, 147–161.

Kubler-Ross, E. (1969). *On Death and Dying*. New York: Macmillan.

Kulik, J. A. and Mahler, H. I. (1989). Social support and recovery from surgery. *Health Psychology*, 8, 221–238.

Kvale, G., Hugdahl, K., Asbjornsen, A., Rosengren, B., Lote, K. and Nordby, H. (1991). Anticipatory nasuea and vomiting in cancer patients. *Journal of Consulting and Clinical Psychology*, 59, 894–898.

Lalljee, M., Lamb, R. and Carnibella, G. (1993). Lay prototypes of illness: Their content and use. *Psychology and Health*, 8, 33–49.

Landrine, H. and Klonoff, E. A. (1992). Culture and health-related schema: A review and proposal for interdisciplinary integration. *Health Psychology*, 11, 267–276.

Landsbergis, P. A. (1988). Occupational stress among health care workers: A test of the job demands-control model. *Journal of Organisational Behaviour*, 9, 217–238.

Langer, E. J., Janis, I. E. and Wolfer, J. A. (1975). Reduction of psychological stress in surgical patients. *Journal of Experimental Social Psychology*, 11, 155–165.

Langosch, W. (1984). Behavioural interventions in cardiac rehabilitation. In A. Steptoe and A. Mathews (eds), *Health Care and Human Behaviour*. London: Academic Press.

Larsen, R. J. (1992). Nueroticism and selective encoding and recall of symptoms: Evidence from a combined recurrent-retrospective study. *Journal of Personality and Social Psychology*, 62, 480–488.

Larsen, R. J. and Kasimatis, M. (1991). Day-to-day physical symptoms: Individual differences in the occurrence, duration, and emotional concomitants of minor daily illnesses. *Journal of Personality*, 59, 387–423.

Lau, R. R. and Hartman, K. A. (1983). Common-sense representations of common illnesses. *Health Psychology*, 2, 167–185.

Lau, R. R., Bernard, T. M. and Hartman, K. A. (1989). Further explorations of common-sense representations of common illness. *Health Psychology*, 8, 195–219.

Lauver, D. (1987). Theoretical perspectives relevant to breast self-examination. *Advances in Nursing Science*, 9, 16–24.

Lauver, D. and Chang, A. (1991). Testing theoretical explanations of intentions to seek care for a breast cancer symptom. *Journal of Applied Social Psychology*, 21, 1440–1548.

Lauver, D. and Ho, C.-H. (1993). Explaining delay in care seeking for breast cancer symptoms. *Journal of Applied Social Psychology*, 23, 1806–1825.

Lazarus, R. S. (1983). The costs and benefits of denial. In S. Bresnitz (ed.), *Denial of Stress*. New York: International Universities Press.

Lazarus, R. S. and Folkman, S. (1984). *Stress, Appraisal, and Coping*. New York: Springer.

Leenaars, P. E. M., Rombouts, R. and Kok, G. (1993). Seeking medical care for a sexually transmitted disease: Determinants of delay-behavior. *Psychology and Health*, 8, 17–32.

Leigh, H. and Reiser, M. F. (1985). *The Patient: Biological, psychological and social dimensions of medical practice*. New York: Plenum Press.

Leirer, V. O., Morrow, D. G., Tanke, E. D. and Pariante, G. M. (1991). Elders' nonadherence: Its assessment and medication reminding by voice mail. *The Gerontologist*, 31, 514–520.

Leon, A. S., Connett, J., Jacobs, D. R. and Rauramaa, R. (1987). Leisure-time physical activity levels and risk of coronarty heart disease and death: The multiple risk factor intervention trial. *Journal of the American Medical Association*, 258, 2388–2395.

Lerman, C., Rimer, B., Trock, B., Balsham, A. A. and Engstrom, P. F. (1990). Factors associated with repeat adherence to breast cancer screening. *Preventive Medicine*, 19, 279–290.

Lerman, C., Trock, B., Rimer, B. K., Jepson, C. and Boyce, A. (1991). Psychological side effects of breast cancer screening. *Health Psychology*, 10, 259–267.

Levenson, H. (1973). Multidimensional health locus of control in psychiatric patients. *Journal of Consulting and Clinical Psychology*, **41**, 397–404.

Leventhal, E. A. and Prohaska, T. R. (1986). Age, symptom interpretation, and health behavior. *Journal of the American Geriatrics Society*, **34**, 185–191.

Leventhal, H. (1983). Behavioral medicine: Psychology in health care. In D. Mechanic (ed.), *Handbook of Health, Health Care, and the Health Professions*. New York: Free Press.

Leventhal, H. (1986). Symptom reporting: A focus on process. In S. McHugh and T. M. Vallis (eds), *Illness Behavior: A multidisciplinary model*. New York: Plenum Press.

Leventhal, H. (1993). Theories of compliance, and turning necessities into preferences: application to adolescent health action. In N. A. Krasnegor, L. Epstein, S. B. Johnson and S. F. Yaffe (eds), *Developmental Aspects of Health Behavior*. New Jersey: Lawrence Erlbaum Associates.

Leventhal, H. and Cameron, L. (1987). Behavioral theories and the problem of compliance. *Patient Education and Counselling*, **10**, 117–138.

Leventhal, H. and Leventhal, E. A. (1993). Affect, cognition, and symptom perception. In C. R. Chapman and K. M. Foley (eds) *Current and Emerging Issues in Cancer Pain: Research and practice*. New York: Raven Press.

Leventhal, H., Benyamini, Y., Brownlee, S., Diefenbach, M., Leventhal, E. A., Patrick-Miller, L. and Robitaille, C. (1997). Illness representations: Theoretical foundations. In K. J. Petrie and J. A. Weinman (eds), *Perceptions of Health and Illness*. Amsterdam: Harwood Academic Publishers.

Leventhal, H., Meyer, D. and Nerenz, D. (1980). The common sense representation of illness danger. In Rachman, S. (ed.), *Contributions to Medical Psychology*, Vol. II. Oxford: Pergamon Press.

Leventhal, H., Nerenz, D. R. and Steele, D. J. (1984). Illness representations and coping with health threats. In A. Baum, S. E. Taylor and J. E. Singer (eds), *Handbook of Psychology and Health, Vol. IV. Social psychological aspects of health*. Hillsdale, NJ: Lawrence Erlbaum Associates.

Leventhal, H., Nerenz, D. and Strauss, A. (1982). Self-regulation and the mechanisms of symptom appraisal. In D. Mechanic (ed.), *Symptoms, Illness Behavior and Help-seeking*. New York: Prodist.

Levin, L. and Idler, E. (1983). Self-care in health. *Review of Public Health*, **4**, 108–201.

Levin, L. S., Katz, A. H. and Holst, E. (1976). *Self Care: Lay initiatives in health*. New York: Prodist.

Levinson, W., Stiles, W. B., Inui, T. S. and Engle, R. (1993). Physician frustration in communicating with patients. *Medical Care*, **31**, 285–295.

Levkoff, S. E., Cleary, P. D., Wetle, T. and Besdine, R. W. (1988). Illness behavior in the aged. Implications for clinicians. *Journal of the American Geriatrics Society*, **36**, 622–629.

Levy, R. (1983). Social support and compliance. *Social Science and Medicine*, **17**, 1329–1338.

Levy, S. M. (1985). *Behavior and Cancer*. San Francisco: Jossey-Bass.

Levy, S. M. (1990). Humanizing death: Psychotherapy with terminally ill patients. In P. T. Costa and G. R. Vandenbos (eds), *Psychological Aspects of Serious Illness: Chronic conditions, fatal diseases, and clinical care*. Washington, DC: American Psychological Association.

Levy, S. M., Herberman, R. B., Whiteside, T., Sanzo, K., Lee, J. and Kirkwood, J. (1990). Perceived social support and tumor estrogen/progesterone receptor status as predictors of natural killer cell activity in breast cancer patients. *Psychosomatic Medicine*, **52**, 73–85.

Lewith, G. T. and Aldridge, D. A. (1991). *Complementary Medicine and the European Community*. Saffron Walden: C. W. Daniel.

Ley, P. (1979). Memory of medical information. *British Journal of Social and Clinical Psychology*, **18**, 245–255.

Ley, P. (1983). Patients' understanding and recall in clinical communication failure. In D. Pendelton and J. Hasler (eds), *Doctor–Patient Communication*. London: Academic Press.

Ley, P. (1988). *Communicating with Patients*. London: Croom Helm.

Ley, P. (1989). Improving patients' understanding, recall, satisfaction and compliance. In A. Broome (ed.), *Health Psychology: Process and applications* (1st edn). London: Chapman & Hall.

Ley, P. and Llewelyn, S. (1995). Improving patients' understanding, recall, satisfaction and compliance. In A. Broome and S. Llewelyn (eds), *Health Psychology: Process and application* (2nd edn). London: Chapman & Hall.

Lieberman, M. A. and Fisher, L. (1995). The impact of chronic illness on the health and well-being of family members. *The Gerontologist*, **35**, 94–102.

Lierman, L. M., Young, H. M., Kasprzyk, D. and Benoliel, J. Q. (1990). Predicting breast self-examination using the theory of reasoned action. *Nursing Research*, **39**, 97–101.

Light, E. and Lebowitz, B. D. (eds) (1989). *Alzheimer's Disease Treatment and Family Stress: Directions for research*. Rockville, MD: National Institute of Mental Health.

Lindemann, E. (1944). Symptomatology and management of acute grief. *American Journal of Psychiatry*, **101**, 141–148.

Linden, M., Horgas, A. L., Gilbert, R. and Steinhagen-Thiesses, E. (1997). Predicting health care utilization in the very old: The role of physical health, mental health, attitudinal and social factors. *Journal of Aging and Health*, **9**, 3–27.

Lipowski, Z. J. (1986). What does the word 'psychosomatic' really mean? A historical and semantic inquiry. In M. J. Christie and P. G. Mellett (eds), *The Psychosomatic Approach: Contemporary practice and whole person care*. New York: Wiley.

Lipton, J. A. and Marbach, J. J. (1984). Ethnicity and the pain experience. *Social Science and Medicine*, **19**, 1279–1298.

Littlefield, C. H., Rodin, G. M., Murray, M. A. and Craven, J. L. (1990). Influence of functional impairment and social support on depressive symptoms in persons with diabetes. *Health Psychology*, **9**, 737–749.

Livingstone, M. G. and Brooks, D. N. (1988). The burden on families of the brain injured: A review. *Journal of Head Trauma Rehabilitation*, **2**, 6–15.

Livingstone, M. G., Brooks, D. N. and Bond, M. R. (1985). Three months after severe head injury: Psychiatric and social impact on relatives. *Journal of Neurology, Neurosurgery and Psychiatry*, **48**, 870–875.

Lloyd, G. G. and Deakin, H. G. (1975). Phobias complicating treatment of uterine carcinoma. *British Medical Journal*, **5**, 440.

Long, C. L. (1989). Renal care. In A. Broome (ed.), *Health Psychology: Process and applications*. London: Chapman & Hall.

Lorenc, L. and Branthwaite, A. (1993). Are older adults less compliant with prescribed medication than younger adults? *British Journal of Clinical Psychology*, **32**, 485–492.

Lorig, K., Chastain, R. L., Ung, E., Shoor, S. and Holman, H. (1989). Development and evaluation of a scale to measure perceived self-efficacy in people with arthritis. *Arthritis and Rheumatism*, **32**, 37–44.

Ludwick-Rosenthal, R. and Neufeld, R. W. J. (1988). Stress management during noxious medical procedures: An evaluative review of outcome studies. *Psychological Bulletin*, **104**, 326–342.

Ludwick-Rosenthal, R. and Neufeld, R. W. J. (1993). Preparation forundergoing an invasive medical procedure: Interacting effects of information and coping style. *Journal of Consulting and Clinical Psychology*, **61**, 156–164.

Lunt, B. and Hillier, P. (1981). Terminal care. *British Medical Journal*, **283**, 595–598.

Lupton, D. (1994). *Medicine as Culture: Illness, disease and the body in western societies*. London: Sage.

Luscher, T. F. and Vetter, W. (1990). Adherence to medication. *Journal of Human Hypertension*, **4**, 43–46.

Lyons, R. F., Sullivan, M. J. L. and Ritvo, P. G. (1995). *Relationships in Chronic Illness and Disability*. London: Sage.

MacAlpine, I. (1957). Syphilophobia. *British Journal of Venereal Disease*, **33**, 92–99.

McAuley, E. (1992). The role of efficacy cognitions in the prediction of exercise behavior in middle-aged adults. *Journal of Behavioral Medicine*, **15**, 65–87.

McAuley, E. (1993). Self-efficacy and the maintenance of exercise participation in older adults. *Journal of Behavioral Medicine*, **16**, 103–113.

McAuley, E. and Courneya, K. S. (1992). Self-efficacy relationships with affective and assertion responses to exercise. *Journal of Applied Social Psychology*, **22**, 312–326.

McAuley, E. and Jacobson, L. (1991). Self-efficacy and exercise participation in sedentary adult females. *American Journal of Health Promotion*, **5**, 65–88.

MacBryde, C. M and Blacklow, R. S. (1970). *Signs and Symptoms: Applied pathologic physiology and clinical interpretations* (5th edn). Philadelphia: Lippincott.

McCaul, K. D., Branstetter, A. D., Schroeder, D. M. and Glasgow, R. E. (1996). What is the relationship between breast cancer risk and mammography screening? A meta-analytic review. *Health Psychology*, **15**, 423–429.

McCaul, K. D., Schroeder, D. M. and Reid, P. A. (1996). Breast cancer worry and screening: Some prospective data. *Health Psychology*, **15**, 430–433.

McCranie, E. W., Lambert, V. A. and Lambert, C. E. (1987). Work stress, hardiness, and burnout among hospital staff nurses. *Nursing Research*, **36**, 374–378.

McCulloch, D. K., Mitchell, R. D., Ambler, J. and Tattersall, R. B. (1983). Influence of imaginative teaching of diet on compliance and metabolic control in insulin dependent diabetes. *British Medical Journal*, **287**, 1858–1861.

McEvedy, C. J. and Basquille, J. (1997). BSE, public anxiety and private neurosis. *Journal of Psychosomatic Research*, **42**, 485–486.

McEwan, J. (1979). Self-medication in the context of self-care: A review. In J. A. D. Anderson (ed.), *Self-Medication*. Lancaster: MTP Press.

McFarland, C., Ross, M. and DeCourville, N. (1989). Women's theories of menstruation and biases in recall of menstrual symptoms. *Journal of Personality and Social Psychology*, **57**, 522–531.

MacFarlane, E. M. and Sony, S. D. (1992). Women, breast lump discovery, and associated stress. *Health Care for Women International*, **13**, 23–32.

MacGregor, G. A., Markandu, N. D., Best, F. E., Elder, D. M., Cam, J. M., Sagnella, G. A. and Squires, M. (1982). Double-blind randomised crossover trial of moderate sodium restriction in essential hypertension. *Lancet*, **1**, 351–355.

MacGregor, G. A., Markandu, N. D., Sagnella, G. A., Singer, D. J. and Cappuccio, F. P. (1989). Double-blind study of three sodium intakes and long-term effects of sodium restriction in essential hypertension. *Lancet*, **2**, 1244–1247.

MacIntyre, S. (1993). Gender differences in the perceptions of common cold symptoms. *Social Science and Medicine*, **36**, 15–20.

McIvor, G., Riklan, M. and Reznikoff, M. (1984). Depression in multiple sclerosis patients as a function of length and severity of illness, age, remissions, and perceived social support. *Journal of Clinical Psychiatry*, **40**, 1028–1033.

McKee, J. (1988). Holistic health and the critique of western medicine. *Social Science and Medicine*, **26**, 775–784.

McKinlay, J. B. (1975). Who is really ignorant – physician or patient? *Journal of Health and Social Behaviour*, **16**, 3–11.

McKinlay, J. B., Potter, D. A. and Feldman, H. A. (1996). Non-medical influences on medical decision making. *Social Science and Medicine*, **42**, 769–776.

McKinlay, W. W., Brooks, D. N., Bond, M. R., Martinage, M. M. and Marshall, M. (1981). The short-term outcome of severe blunt head injury as reported by relatives of injured persons. *Journal of Neurology, Neurosurgery and Psychiatry*, **44**, 527–533.

Maddi, S. E. (1990). Prolonging life by heroic measures: A humanistic existential measure. In P. T. Costa and G. R. VandenBos (eds), *Psychological Aspects of Serious Illness: Chronic conditions, fatal diseases, and clinical care*. Washington DC: American Psychological Association.

Maddux, J. E. (1993). Social cognitive models of health and exercise behavior: An introduction and review of conceptual issues. *Journal of Applied Sport Psychology*, **5**, 116–140.

Maeland, J. G. and Havik, O. E. (1987). Psychological predictors for return to work after a myocardial infarction. *Journal of Psychosomatic Research*, **31**, 471–481.

Magnus, K., Matroos, A. and Strackee, J. (1979). Walking, cycling or gardening, with or without seasonal interruption, in relation to acute coronary events. *American Journal of Epidemiology*, **110**, 724–733.

Maguire, P., Fairburn, S. and Fletcher, C. (1986). Consultation skills of young doctors: I. Benefits of feedback training in interviewing as students persist. *British Medical Journal*, **292**, 1573–1576.

Maheux, B., Dufort, F., Beland, F., Jacques, A. and Levesque, A. (1990). Female medical practitioners: More preventive and patient oriented? *Medical Care*, **28**, 87–92.

Manne, S. and Sandler, I. (1984). Coping and adjustment to genital herpes. *Journal of Behavioral Medicine*, **7**, 391–410.

Manne, S. L. and Zautra, A. J. (1989). Spouse criticism and support: Their association with coping and psychological adjustment among women with rheumatoid arthiritis. *Journal of Personality and Social Psychology*, **56**, 608–617.

Manstead, A. S. R., Proffitt, C. and Smart, J. L. (1983). Predicting and understanding mother's infant-feeding intentions and behavior: Testing the theory of reasoned action. *Journal of Personality and Social Psychology*, **44**, 657–671.

Manuel, G. M., Roth, S., Keefe, F. J. and Brantly, B. A. (1987). Coping with cancer. *Journal of Human Stress*, **13**, 149–158.

Marchandise, B., Bourassa, M. G., Chaitman, B. R. and Lesperance, J. (1978). Angiographic evaluation of the natural history of normal coronary atheroslecrosis. *American Journal of Cardiology*, **41**, 216–220.

Marcus, B. H. and Owen, N. (1992). Motivational readiness, self-efficacy and decision making for exercise. *Journal of Applied Social Psychology*, **22**, 3–16.

Marcus, B. H., Selby, V. C., Niaura, R. S., Rossi, J. S. and Abrams, D. B. (1992). The stages and processes of exercise adoption and maintenance in a worksite sample. *Health Psychology*, **11**, 386–395.

Marks, I. (1987). *Fear, Phobias, and Rituals*. Oxford: Oxford University Press.

Marks, I. (1988). Blood-injury phobia: A review. *American Journal of Psychiatry*, **145**, 1207–1213.

Marmot, M. G., Davey Smith, G., Stansfield, S., Patel, C. and North, F. (1991). Health inequalities among British civil servants: The Whitehall II Study. *Lancet*, **337**, 1387–1393.

Marshall, J. R. and Funch, D. P. (1986). Gender and illness behaviour among colerectal cancer patients. *Women and Health*, **11**, 67–82.

Marshall, J. R., Gregorio, D. I. and Walsh, D. (1982). Sex differences in illness behavior: Care seeking among cancer patients. *Journal of Health and Social Behavior*, **23**, 197–204.

Marteau, T. M. (1989). Health beliefs and attributions. In A. K. Broome (ed.), *Health Psychology*. London: Chapman & Hall.

Marteau, T. M. (1993). Health-related screening: Psychological predictors of uptake and impact. In S. Maes, H. Leventhal and M. Johnston (eds), *International Review of Health Psychology*, Vol. II. Chichester: Wiley.

Marteau, T. M., Bloch, S. and Baum, J. D. (1987). Family life and diabetes control. *Journal of Child Psychology and Psychiatry*, **28**, 823–833.

Marteau, T.M., Cook, R., Kidd, J., Michie, S., Johnson, M., Slack, J. and Shaw, R.W. (1992). The psychological effects of false positive results in prenatal screening for fetal abnormality: A prospective study. *Prenatal Diagnosis*, **12**, 205–214.

Marteau, T. M., Johnston, M., Kidd, J., Michie, S., Cook, R., Slack, J. and Shaw, R. (1992). Psychological models in predicting uptake of prenatal screening. *Psychology and Health*, **6**, 13–22.

Marteau, T. M., Kidd, J., Cook, R., Johnston, M., Mitchie, S., Shaw, R. W. and Slack, J. (1988). Screening for Down's syndrome. *British Medical Journal*, **297**, 1469.

Marteau, T. M., Slack, J., Kidd, J. and Shaw, W. (1992). Presenting a routine screening test in antenatal care: Practice observed. *Public Health*, **106**, 131–141.

Martelli, M. F., Auerbach, S. M., Alexander, J. and Mercuri, L. (1987). Stress management in the health care setting: Matching interventions with patient coping styles. *Journal of Consulting and Clinical Psychology*, **55**, 201–207.

Martin, J. E. and Dubbert, P. M. (1982). Exercise and health: The adherence problem. *Behavioral Medicine Update*, **4**, 17–24.

Martin, S. C., Arnold, R. M. and Parker, R. M. (1988). Gender and medical socialization. *Journal of Health and Social Behavior*, **29**, 333–343.

Maslach, C. (1976). Burned out. *Human Behavior*, **5**, 16–22.

Maslach, C. (1982). *Burnout: The cost of caring*. Prentice Hall, NJ: Englewood Cliffs.

Maslach, C. and Jackson, S. (1982). Burnout in health professions: A social psychological analysis. In G. Sanders and J. Suls (eds), *Social Psychology of Health and Illness*. Hillsdale, NJ: Erlbaum.

Matarazzo, J. D. (1980). Behavioral health and behavioral medicine: Frontiers for a new health psychology. *American Psychologist*, **35**, 807–817.

Matson, N. (1994). Coping, caring and stress: A study of stroke carers and carers of older confused people. *British Journal of Clinical Psychology*, **33**, 333–344.

Matthews, K. A., Siegel, J. M., Kuller, C. H., Thompson, M. and Varat, M. (1983). Determinants of decisions to seek medical treatment by patients with acute myocardial infarction symptoms. *Journal of Personality and Social Psychology*, **44**, 1144–1156.

Matthews, S. H. and Rosner, T. T. (1988). Shared filial responsibility: The family as primary caregiver. *Journal of Marriage and the Family*, **50**, 185–195.

Mayer, J. A. and Solomon, L. J. (1992). Breast self-examination skill and frequency: A review. *Annals of Behavioral Medicine*, **14**, 189–196.

Mayou, R. (1973). Chest pain, angina pectoris, and disability. *Journal of Psychosomatic Research*, **17**, 287–291.

Mechanic, D. (1962). The concept of illness behavior. *Journal of Chronic Disease*, **15**, 189–194.

Mechanic, D. (1968). *Medical Sociology*. New York: Free Press.

Mechanic, D. (1972). Social psychologic factors affecting the presentation of bodily symptoms. *New England Journal of Medicine*, **286**, 1132–1139.

Mechanic, D. (1974). Discussion of research programs on relations between stressful life events and episodes of physical illness. In B. S. Dohrenwend and B. P. Dohrenwend (eds), *Stressful Life Events: Their nature and effects*. New York: Wiley.

Mechanic, D. (1976). Sex, illness behavior and the use of health services. *Journal of Human Stress*, **2**, 29–40.

Mechanic, D. (1978). *Medical Sociology* (2nd edn). New York: Free Press.

Mechanic, D. (1980). The experience and reporting of common physical complaints. *Journal of Health and Social Behavior*, **21**, 146–155.

Mechanic, D. (1983). Adolescent health and illness behavior: Review of the literature and a new hypothesis for the study of stress. *Journal of Human Stress*, **9**, 4–13.

Mechanic, D. (1986). Illness behaviour: An overview. In S. McHugh and T. M. Vallis (eds), *Illness Behavior: A multidisciplinary model*. New York: Plenum Press.

Meeuwesen, L., Schaap, C. and Van der Staak, C. (1991). Verbal analysis of doctor–patient communication. *Social Science and Medicine*, **32**, 1143–1150.

Meichenbaum, D. H. and Turk, D. C. (1987). *Facilitating Treatment Adherence: A practitioner's guidebook*. New York: Plenum Press.

Meininger, J. C. (1986). Sex differences in factors associated with use of medical care and alternative illness behaviors. *Social Science and Medicine*, **22**, 285–292.

Melamed, B. G., Yurcheson, R., Fleece, L., Hucherson, S. and Hawes, R. (1978). Effects of film modeling on the reduction of anxiety-related behaviors in individuals varying in levels of previous experience in the stress situation. *Journal of Consulting and Clinical Psychology*, **46**, 1357–1367.

Meyer, D., Leventhal, H. and Gutmann, M. (1985). Common-sense models of illness: The example of hypertension. *Health Psychology*, **4**, 115–135.

Michela, J. (1986). Interpersonal and individual impacts of a husband's heart attack. In A. Baum and J. E. Singer (eds), *Handbook of Psychology and Health: Vol. V. Stress and coping*. Hillsdale, NJ: Erlbaum.

Midence, K., Fuggle, P. and Davies, S. (1993). Psychosocial aspects of sickle cell disease (SCD) in childhood and adolescence: A review. *British Journal of Clinical Psychology*, **32**, 271–280.

Miller, A., Chamberlain, A. and Tschchkovski, M. (1985). Self-examination in the early detection of breast cancer. *Journal of Chronic Diseases*, **38**, 527–540.

Miller, B. and Montgomery, A. (1990). Family caregivers and limitations in social activities. *Research on Aging*, **12**, 72–93.

Miller, D., Acton, T. M. G. and Hedge, B. (1988). The worried well: Their identification and management. *Journal of the Royal College of Physicians of London*, **22**, 158–165.

Miller, D., Green, J., Farmer, R. and Carroll, G. (1985). A 'pseudo-AIDS' syndrome following from a fear of AIDS. *British Journal of Psychiatry*, **146**, 550.

Miller, S. M., Brody, D. S. and Summerton, J. (1988). Styles of coping with threat: Implications for health. *Journal of Personality and Social Psychology*, **54**, 142–148.

Miller, S. M. and Mangan, C. E. (1983). Interacting effects of coping style in adapting to gynecologic stress: Should the doctor tell all? *Journal of Personality and Social Psychology*, **45**, 223–236.

Miller-Johnson, S., Emery, R. E., Marvin, R. S., Clarke, W., Lovinger, R. and Marin, M. (1994). Parent–child relationships and management of insulin-dependent diabetes mellitus. *Journal of Consulting and Clinical Psychology*, **62**, 603–610.

Millstein, S. G. and Irwin, C. E. (1987). Concepts of health and illness: Different constructs or variations on a theme. *Health Psychology*, **6**, 515–524.

Minden, S. L., Oran, J. and Reich, P. (1987). Depression in multiple sclerosis. *General Hospital Psychiatry*, **9**, 426–434.

Montano, D. E. and Taplin, S. H. (1991). A test of an expanded theory of reasoned action to predict mammography participation. *Social Science and Medicine*, **32**, 733–741.

Montgomery, R. J. V. (1989). Investigating caregiver burden. In K. S. Markides and C. L. Cooper (eds), *Aging, Stress and Health*. Chichester: Wiley.

Moore, S. M., Barling, N. R. and Hood, B. (1998). Predicting testicular and breast self-examination behavior: A test of the theory of reasoned action. *Behaviour Change*, **15**, 41–49.

Moos, R. H. (1977). *Coping with Physical Illness*. New York: Plenum.

Moos, R. H. and Schaefer, J. A. (1984). The crisis of physical illness: An overview and conceptual approach. In R. H. Moos (ed.), *Coping with Physical Illness: New perspectives*. Vol. II. New York: Plenum Press.

Moos, R. H. and Schaefer, J. A. (1987). Evaluating health care work settings: A holistic conceptual framework. *Psychology and Health*, **1**, 97–122.

Mor, V. and Hiris, J. (1983). Determinants of site of death among hospice cancer patients. *Journal of Health and Social Behavior*, 24, 384–396.

Morisky, D. (1983). Five-year blood pressure control and mortality following health education for hypertensive patients. *American Journal of Public Health*, **73**, 153–162.

Morris, J. N., Everitt, M. G., Pollard, R., Chave, S. P. W. and Semmence, A. M. (1980). Vigorous exercise in leisure-time: Protection against coronary heart-disease. *Lancet*, **2**, 1207–1210.

Morris, L. W., Morris, R. G. and Britton, P. G. (1988). The relationship between marital intimacy and perceived strain and depression in spouse caregivers of dementia sufferers. *British Journal of Medical Psychology*, **61**, 231–236.

Morris, R. G., Morris, L. W. and Britton, P. G. (1988). Factors affecting the emotional well-being of the caregivers of dementia sufferers. *British Journal of Psychiatry*, **153**, 147–156.

Morris, R. G., Woods, R. T., Davies, K. S. and Morris, L. W. (1991). Gender differences in carers of dementia sufferers. *British Journal of Psychiatry*, **158**, 69–74.

Morris, T., Greer, S. and White, P. (1977). Psychological and social adjustment to mastectomy: A 2-yr follow up study. *Cancer*, **40**, 2381–2387.

Morrow, G. R. (1986). Effect of the cognitive heirarchy on the systematic desensitisation of anticipatory nausea in cancer patients: A component comparison with relaxation only, counselling and no treatment. *Cognitive Therapy and Research*, **10**, 421–466.

Morrow, G. R. and Dobkin, P. L. (1988). Anticipatory nausea and vomiting in cancer patients undergoing chemotherapy treatment: Prevalence, etiology, and behavioral interventions. *Clinical Psychology Review*, 8, 517–556.

Morrow, G. R., Lindke, J. and Black, P. M. (1991). Anticipatory nausea in cancer patients: Replication and extension of a learning model. *British Journal of Psychology*, **82**, 61–72.

Murdoch, G. P. (1980). *Theories of Illness: A world survey*. Pittsburgh: University of Pittsburgh Press.

Myers, L. B. and Midence, K. (eds) (1998). *Adherence to Treatment in Medical Conditions*. Amsterdam: Harwood Academic Publishers.

Myers, M. F. (1996). When helping starts to hurt: A new look at burnout among psychotherapists. *Journal of Psychosomatic Research*, **40**, 215.

Myers, R. E., Ross, E. A., Wolf, T. A., Balshem, A., Jepson, C. and Millner, L. (1991). Behavioral interventions to increase adherence in colocectal cancer screening. *Medical Care*, **29**, 1039–1050.

Nagy, V. T. and Wolfe, G. R. (1984). Cognitive predictors of compliance in chronic disease patients. *Medical Care*, **22**, 912–921.

Nail, L. M., King, K. B. and Johnson, J. E. (1986). Coping with radiation treatment for gynecologic cancer: Mood and disruption in usual function. *Journal of Psychosomatic Obstetrics and Gynaecology*, **5**, 271–281.

Nathanson, C. A. (1975). Illness and the feminine role: A theoretical review. *Social Science and Medicine*, **9**, 57–62.

Nathanson, C. A. (1977). Sex, illness and medical care: A review of data, theory and method. *Social Science and Medicine*, **11**, 13–25.

Naysmith, A. and O'Neill, W. (1989). Hospice. In L. Sherr (ed.), *Death, Dying and Bereavement*. Oxford: Blackwell Scientific Publications.

Neale, A. V., Tilley, B. C. and Vernon, S. W. (1986). Marital status, delay in seeking treatment and survival from breast cancer. *Social Science and Medicine*, **23**, 305–312.

Nelson, L., Jennings, G. L., Elser, M. D. and Korner, P. I. (1986). Effect of changing levels of physical activity on blood pressure and haemodynamics in essential hypertension. *Lancet*, **2**, 473–476.

Nerenz, D. R. and Leventhal, H. (1983), Self-regulation theory in chronic illness. In T. G. Burish and L. A. Bradley (eds), *Coping with Chronic Disease: Research and applications*. New York: Academic Press.

Neuling, S. J. and Winefield, H. R. (1988). Social support and recovery from breast cancer: Frequency and correlates of supportive behavior by family, friends and surgeon. *Social Science and Medicine*, **27**, 385–392.

Newacheck, P. W., McManus, M. A. and Fox, H. B. (1991). Prevalence and impact of chronic illnesses among adolescents. *American Journal of Diseases of Childhood*, **145**, 1367–1373.

Nicassio, P.M. and Smith, T.W. (eds) (1995) *Managing Chronic Illness: A biopsychosocial perspective*. Washington, DC: American Psychological Association.

Nicassio, P. M., Wallston, K. A., Callahan, L. F., Herbert, M. and Pincus, T. (1985). The measurement of helplessness in rheumatoid arthritis: The development of the Arthritis Helplessness Index. *Journal of Rheumatology*, **12**, 462–467.

Nichols, K. A. (1987). Teaching nurses psychological care. In D. Miller (ed.), *Teaching Nurses Psychological Skills*. Leicester: British Psychological Society.

Noble, L. M. (1998). Doctor–patient communication and adherence to treatment. In Myers, L. and Midence, K. (eds), *Adherence to Treatment in Medical Conditions*. Amsterdam: Harwood Academic Publishers.

Norman, P. (1991). Social learning theory and the prediction of attendance at screening. *Psychology and Health*, **5**, 231–239.

Norman, P. and Conner, M. (1993). The role of social cognition models in predicting attendance at health checks. *Psychology and Health*, **8**, 447–462.

Novack, D. H., Plumer, R., Smith, R. L., Ochitill, H., Morrow, G. R. and Bennett, J. M. (1979). Changes in physicians' attitudes toward telling the cancer patient. *Journal of the American Medical Association*, **241**, 897–900.

O'Brien, M. K., Petrie, K. and Raeburn, J. (1992). Adherence to medication regimens: Updating a complex medical issue. *Medical Care Review*, **49**, 435–454.

O'Connor, D. W., Pottitt, P. A., Roth, M., Brook, C. P. B. and Reiss, B. B. (1990). Problems reported by relatives in a community study of dementia. *British Journal of Psychiatry*, **156**, 835–841.

O'Dowd, T. C. (1988). Five years of heartsink patients in general practice. *British Medical Journal*, **297**, 528–532.

O'Leary, A., Shoor, S., Lorig, K. and Holman, H. R. (1988). A cognitive–behavioral treatment for rheumatoid arthritis. *Health Psychology*, **7**, 527–544.

Office of Population and Census Surveys (OPCS) (1984) *Causes of Death*. London: Government Statistical Service.

Ogden, J. (1996). *Health Psychology: A textbook*. Buckingham: Open University Press.

Oja, P., Vuori, I. and Olavi, O. (1998). Daily walking and cycling to work: Their utility as health-enhancing physical activity. *Patient Education and Counselling*, **33**, S87–S94.

Oken, D. (1961). What to tell cancer patients: A study of medical attitudes. *Journal of the American Medical Association*, **175**, 1120–1128.

Oldridge, N. B. (1982). Compliance and exercise in primary and secondary prevention of coronary heart disease: A review. *Preventive Medicine*, **11**, 56–70.

Oliver, R. L. and Berger, P. K. (1979). A path analysis of preventive health care decision models. *Journal of Consumer Research*, **6**, 113–122.

Ong, L. M. L., de Haes, J. C. J. M., Hoos, A. M. and Lammes, F. B. (1995). Doctor–patient communication: A review of the literature. *Social Science and Medicine*, **40**, 903–918.

Orbell, S. and Gillies, B. (1993). What's stressful about caring? *Journal of Applied Social Psychology*, **23**, 272–290.

Orbell, S. and Sheeran, P. (1993). Health psychology and uptake of preventive health services: A review of 30 years' research on cervical screening. *Psychology and Health*, **8**, 417–433.

Orbell, S., Crombie, I. and Johnston, G. (1996). Social cognition and social structure in the prediction of cervical cancer. *British Journal of Health Psychology*, **1**, 35–50.

Orme, C. M. and Binik, Y. M. (1989). Consistency of adherence across regimen demands. *Health Psychology*, **8**, 27–43.

Osterweiss, M., Solomon, F. and Green, M. (eds) (1984). *Bereavement: Reactions, consequences and care*. Washington, DC: National Academy Press.

Owens, R. G. and Heron, K. (1989). Accuracy of estimates of delay in seeking breast cancer diagnosis and treatment. *Journal of Psychosocial Oncology*, **7**, 193–197.

Pachter, L. M. (1994). Culture and clinical care: Folk illness beliefs and behaviors and their implications for health care delivery. *Journal of the American Medical Association*, **271**, 690–694.

Paffenbarger, R. S., Hyde, R. T. and Wing, A. L. (1987). Physical activity and incidence of cancer in diverse populations: A preliminary report. *American Journal of Clinical Nutrition*, **45**, 312–317.

Paffenbager, R. S., Hydfe, R. T., Wing, A. L. and Hsieh, C. (1986). Physical activity, all-cause mortality, and longevity of college alumni. *New England Journal of Medicine*, **314**, 605–613.

Paffenbager, R. S., Hyde, R. T., Wing, A. L. and Steinmetz, C. H. (1984). A natural history of athleticism and cardiovascular health. *Journal of the American Medical Association*, **252**, 491–495.

Paffenbarger, R. S., Thorne, M. C. and Wing, A. L. (1968). Chronic disease in former college students. VIII. Characteristics in youth predisposing to hypertension in later years. *American Journal of Epidemiology*, **88**, 25–32.

Paffenbarger, R. S., Wing, S. L., Hyde, R. T. and Jung, D. L. (1983). Physical activity as an index of hypertension in college alumni. *American Journal Epidemiology*, **108**, 161–175.

Page, L. B. (1983). Epidemiology of hypertension. In J. Genest, O. Kuchel, P. Hamet and M. Cantin (eds), *Hypertension* (2nd edn). New York: McGraw-Hill.

Pagel, M. D., Erdly, W. W. and Becker, J. (1987). Social networks: We get by with (and in spite of) a little help from our friends. *Journal of Personality and Social Psychology*, **53**, 793–804.

Paradis, C.F. and Cummings, S.B. (1986) The evolution of the hospice in America toward organisational homogeneity. *Journal of Health and Social Behavior*, **27**, 370–386.

Parker, J. C., Frank, R. G., Beck, N. C., Smarr, K. L., Buescher, K. L., Phillips, L. R., Smith. E. I., Anderson, S. K. and Walker, S. E. (1988). Pain management in rheumatoid arthritis patients: A cognitive-behavioural approach. *Arthritis and Rheumatism*, **31**, 593–601.

Parker, J. D., Bagby, R. M. and Taylor, G. J. (1989). Toronto alexithymia scale, EPQ, and self-report measures of somatic complaints. *Personality and Individual Differences*, **10**, 599–604.

Parkes, C. M. (1972). *Bereavement: Studies of grief in adult life*. New York: International Universities Press.

Parkes, C. M. (1975). Determinants of grief following bereavement. *Omega*, **6**, 303–323.

Parkes, C. M. (1980). Terminal care: An evaluation of an advisory domiciliary service at St Christopher's Hospice. *Postgraduate Medical Journal*, **56**, 685–689.

Parkes, C. M. (1981). Evaluation of a bereavement service. *Journal of Preventive Psychiatry*, **1**, 179–188.

Parkes, C. M. and Parkes, J. (1984). 'Hospice' versus 'hospital' care-re-evaluation after ten years as seen by surviving spouses. *Postgraduate Medical Journal*, **60**, 120–124.

Parkes, C. M. and Weiss, R. S. (1983). *Recovery from Bereavement*. New York: Basic Books.

Parkes, K. (1982). Occupational stress among student nurses: A natural experiment. *Journal of Applied Psychology*, **67**, 784–796.

Parkes, K. (1985). Stressful episodes reported by first year student nurses: A descriptive account. *Social Science and Medicine*, **20**, 945–953.

Parrott, R., Burgoon, J. K., Burgoon, M. and LePoire, B. A. (1989). Privacy between physicians and patients: More than a matter of confidentiality. *Social Science and Medicine*, **29**, 1381–1384.

Parsons, T. (1951a). Illness and the role of the physician: A sociological perspective. *American Journal of Orthopsychiatry*, **21**, 452–460.

Parsons, T. (1951b). *The Social System*. New York: Free Press.

Partridge, C. and Johnston, M. (1989). Perceived control of recovery from physical disability: Measurement and prediction. *British Journal of Clinical Psychology*, **281**, 53–60.

Paskett, E. D. and Rimer, B. K. (1995). Psychosocial effects of abnormal Pap tests and mammograms: A review. *Journal of Women's Health*, **4**, 73–82.

Patterson, J. M. and Garwick, A. W. (1994). The impact of chronic illness on families: A family systems perspective. *Annals of Behavioral Medicine*, **16**, 131–142.

Pearlin, L. I., Mullan, J. T., Semple, S. J. and Skaff, M. M. (1990). Caregiving and the stress process: An overview of concepts and their measures. *The Gerontologist*, **30**, 583–594.

Pendleton, D. (1983). Doctor–patient communication: A review. In D. Pendleton and J. Hasler (eds), *Doctor–Patient Communication*. London: Academic Press.

Pendelton, D. A. and Bochner, S. (1980). The communication of medical information in general practice consultations as a function of patients' social class. *Social Science and Medicine*, **14A**, 669–673.

Pennebaker, J. W. (1982). Social and perceptual factors affecting symptom reporting and mass psychogenic illness. In M. J. Colligan, J. W. Pennebaker and L. R. Murphy (eds), *Mass Psychogenic Illness: A social psychological analysis*. Hillsdale, NJ: Erlbaum.

Pennebaker, J. W. (1983). Accuracy of symptom perception. In A. Baum, S. E. Taylor and J. Singer (eds), *Handbook of Psychology and Health*, Vol. IV. Hillsdale, NJ: Erlbaum.

Pennebaker, J. W. and Brittingham, G. L. (1982). Environmental and sensory cues affecting the perception of physical symptoms. In A. Baum and J. Singer (eds), *Advances in Environmental Psychology*, Vol. IV. Hillsdale, NJ: Lawrence Erlbaum.

Pennebaker, J. W. and Lightner, J. M. (1980). Competition of internal and external information in an exercise setting. *Journal of Personality and Social Psychology*, **35**, 167–174.

Pennebaker, J. W. and Skelton, J. A. (1981). Selective monitoring of bodily sensations. *Journal of Personality and Social Psychology*, **41**, 213–233.

Perkins, K. A. and Epstein, L. A. (1988). Methodology in exercise adherence research. In R. K. Dishman (ed.), *Exercise Adherence: Its impact on public health*. Champaign, IL: Human Kinetics.

Persson, L.-O., and Sjoberg, L. (1987). Mood and somatic symptoms. *Journal of Psychosomatic Research*, **31**, 499–511.

Peters, R. K., Moraye, B., Bear, M. S. and Thomas, D. (1989). Barriers to screening for cancer of the cervix. *Preventive Medicine*, **18**, 133–146.

Peterson, L., Schultheis, K., Ridley-Johnson, R., Miller, D. J. and Tracy, K. (1984). Comparison of three modeling procedures on the presurgical and postsurgical reactions of children. *Behavior Therapy*, **15**, 197–203.

Peterson, L. and Shigetomi, C. (1981). One-year follow-up of elective surgery child patients receiving preoperative prearation. *Journal of Pediatric Psychology*, **7**, 43–48.

Petrie, K. J. and Weinman, J. A. (eds) (1997). *Perception of Health and Illness*. Amsterdam: Harwood Academic Publishers.

Pettegrew, L. S. and Logan, R. (1987). The health care context. In C. R. Berger and S. H. Chaffee (eds), *Handbook of Communication Science*. Newbury Park, CA: Sage.

Pettingale, K. W., Morris, T., Greer, S. and Haybittle, J. L. (1985). Mental attitudes to cancer: an additional prognostic factor. *Lancet*, **1**, 750.

Pickett, C. and Clum, G. A. (1982). Comparative treatment strategies and their interaction with locus of control in the reduction of surgical pain and anxiety. *Journal of Consulting and Clinical Psychology*, **50**, 439–441.

Pill, R. and Stott, N. C. H. (1982). Concepts of illness causation and responsibility: Some preliminary data from a sample of working class mothers. *Social Science and Medicine*, **16**, 43–52.

Pilowsky, I. (1967). Dimensions of hypochondriasis. *British Journal of Psychiatry*, **113**, 88–93.

Pilowsky, I. (1997). *Abnormal Illness Behaviour*. Chichester: Wiley.

Pinto, R. P. and Hollandsworth, J. G. (1989). Using videotape modelling to prepare children psychologically for surgery: Influence of parents and costs versus benefits of providing preparation services. *Health Psychology*, **8**, 79–95.

Plante, A. and Bouchard, L. (1995). Occupational stress, burnout, and professional support in nurses working with dying patients. *Omega: Journal of Death and Dying*, **32**, 93–109.

Plaud, J. J., Dubbert, P. M., Holm, J. and Wittrock, D. (1996). Erectile dysfunction in men with chronic medical illness. *Journal of Behavior Therapy and Experimental Psychiatry*, **27**, 11–19.

Pliskin, J. S. and Pliskin, N. (1980). Decision analysis in clinical practice. *European Journal of Operational Research*, **4**, 153–159.

Poll, I. and Kaplan De-Nour, A. (1980). Locus of control and adjustment to chronic haemodialysis. *Psychological Medicine*, **10**, 153–157.

Porter, M. (1990). Professional–client relationships and women's reproductive health care. In S. Cunningham-Burley and N. P. McKeganay (eds), *Readings in Medical Sociology*. London: Routledge.

Posner, T. (1991). What's in a smear? Cervical screening, medical signs and metaphors. *Science as Culture*, **2**, 166–187.

Powell, K. E., Caspersen, C. J., Koplan, J. P. and Ford, E. S. (1989). Physical activity and chronic disease. *American Journal of Clinical Nutrition*, **49**, 999–1006.

Powell, K. E., Thompson, P. D., Caspersen, C. J. and Kendrick, J. S. (1987). Physical activity and the incidence of coronary heart disease. *Annual Review of Public Health*, **8**, 253–287.

Pratt, C., Schmall, V., Wright, S. and Cleland, M. (1985). Burden and coping strategies of caregivers to Alzheimer patients. *Family Relations*, **34**, 27–33.

Prochaska, J. O. and DiClemente, C. C. (1984). *The Transtheoretical Approach: Crossing traditional boundaries of therapy*. Homewood, IL: Dow Jones Irwin.

Prohaska, T. R., Funch, D. and Blesch, K. S. (1990). Age patterns in symptom perception and illness behavior among colorectal cancer patients. *Behavior, Health, and Aging*, **1**, 27–39.

Prohaska, T. R., Keller, M. L., Leventhal, E. A. and Leventhal, H. (1987). Impact of symptoms and aging attributions on emotions and coping. *Health Psychology*, **6**, 495–514.

Pruchno, R. A. and Potashnik, S. L. (1987). Caregiving spouses: Physical and mental health in perspective. *Journal of the American Geriatrics Society*, **37**, 697–705.

Pruchno, R. A. and Resch, N. L. (1989). Hubands and wives as caregivers: Antecedents of depression and burden. *The Gerontologist*, **29**, 159–165.

Prugh, D. and Eckhardt, L. (1980). Children's reactions to illness, hospitalization and surgery. In H. Kaplan, A. M. Freedman and A. J. Saddock (eds), *Comprehensive Textbook of Psychiatry*. Vol. III. Baltimore: Williams & Wilkins.

Putnum, D. E., Finney, J. W., Barkley, P. L. and Bonner, M. J. (1994). Enhancing commitment improves adherence to a medical regimen. *Journal of Consulting and Clinical Psychology*, **62**, 191–194.

Putnam, S. M., Stiles, W. B., Jacob, C. M. and James, S. A. (1985). Patient exposition and physician explanation in initial medical interviews and outcomes of clinic visits. *Medical Care*, **23**, 74–83.

Putnam, S. M., Stiles, W. B., Jacob, C. M. and James, S. A. (1988). Teaching the medical interview: An intervention study. *Journal of General Internal Medicine*, **3**, 38–47.

Radley, A. (1994). *Making Sense of Illness: The social psychology of health and disease*. London: Sage.

Rakowski, W., Dube, C. E., Marcus, B. H., Prochaska, J. O., Velicer, W. F. and Abrams, D. D. (1992). Assessing elements of women's decisions about mammography. *Health Psychology*, **11**, 111–118.

Rakowski, W., Julius, M., Hickey, T., Verbrugge, L. M. and Halter, J. B. (1988). Daily symptoms and behavioral responses. *Medical Care*, **26**, 278–297.

Ramiriez, A. J., Graham, J., Richards, M. A., Cull, A. and Gregory, W. M. (1996). Mental health of hospital consultants: The effects of stress and satisfaction at work. *Lancet*, **347**, 724–728.

Ransford, E. H. and Smith, M. L. (1991). Grief resolution among the bereaved in hospice and hospital wards. *Social Science and Medicine*, **32**, 295–304.

Redd, W. H., Jacobsen, P. B., Die-Trill, M., Dermatis, H., McEvoy, M. and Holland, J. C. (1987). Cognitive/attentional distraction in the control of conditioned nausea in pediatric cancer patients receiving chemotherapy. *Journal of Consulting and Clinical Psychology*, **55**, 394–395.

Revenson, T. A., Schiaffino, K. M., Majerovitz, D. and Gibofsky, A. (1991). Social support as a double-edged sword: The relation of positive and problematic support to depression among rheumatoid arthritis patients. *Social Science and Medicine*, **33**, 807–813.

Reynolds, F. (1996). Models of health and illness. In V. Aitken and H. Jellico (eds), *Behavioural Sciences for Health Professionals*. London: W. B. Saunders Company Ltd.

Richardson, P. (1989). Placebos: Their effectiveness and modes of action. In A. K. Broome (ed.), *Health Psychology, Process and Applications*. London: Chapman & Hall.

Ridgeway, V. and Mathews, A. (1982). Psychological preparation for surgery: A comparison of methods. *British Journal of Clinical Psychology*, **21**, 271–280.

Rimer, B. K. (1992). Understanding the acceptance of mammography by women. *Annals of Behavioral Medicine*, **14**, 197–203.

Rimer, B. K., Trock, B., Engstrom, P. F., Lerman, C. and King, E. (1991). Why do some women get regular mammograms? *American Journal of Preventive Medicine*, **7**, 69–74.

Ritchey, F. J., La Gory, M. and Mullis, J. (1991). Gender differences in health risks and physical symptoms among the homeless. *Journal of Health and Social Behavior*, **32**, 33–48.

Roberts, A. K., Kewman, D. G., Mercier, L. and Hovell, M. (1993). The power of nonspecific effects in healing: Implications for psychosocial and biological treatments. *Clinical Psychology Review*, **13**, 375–391.

Rodin, G. and Voshart, K. (1986). Depression in the medically ill: An overview. *American Journal of Psychiatry*, **143**, 696–705.

Rodin, G., Craven, J. and Littlefield, C. (1991). *Depression in the Medically Ill: An integrated approach*. New York: Brunner/Mazel.

Rogers, R. W. (1983). Cognitive and psychological processes in fear appeals and attitude change: A revised theory of protection motivation. In J. T. Cacioppo and R. E. Petty (eds), *Social Psychophysiology: A sourcebook*. New York: Guildford Press.

Ronis, D. L. (1992). Conditional health threats: Health beliefs, decisions, and behaviors among adults. *Health Psychology*, **11**, 127–134.

Ronis, D. L. and Harel, Y. (1989). Health beliefs and breast examination behaviors: Analysis of linear structural relations. *Psychology and Health*, **3**, 259–285.

Rosenbaum, M. and Palmon, N. (1984). Helplessness and resourcefulness in coping with epilepsy. *Journal of Consulting and Clinical Psychology*, **52**, 244–253.

Rosenstock, I. M. (1974). Historical origins of the health belief model. *Health Education Monographs*, **2**, 328–335.

Ross, M. and Olson, J. M. (1981). An expectancy-attribution model of the effects of placebos. *Psychological Review*, **88**, 408–437.

Roter, D. L. (1989). What facets of communication have strong effects on outcome – a meta analysis. In M. A. Stewart and D. L. Roter (eds), *Communicating with Medical Patients*. Newbury Park, CA: Sage.

Roter, D. L. and Hall, J. A. (1989). Studies of doctor–patient interaction. *Annual Review of Public Health*, 10, 163–180.

Roter, D. L. and Hall, J. A. (1992). *Doctors Talking with Patients/Patients Talking with Doctors*. Westport, CT: Auburn House.

Roter, D. L., Hall, J. A. and Katz, N. R. (1988). Patient–physician communication: A descriptive review of the literature. *Patient Education and Counselling*, 12, 99–119.

Roter, D., Lipkin, M. and Korsgaard, A. (1991). Sex differences in patients' and physicians' communication during primary care medical visits. *Medical Care*, 29, 1083–1093.

Roter, D. L., Stewart, M., Putnam, S. M., Lipkin, M. (1997). Communication patterns in primary care physicians. *Journal of the American Medical Association*, 277, 350–356.

Roth, H. P. (1987). Measurement of compliance. *Patient Education and Counseling*, 10, 107–116.

Rotter, J. B. (1954). *Social Learning and Clinical Psychology*. Englewood Cliffs, NJ: Prentice Hall.

Rotter, J. B. (1966). Generalised expectancies for internal versus external control of reinforcement. *Psychological Monographs*, 80 (1, whole no. 609).

Rowe, J. W. and Besdine, R. W. (eds) (1982). *Health and Disease in Old Age*. Boston: Little Brown & Co.

Ruble, D. N. (1977). Premenstrual symptoms: A reinterpretation. *Science*, 197, 291–292.

Rudd, P. and Marshall, G. (1987). Resolving problems of measuring compliance with medication monitors. *Journal of Compliance in Health Care*, 2, 23–35.

Rutledge, D. N., Hartmann, W. H., Kinman, P. O. and Winfield, A. C. (1988). Exploration of factors affecting mammography behaviors, *Preventive Medicine*, 17, 412–422.

Ryan, C. M. and Morrow, L. A. (1992). Dysfunctional buildings or dysfunctional people: An examination of the sick building syndrome and allied disorders. *Journal of Consulting and Clinical Psychology*, 60, 220–224.

Ryle, J. A. (1948). Nosophobia. *Journal of Mental Science*, 94, 1–17.

Rynearson, E. K. (1990). Pathologic grief: The Queen's croquet ground. *Psychiatric Annals*, 20, 295–303.

Safer, M. A., Tharps, Q. J., Jackson, T. C. and Leventhal, H. (1979). Determinants of three stages of delay in seeking care at the medical clinic. *Medical Care*, 17, 11–29.

Saile, H., Burgmeier, R. and Schmidt, L. R. (1988). A meta-analysis of studies on psychological preparation of children facing medical procedures. *Psychology and Health*, 2, 107–132.

Salkovskis, P. M. and Warwick, H. M. C. (1986). Morbid preoccupations, health anxiety and reassurance: A cognitive behavioural approach to hypochondrisais. *Behaviour Research and Therapy*, 24, 597–602.

Sallis, J. F., Nader, P. R., Broyles, S. L., Berry, C. C., Elder, J. P., McKenzie, T. L. and Nelson, J. A. (1993). Correlates of physical activity at home in Mexican–American and Anglo-American preschool children. *Health Psychology*, 12, 390–398.

Salmon, P. (1992). Psychological factors in surgical stress: Implications for management. *Clinical Psychology Review*, 12, 681–704.

Salmon, P. and Quine, J. (1989). Patient's intentions in primary care: Measurement and preliminary investigation. *Psychology and Health*, 3, 103–110.

Salmon, P., Evans, R. and Humphrey, D. (1986). Anxiety and endocrine changes in surgical patients. *British Journal of Clinical Psychology*, 25, 135–141.

Salonen, J. T., Puska, P. and Tuomilehto, J. (1982). Physical activity and risk of myocardial infarction, cerebral stroke, and death. *American Journal of Epidemiology*, 115, 525–537.

Salovey, P. and Birnbaum, D. (1989). Influence of mood on health-relevant cognitions. *Journal of Personality and Social Psychology*, 57, 539–551.

Salovey, P., O'Leary, A., Stretton, M. S., Fishkin, S. A. and Drake, C. A. (1991). Influence of mood on judgments about health and illness. In J. P. Forgas (ed.), *Emotion and Social Judgments*. Oxford: Pergamon Press.

Samet, J. M., Hunt, W. C., Lerchen, M. L. and Goodwin, J. S. (1988). Delay in seeking care for cancer symptoms: A population-based study of elderly New Mexicans. *Journal of the National Cancer Institute*, 80, 432–438.

Sanders, C. M. (1988). Risk factors in bereavement outcome. *Journal of Social Issues*, 44, 97–111.

Sanders, G. S. (1982). Social comparison and perceptions of health and illness. In G. S. Sanders and J. Suls (eds), *Social Psychology of Health and Illness*. Hillsdale, NJ: Lawrence Erlbaum.

Sanders, K. J., Pilgrim, C. A. and Pennypacker, H. S. (1986). Increased proficiency of search in breast self-examination. *Cancer*, 58, 2531–2537.

Sarafino, E. P. (1994). *Health Psychology* (2nd edn). New York: Wiley.

Sarason, I. G., Sarason, B. R., Poter, B. H. and Antoni, M. H. (1985). Life events, social support, and illness. *Psychosomatic Medicine*, 47, 156–163.

Satariano, W. A. and Syme, S. L. (1981). Life changes and diseases in elderly populations: Coping with change. In G. H. March (ed.), *Aging: Biology and behavior*. New York: Academic Press.

Saunders, C. and Baines, M. (1983). *Living with Dying: The management of terminal disease*. New York: Oxford University Press.

Saylor, C. F., Pallmeyer, T. P., Finch, A. J., Eason, L., Trieber, F. and Folgar, C. (1987). Predictors of psychological distress in hospitalised paediatric patients. *Journal of the American Academy of Child and Adolescent Psychiatry*, 232–236.

Scambler, A., Scambler, G. and Craig, D. (1981). Kinship and friendship networks and women's demand for primary care. *Journal of the Royal College of General Practitioners*, 26, 746–750.

Schaalma, H., Kok, G. and Peters, L. (1993). Determinants of consistent condom use by adolescents: The impact of experience of sexual intercourse. *Health Education Research*, 8, 255–269.

Schachter, S. (1982). Recidivism and self-cure of smoking and obesity. *American Psychologist*, 37, 436–444.

Scharlach, A. E., Sobel, E. L. and Roberts, R. E. L. (1991). Employment and caregiver strain: An integrative model. *The Gerontologist*, 31, 778–787.

Scharloo, M. and Kaptein, A. (1997). Measurement of illness perceptions in patients with ichonic somatic illness: A review. In J.A. Weinmann and KJ. Petrie (eds), *Perceptions of Health and Illness*. Amsterdam: Harwood Academic Publishers.

Scharloo, M., Kaptein, A. A., Weinman, J., Hazes, J. M., Willems, L. N. A., Bergman, W. and Rooijmans, H. G. M. (1998). Illness perceptions, coping and functioning in patients with rheumatoid arthritis, chronic obstructive pulmonary disease and psoriasis. *Journal of Psychosomatic Research*, 44, 573–585.

Schiaffino, K. M., Shawaryn, M. A. and Blum, D. (1998). Examining the impact of illness representations on psychological adjustment to chronic illness. *Health Psychology*, 17, 262–268.

Schleifer, S. J., Bhardwaj, S., Lebovits, A., Tanaka, J. S., Messe, M. and Strain, J. J. (1991). Predictors of physician nonadherence to chemotherapy regimens. *Cancer*, 67, 945–951.

Schleifer, S. J., Keller, S., Camerino, M., Thornton, J. C. and Stein, M. (1983). Suppression of lymphocyte stimulation following bereavement. *Journal of the American Medical Association*, 259, 374–377.

Schneider, M. S., Friend, R., Whitaker, P. and Wadhwa, N. K. (1991). Fluid noncompliance and symptomatology in end-stage renal disease: Cognitive and emotional variables. *Health Psychology*, 10, 209–215.

Schneidman, E. S. (1978). Some aspects of psychotherapy with dying persons. In C. A. Garfield (ed.), *Psychological Care of the Dying Patient*. New York: McGraw-Hill.

Schottenfeld, D., Warshauer, M. E., Sherlock, S., Zauber, A. G., Leder, M. and Payne, R. (1980). The epidemiology of testicular cancer in young adults. *American Journal of Epidemiology*, 112, 232–246.

Schubert, D. S. P. and Folliart, R. H. (1993). Increased depression in multiple sclerosis patients. *Psychosomatics*, 34, 124–130.

Schultheis, W., Peterson, L. and Selby, V. (1987). Preparation for stressful medical procedures and person x treatment interactions. *Clinical Psychology Review*, 7, 329–352.

Schulz, R. and Decker, S. (1985). Long-term adjustment to physical disability: The role of social support, perceived control, and self-blame. *Journal of Personality and Social Psychology*, 48, 1162–1172.

Schulz, R., Tompkins, C. A. and Rau, M. T. (1988). A longitudinal study of psychosocial impact of stroke on primary support persons. *Psychology and Aging*, 3, 131–141.

Schulz, R., Visintainer, P. and Williamson, G. (1990). Psychiatric and physical morbidity effects of caregiving. *Journal of Gerontology: Psychological Sciences*, 45, P181–P191.

Schulze, C., Florin, I., Matschin, E., Sougioultzi, C. and Schulze, H.-H. (1988). Psychological distress after hysterectomy – a predictive study. *Psychology and Health*, 2, 1–12.

Schwartz, G. E. (1982). Testing the biopsychosocial model: the ultimate challenge facing behavioral medicine? *Journal of Consulting and Clinical Psychology*, 50, 1040–1053.

Schwarzer, R. (1992). Self efficacy in the adoption and mainenance of health behaviours: Theoretical approaches and a new model. In R. Schwazer (ed.), *Self Efficacy: Thought control of action*. Washington, DC: Hemisphere.

Schwenk, T. L., Marquez, J. T., Lefever, D. and Cohen, M. (1989). Physician and patient determinants of difficult physician–patient relationships. *The Journal of Family Practice*, 28, 59–63.

Seale, C. (1989). What happens in hospices: A review of research evidence. *Social Science and Medicine*, 28, 551–559.

Seale, C. (1990). Caring for people who die: The experience of family and friends. *Aging and Society*, 10, 413–428.

Seale, C. (1991a). A comparison of hospice and conventional care. *Social Science and Medicine*, 32, 147–152.

Seale, C. (1991b). Communication and awareness about death: A study of a random sample of dying people. *Social Science and Medicine*, 32, 943–952.

Seale, C. (1992). Community nurses and the care of the dying. *Social Science and Medicine*, 34, 375–382.

Seale, C. and Kelly, M. (1997). A comparison of hospice and hospital care for the spouses of people who die. *Palliative Care*, 11, 101–106.

Seeman, M. and Seeman, T. E. (1983). Health behavior and personal autonomy: A longitudinal study of the sense of control in illness. *Journal of Health and Social Behavior*, 24, 114–160.

Seydel, E., Taal, E. and Wiegman, O. (1990). Risk appraisal, outcome and self-efficacy expectancies: Cognitive factors in preventive behaviour related to cancer. *Psychology and Health*, 4, 99–109.

Shapiro, A. K. (1960). A contribution to the history of the placebo effect. *Behavioral Science*, 5, 109–135.

Shapiro, A. K. (1964). Factors contributing to the placebo effect: Their implications for psychotherapy. *American Journal of Psychotherapy*, 18, 73–88.

Shapiro, A. K. and Morris, L. A. (1978). The placebo effect in medical and psychological therapies. In A. E. Bergin and S. Garfield (eds), *Handbook of Psychotherapy and Behavior Change* (2nd edn). New York: J. Wiley.

Sharma, U. (1992). *Complementary Medicine Today: Practitioners and Patients*. London: Routledge.

Shepperd, S. L., Solomon, L. J., Atkins, E., Foster, R. S. Jr. and Frankowski, B. (1990). Determinants of breast self-examination among women of lower income and lower education. *Journal of Behavioral Medicine*, 13, 359–371.

Sherbourne, C. D., Hays, R. D., Ordway, L., DiMatteo, M. R., and Kravitz, R. L. (1992). Antecedents of adherence to medical recommendations: Results from the Medical Outcomes Study. *Journal of Behavioral Medicine*, 15, 447–468.

Sherman, B. R. (1995). Impact of home-based respite care on families of children with chronic illness. *Children's Health Care*, 24, 33–45.

Shillitoe, R. W. (1988). *Psychology and Diabetes: Psychosocial factors in management and control*. London: Chapman & Hall.

Shipley, R. H., Butt, J. H. and Horwitz, B. (1979). Preparation to reexperience a stressful medical examination: Effect of repetitious videotape exposure and coping style. *Journal of Consulting and Clinical Psychology*, 47, 485–492.

Shipley, R. H., Butt, J. H., Horwitz, B. and Farbry, J. E. (1978). Preparation for a stressful medical procedure: Effect of amount of stimulus exposure and coping style. *Journal of Consulting and Clinical Psychology*, 46, 499–507.

Shontz, F. C. (1975). *The Psychological Aspects of Physical Illness and Disability*. New York: Macmillan.

Shulz, R. and Aderman, D. (1974). Clinical research and the stages of dying. *Omega*, 5, 137–144.

Siegel, L. J. and Peterson, L. (1980). Stress reduction in young dental patients through coping skills and sensory information. *Journal of Consulting and Clinical Psychology*, 48, 785–787.

Siegler, I. C., Feaganes, J. R. and Rimer, B. K. (1995). Predictors of adoption of mammography in women under age 50. *Health Psychology*, 14, 274–278.

Silliman, R. A., Earp, J. L., Fletcher, R. H. and Wagner, E. H. (1987). Stroke: The perspective of family caregivers. *Journal of Applied Gerontology*, 6, 363–371.

Silverman, D. C. (1993). Psychological impact of HIV-related caregiving on health providers: A review and recommendation for the role of psychiatry. *American Journal of Psychiatry*, 150, 705–712.

Sime, A. M. (1976). Relationship of pre-operative fear, type of coping, and information received about surgery to recovery from surgery. *Journal of Personality and Social Psychology*, 34, 716–724.

Singer, M. (1989). The limitations of medical ecology: The concept of adaptation in the context of social stratification and social transformation. *Medical Anthropology*, 10, 223–234.

Sirois, R. (1982). Perspectives on epidemic hysteria. In Colligan, M. J.,Pennebaker, J. W. and Murphy, L. R. (eds), *Mass Psychogenic Illness*. Hillsdale, NJ: Lawrence Erlbaum Associates.

Sitzia, J. and Wood, N. (1997). Patient satisfaction: A review of issues and concepts. *Social Science and Medicine*, 45, 1829–1843.

Skelton, J. A. and Croyle, R. T. (1991). Mental representation in health and illness: An introduction. In J. A. Skelton and R. T. Croyle (eds) (1991) *Mental Representation in Health and Illness*. New York: Springer-Verlag.

Skelton, J. A. and Croyle, R. T. (eds)(1991) *Mental Representation in Health and Illness*. New York: Springer-Verlag.

Skelton, J. A. and Pennebaker, J. W. (1982). The psychology of physical symptoms and sensations. In G. S. Sander and J. Suls (eds), *Social Psychology of Health and Illness*. Hillsdale, NJ: Lawrence Earlbaum.

Skelton, J. A. and Strohmetz, D. B. (1990). Priming symptom reports with health-related cognitive activity. *Personality and Social Psychology Bulletin*, 16, 449–464.

Skevington, S. M. (1993). Depression and causal attributions in the early stages of a chronic painful disease: A longitudinal study of early synovitis. *Psychology and Health*, 8, 51–64.

Slade, P. (1984). Premenstrual emotional changes in normal women: Fact or fiction? *Journal of Psychosomatic Research*, 28, 1–7.

Small, G. W. and Borus, J. F. (1983). Outbreaks of illness in a school chorus: Toxic poisoning or mass hysteria? *New England Journal of Medicine*, 308, 632–635.

Small, G. W., Feinberg, D. T., Steinberg, D. and Collins, M. T. (1994). A sudden outbreak of illness suggestive of mass hysteria in schoolchildren. *Archives of Family Medicine*, 3, 711–716.

Smetena, J. G. and Adler, N. E. (1980). Fishbein's value × expectancy model: An examination of some assumptions. *Personality and Social Psychology Bulletin*, **6**, 89–96.

Smith, M. D., Hong, B. A. and Robson, A. M. (1985). Diagnosis of major depression in patients with end stage renal disease: Comparative analysis. *American Journal of Medicine*, **79**, 160–166.

Smith, T. (1983). Alternative medicine (editorial). *British Medical Journal*, **287**, 307–308.

Smith, T. W., Pope, M. K., Rhodewalt, F. and Poulton, J. L. (1989). Optimism, neuroticism, coping, and symptom reports: An alternative interpretation of the life orientation test. *Journal of Personality and Social Psychology*, **36**, 640–648.

Smith, T. W., Snyder, C. R. and Perkins, S. C. (1983). The self-serving function of hypochondria-cal complaints: Physical symptoms as self-handicapping strategies. *Journal of Personality and Social Psychology*, **44**, 787–797.

Snow, L. (1978). Sorcerers, saints, and charlatans: Black folk healers in urban America. *Culture, Medicine and Psychiatry*, **2**, 69–106.

Sorensen, J. R. , Levy, H. L., Mangione, T. W. and Sepe, S. F. (1984). Parental response to repeat testing of infants with 'false positive' results in a newborn screening programme. *Paediatrics*, **73**, 183–187.

Soskoline, C. and De-Nour, A. K. (1989). The psychosocial adjustment of patients and spouses in dialysis treatment. *Social Science and Medicine*, **29**, 497–502.

Sox, H. C., Blatt, M. A., Higgins, M. C. and Marton, K. I. (1988) *Medical Decision Making*. Boston: Butterworths.

Speck, P. (1985). Counselling on death and dying. *British Journal of Guidance and Counselling*, **13**, 89–97.

Spector, R. E. (1991). *Cultural Diversity in Health and Illness* (3rd edn). Norwalk, CA: Appleton and Lange.

Spiegel, D., Blom, J. and Yalom, I. (1981). Group support for patients with metastatic cancer. *Archives of General Psychiatry*, **38**, 527–533.

Spiegel, D., Kraemer, H., Bloom, J. and Gottheil, E. (1989). Effect of psychosocial treatment on survival of patients with metastatic breast cancer. *Lancet*, 888–891.

Spirito, A., Stark, L. J. and Tyc, V. L. (1994). Stressors and coping strategies described during hospitalization by chronically ill children. *Journal of Clinical Child Psychology*, **23**, 314–322.

Spurgeon, A., Gompertz, D. and Harrington, J. M. (1997). Non-specific symptoms in response to hazard exposure in the workplace. *Journal of Psychosomatic Research*, **43**, 43–49.

Squier, R. W. (1990). A model of empathic understanding and adherence to treatment regimens in practitioner–patient relationships. *Social Science and Medicine*, **30**, 325–339.

Stacy, A. W., Widaman, K. W., Hays, R. and DiMatteo, M. R. (1985). The validity of self-reports of alcohol and other drug use: A multitrait-multimethod assessment. *Journal of Personality and Social Psychology*, **49**, 2190–232.

Stainton Rogers, W. (1991). *Explaining Health and Illness*: *An exploration of diversity*. Hemel Hempstead: Harvester Wheatsheaf.

Stamler, J., Wentworth, D. and Neaton, J. D. (1986). Is relationship between serum cholesterol and risk of premature death from coronary heart disease continuous and graded? Findings in 356,222 primary screenees of the Multiple Risk Factor Intervention Trial (MRFIT). *Journal of the American Medical Association*, **256**, 2823–2828.

Stamler, R., Stamler, J., Gosch, F. C., Civinelli, J., Fishman, J., McKeever, P., McDonald, A. and Dyer, A. R. (1989). Primary prevention of hypertension by nutritional-hygienic means: Final report of a randomized, controlled trial. *Journal of the American Medical Association*, **262**, 1801–1807.

Stanton, A. L. (1987). Determinants of adherence to medical regimens by hypertensive patients. *Journal of Behavioral Medicine*, **10**, 377–394.

Steffen, V. J. (1990). Men's motivation to perform the testicle self-exam: Effects of prior knowledge and an educational brochure. *Journal of Applied Social Psychology*, **20**, 681–702.

Steffen, V. J., Sternberg, L., Teegarden, L. A. and Shepherd, K. (1994). Practice and persuasive frame: Effects on beliefs, intention, and performance of a cancer self-examination. *Journal of Applied Social Psychology*, **24**, 897–925.

Stein, J. A., Fox, S. A. and Murata, P. J. (1991). The influence of ethnicity, socioeconomic status, and physician barriers on use of mammography. *Journal of Health and Social Behavior*, **32**, 101–113.

Stein, J. A., Fox, S. A., Murata, P. J. and Morisky, B. D. (1992). Mammography usage and the health belief model. *Health Education Quarterly*, **19**, 447–462.

Stenbak, E. (1982). Preparation of healthy children for a hospital environment. *Child Abuse and Neglect*, **6**, 485–486.

Stephens, M. A. P., Franks, M. M. and Townsend, A. L. (1994). Stress and rewards in women's multiple roles: The case of women in the middle. *Psychology and Aging*, **9**, 45–52.

Stephens, T., Jacob, D. R. Jr., and White, C. C. (1985). A descriptive epidemiology of leisure time physical activity. *Public Health Reports*, **100**, 147–158.

Steptoe, A. and O'Sullivan, J. (1986). Monitoring and blunting styles in women prior to surgery. *British Journal of Clinical Psychology*, **25**, 143–144.

Steptoe, A., Sutcliffe, I., Aleen, B. and Coombes, C. (1991). Satisfaction with communication, medical knowledge, and coping style in patients with metastatic cancer, *Social Science and Medicine*, **32**, 627–632.

Steptoe, A., Wardle, J., Fuller, R., Holte, A., Justo, J., Sanderman, R. and Wichstrom, L. (1997). Leisure-time physical exercise: Prevalence, attitudinal correlates, and behavioral correlates among young Europeans from 21 countries. *Preventive Medicine*, **26**, 845–854.

Stern, M. J., Pascale, L. and Ackerman, A. (1977). Life adjustment post myocardial infarction: Determining predictive variables, *Archives of Internal Medicine*, **137**, 1680–1685.

Stewart, M. (1983). Patient characteristics which are related to the doctor–patient interaction. *Family Practice*, **1**, 30–36.

Stewart, M. A. (1984). What is a successful doctor–patient interview? A study of interactions and outcomes. *Social Science and Medicine*, **19**, 167–175.

Stoate, H. (1989). Can health screening damage your health? *Journal of the Royal College of General Practitioners*, **39**, 193–195.

Stock, R. (1983). Distance and the utilization of health care facilities in rural Nigeria. *Social Science and Medicine*, **17**, 563–570.

Stoeckle, J. D., Zola, I. K. and Davidson, G. E. (1963). On going to see the doctor: The contributions of the patient to the decision to seek medical aid. *Journal of Chronic Disease*, **16**, 975–989.

Stoller, E. P. (1993). Interpretations of symptoms by older people. *Journal of Aging and Health*, **5**, 58–81.

Stoller, E. P., Forster, L. A. and Portugal, S. (1993). Self-care responses to symptoms by older people. *Medical Care*, **31**, 24–42.

Stone, G. C. (1979). Patient compliance and the role of the expert, *Journal of Social Issues*, **35**, 34–59.

Stone, R., Cafferata, G. L. and Sangl, J. (1987). Caregivers of the frail elderly: A national profile. *The Gerontologist*, **27**, 616–626.

Strauss, L. M., Solomon, L. J., Costanza, M. C., Worden, J. K. and Foster, R. S. (1987). Breast self-examination practices and attitudes of women with and without a history of breast cancer. *Journal of Behavioral Medicine*, **10**, 337–350.

Street, R. L. (1991). Information-giving in medical consultations: The influence of patients' communication styles and personal characteristics. *Social Science and Medicine*, **32**, 541–548.

Street, R. L. and Bulker, D. B. (1988). Patient's characteristics affecting physician–patient non-verbal communication. *Human Communication Research*, **15**, 60–72.

Strecher, V. J., DeVellis, B. M., Becker, M. H. and Rosenstock, I. M. (1986). The role of self-efficacy in acheiving health behavior change. *Health Education Quarterly*, **13**, 73–91.

Stroebe, M. S. and Stroebe, W. (1983). Who suffers more? Sex differences in health risks of the widowed. *Psychological Bulletin*, **93**, 279–301.

Stroebe, W. and Stroebe, M. S. (1995). *Social Psychology and Health*. Buckingham: Open University Press.

Suchman, C. A. (1965). Stages of illness and medical care. *Journal of Health and Social Behavior*, **6**, 114–128.

Sudnow, D. (1965). *Passing on: The social organisation of dying*. Englewood Cliffs, NJ: Prentice Hall.

Suls, J. and Wan, C. K. (1989). Effects of sensory and procedural information on coping with stressful medical procedures and pain: A meta-analysis. *Journal of Consulting and Clinical Psychology*, **57**, 372–379.

Sutton, S. (1987). Social-psychological approaches to understanding addictive behaviours: Attitude-behaviour and decision-making models. *British Journal of Addiction*, **82**, 355–370.

Sutton, S. (1998). Predicting and explaining intentions and behavior: How well are we doing? *Journal of Applied Social Psychology*, **28**, 1317–1338.

Sutton, S., Bickler, G., Sancho-Aldridge, A. and Saidi, G. (1994). Prospective study of predictors of attendance for breast screening in inner London. *Journal of Epidemiology and Community Health*, **48**, 65–73.

Sutton, S., Saidi, G., Bickler, G. and Hunter, J. (1995). Does routine screening for breast cancer raise anxiety? Results from a three wave prospective study in England. *Journal of Epidemiology and Community Health*, **49**, 413–418.

Sweet, J.J., Rozensky, R.H. and Tovian, S.M. (eds) (1991) *Handbook of Clinical Psychology in Medical Settings*. New York: Plenum Press.

Sweeting, H. N. and Gilhooly, M. L. M. (1990). Anticipatory grief: A review. *Social Science and Medicine*, **30**, 1073–1080.

Szasz, T. S., Knoff, W. F. and Hollender, M. H. (1958). The doctor–patient relationship and its historical context. *American Journal of Psychiatry*, **115**, 522–528.

Tagliacozzo, D. L. and Mauksch, H. O. (1972). The patient's view of the patient's role. In E. G. Jaco (ed.), *Patients, Physicians, and Illness* (2nd edn). New York: Free Press.

Taylor, M. R. H. and O'Connor, P. (1989). Resident parents and shorter hospital stays. *Archives of Disease in Childhood*, **64**, 274–276.

Taylor, S. E. (1979). Hospital patient behavior: Reactance, helplessness, or control? *Journal of Social Issues*, **35**, 156–184.

Taylor, S. E. (1983). Adjustment to threatening events: A theory of cognitive adaptation. *American Psychologist*, **38**, 1161–1173.

Taylor, S. E. (1995). *Health Psychology* (3rd edn). New York: McGraw-Hill.

Taylor, S. E. and Aspinwall, L. G. (1990). Psychosocial aspects of chronic illness. In P. T. Costa and G. R. VandenBos (eds), *Psychological Aspects of Serious Illness: Chronic conditions, fatal diseases and clinical care*. Washington, DC: American Psychological Association.

Taylor, S. E. and Clarke, L. F. (1986). Does information improve adjustment to noxious medical procedures? In M. J. Saks and L. Saxe (eds), *Advances in Applied Social Behavior*. Hillsdale, NJ: Erlbaum.

Taylor, S. E., Helgeson, V. S., Reed, G. M. and Skokan, L. A. (1991). Self-generated feelings of control and adjustment to physical illness. *Journal of Social Issues*, **47**, 91–109.

Taylor, S. E., Lichtman, R. R. and Wood, J. V. (1984). Attributions, beliefs about control, and adjustment to breast cancer. *Journal of Personality and Social Psychology*, **46**, 489–502.

Telch, C. F. and Telch, M. J. (1985). Psychological approaches for enhancing coping among cancer patients: A review. *Clinical Psychology Review*, 5, 325–344.

Telch, C. F. and Telch, M. J. (1986). Group coping skills instruction and supportive group therapy for cancer patients: A comparison of strategies. *Journal of Consulting and Clinical Psychology*, 54, 802–808.

Temoshok, L., DiClemente, R. J., Sweet, D. M., Blois, M. S. and Sagabiel, R. W. (1984). Factors related to patient delay in seeking medical attention for cutaneous malignant melanoma. *Cancer*, 12, 3048–3053.

Tempelaar, R., De Haes, J. C. J. M., De Ruiter, J. H., Bakker, D., Van Den Heuvel, W. J. A. and Nieuwenhuijzen, M. B. (1989). The social experiences of cancer patients under treatment: A comparative study. *Social Science and Medicine*, 29, 635–642.

Tennen, H., Affleck, G., Allen, P. A., McGrade, B. J. and Ratzan, S. (1984). Causal attributions and coping with insulin dependent diabetes. *Basic and Applied Social Psychology*, 5, 131–142.

Tennen, H., Affleck, G. and Greshman, K. (1986). Self-blame among parents of infants with perinatal complications: The role of self-protective motives. *Journal of Personality and Social Psychology*, 50, 690–696.

Teno, J. M., Licks, S., Lynne, J., Wenger, N., Connors, A. F., Philips, R. S., O'Connor, M. A., Murphy, D. P., Fulkerson, W. J., Desbiens, N. and Knaus, W. A. (1997). Do advance directives provide instructions that direct care? *Journal of the American Geriatrics Society*, 45, 508–512.

Tessler, R., Mechanic, D. and Dimond, M. (1976). The effect of psychological distress on physician utilization: A prospective study. *Journal of Health and Social Behavior*, 17, 353–364.

Thomas, K. J., Carr, J., Westlake, L. and Williams, B. T. (1991). Use of non-orthodox and conventional healthcare in Great Britian. *British Medical Journal*, 302, 207–210.

Thompson, D. and Haran, D. (1985). Living with an amputation: The helper. *Social Science and Medicine*, 20, 319–323.

Thompson, D. R. and Meddis, R. (1990). A prospective evaluation of in-hospital counselling for first time myocardial infarction men. *Journal of Psychosomatic Research*, 34, 327–348.

Thompson, D. R., Webster, R. A., Cordle, C. J. and Sutton, T. W. (1987). Specific sources and patterns of anxiety in male patients with first time myocardial infarction. *British Journal of Medical Psychology*, 60, 343–348.

Thompson, R. H. and Vernon, D. (1993). Research on children's behavior after hospitalization: A review and synthesis. *Developmental and Behavioral Pediatrics*, 14, 28–35.

Thompson, R. J. Jr., Gil, K. M., Abrams, M. R. and Phillips, G. (1992). Stress, coping, and psychological adjustment of adults with sickle cell disease. *Journal of Consulting and Clinical Psychology*, 60, 433–440.

Thompson, S. C. (1981). Will it hurt less if I can control it? A complex answer to a simple question. *Psychological Bulletin*, 90, 89–101.

Thompson, S. C. (1991). The search for meaning following a stroke. *Basic and Applied Social Psychology*, 12, 81–96.

Thompson, S. C., Armstrong, W. and Thomas, C. (1998). Illusions of control, underestimations, and accuracy: A control heuristic explanation. *Psychological Bulletin*, 123, 143–161.

Thompson, S. C., Nanni, C. and Schwankovsky, L. (1990). Patient-oriented interventions to improve communication in a medical office visit. *Health Psychology*, 9, 390–404.

Thompson, S. C., Sobolew-Shubin, A., Graham, M. A. and Janigian, A. S. (1989). Psychosocial adjustment following a stroke. *Social Science and Medicine*, 28, 239–247.

Thomsen, S., Dallender, J., Soares, J., Nolan, P. and Arnetz, B. (1998). Predictors of a healthy workplace for Swedish and English psychiatrists. *British Journal of Psychiatry*, 173, 80–84.

Thorogood, M., Coulter, A., Jones, L., Yudkin, P., Muir, J. and Mant, D. (1993). Factors affecting response to an invitation to attend for a health check. *Journal of Epidemiology and Community Health*, 47, 224–228.

Thyer, B. A., Himle, J. and Curtis, G. C. (1985). Blood-injury-illness phobia: A review. *Journal of Clinical Psychology*, **41**, 451–459.

Timko, C. (1987). Seeking medical care for a breast cancer symptom: Determinants of intentions to engage in prompt or delay behavior. *Health Psychology*, **6**, 305–328.

Tobin, J. N., Wassertheil-Smoller, S., Wexler, J. P., Steingart, R. M., Budner, N., Lense, L. and Wachspress, J. (1987). Sex bias in considering coronary bypass surgery. *Annals of Internal Medicine*, **107**, 19–25.

Tomkins, C. A., Schulz, R. and Rau, M. T. (1988). Post-stroke depression in primary support persons: Predicting those at risk. *Journal of Consulting and Clinical Psychology*, **56**, 501–508.

Totman, R. (1975). Cognitive dissonance and the placebo response: The effect of differential justification for undergoing dummy injections. *European Journal of Social Psychology*, **5**, 441–456.

Totman, R. (1987). *The Social Causes of Illness* (2nd edn). London: Souvenir Press.

Townsend, P. and Davidson, N. (1982). *Inequalities in Health: The Black Report*. Harmondsworth: Penguin Books.

Townsend, P., Davidson, N. and Whitehead, M. (1992). *Inequalities in Health* (2nd edn). Reprinted with revisions. Harmondsworth: Penguin Books.

Townsend, P., Phillimore, P. and Beattie, A. (1988). *Health and Deprivation: Inequality in the North*. London: Croom Helm.

Tuckett, D., Boulton, M. and Olson, C. (1985). A new approach to the measurement of patients' understanding of what they are told in medical consultations. *Journal of Health and Social Behavior*, **26**, 27–38.

Tuckett, D., Boulton, M., Olson, C. and Williams, A. (1986). *Meetings between Experts*. London: Tavistock.

Turk, D. C., Litt, M. D., Salovey, P. and Walker, J. (1985). Seeking urgent pediatric treatment: Factors contributing to frequency, delay, and appropriateness. *Health Psychology*, **4**, 43–59.

Turk, D. C. and Meichenbaum, D. (1991). Adherence to self-care regimens: The patient's perspective. In J. J. Sweet, R. H. Rozensky and S. M. Tovian (eds), *Handbook of Clinical Psychology in Medical Settings*. New York: Plenum Press.

Turk, D. C. and Speers, M. A. (1984). Diabetes mellitus: Stress and adherence. In T. Burish and L. Bradley (eds), *Coping with Chronic Disease*. New York: Academic Press.

Turk, D. C., Salovey, P. and Litt, M. D. (1985). Adherence: A cognitive-behavioral perspective; In K. E. Gerber and A. M. Nehemkis (eds), *Compliance: The dilemma of the chronically ill*. New York: Springer.

Turner, B. S. (1984). *The Body and Society: Explorations in social theory*. Oxford: Basil Blackwell.

Turnquist, D. C., Harvey, J. H. and Anderson, B. (1988). Attributions and adjustment to life threatening illness. *British Journal of Clinical Psychology*, **27**, 55–65.

Tymstra, T. and Bieleman, B. (1987). The psychosocial impact of mass screening for cardiovascular risk factors. *Family Practice*, **4**, 287–290.

Tyrer, P. (1976). *The Role of Bodily Feelings in Anxiety*. London: Oxford University Press.

Vachon, M. L. S. (1995). Staff stress in hospice/palliative care: A review. *Palliative Medicine*, **9**, 91–122.

van Ryn, M., Lytle, A. and Kirscht, J. P. (1996). A test of the theory of planned behavior for two health-related practices. *Journal of Applied Social Psychology*, **26**, 871–883.

van Wijk, C. M. T. G. and Kolk, A. M. (1997). Sex differences in physical symptoms: The contribution of symptom perception theory. *Social Science and Medicine*, **45**, 231–246.

Verbrugge, L. M. (1979). Female illness rates and illness behavior: Testing hypotheses about sex differences in health. *Women and Health*, **4**, 61–79.

Verbrugge, L. M. (1980). Sex differences in complaints and diagnosis. *Journal of Behavioral Medicine*, **3**, 327–356.

Verbrugge, L. M. (1982). Sex differentials in health. *Public Health Reports*, **97**, 417–437.

Verbrugge, L. M. (1985). Gender and health: An update on hypotheses and evidence. *Journal of Health and Social Behavior*, **26**, 156–182.

Verbrugge, L. M. (1989). The twain meet: Empirical explanations of sex differences in health and mortality. *Journal of Health and Social Behavior*, **30**, 282–304.

Verbrugge, C. and Ascione, F. J. (1987). Exploring the iceberg: Common symptoms and how people care for them. *Medical Care*, **25**, 539–569.

Verkes, R. J. and Thung, P. J. (1990). Medical decision analysis and the coming moral crisis in health care. In J. J. Jensen and G. Mooney (eds), *Changing Values in Medical and Health Care Decision Making*. Chichester: Wiley.

Vernon, D. T. W. and Bigelow, D. W. (1974). Effect of information about a potentially stressful situation on responses to stress impact. *Journal of Personality and Social Psychology*, **29**, 50–59.

Vernon, S. W., Laville, E. A. and Jackson, G. L. (1990). Participation in breast screening programs: A review. *Social Science and Medicine*, **30**, 1107–1118.

Victor, C. R. (1989) Income inequality in later life. In M. Jeffreys (ed.), *Growing Old in the Twentieth Century*. London: Routledge.

Victor, C. R. (1993). Health policy and services for dying people and their carers. In D. Dickenson and M. Johnson (eds), *Death, Dying and Bereavement*. London: Sage.

Vincent, C. A. and Furnham, A. (1994). The perceived efficacy of orthodox and complementary medicine. *Complementary Therapies in Medicine*, **2**, 128–134.

Vincent, C. and Furnham, A. (1996). Why do patients turn to complementary medicine? An empirical study. *British Journal of Clinical Psychology*, **35**, 37–48.

Vogele, C. and Steptoe, A. (1986). Physiological and subjective stress responses in surgical patients. *Psychosomatic Research*, **30**, 205–215.

Vuori, I. (1998). Does physical activity enhance health? *Patient Education and Counselling*, **33**, S95–S103.

Wade, D. T., Leigh-Smith, J. and Hewer, R. L. (1986). Effects of living with and looking after survivors of a stroke. *British Medical Journal*, **293**, 418–420.

Waitzkin, H. (1984). Doctor–patient communication. Clinical implications of social scientific research. *Journal of the American Medical Association*, **252**, 2441–2446.

Waitzkin, H. (1985). Information giving in medical care. *Journal of Health and Social Behavior*, **26**, 81–101.

Waitzkin, H. (1989). A critical theory of medical discourse. *Journal of Health and Social Behavior*, **30**, 220–239.

Waldron, I. (1983). Sex differences in illness incidence, prognosis and mortality: Issues and evidence. *Social Science and Medicine*, **17**, 1107–1123.

Wallace, L. (1984). Psychological preparation as a method of reducing the stress of surgery. *Journal of Human Stress*, **10**, 62–79.

Wallston, B. S., Alagna, S. W., DeVellis, M. B. and DeVellis, R. F. (1983). Social support and physical health. *Health Psychology*, **2**, 367–391.

Wallston, K. A. and Wallston, B. S. (1982). Who is responsible for your health? The construct of health locus of control. In G. S. Sanders and J. Suls (eds), *Social Psychology of Health and Illness*. Hillsdale, NJ: Lawrence Erlbaum.

Wallston, K. A., Burger, C., Smith, R. A. and Baugher, R. J. (1988). Comparing the quality of death for hospice and non-hospice cancer patients. *Medical Care*, **26**, 177–182.

Wallston, K. A., Wallston, B. S. and DeVellis, R. (1978). Development of the multidimensional health locus of control (MHLC) scales. *Health Education Monographs*, **6**, 160–170.

Walsh, A. and Walsh, P. A. (1989). Love, self-esteem, and multiple sclerosis. *Social Science and Medicine*, **29**, 793–798.

Walterhouse, D. M., Calzone, K. A., Mele, C. and Brenner, D. E. (1993). Adherence to oral tamoxifen: A comparison of patient self report, pill counts and microelectronic monitoring. *Journal of Clinical Oncology*, **11**, 2547–2548.

Waltz, M. (1986). Marital context and post-infarction quality of life: Is it social support or something more? *Social Science and Medicine*, **22**, 791–805.

Waltz, M., Badura, B., Pfaff, H. and Schott, T. (1988). Marriage and the psychological consequences of a heart attack: A longitudinal study of adaptation to chronic illness after 3 years. *Social Science and Medicine*, **27**, 149–158.

Wanzer, S. H., Adelstein, S. J., Cranford, R. E., Federman, D. D., Hook, E. D., Moertel, C. G., Safer, P., Stone, A., Taussig, H. B. and van Eys, J. (1984). The physician's responsibility toward hopelessly ill patients. *The New England Journal of Medicine*, **310**, 240–241.

Wanzer, S. H., Federman, D. D., Adelstein, S. J., Cassel, C. K., Casses, E. H., Crawford, R. E., Hook, E. W., Lo, B., Moertel, C. G., Safer, P., Stone, A. and van Eys, J. (1989). The physician's responsibility toward hopelessly ill patients: A second look. *New England Journal of Medicine*, **320**, 844–849.

Wardle, J. (1989). The management of obesity. In S. Pearce and J. Wardle (eds), *The Practice of Behavioural Medicine*. British Psychological Society/Oxford University Press.

Wardle, J. and Pope, R. (1992). The psychological costs of screening for cancer. *Journal of Psychosomatic Research*, **36**, 609–624.

Wardle, J., Pernet, A. and Stephens, D. (1995). Psychological consequences of positive results in cervical cancer screening. *Psychology and Health*, **10**, 185–194.

Wardle, J., Steptoe, A., Burckhardt, R., Vogele, C., Vila, J. and Zarczynski, Z. (1994). Testicular self-examination: Attitudes and practices among young men in Europe. *Preventive Medicine*, **23**, 106–210.

Warwick, H. M. C. (1989). A cognitive-behavioural approach to hypochondriasis and health anxiety. *Journal of Psychosomatic Research*, **33**, 705–711.

Warwick, H. M. C. and Salkovskis, P. M. (1990). Hypochondriasis. *Behaviour Research and Therapy*, **28**, 105–117.

Watkins, J. D., Williams, T. F., Martin, D. A., Hogan, M. D. and Anderson, E. (1967). A study of diabetic patients at home. *American Journal of Public Health*, **37**, 452–459.

Watson, D. and Pennebaker, J. W. (1989). Health complaints, stress, and distress: Exploring the central role of negative affectivity. *Psychological Review*, **96**, 234–254.

Watson, D. and Pennebaker, J. W. (1991). Situational, dispositional, and genetic bases of symptom reporting. In Skelton, J. A. and Croyle, R. T. (eds), *Mental Representation in Health and Illness*. New York: Springer-Verlag.

Watson, M. (1993). Anticipatory nausea and vomiting: Broadening the scope of psychological treatments. *Support Care Cancer*, **1**, 171–177.

Watson, M. and Marvell, C. (1992). Anticipatory nausea and vomiting among cancer patients: A review. *Psychology and Health*, **6**, 97–106.

Webb, K. L., Dobson, A. J., O'Connell, D. L., Tupling, H. E., Harris, G. W., Moxon, J. A., Sulway, M. J. and Leeder, S. R. (1984). Dietary compliance among insulin-dependent diabetics. *Journal of Chronic Disease*, **37**, 633–643.

Weinman, J. and Johnston, M. (1988). Stressful medical procedures: An analysis of the effects of psychological interventions and of the stressfulness of the procedures. In S. Maes, C. D. Spielberger, P. B. Defares and J. G. Sarason (eds), *Topics in Health Psychology*. Chichester: Wiley.

Weinstein, M. C. and Fineberg, H. V. (1980). *Clinical Decision Analysis*. Philadelphia: Saunders.

Weinstein, N. D. (1982). Unrealistic optimism about susceptibility of health problems. *Journal of Behavioural Medicine*, **2**, 125–140.

Weinstein, N. D. (1983). Reducing unrealistic optimism about illness susceptibility. *Health Psychology*, **2**, 11–20.

Weinstein, N. D. (1984). Why it won't happen to me: Perceptions of risk factors and susceptibility. *Health Psychology*, **3**, 431–457.

Weinstein, N. D. (1987). Unrealistic optimism about susceptibility to health problems: Conclusions from a community-wide sample. *Journal of Behavioral Medicine*, **10**, 481–500.

Weinstein, N. D. (1988). The precaution adoption process. *Health Psychology*, **7**, 355–386.

Weinstein, N. D. (1993). Testing four competing theories of health-protective behavior. *Health Psychology*, **12**, 324–333.

Weisenberg, M., Kegeles, S. S. and Lund, A. K. (1980). Children's health beliefs and acceptance of dental preventive activity. *Journal of Health and Social Behavior*, **21**, 59–74.

Weisman, A. D. (1972). *On Dying and Denying: A psychiatric study of terminality*. New York: Behavioral Publications.

Weisman, A. D. (1974). *The Realization of Death*. New York: Jason Aronson.

Weisman, C. S. and Nathanson, C. A. (1985). Professional satisfaction and client outcomes: A comparative organizational analysis. *Medical Care*, **23**, 1179–1192.

Weisman, C. S. and Teitelbaum, M. A. (1989). Women and health care communication. *Patient Education and Counselling*, **13**, 183–199.

Wells, J. K., Howard, G. S., Nowlin, W. F. and Vargas, M. J. (1986). Presurgical anxiety and post-surgical pain and adjustment: Effects of a stress inoculation procedure. *Journal of Consulting and Clinical Psychology*, **54**, 831–835.

Wennberg, J. E. (1987). The paradox of appropriate care. *Journal of the American Medical Association*, **258**, 2568–2570.

West, C. (1984). When the doctor is a 'lady': Power, status, and gender in physician–patient encounters. *Symbolic Interaction*, **7**, 87–106.

Whelan, T. A. and Kirkby, R. J. (1998). Advantages for children and their families of psychological preparation for hospitalisation and surgery. *Journal of Family Studies*, **4**, 35–51.

White, A. R., Resch, K.-L. and Ernst, E. (1997). Complementary medicine: Use and attitudes among GPs. *Family Practice*, **14**, 302–306.

White, L., Tursky, B. and Schwartz, G. E. (1985). *Placebo: Theory, research and mechanisms*. New York: Guildford Press.

Whitehead, M. (1990). *The Health Divide*. Harmondsworth: Penguin Books.

Whitehead, M. (1992). The health divide. In P. Townsend, N. Davidson and M. Whitehead, *Inequalities in Health*. Harmondsworth: Penguin Books.

Whitehead, W. E., Busch, C. M., Heller, B. R. and Costa, P. T. (1986). Social learning influences on menstrual symptoms and illness behavior. *Health Psychology*, **5**, 13–23.

Wiener, C. (1975). The burden of rheumatoid arthritis: Tolerating the uncertainty. *Social Science and Medicine*, **9**, 97–104.

Wilhelmson, L., Sane, H., Elmfeldt, D., Tibbin, B., Grimby, G. and Wedel, G. (1975). A controlled trial of physical training after myocardial infarction. *Preventive Medicine*, **4**, 491–508.

Wilkinson, R. G. (1996). *Unhealthy Societies: The afflictions of inequality*. London: Routledge.

Williams, R. (1983). Concepts of health: An analysis of lay logic. *Sociology*, **17**, 185–204.

Williams, R. (1990). *A Protestant Legacy: Attitudes to death and illness among older Aberdonians*. Oxford: Clarendon Press.

Williams, S. J. (1989). Chronic respiratory illness and disability: A critical review of the psychosocial literature. *Social Science and Medicine*, **28**, 791–803.

Williams, S. J. and Bury, M. R. (1989). Impairment, disability and handicap in chronic respiratory illness. *Social Science and Medicine*, **29**, 609–616.

Williamson, J. D. and Danaher, K. (1978). *Self-care in Health*. London: Croom Helm.

Wilson, C. (1989). Terminal care: Using psychological skills with the terminally ill. In A. K. Broome (ed.), *Health Psychology: Process and applications*. London: Chapman & Hall.

Wilson, D. (1997). A report of an investigation of end-of-life care practices in health care facilities and the influences on those practices. *Journal of Palliative Care*, 13, 34–40.

Wilson, J. F. (1981). Behavioral preparation for surgery: Benefit or harm? *Journal of Behavioral Medicine*, 4, 79–102.

Wilson, S. and Walker, A. (1993) Unemployment and health: A review. *Public Health*, 107, 153–162

Winefield, H. R. (1992). Doctor–patient communication: An interpersonal helping process. In S. Maes, H. Leventhal and M. Johnston (eds), *International Review of Health Psychology*. Vol. I. Chichester: J. Wiley.

Wing, R. R., Caggiula, A. W., Nowalk, M. P., Koeske, R., Lee, S. and Langford, H. (1984). Dietary approaches to the reduction of blood pressure: The independence of weight and sodium/potassium interventions. *Preventive Medicine*, 13, 233–244.

Wing, R. R., Epstein, L. H., Nowalk, M. P. and Lamparski, D. M. (1986). Behavioral self-regulation in the treatment of patients with diabetes mellitus. *Psychological Bulletin*, 99, 78–89.

Wing, R. R., Koeske, R., Epstein, L. H., Nowalk, M. P., Gooding, W. and Becker, D. (1987). Long-term effects of modest weight loss in Type II diabetes patients. *Archives of Internal Medicine*, 147, 1749–1753.

Wolinsky, F. D. (1978). Assessing the effects of predisposing, enabling, and illness-morbidity characteristics on health service utilization. *Journal of Health and Social Behavior*, 19, 384–396.

Wolinsky, F. D. and Coe, R. M. (1984). Physician and hospital utilization among non-institutionalized elderly adults: An analysis of the Health Interview Survey. *Journal of Gerontology*, 39, 334–341.

Wolinsky, F. D. and Johnson, R. J. (1991). The use of health services by older adults. *Journal of Gerontology*, 46, S345–S357.

Wong, P. T. P. and Weiner, B. (1981). When people ask 'Why' questions, and the heuristics of attributional research. *Journal of Personality and Social Psychology*, 40, 650–663.

Woolley, H., Stein, A., Forrest, G. and Baum, J. D. (1989). Staff stress and job satisfaction at a children's hospice. *Archives of Diseases of Childhood*, 64, 114–118.

Worden, J. W. (1991). *Grief Counseling and Grief Therapy: A handbook for the mental health practitioner* (2nd edn). New York: Springer.

Worden, J. W. and Weisman, A. D. (1984). Preventive psychosocial intervention with newly diagnosed cancer patients. *General Hospital Psychiatry*, 6, 243–249.

World Health Organization (1948). *Constitution of the World Health Organization*. Geneva: WHO Basic Documents.

World Health Organization (1981). *Global Strategy for Health for All by the Year 2000*. Geneva: World Health Organization.

Wortman, C. B. and Dunkel-Schetter, C. (1979). Interpersonal relationships and cancer: A theoretical analysis. *Journal of Social Issues*, 35, 120–155.

Wortman, C. B. and Silver, R. C. (1989). The myths of coping with loss. *Journal of Consulting and Clinical Psychology*, 57, 349–357.

Wortman, D. and Lehman, D. (1985). Reactions to victims of life crisis: Support attempts that fail. In I.G. Sarason and B. R. Sarason (eds), *Social Support: Theory, research and applications*. Dordtrecht, The Netherlands: Martinus Nijhoff.

Wright, J. and Weber, E. (1987). *Homelessness and Health*. Washington, DC: McGraw-Hill.

Wright, S. D., Lund, D. A., Caserta, M. S. and Pratt, C. (1991). Coping and caregiver well being: the impact of maladaptive strategies. *Journal of Gerontological Social Work*, 17, 75–91.

Wurtele, S. K. and Maddux, J. E. (1987). Relative contributions of protection motivation theory components in predicting exercise intentions and behavior. *Health Psychology*, **6**, 453–466.

Wysocki, T., Green, L. and Huxtable, K. (1989). Blood glucose monitoring by diabetic adolescents: Compliance and metabolic control. *Health Psychology*, **8**, 267–284.

Yoong, A. F. E., Lim, J., Hudson, C. N. and Chard, T. (1992). Audit of compliance with antenatal protocols. *British Medical Journal*, **305**, 1184–1186.

Yorkston, N. J., McHugh, R. B., Brady, R., Serber, M. and Sergeant, H. G. S. (1974). Verbal desensitization in bronchial asthma. *Journal of Psychosomatic Research*, **18**, 371–376.

Young, A. (1981). *Medical Choice in a Mexican Village*. New Brunswick, NJ: Rutgers University Press.

Young, A. (1982). The anthropology of sickness and the anthropology of illness. *Annual Review of Anthropology*, **11**, 257–285.

Young, J. and Garro, L. Y. (1982). Variation in the choice of treatment in two Mexican communities. *Social Science and Medicine*, **16**, 1453–1466.

Young, M., Benjamin, B. and Wallis, C. (1963). Mortality of widowers. *Lancet*, **2**, 454–456.

Zarit, S. H. (1989). Do we need another 'stress and caregiving' study? *The Gerontologist*, **29**, 147–148.

Zarit, S. H., Reever, K. E. and Bach-Peterson, J. (1980). Relatives of the impaired elderly: Correlates of feelings of burden. *The Gerontologist*, **20**, 649–655.

Zarit, S. H, Todd, P. A. and Zarit, J. M. (1986). Subjective burdens of husbands and wives as caregivers: A longitudinal study. *The Gerontologist*, **26**, 260–266.

Zborowski, M. (1952). Cultural components in response to pain. *Journal of Social Issues*, **8**, 16–30.

Zich, J. and Temoshok, L. (1987). Perceptions of social support in men with AIDS and ARC: Relationships with distress and hardiness. *Journal of Applied Social Psychology*, **17**, 193–215.

Zimmerman, J. (1981). *Hospice: Complete care for the terminally ill*. Baltimore and Munich: Urban and Schearzenberg.

Zisook, S. (1994). Bereavement, depression and immune function. *Psychiatry Research*, **52**, 1–10.

Zisook, S., Peterkin, J. J., Shuchter, S. R. and Bardone, A. (1995). Death, dying and bereavement. In P. M. Nicassio and T. W. Smith (eds), *Managing Chronic Illness. A biopsychosocial perspective*. Washington, DC: American Psychological Association.

Zola, I. K. (1966). Culture and symptoms – An analysis of patients' presenting complaints. *American Sociological Review*, **31**, 615–630.

Zola, I. K. (1972). Medicine as an institution of social control. *Sociological Review*, **29**, 487–504.

Zola, I. K. (1973). Pathways to the doctor – from person to patient. *Social Science and Medicine*, **7**, 677–689.

INDEX